WATER RESEARCH

Papers presented at the Seminars in Water Resources Research, sponsored by Resources for the Future and the Western Resources Conference, at Colorado State University, July 1965

Papers by

William C. Ackermann
Henry W. Anderson
Kenneth J. Arrow
Joe S. Bain
Blair T. Bower
Norman H. Crawford
Paul Davidson, F. Gerard Adams, Joseph Seneca
Robert K. Davis
Willis H. Ellis
Myron B. Fiering
Irving K. Fox
Earnest F. Gloyna
J. A. Harder
L. M. Hartman and D. A. Seastone
Maynard M. Hufschmidt
Allen V. Kneese
Jack L. Knetsch and Robert K. Davis
John V. Krutilla
Arthur Maass
Hubert Marshall
J. W. McCutchan and Walter M. Pollit
Roland R. Renne
Stephen C. Smith
Peter O. Steiner
G. S. Tolley
Gilbert F. White
Vujica M. Yevdjevich

WATER RESEARCH

Economic analysis, Water management, Evaluation problems,
Water reallocation, Political and administrative problems,
Hydrology and engineering, Research programs and needs

Edited by
Allen V. Kneese and Stephen C. Smith

Published for
Resources for the Future, Inc.
by
The Johns Hopkins Press
Baltimore and London

RESOURCES FOR THE FUTURE, INC.

1755 Massachusetts Avenue N.W., Washington, D.C. 20036

Resources for the Future is a nonprofit corporation for research and education in the development, conservation, and use of natural resources. It was established in 1952 with the co-operation of the Ford Foundation and its activities since then have been financed by grants from that Foundation. Part of the work of Resources for the Future is carried out by its resident staff, part supported by grants to universities and other nonprofit organizations. Unless otherwise stated, interpretations and conclusions in RFF publications are those of the authors; the organization takes responsibility for the selection of significant subjects for study, the competence of the researchers, and their freedom of inquiry.

This book is based on papers prepared by authorities who participated in the Seminars in Water Resources Research, 1965 Western Resources Conference, sponsored by Resources for the Future, University of Colorado, Colorado State University, and Colorado School of Mines.

RFF staff editors: Henry Jarrett, Vera W. Dodds, Nora E. Roots, Sheila M. Ekers.

Contents

v

RESEARCH ON EVALUATION PROBLEMS

STUDIES OF WATER REALLOCATION

POLITICAL AND ADMINISTRATIVE STUDIES

RESEARCH ON HYDROLOGY AND ENGINEERING

MAJOR RESEARCH PROGRAMS AND NEEDS

WATER RESEARCH

Introduction:
New Directions in Water Resources Research

Allen V. Kneese*

T his volume consists of papers presented at the Western Resources Conference, held in Fort Collins, Colorado, in July, 1965. In many instances the papers have been substantially revised and edited; nevertheless, they reflect the quality of the Conference and we hope that they will communicate to the reader some of the excitement which the participants felt.

The Conference could look back upon and reap the fruits of several years of vigorous research activity on problems of planning and managing water resources—the problems around which it was centered. A significant current in this stream of activity was the Resources for the Future program of staff and grant research. By 1965, this program had reached a point where the outcome of some major projects could usefully be summarized or important early results reported. For this reason, Resources for the Future joined with the University of Colorado, Colorado State University, and the Colorado School of Mines in sponsoring the Conference—the seventh in a series that has come to be a respected institution among the many scholars and others interested in resources research and policy.[1] Of the twenty-six papers in this volume, fifteen report on RFF staff research or grant research wholly or partly sponsored by Resources for the Future.

---

* Director, Water Resources Program and Quality of the Environment Program, Resources for the Future, Inc.
[1] Books resulting from the first six conferences in the series are listed at the end of this Introduction [ref. 1].

Far the major portion of the Conference was devoted to reports on the results or status of current research. In this Introduction, I will briefly look back over the last decade or so of research on the planning and management of water resources, in order to trace the main streams of development that have led to the present state of water research.

Although they frequently overlapped, these developments can be dealt with in the following rough chronological order:

1) Clarification and more far-reaching applications of economic concepts to water development and use.

2) An increasing emphasis on cross-disciplinary research.

3) The application of high-speed electronic computers to water management research.

4) New emphasis on problems of recreation, water quality, and management of water-associated land uses.

5) Greater research emphasis on political, administration, and institutional factors.

6) The new role of the federal agencies with respect to research on water management.

7) The passage of the Water Resources Research Act in 1964.

1. Beginning in the mid-fifties, several books were published setting out in detail the economic theory relevant to water resources development and use and demonstrating its applicability and significance by means of case studies. This was undoubtedly a major development. Today these books, especially those of Krutilla, Eckstein, and McKean and of Hirshleifer, Milliman, and De Haven [ref. 2, 3, 4, 5], are cited wherever the economics of water resources is discussed. They are distinguished not only for their pioneering work in bringing economic theory to bear on water problems, using it to illuminate issues that previously had been obscure, but also because they made an honest effort to communicate research results to persons involved in the decision-making process, whatever their professional background might be.

There had, of course, been earlier contributions relating to the economic and management aspects of water resources development and use. Perhaps the most important among them came not from the academic and research communities but from within the government agencies. The agencies responsible for water resources development had for long been aware of the need for economic evaluation. Fox [ref. 6] has noted that from 1808, when Albert Gallatin brought out his report on a transportation program for the new nation, to the present day, public water development agencies have found it necessary and desirable to systematically compare estimated benefits with the costs of proposed improvements.

2

The Federal Reclamation Act in 1902 required economic analysis of projects, the Flood Control Act of 1936 proposed the welfare economics feasibility test that benefits to whomsoever they accrue must exceed costs. In 1946, the Federal Inter-Agency River Basin Committee appointed a subcommittee on benefits and costs to reconcile the practices of federal agencies in making benefit-cost analyses. In 1950, this subcommittee issued a landmark report, entitled *Proposed Practices for Economic Analysis of River Basin Projects* [ref. 7]. While never fully accepted either by the parent committee or the federal agencies, this report was remarkably sophisticated in its use of economic analysis and laid an intellectual foundation for research and debate in the water area which still sets it apart from other major reports in the realm of public expenditure. Some high-quality commentary from the academic community also preceded the publications I have singled out for attention. The name of S. V. Ciriacy-Wantrup is especially notable in this connection.

Nevertheless, the more recent books have gone much farther than ever before in clarifying the concepts of welfare economics applicable to water resources use and development, in exploring the fundamental rationale for government activity in the area, and in focusing strong attention upon the problems of empirical measurement. Finally—and perhaps this point applies chiefly to the work of Krutilla and McKean—they helped lay the foundation for economic systems analysis by emphasizing the external effects of water development and the impossibility of arriving at optimum development and use unless these are taken explicitly into account. Many current water resource research projects are the progeny of these distinguished fathers.

2. Another major current—perhaps the most important to develop during the decade from the mid-fifties to the mid-sixties—brought the disciplines of engineering, hydrology, economics and, to a lesser extent, political science into an intimate and meaningful nexus. The thought has now penetrated deeply that economic analysis is not something to be tacked onto a piece of engineering analysis after it is finished, in order to justify it. Rather, it is deemed an integral element with hydrology and engineering in searching for optimum ways to combine resources into valuable outputs. The point is well illustrated by a few major research programs of the past several years. The Harvard Program, as well as contributing to the application of operations research methods to water resource system design, made much progress in extending understanding of the cross-disciplinary approach in water resources research. The Harvard book *Design of Water-Resource Systems,* which appeared in 1962, must stand as a landmark of co-ordinated, highly articulated

3

research among several disciplines [ref. 8]. Two papers in the present volume are direct outgrowths of the interdisciplinary effort at Harvard, and several others have been influenced by it.

A similar conception has underlain teaching and thought on water resources at Stanford University for some years, even though it has only comparatively recently blossomed into a full-scale engineering-economic program of instruction and research. Early results of the research done under this program clearly justify this effort. Stanford is strongly represented in the papers found in this book.

A large part of the Resources for the Future staff and grant program has been directed toward improving knowledge in the social sciences with respect to water resources. It is clear to those participating that only close working relationships with competent engineers and hydrologists can produce the meaningful results sought. This viewpoint is apparent in several of the papers by RFF staff members in the present volume.

Another event testifying to the growing appreciation of multidisciplinary water resources research is the formation of the Universities Council on Water Resources, which held its meeting in Fort Collins at the close of the Western Resources Conference. This organization had a predecessor, the Universities Council on Hydrology, which was established in 1962 as a result of a conference sponsored and financed by the University of California Water Resources Center. The primary objective of the Universities Council on Hydrology was to represent the university community in activities aimed at encouraging the growth of education and research in hydrology. The study of hydrology is itself multidisciplinary in nature, as is evident from the following definition proposed by a group of hydrologists several years ago: "Hydrology is the science that treats of the waters of the earth, their occurrence, circulation, and distribution, their chemical and physical properties, and their reaction with their environment, including their relation to living things. The domain of hydrology embraces the full life history of water on the earth." [Ref. 9.] So broad a definition can incorporate almost the full range of water resources research. It is not surprising, therefore, that several of the hydrology papers in this volume reflect the cross-disciplinary interests of their authors.

In 1963, the University of California Water Resources Center sponsored a meeting of social scientists interested in water resources. A task group on education and training recommended the formation of an organization which would represent the physical, biological, and social science faculties of American universities engaged in active water resource programs. The group also recommended exploring the possibility of combining the suggested organization with the Universities Council on

Hydrology—a logical move in view of the broad conception of hydrology quoted above.

Out of the resulting negotiations grew the broad interdisciplinary group which is now the Universities Council on Water Resources. The objectives are: (1) to give leadership in the search for common ground among the several disciplines working on problems of water resources; (2) to provide an organization for the systematic exchange of information; (3) to assist in establishing a liaison between universities and public agencies which execute action in research programs in the water field; and (4) to represent the universities before foundations, public agencies, and congressional committees in an effort to broaden the base of financial support for training and research in the social sciences aspects of water management. This organization will undoubtedly play a significant role in the activities of the new university institutes created by the Water Resources Research Act.

3. As in so many other fields of research, the development of the electronic computer has had a profound impact on water studies, especially during the last six or seven years. One need not belabor the point that the computer is not just a faster way to do calculations—this is now widely understood. Several of the studies reported in this volume would not have been done at all without computers, for to contemplate undertaking a large system simulation, multiple-regression, or factor-analysis problem without these devices is quite impractical. The use of computers imposes its own form of discipline. Precise definitions, clear and accurate determination of relationships, and specific quantitative data become absolutely essential. Not the least of the contributions computers have made to research is to make us aware that our ability to calculate now vastly exceeds our ability to form useful hypotheses and obtain meaningful, accurate data.

4. Another major development affecting research in the past few years and posing problems for us today results from new activities of the federal government which reflect underlying changes in the character of water problems. It is true that studies of water policy have been pursued at the federal level for some time. One has only to mention the temporary Water Resources Policy Commission established by President Truman; the Second Hoover Commission, which focused attention on federal water resources investments; and the Cabinet-level committee established by President Eisenhower to examine water policy. More recently, however, two large federal studies have had a profound effect on water policy and water research. In 1958, the U.S. Senate established a special select com-

mittee, under the chairmanship of the late Senator Robert S. Kerr, to assess the national water resources situation. The resulting study was by far the most intensive and extensive study of the national water situation and prospects ever conducted. Among its major results was a much greater emphasis on problems of water quality. Widespread attention toward quality problems was also generated by a national conference on water pollution sponsored by the Department of Health, Education, and Welfare in 1960. In addition, the Outdoor Recreation Resources Review Commission, after massive study of outdoor recreation problems, strongly stressed the recreational values of water.

Accompanying and associated with these developments were major changes in public water resource policy. The federal government broadened its activities and responsibilities in regard to water resources in many ways. These included making municipal and industrial water supply and outdoor recreation fully legitimate purposes of multipurpose federal development projects; permitting water quality benefits to be counted in the justification of multipurpose reservoirs; greatly expanding federal enforcement powers with respect to water pollution control; and providing for flood damage studies to guide state and local agencies in land use planning. These policy changes were largely embodied in a new planning principles document, commonly known as Senate Document No. 97 [ref. 10], which was prepared under the sponsorship of and approved by the President's Water Resources Council consisting of the Secretaries of the Army, Interior, Agriculture, and of Health, Education, and Welfare.

The greater importance of recreation and water quality benefits and planning of water-associated land uses has presented some extraordinarily difficult challenges to water resources research. Benefits are claimed for reservoir-based recreation and improved water quality on the order of many millions of dollars. For example, $140 million of recreation benefit was claimed for the half-billion dollar Potomac projects which were proposed in 1964, and much of the rest of the justification was for water quality improvement which ultimately is also largely in the interest of recreation. Several papers in this book endeavor to pioneer a constructive response to the challenge of measuring meaningful values for these purposes—the evaluation of which now ranges from the arbitrary to the irrelevant.

On the matter of planning water-related land use, there is a larger background of research on flood problems than in any other area. Nevertheless, major difficulties remain in attempting to articulate fully the opportunities for combining land use management and other alternatives with the more conventional reservoir storage and channel modifications.

As one of the papers in this collection points out, major obstacles remain in the way of devising optimal measures for the control of flood damages. Among these, some of the most difficult are institutional.

5. Indeed, an outstanding development of the past few years is the increased research focus upon the institutions through which water resources are developed and allocated and their quality managed. This is a research area which could benefit from more attention. Political scientists such as James Fessler, Arthur Maass, Charles McKinley, Albert Lepawsky, and Irving Fox, and a handful of economists—Stephen Smith for example—have a long-standing interest in organizational arrangements for water resources development and use, but they are few in comparison with the dimensions of the problem area. As time has passed, more complex difficulties have arisen, such as those associated with flood control, recreation, and the many alternative modes for controlling water quality in entire regions. The decade from the mid-fifties to the mid-sixties brought these problems strongly to the fore and at the time of the Conference steps toward their solution were more urgent than ever before. Nowhere was this more evident than in the West, where the institutional obstacles to water transfer from irrigation to municipal, industrial, recreational, and other uses contributed strongly toward propelling the nation toward vast and costly engineering solutions. In 1962, Nathaniel Wollman and several associates at the University of New Mexico published a pioneering but limited study of the water transfer problem [ref. 11]. Two papers in the present book record further advances on this front, and several others on institutional and organizational aspects of water management attest to the fact that this area of study is becoming an integral part of the water resources research effort. Nevertheless, some of the most profound and least understood problems continue to be in this area.

6. Another major development of the past few years has been a significant increase of interest on the part of federal agencies in research on economic and institutional aspects of water management. The Economic Research Service of the Department of Agriculture has, of course, for some time conducted a large program of studies bearing more or less directly upon the development and use of water resources for agriculture. But until recent years other federal agencies with major responsibilities for water resource planning and development had shown less interest. By 1965, at the time the Conference was held, this situation was changing markedly. The Department of Health, Education, and Welfare, for example, was undertaking projects on economics and systems analysis

as applied to water quality management problems. Similarly, the Corps of Engineers was helping to support some important projects, including most notably the work on large-scale system simulation at Harvard. The Corps also had made a grant to pursue research on the economics of transportation systems as related to inland navigation. As part of its responsibilities with regard to planning for water resources development in depressed areas, the Corps was sponsoring research to determine how benefit-cost calculation may be applied under conditions where resources are not fully employed. A project of this nature is reported upon in this book.

Despite all of these favorable signs, a look at the longer-term research plans of the federal agencies in 1965 indicated an intention to spend only a tiny percentage of their research budget on studies of economics, systems analysis, institutions, and other matters bearing directly upon making decisions leading toward effective and efficient use of water resources. A disinterested appraisal would have to conclude that there was fundamental disproportion between the importance of these problems and the resources allocated to them.

7. The last major development to occur before the Conference was the passage of the Water Resources Research Act of 1964. This Act gave large financial assistance to university research and caused water resource research institutes to be established in each of the fifty states and in Puerto Rico. With its passage the nation broke new ground in the support of water resources research. As has been noted, in some universities a strong research effort was already under way. In some others interest was stimulated by the availability of funds and the dramatic emphasis which water resource problems had received in recent years. Many observers have reservations about the extremely wide research base facilitated by the Act in universities across the land. Nevertheless, it is an experiment on a massive scale and certainly the most important single recent development bearing upon water resource research.

The Conference thus stood at the threshold of a new era in university research. For those participating, it was pleasant to view this prospect from a land grant institution whose president was a central force behind passage of the Act and which was one of the first to have its institute approved under the Act. Colorado State University has built upon a long record of distinguished research in hydrology. In recent years it has greatly increased its capability in matters of economics and management. The University and other centers of real competence in Colorado and across the nation offer the promise that the most exciting period for water resource research lies ahead.

REFERENCES

[1] *Proceedings*—Western Resources Conference, 1959–64:
Pollak, Franklin S. (ed.). *Resources Development: Frontiers for Research*. Boulder: University of Colorado Press, 1960.
Amoss, Harold L. (ed.). *Water: Measuring and Meeting Future Requirements*. Boulder: University of Colorado Press, 1961.
Amoss, Harold L., and McNickle, Roma K. (eds.). *Land and Water: Planning for Economic Growth*. Boulder: University of Colorado Press, 1962.
Frush, Charles O., and Lentz, Oscar H. (eds.). *Minerals and Energy: Problems, Practices and Goals* (Vol. I); Lentz, Oscar H., and Frush, Charles O. (eds.). *Minerals and Energy: Problems, Practices and Goals* (Vol. II). Golden: Colorado School of Mines, 1962 and 1963.
McNickle, Roma K. (ed.). *Water: Development, Utilization, Conservation*. Boulder: University of Colorado Press, 1964.
Garnsey, Morris E. (ed.). *New Horizons for Resources Research: Issues and Methodology*. Boulder: University of Colorado Press, 1965.
[2] Krutilla, John V., and Eckstein, Otto. *Multiple Purpose River Development: Studies in Applied Economic Analysis*. Baltimore: Johns Hopkins Press, 1958.
[3] Eckstein, Otto. *Water Resource Development: The Economics of Project Evaluation*. Cambridge: Harvard University Press, 1958.
[4] McKean, Roland N. *Efficiency in Government through Systems Analysis, with Emphasis on Water Resources Development*. New York: John Wiley and Sons, 1958.
[5] Hirshleifer, Jack, Milliman, Jerome W., and De Haven, James C. *Water Supply: Economics, Technology, and Policy*. Chicago: University of Chicago Press, 1960.
[6] Fox, Irving K. "New Horizons in Water Resources Administration," *Public Administration Review,* March 1965. (Also RFF Reprint No. 51. Washington: Resources for the Future, Inc., 1965.)
[7] U.S. Federal Inter-Agency River Basin Committee, Subcommittee on Benefits and Costs. *Proposed Practices for Economic Analysis of River Basin Projects*. Washington, May 1950.
[8] Maass, Arthur, Hufschmidt, Maynard M., Dorfman, Robert, Thomas, Harold A., Jr., Marglin, Stephen A., and Fair, Gordon Maskew. *Design of Water-Resource Systems*. Cambridge: Harvard University Press, 1962.
[9] Federal Council for Science and Technology. *Scientific Hydrology*. Washington: June 1962, p. 2.
[10] President's Water Resources Council. *Policies, Standards, and Procedures in the Formulation, Evaluation, and Review of Plans for Use and Development of Water and Related Land Resources*. S. Doc. No. 97, 87th Congress, 2nd Session, May 29, 1962.
[11] Wollman, Nathaniel. *The Value of Water in Alternative Uses*. Albuquerque: University of New Mexico Press, 1962.

ISSUES IN THEORETICAL ECONOMIC ANALYSIS

Discounting and Public Investment Criteria

Kenneth J. Arrow*

Public investments, like other investments, generate streams of benefits and costs beginning with the present and extending into the more or
less distant future. To decide whether or not an investment project is
worth while, it is necessary to add together in some form future benefits
and costs over the future to see if the algebraic sum is positive or negative. More specifically, it is usual to assign a discount factor to each time
in the future and then compare the sums of discounted benefits and costs.
The discount factors are assumed to be less than one, and to decrease as
the time into the future increases. A system of discount factors implies,
by well-known identities of financial mathematics, a term structure of
interest rates. A special case, appropriate for conditions of steady growth,
is that in which the interest rate is anticipated to be constant, so that the
discount factors decrease geometrically.

What can be said of the discount factors appropriate to public investment decisions? One can approach the question from two directions
which must, however, come to the same destination. One way is to ask
if there is any special problem in discounting the returns to public investment: can we not simply use the market rate of interest? An alternative
approach is more fundamental and frequently clearer: to formulate
explicitly the optimization problem and then seek the solution. I will use
a little of both approaches but will emphasize perhaps more heavily that
of explicit optimization.

* Professor of Economics and Statistics, Stanford University. This work was
carried out under a grant from Resources for the Future, Inc.

If the private capital market were perfect, and if there were no divergences between social and private benefit (and cost), the discount rate on public investments would be the same as that found on the private market. The argument for this proposition is the standard one in welfare economics and need not be repeated in detail here—if the public investment program were determined by evaluating benefits according to some rate different from the market, then there would always be a way to increase total output by some reallocation of investment resources between the public and private sectors.

The divergence between social and private benefits in the capital market has sometimes been argued on the basis of a special collective responsibility for future generations (see especially the view of Sen [ref. 1] and Marglin [ref. 2], and the critical comments of Tullock [ref. 3] and Lind [ref. 4]). No comment is made on this question here, not because it is unimportant (though I am inclined to believe the magnitude of the divergence cannot be great), but because greater stress should be placed on the imperfections of the capital market.

The view that the capital market is imperfect derives immediately from the observation that many different rates of return appear to be available in our economy. The opportunities for investment range from cash, with zero return, up through various forms of time deposits, government bonds, personal finance loans, consumer installment credit, and direct investments—a wide range indeed. It is to be noted further that while some of these rates are market prices in a reasonably strict sense, others have to be imputed, sometimes by methods of such subtlety that experts find themselves in sharp disagreement. In point is the current discussion of the rate of return on human capital (e.g., Becker [ref. 5]).

It is, of course, not sufficient to look at these gross facts; to interpret them requires more analysis of the different services rendered by different capital markets than would be consistent with the scope of this paper. The risk-bearing components of different capital markets will, however, be referred to again in the last section. But it is crucial in welfare evaluation to examine the extent to which observed rates of interest reflect time preference, and this question will be briefly discussed in Section I.

Public investment policy by definition involves commitment over time and, as modern economic theory makes clear, must be judged in the context of a growing economy. Fundamentally, growth here means increases in population and technological knowledge, though the course of capital accumulation also enters as both cause and effect. In Section II, the now familiar elementary propositions about the time development of growing economies will be recapitulated, and the concept of the "natural rate of growth" stressed. One aspect that seems a little less familiar is that of the

14

interest rate implied by growing per capita consumption; the "natural rate of interest" is introduced in Section III as a value counterpart of the natural rate of growth.

Explicit introduction of a growth model will clarify much of the current discussion of the effect of time patterns of return on the choice among projects. Much effort (see Eckstein [ref. 6, pp. 94–104], Marglin [ref. 7]) has gone into explicit consideration of reinvestment of the so-called "throw-off." But this discussion has been unnecessarily complicated by failing to observe that the policy maker who is optimizing with respect to a current decision is also in a position to optimize with respect to reinvestment. The problem, correctly posed, is not that of optimizing a current decision, taking as given all future behavior on the part of the government and of private individuals. Rather, the problem is that of choosing an optimal policy, i.e., a rule for decision making to be applied now and in the future. The approach is that of dynamic programming, which has been applied so successfully to multistage decision problems in industry and engineering.

One consequence of this viewpoint is that the choice criterion for an investment project is that the present value (sum of discounted net benefits) be positive. Variations in the time pattern of returns affect choice only to the extent that they affect the present value. Of course, the discount rates used must be the proper ones, and the rates of interest underlying them need not be constant over time.

Intimately related with this view is another, which may be less familiar. In an appropriate sense, all investment is short run, at least in a growing economy. In such a case, the marginal investment is always the new one. It follows that the investment should be made on what may be termed "myopic" grounds; the marginal productivity of capital at any instant should be equated to the short-term rate of interest (see Marglin [ref. 8, pp. 20–27]; Arrow [ref. 9]). To avoid misunderstanding, two remarks may be helpful: (1) the current investment decision still depends on the whole future, in that the "correct" short-term rate of interest must in full equilibrium reflect future movements of profitability; (2) the short-term interest rate needed for this computation is the one appropriate to a non-monetary full-employment economy; the rate actually observed is probably overly influenced by monetary and cyclical factors.

Instead of defending these views polemically, I will outline in Section IV a simple aggregative model expressing some generally accepted current views on optimal economic growth, stemming ultimately from the seminal work of Ramsey in 1928 [ref. 10]. Here, it will be seen that current investment is governed by the above "myopic" rule with a short-term rate of interest, which tends over time to the natural rate of interest.

15

In a state of steady balanced growth, the natural rate of growth would prevail at all points along the path.

This model is applicable to a perfectly planned economy or to a system with perfect capital markets. The opportunity cost of capital and the rate of interest to the consumer are identical, as they must be for full optimality, and the present value of any proposed new investment project must be computed using discount rates derived from the present and future values of the short-term rate of interest.

Section V returns to the assumption of imperfect capital markets. This will be expressed by the usual consumption function: individual savings is a constant fraction of disposable income, independent of future earnings and of interest rates. (It will be clear from the argument that generalizations, such as the permanent-income hypothesis in its usual forms, will not affect the qualitative results.) Suppose further that there are two kinds of capital, private and public, and that all public investment is financed by taxation. Then the optimal policy will imply two interest rates, one for each kind of capital. They will be in general unequal and will remain so even in a steady state of growth. Nevertheless, the rate appropriate for discounting public investment will tend ultimately to the natural rate of interest, the same as in the perfect economy, even though the rate used in the private sector is different even in the limit. This result is a somewhat surprising departure from the usual static theory of the "second-best," in which it is held that a departure from optimality in one part of the economy requires a corresponding departure elsewhere in order to do as well as possible. For example, if private industry is monopolistic and hence charges a markup over marginal cost, it is sometimes held that the prices charged by the public sector should have the same markup. However, this is strictly valid only if factor supplies are regarded as constant. (On this, see Meade [ref. 11, ch. 7]; Lerner [ref. 12, pp. 100–105].) In the present case, the government, by its tax policy, is actually changing the supply of savings to the economy.

In Section VI, the effects of permitting the government to finance public investment by bonds as well as by taxation are examined. It is shown that an optimal mix of the two will permit the achievement of a fully optimal pattern. In that case, the rates of return in the two sectors should be equated at every instant of time, but the government through its bond and tax policies should aim at driving the common rate of return towards the natural rate of interest. The optimal policy may well involve negative bond financing, i.e., government lending or retirement of the national debt.

Finally, in Section VII, a collateral but important issue is discussed— the relation between discounting and risk. It is argued that on the basis of plausible assumptions, the government should not act as a risk averter. That is, the optimal policy for the government is to reckon uncertain benefits and costs at their expected value and then discount the resulting stream at the same rates as used for riskless investments.

I

THE IMPERFECTIONS OF THE CAPITAL MARKET

The welfare interpretation of interest rates requires that they correspond to time preference on the part of individuals. Thus, if an observed interest rate is to be used for discounting investments, it ought to be true that individuals make their choice between saving and spending on the basis of that rate. Under perfectly competitive conditions, an individual's consumption should be a function of his wealth and of the rate of interest, wealth itself being defined in turn as the sum of discounted returns to both currently held material assets and personal skills and qualities. The present and future values of the rate of interest thus enter both directly and through the measurement of wealth.[1]

Although there have been many empirical investigations of savings behavior, none to my knowledge has been completely compatible with this hypothesis. Among the innumerable time series analyses of the consumption function, none that I know of has introduced any version of the rate of interest as an explanatory variable. Further, the very concept of a consumption function, especially in its original Keynesian form, is a denial of a purely competitive theory, for it relates consumption to current income rather than to wealth in any form; indeed, the explanatory power of the consumption function for business cycles (and for employment policy) depends on its sensitivity to current income. More modern analysis, particularly the vital investigations of Modigliani and Brumberg [ref. 13] and Friedman [ref. 14] have placed greater emphasis on some kind of lifetime average of income, a concept more closely related to wealth. But when Friedman makes explicit use of time-series analysis, "permanent income" turns out to be an average of about three or four years' previous income, with adjustment for trends in income. (See [ref. 14, pp. 142–52, especially p. 150].)

In any case, the evidence from time series data of aggregate consump-

[1] It is possible for consumption to depend only on wealth (as defined above), if the individual is maximizing a discounted sum of utilities of consumption at the successive time points in the future, where the utility of consumption at any given time point is its logarithm. But even then the wealth must in general depend on present and future rates of interest, through the discounting of future returns. It can be shown that, in general, consumption (or savings) can never be independent of the rate of interest under perfectly competitive conditions.

tion and income does not cast much light on the way individuals allocate their resources over time. The perfectly competitive hypothesis would imply that two individuals with the same wealth (defined as material wealth plus the sum of discounted future earnings from personal services) would consume that same amount at a given age regardless of the way income is distributed over their lifetime. More strongly, if it is assumed that the utility function for consumption does not vary with age, then consumption should be either steadily increasing or steadily decreasing as a function of time (see Yaari [ref. 15, p. 309]). Casual observation suggests that neither of these statements is valid, at least for individuals whose primary wealth is derived from wages and salaries; on the contrary, consumption profiles over time bear a distinct relation to income profiles. Medical students with high expected incomes do not typically live as well as they will when in practice, though the perfectly competitive hypothesis would imply that they could borrow for current consumption against their future incomes.

The inapplicability of the perfectly competitive hypothesis is also suggested by the variety of interest rates facing the individual. He may receive 4 or 5 per cent in time deposits and government bonds, and perhaps double (after taxes) by investing in stocks; but he may have to pay 30 per cent or more for personal finance or consumer credit. With these rates we may also compare some computed in various indirect fashions. Certain writers on the consumption function have attempted to infer the rate of interest implicit in their estimates. Hamburger [ref. 16] found a rate of 16⅔ per cent for discounting future wages and salaries, which he attributes to "interest, uncertainty discount, and the effect of the illiquidity of human wealth" (p. 10). Friedman has, by different methods, found the even higher rate of 33⅓ per cent [ref. 17, p. 23]. Perhaps even more relevant are the rates of return on investment in human capital, in the form of education. For college education, Becker [ref. 5, p. 114] finds a rate of 12 per cent, to which must be added the considerable nonpecuniary consumption benefits to the student.

There is no pretense here of a complete re-analysis of the empirical evidence on consumption and savings from the viewpoint of the perfectly competitive hypothesis. Enough has been said here, it is hoped, to make plausible the assumption that borrowing against future earnings cannot in general be carried out at the usual market rates of interest. The resulting divergence between the rate of interest implicit in consumption decisions and any market rate is so great that it must be accepted that savings is largely independent of the latter and that current income plays a major role in determining the individual's opportunities for consuming and saving.

To express this conclusion simply, I will follow the Keynesian assumption in the form which Harrod and others have applied to growth theory —namely, to make consumption simply proportional to disposable income. The results that follow would not be changed in any essential way if consumption were to depend on lagged as well as current income.

II

ELEMENTARY PROPOSITIONS ON ECONOMIC GROWTH

The type of growth theory which started with Harrod [ref. 18] and was developed by Solow [ref. 19] and Swan [ref. 20] may be briefly summarized as follows: Assume a single commodity which may be either consumed or saved and therefore added to the stock of capital. Following the thought of the previous section, consumption is proportional to output (equals income) at any moment of time (in the absence of an estate, disposable and total income are the same). At any moment of time, output is a function of capital and labor, but this function is shifting over time due to technological progress. For simplicity, we assume that technological progress is always exactly equivalent to increasing the number of workers; that is, it simply increases the efficiency of each worker; the shifts in the production function are then said to be *Harrod-neutral*. We further assume that the rate of technological progress in this sense is a constant exponential growth. In symbols, let Y be income, K be capital, $\dot{K}$ be saving (equals capital accumulation), L be labor, and τ be the rate of technological progress. Then the savings assumption is

$$\dot{K} = sY , \qquad (1)$$

and the production function assumption is

$$Y = F(K, e^{\tau t} L) . \qquad (2)$$

The production function is also assumed to have the usual properties of constant returns to scale and concave isoquants. Finally, the labor force, L, is assumed to be growing at a constant rate, π.

Then it has been shown that the growing system will be characterized by a *natural rate of growth*, γ, where

$$\gamma = \pi + \tau , \qquad (3)$$

i.e., the sum of rate of growth of labor force and the rate of (Harrod-neutral) technological progress. Starting from any initial situation with regard to capital and labor, the capital-output ratio will gradually tend to a constant limit (given by s/γ). When this limit is reached, capital and

19

output will necessarily be growing at the same rate, which will in fact be the natural rate γ. If the capital-output ratio at any moment of time is below its long-run equilibrium value, then both output and capital grow more rapidly than the natural rate, with capital growing the more rapidly, and vice versa.

It should be noted that since output is ultimately increasing at the rate γ, while labor force and population (assumed proportional to each other) are increasing at the rate π, it follows from (3) that output per capita increases in the long run at the rate τ, the rate of technological progress.

III

THE NATURAL RATE OF INTEREST

Consider now a representative individual with income growing at rate τ, and therefore consumption growing at the same rate, since consumption is proportional to income. Assuming that the individual has a utility function for consumption streams, what is the rate of interest implicit in his consumption pattern? I restate the treatment originally developed by Eckstein [ref. 21]: by considering time to be continuous, rather than discrete, I hope to simplify the exposition and the resulting formulas.

Some elementary definitions will be helpful. Suppose we have for each time t in the future a discount factor; it is a decreasing function of time. The *interest rate* at time t implied by the discount factors is the negative of the rate of change of the discount factor with respect to t. (The term "rate of change" is understood to mean "relative rate of change," or "logarithmic derivative.") The discount factor and the corresponding rates of interest may be applied either to the commodity consumed or to its utility, and we distinguish accordingly between consumption discount factors and rates of interest and utility discount factors and rates of interest.

I will assume that the utility function for consumption at any moment of time is a given function, $u(c)$. However, the utility of consumption at time t, viewed from the present (time 0) may have a discount factor. The same will be true of the marginal utility of future consumption. The consumption discount factor for time t is simply the marginal rate of substitution between future and present consumption, and hence is the ratio of their marginal utilities as viewed from the present.

Consumption discount factor

$$= (\text{utility discount factor}) \times \left(\frac{\text{marginal utility of future consumption}}{\text{marginal utility of present consumption}}\right).$$

Since the rate of change of a product is the sum of the rates of change, it follows from the preceding remarks that

consumption rate of interest

= (utility rate of interest) − (rate of change of marginal utility of consumption).

If we think of the meaning of the last term, it will become evident that rate of change of marginal utility of consumption

= (elasticity of marginal utility of consumption) × (rate of change of consumption).

In the long-term growth pattern, the rate of change of consumption has been seen to be τ. Define

ω = consumption rate of interest in steady growth (*natural rate of interest*),

ρ = utility rate of interest,

v = elasticity of marginal utility of consumption (with sign reversed).

Then we have the simple formula,

$$\omega = \rho + v\tau. \tag{4}$$

As Frisch [ref. 22] has noted with respect to a similar formula, the first term is Böhm-Bawerk's second ground for the existence of interest, the systematic underevaluation of future utilities, while the second term is Böhm-Bawerk's first ground, the lower marginal utility of consumption in the future owing to expected growth in wealth.

This analysis holds for a single individual or for a representative individual in a stationary population. There is a divergence of opinion in the literature as to the valuation of future states when the population is growing. One school argues that only future per capita income counts; apparently only the quality, not the quantity, of life should count. The view expressed by Meade, with which I strongly concur [ref. 11, ch. 6, especially pp. 87–89], argues that one should add up the utilities of all individuals in a generation to arrive at the social utility; if more people benefit, that is so much the better. Hence, in this view, the total utility for a time point t units is the population at that time multiplied by the utility of per capita income. Consider then a unit increase in total consumption divided equally among all individuals. Then the increment in utility for each comes to

$$\frac{\text{Marginal utility of per capita consumption}}{\text{population}},$$

and the gain in utility to the entire community is obtained by multiplying this by the population. Hence, the marginal social utility of total consumption is equal to the marginal utility of per capita consumption, and the entire analysis leading up to equation (4) remains valid. (If future utility were judged solely by per capita consumption, the natural rate of interest would be increased by π.)

IV

A SIMPLE OPTIMAL GROWTH MODEL

Suppose this to be a one-commodity world, as considered in the last two sections, with the production relation equation (2) (i. e., constant returns to scale and exponential Harrod-neutral technological progress) and the labor force increasing exponentially at the rate π. Suppose further, a perfectly planned economy, so that the savings at each moment of time can be determined optimally. The criterion of optimality is the maximization of the sum of discounted utilities of consumption for all members of the society.

This problem was first successfully analyzed by Ramsey [ref. 10]. Unfortunately, any analysis requires the use of a family of fairly sophisticated mathematical tools, the calculus of variations, dynamic programming, and optimal control theory. The modern mathematical work basic to the currently developing theory of optimal economic growth has appeared in the works of Bellman [ref. 23], and of Pontryagin and his associates [ref. 24]. The best heuristic introductions to these works are Bellman and Dreyfus [ref. 25] (in particular, see pp. 190–200 for a well-motivated introduction to the calculus of variations), and Kalman [ref. 26]. For applications of these methods to the problem of economic growth, see Stoleru [ref. 27] and Mirrlees [ref. 28].

A simple exposition of the results is given here. Intuitively, it is reasonable to expect that the optimal savings ratio tends to some constant limit, say s^*. If the savings ratio is steadily at s^*, then the economy satisfies all the conditions of the model of Section II so that it grows eventually at the natural rate of growth, γ. The rate of interest implicit in the consumption pattern is the natural rate of interest developed in the last section. Hence, along the path of steady growth, optimality requires that

marginal productivity of capital = natural rate of interest.   (5)

Note that this condition determines what the optimal savings ratio is. For, from the nature of Harrod-neutral technological progress, the labor force measured in efficiency units is growing at the natural rate, γ.

Under constant returns, the marginal productivity of capital is determined by the ratio of capital to labor, again in efficiency terms. Since this ratio must be constant, capital is also growing at the rate γ, and its magnitude at any time, t, is determined by equation (5). It follows that investment, the rate of accumulation of capital, is also growing at the rate γ; finally, since output must also be growing at the same rate, the ratio of saving (equals investment) in income must be a determined constant.[2]

Suppose now that initially the capital-labor ratio is not that which is optimal in the long run. Then there must occur a process of adjustment to the long-run optimum. The rate of interest at the beginning must equal the marginal product of capital as determined by the initial conditions and gradually move to the natural rate. Thus, there is no constant rate of interest to be applied to an investment.

The exact solution can be presented as follows. For any given initial stock of capital, K, there is a maximum possible sum of discounted utilities of consumption possible, that obtained by following the optimal policy. Let $V(K)$ be this maximum, and let $p = V'(K)$ be the marginal contribution of K to V. We can term p the *utility price of capital*. Then it can be shown that at any moment of time, capital should be so chosen that

marginal productivity of capital = consumption rate of interest
$$= \omega - (\dot{p}/p) , \tag{6}$$

where the dot denotes differentiation with respect to time, so that $\dot{p}/p$ is the rate of change of the utility price of capital. Thus, the marginal productivity of capital is equated to the natural rate of interest modified, as usual, by speculation on the changes in the prices of capital goods. Together with this rule we have the obvious rule for consumption:

$$\text{marginal utility of consumption} = p . \tag{7}$$

These two principles together with the production relation equation (2) provide a system of relations for determining the optimal course of the economy.

So far a perfectly planned economy has been assumed. However, these results can be given two important alternative institutional interpretations.

First, clearly all results remain valid for a perfectly competitive economy. It would have to be supposed, though, that the interests of unborn generations are somehow being represented on any current market. The most natural mechanism for this is responsibility of each current individual for his heirs.

---

[2] The validity of this analysis depends on the assumption that $\omega > \gamma$, so that the discounted value of future output is finite; otherwise, infinite values for discounted utility streams are possible, which so far have been hard to interpret.

Second, suppose that individuals are faced with an imperfect capital market, as postulated in Section I, and, therefore, they save a fixed fraction of disposable income. Suppose at the same time we introduce a public sector which can tax and use the proceeds for investment; public capital is for the moment assumed indistinguishable from private. Let T be the volume of taxes. Then capital formation is the sum of private saving and taxes.

$$\dot{K} = s(Y - T) + T = sY + (1 - s)T . \tag{8}$$

Clearly, by suitable choice of T, the public sector can make the rate of capital formation anything it desires. In particular, then, taxes can so be chosen as to achieve the highest possible optimum. In effect, the assumption of a fixed saving ratio removes one degree of freedom from the private sector, and this is exactly compensated by giving the government a compensatory degree of freedom. In Tinbergen's terminology [ref. 29, ch. 2, 4, 5], we have one target of policy, achievement of an optimum savings ratio, and one instrument, taxation, so the target can always be achieved.[3]

V

PUBLIC AND PRIVATE CAPITAL WITH FIXED SAVINGS RATIO AND TAX FINANCING

Now suppose there are two kinds of capital, public and private. Output is a function of the amounts of both kinds of capital and of the labor force, and again we assume Harrod-neutral technological progress. Let K_1 and K_2 be the amounts of private and public capital, respectively. Then the production relation equation (2) is replaced by

$$Y = F(K_1, K_2, e^{\tau t}L) , \tag{9}$$

where again F has constant returns to scale and isoquants which are convex to the origin.

Suppose again that we have a perfectly planned economy which can determine both kinds of investment. Then it is easy to see that the marginal productivities of the two kinds of capital must be equal at each moment of time. If we let F_1 and F_2 be the marginal productivities of private and public capital, respectively, then we are requiring

---

[3] There may be some difficulty if the private rate of saving, s, exceeds the optimal; then T would have to be negative (subsidies), and the public would have to disinvest. This will be impossible if publicly owned capital is already zero. Hence, the economy will fall short of its optimum; in the long run, the capital-output ratio will be too high.

$$F_1 = F_2 . \tag{10}$$

Once this rule is followed, the two kinds of capital are in effect one. They have the same utility price in the sense defined in the last section, and, for an optimum, equations (6) and (7) must still hold. In the long run, the system tends towards a steady growth at the natural rate, γ, with the common marginal productivity of the two kinds of capital being equated to the natural rate of interest, ω.

Thus, the optimal discount rule for public investment is that it use the rates of return to private capital. But this is only valid in the context of a more inclusive policy in which aggregate capital is being adjusted to a long-run position where the natural rate of interest is governing.

Again, note that a perfectly competitive capital market will achieve this optimum.

We now turn to the central issue, the effect of imperfect capital markets. It is further assumed at this point that private and public capital formation are separated; private capital formation is governed by private savings out of disposable income, while the formation of public capital is simply equal to taxation. (I abstract from current government expenditures, which can easily be introduced into the model.) This is essentially the model studied by Eckstein [ref. 6, pp. 94–104] and subsequently by Steiner [ref. 30] and Marglin [ref. 7]. Let T be total taxes collected. Then the assumptions on capital formation are

$$\dot{K}_1 = s(Y - T) , \tag{11}$$

$$\dot{K}_2 = T . \tag{12}$$

The aim of government policy is to choose T at each moment of time so as to maximize the sum of discounted utilities of consumption. A full analysis of the optimal path, starting with given magnitudes of the two stocks of capital, seems impossible without the sophisticated mathematical tools mentioned in Section IV, but I will try to show the nature of the optimal policy under conditions of steady growth.

It will be granted that for an optimal policy the tax rate, T/Y, will approach some limit. In a condition of steady growth, then, we assume T/Y to be constant, but we wish to determine what value it assumes for an optimum. For constant T/Y, it follows from equations (11) and (12) that $\dot{K}_1$ and $\dot{K}_2$ are both constant fractions of Y. Hence, by an extension of the same reasoning as in Section II, the economy will grow at the constant rate, γ, the natural rate. Both kinds of capital will grow at the rate γ, so the ratios among the three quantities, private capital, public capital, and labor force measured in efficiency units, will be constant. Then the marginal productivities of the two kinds of capital will also be constant. Finally, the consumption rate of interest will be, as before, the natural rate of interest, ω.

It is argued that the optimal policy for taxation and public capital formation will be that which equates the marginal productivity of public investment, F_2, to ω. The fundamental point is that the benefits from a public investment project increase national income and therefore are partly saved. Hence, indirectly the returns from public investment include some benefit from private investment projects. It is claimed that this exactly offsets the loss of private investment due to the initial act of public investment.

To see this, consider first any dollar added to the disposable income of the private sector. Some will be consumed immediately, the rest saved. The earnings from the amount saved will again be split between saving and consumption, and the process continued. As stated, F_1 is the rate of return available at all times in the private sector (a constant along the path of steady growth). Then at any instant the individual earns a return of F_1 on this present capital, of which sF_1 constitutes an increase of capital. Thus, the stock of capital grows at the rate sF_1; at a constant rate of return, income rises at the same rate, and hence so does consumption. Under the assumption that $\omega > sF_1$, this exponential increasing stream of consumption will have a finite social value (i.e., when discounted at the natural rate of interest), say v. Thus, the addition of a dollar to disposable income is equivalent to a single act of consumption of value v. Now consider that a government project costing a dollar, and yielding a constant perpetual income of r, is contemplated. The welfare loss to the private sector for the cost is v. In each subsequent time period, however, r dollars are added to the private sector and hence yield a welfare increase of rv. Thus, taking account of all interactions, the rate of return of the government project to the economy is still r, and it should, of course, be undertaken if, and only if, $r \geqq \omega$. Thus, we conclude that

$$F_2 = \omega \text{ along a steady growth path .} \qquad (13)$$

There is no necessity that the rate of return on private capital also equal ω along the path of steady growth; on the contrary, except by accident, the two rates will differ. Since K_1, K_2, and the labor force in efficiency units are all growing at the same rate, the steady growth path is determined by two of the ratios among these three variables. One relation among these ratios is that given by equation (13); the other follows from equations (11) and (12), in that the amount of private saving must be enough to maintain private capital formation at the appropriate rate.

If, at the initial stage, the ratios of the two kinds of capital and of labor are not at their long-run values, a process of adjustment must take place. The sum of discounted utilities obtainable by starting at any given moment with given stocks of the two kinds of capital is a function, $V(K_1, K_2)$. By differentiation, we can obtain marginal valuations, p_1 and p_2, for the two types of capital, respectively. Then it can be shown that the optimal path satisfies the conditions

$$(p_2/p_1) F_1 = \omega - (\dot{p}_1/p_1) . \tag{14}$$

$$F_2 = \omega - (\dot{p}_2/p_2) . \tag{15}$$

$$\text{marginal utility of consumption} = (p_2 - sp_1)/(1 - s) . \tag{16}$$

These equations do not lend themselves to completely transparent interpretation. Equation (15) supplies the discount criterion for the government, and is in the typical form of correcting the equilibrium interest rate by a speculative term. Equation (14) has the same form except that output is revalued in the ratio p_2/p_1 . Equation (16) is more meaningful in the form

$$p_2 = sp_1 + (1 - s) \text{ (marginal utility of consumption)};$$

since a dollar of taxes reduces private investment by s and consumption by $1 - s$, the utility price of public capital is the corresponding weighted average of the utility prices of private capital and consumption.

These equations are intended for the government to calculate the volume of taxes needed to carry out the optimal program.

The inequality between the rates of return to the two kinds of capital means, of course, a failure to achieve the optimum possible in a perfectly planned or perfectly competitive world. Essentially, to use again Tinbergen's terminology, there are now two targets, the rates of capital accumulation in the two sectors, and only one instrument, the tax policy.

VI

THE IMPLICATIONS OF BOND FINANCING

Suppose now we permit the government to finance public investment by either bonds or taxes. Now one more instrument is added to the government and, as might be expected, the fully optimal policy is now achievable. Assume that the saver is indifferent as to choice between government bonds and investment in private capital. (The more general assumption that bonds are an imperfect substitute for private investment would not essentially alter the results.) Let B be the flow of new bond issues, in real terms. Then private capital formation is reduced by B from that given in equation (11), while public capital formation is increased by the same amount. Then equations (11) and (12) are replaced by

$$\dot{K}_1 = s(Y - T) - B , \tag{17}$$

$$\dot{K}_2 = T + B . \tag{18}$$

In these equations, it is necessary to define T to mean taxes *less* interest payments on the national debt, since these two magnitudes offset each other both in the disposable income and in the budgetary balance of the government. (This cancellation is the meaning of Franklin D. Roosevelt's famous phrase, "We owe it to ourselves." It does not mean that there is no burden to the debt.)

It is trivial to observe that any desired time path of capital accumulation can be achieved by suitable choice of T and B; in particular, the optimal time path can be followed. In this regime, equation (10) holds; thus, as Hirshleifer, De Haven, and Milliman [ref. 31, p. 120] pointed out, the rate of interest applicable to public investments should equal the private rate, if the government is taking appropriate monetary and fiscal measures to overcome any divergence between true time preference and that observed in market behavior. But this may be a big "if."[4]

VII

RISK AND THE RATE OF RETURN

To conclude, it is argued that the government should not display risk aversion in its behavior. Hence, the proper procedure is to compute the expected values of benefits and costs, and discount them at a riskless rate, contrary to the view of Hirshleifer [ref. 35, p. 85].

Suppose the future to be unknown; it is known that one of a set of states will prevail and their probabilities are known (or believed in). A given state means a complete description of all production possibilities,

---

[4] Even apart from the issue of public investment as such, Tobin has argued the possibility and desirability of government fiscal policy (at full employment) because of the imperfections of the capital market [ref. 32, pp. 12–13]. Notice though that an increase in B decreases private investment. Hence, in the absence of public investment, if private saving is deemed deficient, the cure is a negative value for B. So long as the government has a large debt, this can be handled by budgetary surplus and debt retirement. But in the long run it would require government lending to private industry, which represents a considerable institutional change. In the presence of public investment, total investment is unaffected by bonds, and it is at least possible that the optimal solution will require $B > 0$ in the long run.

It may also be worth noting that the effect of bond financing on physical investment is precisely the "burden of the debt" which Buchanan [ref. 33] and Modigliani [ref. 34] have studied.

so that all uncertainties are resolved when the state is known. To summarize some earlier discussions ([ref. 36]; Debreu [ref. 37, chap 7]; Hirshleifer [ref. 35, pp. 80–85]), we can achieve an optimal allocation if we imagine markets in all possible commodity-options, a commodity-option being an obligation to deliver a fixed amount of a given commodity if, and only if, a given state prevails.

Suppose, for example, that there is only one commodity and, to make matters really simple, only one consumer (or, all consumers are alike). The consumer or consumers start out owning claims on future production. The amount of the commodity they can claim is, of course, a random variable whose outcome depends on the state of nature. Thus, the representative individual is entitled, before trading, to an amount $\bar{y}_s$ if state s occurs. Let Π_s be the probability of state s, and let p_s be the market price of a claim to one unit of the commodity if state s occurs. Using the Ramsey–von Neumann–Morgenstern utility construction, the consumer chooses claims y_s so as to maximize

$$\sum \Pi_s \, U(y_s) \, ,$$

subject to a budget constraint, $\sum p_s y_s = \sum p_s \bar{y}_s$. Hence, by the usual Lagrangian techniques, we have, for any two states s and t,

$$p_s/p_t = (\Pi_s/\Pi_t) \, [U'(y_s)/U'(y_t)] \, .$$

Equality of supply and demand on the market insures that $y_s = \bar{y}_s$, all s. Hence, the price of a claim in state s is relatively higher than the actuarial value, if the marginal utility of income is relatively higher. Under the assumption of risk aversion (diminishing marginal utility), the price is higher than the actuarial value for adverse conditions, and vice versa.

Consider now a small project which will yield a random variable, h_s , depending on the state s. It is worth while introducing this project if $\sum p_s h_s \geqq 0$. Since, as noted, the prices p_s are not proportional to the probabilities, it might appear that something different from an expected value calculation is relevant. Indeed, in general, this is so. But if a plausible condition is added, the criterion is reduced to the expected value. Suppose that the return to the new investment is independent of the variations in income before the investment is made. In the context of public investment, y_s should be interpreted as the total national income, considered as a random variable. The returns to a particular new project are apt to have little statistical relation to the previous national income. The criterion for introducing a new project can be written as

$$\sum_s \Pi_s \, U'(y_s)h_s \geqq 0 \, ,$$

29

the left-hand side being the expectation of the product of random variables $U'(y_s)h_s$. If h_s is independent of y_s, it is also independent of $U'(y_s)$, so that the expectation of the product is the product of the expectations. The criterion becomes

$$E[U'(y_s)]\, E[h_s] \geqq 0 ,$$

and since the first factor is necessarily positive, this is equivalent to the condition $E(h_s) \geqq 0$. Hence, for small investments uncorrelated with previous national income, the government should be risk-neutral.

Indeed, in many cases (e.g., flood control), one would expect that there is a negative relation between y_s and h_s, and hence a positive relation between $U'(y_s)$ and h_s, so that the new project may be justified, even if its expected value is negative, since it reduces aggregate uncertainty.

Consider a private investment of comparable riskiness. In a perfect system of risk markets, such as those suggested above, the firm can reinsure its risks in effect with the whole economy, and therefore would behave as the government should. But in fact these markets do not exist. Hence, the y_s for the firm is basically only the firm's own other income, and this is apt to be positively related to the return on the new investment, so that the criterion for accepting the project becomes more rigid than the expected value criterion. Thus, the firm displays risk aversion, and the government should not be required to observe the same standards.

As in all cases of imperfection, this raises the question of whether the important step might be the institution of risk markets. The trouble here is the difficulty of divorcing risk-taking and responsibility. It is socially desirable to permit insurance against unavoidable risks, but not against a failure of the individual to optimize; and observation does not ordinarily permit a clear distinction, at least not costlessly.

It can be argued that many markets, especially those in equities, do perform some of the functions of risk markets. This is correct, but I would maintain that their performance is far from perfect; the evidence for this assertion is that perfect risk markets would eliminate risk to the *firm,* and we know that this elimination has not occurred.

REFERENCES

[1] Sen, A. K. "On Optimizing the Rate of Saving," *Economic Journal,* Vol. 71 (September 1961).
[2] Marglin, S. A. "The Social Rate of Discount and the Optimal Rate of

Investment," *Quarterly Journal of Economics*, Vol. 77 (February 1963).

[3] Tullock, G. "The Social Rate of Discount and the Optimal Rate of Investment: Comment," *Quarterly Journal of Economics*, Vol. 78 (May 1964).

[4] Lind, R. C. "The Social Rate of Discount and the Optimal Rate of Investment: Further Comment," *Quarterly Journal of Economics*, Vol. 78 (May 1964).

[5] Becker, G. *Human Capital: A Theoretical and Empirical Inquiry*. New York: National Bureau of Economic Research, 1965.

[6] Eckstein, O. *Water Resource Development*. Cambridge: Harvard University Press, 1961.

[7] Marglin, S. A. "The Opportunity Costs of Public Investment," *Quarterly Journal of Economics*, Vol. 77 (May 1963).

[8] ——. *Approaches to Dynamic Investment Planning*. Amsterdam: North-Holland Publishing Co., 1963.

[9] Arrow, K. J. "Optimal Capital Policy, The Cost of Capital, and Myopic Decision Rules," *Annals of the Institute of Statistical Mathematics* (Tokyo), Vol. 16, 1964.

[10] Ramsey, F. P. "A Mathematical Theory of Saving," *Economic Journal*, Vol. 38 (December 1928).

[11] Meade, J. E. *Trade and Welfare*. London, New York, and Toronto: Oxford University Press, 1955.

[12] Lerner, A. P. *The Economics of Control*. New York: Macmillan Co., 1946.

[13] Modigliani, F., and Brumberg, R. "Utility Analysis and the Consumption Function: An Interpretation of Cross-Section Data," chap. 15 in K. K. Kurihara (ed.), *Post-Keynesian Economics*. New Brunswick, N.J.: Rutgers University Press, 1954.

[14] Friedman, M. *A Theory of the Consumption Function*. New York: National Bureau of Economic Research, 1957.

[15] Yaari, M. E. "On the Consumer's Lifetime Allocation Process," *International Economic Review*, Vol. 5 (September 1964).

[16] Hamburger, W. "The Relation of Consumption to Wealth and the Wage Rate," *Econometrica*, Vol. 23 (July 1955).

[17] Friedman, M. "Windfalls, the 'Horizon,' and Related Concepts in the Permanent-Income Hypothesis," in C. Christ and others, *Measurement in Economics*. Stanford: Stanford University Press, 1963.

[18] Harrod, R. F. *Towards a Dynamic Economics*. London: Macmillan Co., 1948.

[19] Solow, R. M. "A Contribution to the Theory of Economic Growth," *Quarterly Journal of Economics*, Vol. 70 (February 1956).

[20] Swan, T. "Economic Growth and Capital Accumulation," *Economic Record*, Vol. 32 (November 1956).

[21] Eckstein, O. "Investment Criteria for Economic Development and the Theory of Intertemporal Welfare Economics," *Quarterly Journal of Economics*, Vol. 71 (February 1957).

[22] Frisch, R. "Dynamic Utility," *Econometrica*, Vol. 32 (July 1964).

[23] Bellman, R. *Dynamic Programming*. Princeton: Princeton University Press, 1957.

31

[24] Pontryagin, L. S., Boltyanskii, V. G., Gamkrelidze, R. V., and Mischenko, E. T. *The Mathematical Theory of Optimal Processes.* New York and London: Interscience Publishers, Inc., 1962.

[25] Bellman, R., and Dreyfus, S. *Applied Dynamic Programming.* Princeton: Princeton University Press, 1962.

[26] Kalman, R. E. "The Theory of Optimal Control and the Calculus of Variations," in R. Bellman (ed.), *Mathematical Optimization Techniques.* Berkeley and Los Angeles: University of California Press, 1963.

[27] Stoleru, L. G. "An Optimal Policy for Economic Growth," *Econometrica,* Vol. 33 (April 1965).

[28] Mirrlees, J. *Optimal Planning for a Dynamic Economy.* Unpublished Ph.D. dissertation, University of Cambridge, 1963.

[29] Tinbergen, J. *On the Theory of Economic Policy.* Amsterdam: North-Holland Publishing Co., 1952.

[30] Steiner, P. O. "Choosing Among Alternative Public Investments," *American Economic Review,* Vol. 49 (December 1959).

[31] Hirshleifer, J., De Haven, J. C., and Milliman, J. W. *Water Supply: Economics, Technology, and Policy.* Chicago: University of Chicago Press, 1960.

[32] Tobin, J. "Economic Growth as an Objective of Government Policy," *American Economic Review Papers and Proceedings,* Vol. 54 (May 1964).

[33] Buchanan, M. *Public Principles of Public Debt.* Homewood, Ill.: Richard D. Irwin, Inc., 1958.

[34] Modigliani, F. "Long-Run Implications of Alternative Fiscal Policies and the Burden of the National Debt," *Economic Journal,* Vol. 71 (December 1961).

[35] Hirshleifer, J. "Efficient Allocation of Capital in an Uncertain World," *American Economic Review Papers and Proceedings,* Vol. 54 (May 1964).

[36] Arrow, K. J. "The Role of Securities in the Optimal Allocation of Risk Bearing," *Review of Economic Studies,* Vol. 31 (April 1964).

[37] Debreu, G. *Theory of Value.* New York: John Wiley and Sons, 1959.

The Role of Alternative Cost in Project Design and Selection

Peter O. Steiner*

Substantial—indeed it seems to me decisive—progress has been made in the past decade in formulating the correct principles of project design and selection with adequate attention to such matters as hidden interactions, incompatibilities, and opportunity costs. No attempt is made here to enlarge on that progress. Rather, an intensely practical problem is addressed, albeit theoretically: Under what conditions can one avoid, limit, or make more manageable the enormously difficult problem of benefit estimation?

While many recent ingenious papers deal with the measurement of benefits of public expenditures in a variety of cases (e.g., [ref. 1]), it is assumed throughout this paper that it is much easier to evaluate the cost of a project than to estimate the benefits that accrue therefrom. This assumption results from the successes as well as the failures in benefit measurement. Benefit measurement is hard and time-consuming, and should be undertaken only when required.

The central question here then is: When and to what extent can the cost of an alternative project substitute for, or provide limits to, benefit measurement? (This reverses the economist's usual substitution, wherein

* Professor of Economics, University of Wisconsin. This paper appeared in substantially the same form in the August 1965 issue of the *Quarterly Journal of Economics*. The author would like to acknowledge the financial support of the Harvard Water Program and the Research Committee of the University of Wisconsin. Helpful suggestions have been received from members of the Harvard Water Program and from the Workshop on the Firm and Market, Social Systems Research Institute, University of Wisconsin.

the cost of A is the benefit lost by not doing B.) There is a good deal of fuzzy folklore to the effect that alternative cost sets an upper limit to benefits. But when the matter is examined systematically, we find that in some cases alternative costs substitute for benefits, in others they provide upper limits to attribution of benefits, and in still others they provide minimum target levels that benefits must reach for the choices that have to be made.

The problem is complicated because a specific proposed public project may have alternatives of different sorts. For example, a dual-purpose public project may have single-purpose public alternatives to each purpose, it may have a variant dual-purpose public alternative, or it may have private alternatives to either or both purposes. These alternatives may be equivalent in quantity, quality, and distribution of services, or they may differ. Furthermore, if the specific public project is not undertaken, the conditions under which a specified alternative will actually come into operation will vary.

The basic strategy of this paper is to set up what appears to be a very limited model in which we consider only two public projects and two private projects. By varying assumptions about:

1) what is alternative to what,
2) what combinations of projects are compatible,
3) what institutional rules govern the selection of projects, and
4) what quantities and qualities of services are provided by individual projects,

we can capture the flavor of the many possibilities of the general problem, and define the extent to which alternative costs substitute for benefit measurement.

I

THE BASIC MODEL

Let us designate initially a specific governmental project P_{1g}. Let x_{1g} represent the "level" of this project. $x_{1g} = 1$ means the project is activated. $x_{1g} = 0$ means the project is not activated.[1] x_{1g}, in other words, is the choice variable for the first governmental project. Let B_{1g} and C_{1g} represent respectively the benefits and costs of the project if it is activated, as evaluated from the public point of view. A second governmental project, P_{2g}, has a choice variable x_{2g}, and benefits and costs B_{2g} and C_{2g}. x_{2g} is limited to the values 0 and 1.

---

[1] A "project" is thus defined as a specific design and pattern of operation. Alternative designs or alternative plans of operation are, in this usage, different projects. This assumption which makes the $x_{1g} = 0, 1$, by definition, is an analytic convenience that implies no loss of generality.

34

Designate further two private projects P_{1p} and P_{2p}, whose levels are x_{1p} and x_{2p}, and whose benefits and costs are B_{1p}, B_{2p}, C_{1p} and C_{2p} respectively. These benefits and costs are evaluated from the public (i.e., governmental) point of view. Again the choice variables x_{1p} and x_{2p} are limited to the values 0 or 1.

Constraints on Choice

Suppose one wishes to regard two of these four projects—say P_{1g} and P_{1p}—as alternatives to one another in the sense that both of them will not be activated. This restriction may be stated in one of two forms:

Either $x_{1g} + x_{1p} = 1$, which says that one project or the other, but not both, will be activated,

or $x_{1g} + x_{1p} \leqq 1$, which states that at most one of these projects will be activated, but it is perfectly possible that neither will be activated.

If we wish to designate two projects—say P_{1g} and P_{2g}—as necessarily joint in the sense that both or neither are to be activated, we use the constraint $x_{1g} = x_{2g}$.

Rules of Choice

We will assume that the government directly or indirectly controls the choice of all the x's because of the institutional rules of the game. The assumption can take one of two forms. The weaker of these is that the government has pre-emptive power of choice in a conflict between private and public projects. In this case, for example, if one supposes P_{1g} and P_{1p} are incompatible in the sense that both cannot be activated, the government gets "first refusal." If it assigns $x_{1g} = 1$, then it implicitly assigns $x_{1p} = 0$. If, however, it assigns $x_{1g} = 0$, then the decision as to whether x_{1p} is equal to 0 or 1 is left to the private sector.

The stronger institutional assumption is that the government has determinative choice. Not only can it assign $x_{1g} = 0$, but it can also assign $x_{1p} = 0$ even though the private sector would like to build the private project.[2]

---

[2] To make this distinction concrete, suppose the government is considering building a dam on the Skunk river which will provide electric power to the inhabitants of the Skunk valley. The privately owned Skunk Power and Light Company would like to build its own dam for a private hydroelectric installation, and if permitted would do so, should the public project not be built. Under *pre-emptive* choice, the government either builds its project or implicitly permits the private project to be built. Suppose the public authorities decide not to build and also to preserve forever the Skunk river for fishing by refusing to allow a private dam. This is *determinative* choice. Of course, the S. P. and L. Co. may have as its second choice a steam plant. Even if the government can exercise determinative choice against the private hydro project, it will be limited to pre-emptive choice against the alternate steam installation.

There is a third possibility.[3] Government may have no authority to prevent a private project, but it may announce a public project that is competitive with a planned private project. This would almost surely make unattractive to private investors a private project that had previously appeared attractive. If this kind of announcement always worked, such a case would analytically be identical with pre-emptive choice. If it worked only sometimes, the situation would be troublesome. If the private project were built anyway, the government would have two choices. It might vindictively build a wasteful, redundant facility in order to strengthen its position in similar situations, or it might withdraw, thus weakening its hand in the future. Analysis of these possibilities invites the use of game theory. I will ignore this case in this paper (except as it fits the pre-emptive choice case) because I think it is not very real in the contemporary political and economic climate.

Explicit and Implicit Sets of Alternatives

Choices are generally made among a specified set of alternatives. Suppose, to keep things simple, we consider a choice set that involves two projects P_A and P_B. Four explicit outcomes to a choice are defined in this set:

$$P_A \text{ but not } P_B$$
$$P_B \text{ but not } P_A$$
$$P_B \quad \text{and} \quad P_A$$
$$\text{neither } P_A \text{ nor } P_B.$$

In the analysis of these alternatives some hitherto unconsidered possibilities may be discovered. These will be referred to as implicit alternatives. For a real example, in the choice between a high public dam at Hells Canyon and a three-low-dam private development, one implicit alternative was a three-low-dam *public* project.

Viable Private Alternatives

A private alternative to the services of a specified public project is defined as "viable" if it is undertaken by the private sector with the permission of the public authorities. Viability is determined in the private sector presumably by attention to revenues, costs, availability of capital, etc. A viable alternative in this sense is genuine, as distinct from hypothetical.

Determining whether there are viable private alternatives is an im-

---

[3] Professor Smithies has called this possibility to my attention. He does not share my view of its unreality.

portant practical problem. In some cases there is direct evidence of both the existence and viability of a private alternative development plan—for example, in applications for permission to develop, and in the activities of interested private groups. In other cases, preliminary announcement of governmental interest may generate a counterproposal from a private group. In still other situations either or both the existence and viability of a private alternative must be determined. Here there is extra work to be done. This work will tend, however, to be much easier than estimating public benefits. Analysis must be from the private point of view and attention can be limited to direct, recoverable sources of revenue. It is not always easy to estimate prices, but it is much easier than estimating a whole demand curve. In my view, defining the existence and viability of private alternatives is a manageable problem; if this view is wrong, the scope of alternative cost is drastically reduced. I assume that it is not wrong.

The Choice Criterion

Government is assumed to choose to maximize the net public benefits over all the choices it controls, subject to whatever constraints are applicable. Letting Z represent net public benefits, we may write the objective function for a four-project (two private, two public) choice set as:

$$Z = (B_{1g} - C_{1g})\, x_{1g} + (B_{2g} - C_{2g})\, x_{2g} \qquad (1)$$
$$+ (B_{1p} - C_{1p})\, x_{1p} + (B_{2p} - C_{2p})\, x_{2p}\,.$$

The government wishes to choose the choice variables under its control so as to maximize (1) subject to all relevant constraints. To give content to this otherwise empty statement we must examine specified cases.

II

CHOICES ONLY AMONG EXPLICIT ALTERNATIVES— GOVERNMENT CHOICE PRE-EMPTIVE (CASES A, B, AND C)

A. Cases in which to each governmental project (or service) there is a viable private alternative project at the same level, quantity and pattern of distribution of service. (Case A)

The assumptions of Case A may be specified formally as:

(a) $\qquad\qquad\qquad B_{1g} = B_{1p};\, B_{2g} = B_{2p}\,.$

(b) $\qquad\qquad\qquad x_{1g} + x_{1p} = 1;\, x_{2g} + x_{2p} = 1\,.$

Conditions (a) reflect the fact that since the physical services are identical the public evaluation of the benefits therefrom is independent of whether the services are privately or publicly provided.

Conditions (b) reflect the fact that to each project there is a viable alternative, which means that the private project will be built unless the public choice pre-empts it.

Substituting (a) and (b) in equation (1) leads us to

$$Z = (C_{1p} - C_{1g}) \, x_{1g} + (C_{2p} - C_{2g}) \, x_{2g} + [B_{1p} + B_{2p} - C_{1p} - C_{2p}] \, .$$

Noting that the expression in square brackets is not a function of the choice variables we rewrite this as:

$$Z_A = (C_{1p} - C_{1g}) \, x_{1g} + (C_{2p} - C_{2g}) \, x_{2g} + K_A \, . \tag{2}$$

It is clear that to maximize Z_A [4] no information about benefits is required. This is the pure domain of comparative cost. The reason is obvious: since the services will be provided in any event, the only issue concerns providing them in the cheapest possible way. This is true for the case in which there is no interrelationship between the public projects (just considered) or subcases in which they are interdependent. Consider two subcases:

Case A.1: The two public projects are alternative competing ways of providing the same set of services.

The assumptions here are, formally, that

(c) $x_{1g} + x_{2g} \leqq 1$.   (At most one will be built.)

(d) $C_{1p} = C_{2p}$.   (Since the services are the same, the private alternative is common to both.)

Examining (c) and equation (2), it is clear that if either of the parenthetical expressions in (2) is positive, Z_A will be maximized by building one of the public projects. That is by

(c') $x_{1g} + x_{2g} = 1$.

In this event, rewrite (2) as:

$$Z_{A.1} = (C_{2g} - C_{1g}) \, x_{1g} + K_{A.1} \, , \tag{3}$$

which says merely that one should pick the cheaper of the two public projects.

Had both parenthetical expressions in (2) been negative, $x_{1g} = x_{2g} = 0$ would maximize Z. This again says the obvious: that if the private

---

[4] The subscript A is used to identify this as Case A.

alternative is equivalent in service to either public project, and is cheaper, it is preferred.[5]

Case A.2: The two public projects are joint (complementary) products of a common project. This dual-purpose project has a common set of costs.

The implied restriction is that $x_{1g} = x_{2g}$. We do both or neither. Assume for simplicity that the common costs, C_g, are truly joint costs.[6] That is, assume $C_g = C_{1g} + C_{2g}$. Substituting these restrictions in (2), leads to:

$$Z_{A.2} = (C_{1p} + C_{2p} - C_g)\, x_{1g} + K_{A.2}\,, \qquad (4)$$

where, if the expression in parentheses is positive, both $x_{1g} = 1$ and $x_{2g} = 1$, and if negative both are zero.

Notice in Cases A, A.1, and A.2 that the choice criterion is wholly a function of comparative costs. There is no need to establish "absolute merit," because the existence of a viable private alternative assures that whatever the decision the services will be provided.

B. Cases in which there is no viable alternative to either government project. (Case B)

We here assume the following restrictions on the general case of equation (1):

(e) $$B_{1p} = B_{2p} = C_{1p} = C_{2p} = 0\,,$$

and the objective function becomes:

$$Z_B = (B_{1g} - C_{1g})\, x_{1g} + (B_{2g} - C_{2g})\, x_{2g}\,, \qquad (5)$$

and there is no escape from benefit measurement. With no additional restrictions on x_{1g} and x_{2g}, it is necessary to establish "absolute-merit" of each project. This is true whether or not the two public projects are alternatives. Even if it is assumed that $B_{1g} = B_{2g}$ and $x_{1g} + x_{2g} \leq 1$ it is not known whether both x_{1g} and x_{2g} should equal zero without demonstrating benefits in excess of cost.

---

[5] I am abstracting throughout this paper from the fact that private and public funds may be differently constrained and thus have different opportunity costs. The C_p as defined here includes an opportunity cost of the private capital involved. On the broader issue, see my earlier paper [ref. 2] for extended discussion. It would complicate but not illuminate to incorporate this modification here, where we are concerned solely with the role of comparative cost in limiting benefit measurement.

[6] We could easily visualize some common costs and some separate costs and visualize three (or more) variants of the public project. But it does not change the essential result that only cost measurement is required.

39

It may be trite to state that where there are no alternatives, alternative cost plays no role.

One subcase is worth noting. Suppose it is stipulated, say by legislative assertion of the need for service, that a public project be undertaken. This adds the constraint:

(f) $$x_{1g} + x_{2g} = 1 ,$$

and equation (5) becomes:

$$Z_{B.1} = [(B_{1g} - B_{2g}) + (C_{2g} - C_{1g})] x_{1g} + K_{B.1} \qquad (6)$$

and if $B_{1g} = B_{2g}$, comparative cost alone need be considered. In this case legislative assertion of absolute merit replaces the need for measurement to establish such merit.

C. Cases in which there is limited or partial existence of viable alternatives. (Case C)

Cases of this kind can arise either if there is a viable private alternative to one but not both public projects, or if the private alternative that will be undertaken (i.e., it is viable) produces a different quantity, quality, or distribution of services. (The subcases will be distinguished below after a development of the general case.)

Let us define
$$\Delta B_1 = B_{1g} - B_{1p}$$
$$\Delta B_2 = B_{2g} - B_{2p}$$

with no restrictions on the signs of ΔB_1 and ΔB_2. (Note for future reference that $B_{1p} = 0$ can be permitted to represent the case of the non-viable alternative. In this usage there is always a private alternative—which may be to do nothing.)

The constraints this case imposes are:

(g) $$x_{1g} + x_{1p} = 1$$
$$x_{2g} + x_{2p} = 1 .$$

Substituting in equation (1) leads us to the very general equation:[7]

$$Z_C = (\Delta B_1 + C_{1p} - C_{1g}) x_{1g} + (\Delta B_2 + C_{2p} - C_{2g}) x_{2g} + K_C \qquad (7)$$

and it is apparent that at least incremental benefit measurement may be required. Consider some subcases.

---

[7] Cases A and B, above, are just special cases of this most general case. In Case A, equation (2), it was assumed that $\Delta B_1 = \Delta B_2 = 0$. In Case B, equation (5), it was assumed that $\Delta B_1 = B_{1g}$, $\Delta B_2 = B_{2g}$, and $C_{1p} = C_{2p} = 0$.

Case C.1: Viable alternative at same level of benefits to one public project, no viable alternative to the other public project.

Let $\Delta B_1 = B_{1g}$ and $C_{1p} = 0$ (No viable private alternative to P_{1g}.)

    $\Delta B_2 = 0$ (Viable private alternative to P_{2g}.)

And equation (7) becomes:

$$Z_{C.1} = (B_{1g} - C_{1g})\, x_{1g} + (C_{2p} - C_{2g})\, x_{2g} + K_C. \qquad (8)$$

Alternative cost substitutes for benefit measurement for P_{2g}, but not for P_{1g}, the absolute merit of which must be established. Half a loaf is better than none. Notice, importantly, that if P_{1g} and P_{2g} are competing with each other—for scarce public funds, or for alternative uses of a river to mention two examples—this formulation may be of some help. Now $x_{1g} + x_{2g} \leqq 1$. Suppose (for simplicity) that $C_{1g} = C_{2g}$.

If $C_{2g} > C_{2p}$, we eliminate P_{2g} from consideration, and consider only the absolute merit of P_{1g}. If $C_{2p} > C_{2g}$, which implies $x_{1g} + x_{2g} = 1$, equation (8) becomes:

$$Z_{C.1}' = (B_{1g} - C_{2p})\, x_{1g} + K_C' \qquad (9)$$

which gives a target level for benefits. It is not necessary to measure benefits precisely. If B_{1g} can be shown to be at least as large as C_{2p} it is known that P_{1g} should be activated and P_{2g} abandoned. In some instances at least, target levels of this kind can save much labor in measurement.

Case C.2: Viable alternatives to both public projects but at lower levels of service (lower either in quantity or quality of service, or in the sense of providing a "less favorable" distribution of output).

Equation (7) now applies directly but we assume both ΔB_1 and ΔB_2 are positive. This may be of some help. For example, suppose the two public projects are compatible (i.e., both may be built). Consider P_{1g}. If $C_{1p} > C_{1g}$, P_{1g} is known to be desirable without any benefit measurement. (It may also be desirable if $C_{1g} > C_{1p}$, but in such a case it would be necessary to compare the extra cost with the extra benefits.)

The formulation in equation (7) may be helpful in other senses. Even if benefit measurement is required it will often be easier to estimate incremental benefits than total benefits, particularly if the size of the increment is a small fraction of the total. Further, by focusing on the target levels of benefits required for decisions, a great deal of detailed labor may be avoided. Many cases will not be close and refined measurement can be avoided.

III

CHOICES ONLY AMONG EXPLICIT ALTERNATIVES GOVERNMENT CHOICE DETERMINATIVE (CASE D)

In the cases to this point it has been assumed that if the government abstained, private developers could move in. This simplified measurement in some cases because something was going to be done with or without government action and only the net differences had to be evaluated.

My own view is that this is characteristic of a great many, perhaps most, public investment decisions for which viable private alternatives exist. But this is a political judgment, not an analytic one, and the analysis may be readily extended to comprehend determinative choices. For example, with respect to a particular governmental project (P_{1g}) which has a viable private alternative (P_{1p}) the government may:

1) build P_{1g}, thus precluding P_{1p};
2) not build P_{1g}, but permit P_{1p} to be built;
3) not build P_{1g}, but prohibit P_{1p}.

This problem may be treated in either of two ways. One would be to regard the third alternative as a second public project, say P_{2g} with no private alternative, with $C_{2g} = 0$, and with B_{2g} equal to the reservation value (if any) of the project site.[8] This straightforward application of the previous analysis shows that the third alternative is employed only when *both* P_{1g} and P_{1p} have less absolute merit than reserving the site. Some absolute judgment of merit is thus required, but the measurement burden seems unlikely to be onerous.

Alternatively, and perhaps with more illumination, let us look at the problem in a different way. Suppose a public project P_g has the viable private alternative P_{1p}, which the government can prohibit as well as preclude. Let P_{2p} be a second-best private alternative[9] that the government cannot prohibit,[10] which will be built if $x_{1g} = 0$ and P_{1p} is prohibited.

The objective function may be written directly as:

$$Z_D = (B_g - C_g)\, x_g + (B_{1p} - C_{1p})\, x_{1p} + (B_{2p} - C_{2p})\, x_{2p} \quad (10)$$

subject to:

$$x_g + x_{1p} + x_{2p} = 1.$$

[8] Only in cases involving natural resources—which I here call "site"—does a determinative policy make institutional sense to me. But my use of this word should not prejudge the issue.

[9] Second best from the private point of view.

[10] I believe this is a sensible way of looking at an alternative to a service.

Suppose the government makes its analyses sequentially. First, it chooses between P_{1p} and P_{2p}. Suppose the level of service is the same, then the choice depends wholly upon a comparison of C_{1P} and C_{2p}.[11] If the level of service is not the same, some attention to incremental benefits as well as costs is required.[12] If P_{1p} is not inferior to P_{2p} (from the public point of view), the case is the pure pre-emptive case discussed in Section II. If P_{1p} is inferior, again there is a pure pre-emptive case between P_g and P_{2p}.

In either case then the analysis of Section II applies. However, the real issue is not the formal one of fitting into the earlier analysis. Rather, it is whether the potentially substantial role of alternative cost as a substitute for benefit measurement is vitiated. It seems to me not to be, partly because *prohibitive* (as distinct from pre-emptive) policies will rarely be in doubt. Where they are in doubt the issues are more likely to be political than economic; where economic analyses will help, the choice is likely to be between alternative private projects, which can frequently be easily made. In a few cases an absolute judgment about the absolute merit of a private project will be required. To that extent, the previous (and subsequent) conclusions require modification.

IV

ADDITION OF IMPLICIT ALTERNATIVES (CASE E)

As seen above, the existence of viable alternatives helps avoid full and complete measurement of benefits.

Two broad types of implicit alternatives with many variations may be considered; these attempt to add to the list of alternatives, and thus potentially serve to substitute labor in choice for labor in measurement. The first is the implicit public alternative. The second is the implicit private alternative. Neither of these devices is fully helpful, but either may gain ground in some cases.

In order to see the issues, consider a particularly simple subcase of Case C.2, that in which a single-purpose public project has a viable private alternative but at a lower level of benefits. Assume first that the lower benefits are the result of the quantity of service rather than its quality or distributional pattern.

In this case, without implicit alternatives, we would specify:

---

[11] Note that if there is a "site reservation value" it is part of C_{1p}. In this way the present approach makes contact with the one discussed above.

[12] If P_{2p} does not exist then a judgment is required of the absolute merit of P_{1p}.

(h) $$\Delta B_1 = B_{1g} - B_{1p} > 0$$
(i) $$B_{2g} = C_{2g} = B_{2p} = C_{2p} = 0$$
(j) $$x_{1p} + x_{1g} = 1 \, ,$$

and write the objective function as:

$$Z_E = (\Delta B_1 + C_{1p} - C_{1g}) \, x_{1g} + K_E \, . \tag{11}$$

Suppose $C_{1g} > C_{1p}$, in order to make the decision depend upon the magnitude of ΔB_1.

Implicit Alternative 1: Let the private project be built, but provide the best possible complementary alternative public project P_{1g}' such that $B_{1g}' = \Delta B_1$ and specify:

$$x_{1p} + x_{1g} = 1 \, , \qquad \text{as before, and}$$
(k) $$x_{1p} = x_{1g}' \qquad \text{(make } P_{1p} \text{ and } P_{1g}' \text{ complementary)}$$

$$\begin{aligned} Z_{E.1} &= (B_{1g} - C_{1g}) \, x_{1g} + (B_{1g}' + B_{1p} - C_{1p} - C_{1g}') \, x_{1g}' \quad (12) \\ &= (C_{1p} + C_{1g}' - C_{1g}) \, x_{1g} + K_{E.1} \, . \end{aligned}$$

If the expression $C_{1p} + C_{1g}' - C_{1g}$ is negative, we know that $x_{1g} = 0$ will maximize $Z_{E.1}$. The public project is rejected and the private project is built. Whether in fact the public should build the alternative P_{1g}' depends upon $B_{1g}' - C_{1g}'$ —its absolute merit.

If $C_{1p} + C_{1g}' - C_{1g}$ is positive, a little ground is gained. We know that P_{1g}' is unpromising, and we are left with the criterion involved in equation (11) which involves measuring incremental benefits.[13]

Implicit Alternative 2: Design an alternative governmental project P_{1g}'' such that $B_{1g}'' = B_{1p}$. (If the original design of the public project had been optimal we know $B_{1g} - C_{1g} > B_{1g}'' - C_{1g}''$. In any event, here contact is made with the design problem.)

That is, we first compare P_{1g}'' and P_{1p} in a case where:

(l) $$B_{1g}'' = B_{1p} \qquad \text{(by definition)}$$
(m) $$x_{1g}'' + x_{1p} = 1 \qquad \text{and finding}$$

$$Z_{E.2} = (B_{1g}'' - C_{1g}'') \, x_{1g}'' + (B_{1p} - C_{1p}) \, x_{1p} \, , \tag{13}$$

substituting (l) and (m) in (13), the equation becomes:

$$Z_{E.2} = (C_{1p} - C_{1g}'') x_{1g}'' + K_{E.2} \, . \tag{14}$$

If $C_{1p} > C_{1g}''$, there is an apparent advantage of public over private

---

[13] C_{1g}' (the cost of P_{1g}') provides the maximum level of benefits one can assign to ΔB_1 as the contribution of P_{1g}. That is to say the incremental benefits assignable to a particular government project cannot exceed the cost of achieving those benefits by an alternative government project. This is the sense in which alternative costs provide an upper limit to benefits of a specific project.

44

provision, independent of the level of service, and some governmental project will be built. The question of scale of the public project remains to be decided. If the original design is known to have been optimal it has already been decided.

If $C_{1p} < C_{1g}''$ no ground has been gained and it is necessary to return to equation (11).

Under determinative, as distinct from pre-emptive, rules of choice there is a third implicit alternative. This is to prohibit the private project P_{1p}, but to permit the private developers to redesign their project into P_{1p}' in such a way that it provides the same level of service as P_{1g}. That is, to prescribe $B_{1p}' = B_{1g}$ if a private project is to be permitted.

From the governmental point of view, the choice between P_{1g} and P_{1p}' depends upon purely cost considerations. See Case A, equation (2), above. If C_{1g} is greater than C_{1p}', it should make the offer (or ultimatum, if you prefer) that this implicit alternative envisages. If the private group rejects this outcome we are left with equation (11).

Should the private developers reject this third alternative, either as a matter of strategy or because the private costs of P_{1p}' exceed its private benefits, or should pre-emptive choice rules apply, there is yet another implicit alternative: offer the private producers a subsidy to substitute P_{1p}' for P_{1p}. This policy may have real merit, but it does not avoid benefit measurement. The reason is that positive governmental action to subsidize requires establishment of the absolute merit of the subsidy. In terms of equation (11), ΔB_1 must be estimated in any case. For that reason, the subsidy alternative is not pursued further in this paper.

To this point, implicit alternatives have been discussed only in the context of quantity of service. If the difference between projects is due to something other than quantity of service, the same formal relations hold, but their meanings change. If, say, $B_{1g} > B_{1p}$ because of a different distribution of output, the implicit alternative may be to allow B_{1p} and adopt a complementary policy that achieves the desired redistribution. If quality of output (e.g., water quality) is the issue, implicit alternatives include such facilities as public or subsidized private water purification plants.

V

SUMMARY AND CONCLUSIONS

Let us start with the obvious conclusion of Case B, where there are no alternatives, explicit or implicit, alternative cost has no role to play, and there is no substitute for showing benefits at least equal to cost in justifying governmental action.

If the only alternative to a governmental project is some other public project, a comparison of costs may eliminate all but one public project. The benefits attributable to a specific governmental action will be limited by the costs of alternative governmental action, but that limitation neither limits the benefits of some governmental action nor does it avoid the necessity of showing absolute merit (benefits greater than cost) of the best public project. The exception to this is the case (B.1) of legislative stipulation of need for service.

Where a viable alternative exists and will be activated in the absence of government action its costs do substitute for benefits. If the list of services is the same, the benefits will be equal. In this case benefit measurement is totally unnecessary, and comparative cost provides necessary and sufficient conditions for choice (Case A). While this condition will not often be precisely met, the range of circumstances in which a substantial part of the benefits will accrue in any case is larger, and in these circumstances comparative costs play a potentially significant role in three ways: first, in narrowing required benefit measurement to incremental benefits, which may be much easier to measure than total benefits;[14] second, in providing sufficient (though not necessary) conditions for choice without benefit measurement that may apply to a significant number of cases; third, in providing target levels of benefits that must be found to justify a project (Case C). I anticipate that in some cases these levels may be so modest that they may be agreed to exist without laborious empirical efforts to establish them.

Implicit alternatives may, but need not, further reduce the need for benefit measurement. The basic strategy in comparing two projects (call them A and C) that differ both as to level of service and as to private versus governmental provision, is to interpose an implicit alternative (call it B), which provides benefits exactly equal to one or the other of the original projects. It may be that we can now show A is preferred to B, and B is preferred to C, thus establishing the choice of A in preference to C. More importantly, implicit alternatives may focus on overlooked projects, and avoid decisions between inferior alternatives. Implicit alternatives rarely avoid the problem of absolute merit, but again may provide either sufficient conditions or target levels that will simplify labor (Case E).

In the foregoing discussion it was assumed that governmental choices were *pre-emptive* rather than *determinative*. If determinative rules apply, we may either lose or gain ground. We lose if nothing ever happens

---

[14] E.g., it may be much easier to estimate a point, or a small region on a demand curve, than to estimate the whole curve.

without governmental permission, because it is then necessary to establish absolute merit of every action. We gain if, because of determinative rules, the government can offer all-or-nothing choices to private developers in such a way as to provide equivalent private alternatives to public projects.

Since the purely determinative cases seem to me to be rather infrequent in our institutional arrangement (but contrast purely socialist economies), the losses seem likely to be small. In mixed cases, alternative cost may well have a decisive role to play (Case D).

What does it all add up to in the end? Alternative cost, while no general substitute for benefit measurement, has a role to play in limiting, perhaps very significantly, the number of cases in which detailed, precise benefit measurement is required. It is true that the "hard" cases remain hard, but perhaps by releasing labor from the easy ones we can facilitate their solution.

REFERENCES

[1] *Measuring Benefits of Government Investments.* Papers presented at the 1963 Brookings Institution Conference on Government Investment Expenditures. Washington: Brookings Institution, 1965.
[2] Steiner, Peter O. "Choosing Among Alternative Public Expenditures," *American Economic Review,* Vol. 49, No. 5, 1959.

CASE STUDIES OF WATER MANAGEMENT

Water Resource Development in California: The Comparative Efficiency of Local, State, and Federal Agencies

Joe S. Bain*

T his is primarily a report on some findings Professor Caves, Professor Margolis, and I reached in a study of Northern California water resource development—conclusions concerning the comparative efficiency of water agencies in developing surface waters for and from the Central Valley of California. [Ref. 1.] We have attempted to make some appraisal of the industry of water agencies in this area with reference to two interrelated dimensions of performance:

a) The level of water resource development.

b) The character of allocation of water among types, sites, and times of use, and among different users of given types.

SOME BASIC CONCEPTS

Among the concepts developed in our analysis of the Central Valley are two referring to the level of water resource development:

1) The level of water usage development.

2) The level of water facilities development.

The level of water usage development refers roughly to the extent to which available water resources have been put to economic uses. Water from any source may be less than fully used or fully used; it becomes

* Professor of Economics, University of California, Berkeley. Numerous findings reported herein are the joint work-product of the author, of Richard E. Caves, Professor of Economics at Harvard University, and of Julius Margolis, Professor of Economics at Stanford University.

fully used as soon as it is an economically scarce good with a positive shadow price at the source. This would mean, in turn, that if properly allocated it would have a positive net marginal value at the source in all alternative uses. It is then clear that the level of water usage development definitionally hits a ceiling as soon as the water becomes economically scarce. One corollary of this definition is that you cannot overdevelop scarce water by further investment in water facilities, but can only reallocate it among uses. Other corollaries are that we may distinguish among water development projects according to whether they are drawing on free water or scarce water, and that if they are drawing on the latter we must insist on counting the opportunity cost of the scarce water as a legitimate part of project costs. It should be understood at this point that in determining the existence or non-existence of scarcity and of full water usage we include all demands for water, including those for non-reimbursable in-stream use. Thus, a full level of water usage development can be entirely consistent with appreciable amounts of water "wasting to the sea," though this situation may or may not be consistent with ideal allocation of the scarce resources.

The second concept, the level of water facilities development, refers to the quantity of non-water resources that have been committed to developing water for use. As long as the facilities are drawing on free water, an increase in the level of facilities development is generally matched by a corresponding increase in usage development, but as soon as water becomes economically scarce, further water facilities development can only reallocate scarce water. Thus, once a threshold of scarce water is passed, an appraisal of the level of water facilities development becomes essentially also an appraisal of the allocation of water among uses.

Before we proceed further with conceptualization, it should be noted that by 1960 water had evidently become a scarce good in all seasons in practically all of the numerous medium-sized and small rivers which flow into the Central Valley (there are no really big ones), with the possible exception of winter water in a few rivers feeding the Sacramento Valley. And on those, clear scarcity was being rapidly brought about by construction to augment interseasonal transfers. Outside that hydrographic region, the flow of the only source that was being tapped for water for the Central Valley—the Trinity River of the North Coastal region—can be presumed to have an appreciable year-round scarcity value deriving from in-stream recreational uses. If this arguable presumption is incorrect, Trinity water is free water so far. It seems, then, that all or practically all of our appraisal of the level of water facilities development in or for the Central Valley refers also to water allocation; we are really not concerned with the question of whether or not free water is being used enough.

Returning to conceptualization, the task of analyzing the allocational accomplishments wrought by water facilities development (and identifying any allocational distortions attributable to insufficient, excessive, or misplaced water facilities) is assisted if we distinguish several allocational frontiers, involving respectively:

1) Allocation among different types of use—such as irrigation, urban water, power, support of navigation, saline repulsion, in-stream recreational use, and so on.

2) Allocation among times of use, embracing interseasonal or interannual transfers, generally through the use of dams and reservoirs.

3) Allocation among places of use, involving particularly inter-basin and long intrabasin transfers of water, but also more local patterns of water distribution within subregions or individual river subbasins.

4) Allocation among customer-members of particular local water agencies, and among the lands of these constituents.

It is obvious that the first three frontiers tend to be highly interrelated either of necessity or in practice. For example, interseasonal transfers generally involve shifting emphasis as among types of use, and the major projects of the Federal Bureau of Reclamation and the California Department of Water Resources have clearly conjoined long-distance water transfers with movements on the first two frontiers. For present purposes, we confine our attention to the interuse, intertemporal, and interspatial allocative frontiers, neglecting the fourth one listed.

TWO SPHERES OF CENTRAL VALLEY
WATER DEVELOPMENT

Now let us turn to an appraisal of the current level of water facilities development and the character of water allocation for and from the Central Valley. It will simplify this evaluation if we first offer one conclusion which emerged from our study after analysis of some evidence referred to below. This is that in the Central Valley there are at present two spheres of water development the performance of which should be distinguished. One is the sphere of local-agency development, undertaken mostly by a variety of types of local public agencies (including irrigation districts and some municipalities) and by two private electric-utility companies—Pacific Gas and Electric and Southern California Edison.

The other is the sphere of the large federal and state producer-wholesalers occupied by the Bureau of Reclamation, the Corps of Engineers, and the California Department of Water Resources.[1]

It is only to a relatively minor degree that these spheres have made contact and developed economic relationships; they are still a long way from integration and co-ordination into a unified system for water development, whatever there is on the drawing boards, and there are very good explanations of the persistence of this situation. Moreover, the agencies in the federal-state sphere have performed differently from those in the local-agency sphere—differently enough to require separate appraisals of the two spheres of Central Valley development. For as comparative newcomers to the Central Valley, the agencies in the federal-state sphere have had to superimpose their operations on the local-agency sphere and, though possessing some inherent advantages over their predecessors, they have encountered important disabilities because of prior development.

How this came about deserves a brief explanation. After the Civil War, the Central Valley began a slow shift from cattle range plus a little dry farming to irrigated agriculture. This movement was greatly accelerated after 1887 with the passage of the Wright Act; this permitted the establishment of public irrigation districts with taxing and bonding powers and thus provided vehicles for local development of irrigation which were operationally superior to private water companies. Development of rivers for irrigation thereafter proceeded rapidly, mostly through local entrepreneurship using public districts as devices—first through the stage of diverting run-of-the-stream flow, and thence into that of building reservoirs for storage and interseasonal transfer. Concurrently, two large private utility companies picked out the most likely rivers for intensive development for hydropower, and constructed a good deal of large-capacity reservoir storage for interseasonal transfers.

If their accomplishment is measured against the present stage of development, local agencies and electric utilities had not proceeded too far with reservoir development before first the Bureau and then other big agencies really entered the area. By 1940 their total water storage capacity in reservoirs with individual capacities of 40,000 acre-feet or more was only about 28 per cent of the large-reservoir capacity of 1962.[2] But one should not be misled by these numbers. A process of economic selection was operating as local agencies developed water. In general, local irrigation agencies concentrated their efforts—within a pattern of

---

[1] The two spheres are further distinguished by the fact that they have, in large part, developed different groups of rivers within or for the Central Valley.

[2] They later added another 8 per cent of that total. See [ref. 2].

development of local sources for local use—on the most attractive river-land combinations (good river flow, good dam sites, and high-grade land adjacent), although they did not necessarily exploit every attractive opportunity. Similarly, the electric utility companies chose to exploit the most promising rivers for power generation, especially the Feather, the San Joaquin, and the Pit; and when the metropolitan agencies of the San Francisco Bay area reached across the Valley to the Sierra Nevada for pure water supplies, they hit on the same general set of rivers. In effect, the local agencies skimmed much of the cream of economically attractive water development opportunities in the Central Valley.

To be sure, these agencies did not and still generally have not developed the "full physical potentials" of their chosen rivers. For several reasons, including budgetary constraints and insularity, they frequently built reservoirs which were suboptimal in scale from the standpoint of multipurpose development. But they tied up the water rights and the dam sites, as well as the natural service areas, of a band of rivers of prime economic potential, thus placing severe barriers in the way of late-coming federal and state agencies should they seek to stir cream into their project benefits or to incorporate this significant series of rivers into any comprehensive plan.

The strategic band of rivers which local-agency and electric-utility development had largely pre-empted before the Bureau got into operation includes the Kings; the San Joaquin and its three principal tributaries, the Merced, Tuolumne, and Stanislaus; some lesser rivers like the Mokelumne just to the north; and in lesser but significant degree the Feather and the Yuba, which feed the Sacramento River about forty miles north of the Delta (for various reasons more or less skipping the American River in between). In the Central Valley, these are the prime rivers serving prime adjacent land in the center of the Valley's eastern slope.

Although this choice area had been more or less carved out of the middle by local development and pre-emption, there remained many good physical or engineering opportunities for bringing water to Valley lands of from moderate to very high grade, especially after ground-water mining began to reach its limit in the Tulare Basin area south of the Kings River. Classified economically, what was left for the federal and state agencies consisted mainly of (a) numerous marginal or submarginal opportunities which could be exploited independently;[3] (b) a very few

[3] It should be noted that in an array of water resource development opportunities in this region according to "quality" or potential economic payoff, there are distinct discontinuities in quality so that increasing demand for water over time did not "promote" most neglected opportunities into a supramarginal class.

better opportunities for augmenting development on rivers already solidly occupied by local agencies, which had not been exploited because of tangled water rights situations (Pine Flat and Friant dams on the Kings and the San Joaquin); and (c) even fewer better opportunities which had been by-passed by local agencies because of huge financial requirements (Shasta on the Sacramento and possibly Oroville on the Feather). Economically feasible projects of certain scales and designs could probably have exploited the opportunities in the latter two categories, though, given the barriers mentioned, they evidently could have effected little more integration in the development of the Valley's water resources. In any event, these possible projects did not offer the superior economic payoffs gained, for example, by watering the alluvial fans of the Kings, Merced, Tuolumne, and Stanislaus from the river flows that traversed them.

In this setting, the federal and state agencies faced severe impediments in any endeavor to effect comprehensive river basin development, even though there was some good "project material" left when the Central Valley Project was launched in the late 1930's. At the same time, these agencies or the legislatures above them were acutely responsive to the pleas and pressures of prospective clients who had been left short of surface water in the course of local-agency development or who were running out of ground water. In consequence, they were led not only to exploit marginal or submarginal opportunities as available, but also generally to exploit the few better opportunities with projects of excessive and uneconomic scale at the dam-reservoir level, incorporating similarly uneconomic facilities to deliver the water.[4] This was done, of course, in the context of a policy of working around the edges of the going concern which the local agencies had established, and which the federal and state agencies did not wish to disrupt, even where the precommitment of fixed facilities by the local agencies might not have made this disruption uneconomic. When the Bureau of Reclamation did break the bind to a limited extent with the basic features of the Central Valley Project (CVP), it did so at a very high economic cost as well as by transfer payments.

Thus it was that the basic features of the Bureau's CVP essentially involved placing a very large dam on the Sacramento River to set in motion a transfer of water to the Tulare Basin 500 miles away, and that it then proceeded further in parallel and comparable endeavors. It is not plausible that the Bureau would have done what it did or in the order that it did it had the Bureau been able to develop the Central Valley

---

[4] A possible exception to this rule is found in the Pine Flat Reservoir on the Kings, built by the Corps of Engineers.

from the beginning. Thus it was also with the developments of the minor rivers feeding the Tulare Basin—the Kaweah, Tule, and Kern—that though none involved a huge investment, each awaited the entrance of the Corps of Engineers to augment the local irrigation water supply while charging most of the cost off to flood control. With respect to the Bureau's CVP works, it is true that the investments involved were beyond the resources of local agencies, so that budgetary constraints alone could have deterred earlier development. But this does not necessarily mean that these investments were previously or then justified on the basis of economic efficiency, if only someone were able to dig up the money. So much for the sketchy establishment of a "second-sphere" classification of Bureau and Corps developments in or serving the Central Valley.

The California Department of Water Resources joined this second sphere by initiating its Feather River Project in 1959, which in the main is to capture 4 million acre-feet per year of winter water from near the mouth of the Feather River, carry about half of it to the southern end of the Tulare Basin for irrigation, and pump the other half across a range of mountains for urban use in the area of Los Angeles. Its operation and position as a marginal operator are quite comparable to those of the Bureau so far as the transfer of irrigation water is concerned, though its pricing policies differ. In its interbasin export of urban water, the demand and benefit situation differs but the marginality of the project is reasonably clear.

DEVELOPMENT AND ALLOCATION IN THE
LOCAL AGENCY SPHERE

Hard evidence on the level of water facilities development and allocation by local agencies is difficult to come by, but we have built up some by supplementing published data with primary research, and have expanded our findings by drawing a few inferences from institutional arrangements. A principal finding, referring to a random sample of eighteen irrigation districts (Table 1), is that on the average from 1952 through 1960 these districts averaged about zero per cent return on price-level-adjusted depreciated investment, which is to say that average revenue was appreciably below long-run average cost. (The dispersion in rates of return within the sample appears principally attributable to differences in the age of district and to the fact that district revenues are set to cover bond amortization rather than calculated depreciation.)

TABLE 1.

Distribution of Average Annual Rates of Return, 1952–1960,
for Eighteen Irrigation Districts

Rate of return	Number of districts
−3.1 to −5.0	1
−1.1 to −3.0	2
−1.0 to 1.0	9
1.1 to 3.0	3
3.1 to 5.0	0
5.1 to 10.0	0
over 10.0	3

Source: Calculated from data supplied by California Districts Securities Commission;
and from California State Controller, *Annual Report of Financial Transactions Concerning
Irrigation Districts of California for the Calendar Year 1952* (Sacramento, 1953), and
Annual Reports, 1953 through 1960.

General evidence concerning the incidence and importance of water
rationing other than by price suggests that the marginal value of water to
users in these districts does not greatly exceed average revenue. Furthermore, economic costs are systematically understated by failure to include
any charge for the opportunity cost of scarce water, or any payment for
the stream-flow regulation service provided to most of the eighteen districts by others on which these districts free-load. Taking these factors
into account, it seems reasonably clear that Central Valley irrigation
districts, so far as they are fairly represented by this random sample,
have tended to invest excessively in water facilities for the service of their
own lands, and correspondingly to overallocate water to irrigating these
lands, at the expense of its use elsewhere in irrigation or in other uses.[5]
On the other hand, surrounding evidence to the effect that irrigation
districts have secured larger water allocations than neighboring actual or
potential irrigators suggests the possibility that the total development of
water facilities for local irrigation is not excessive, but simply maldis-
tributed among irrigators.

Another study of twenty-four irrigation districts and water districts
served by the Bureau of Reclamation with wholesale water showed that
ten of them were predicted to grow crops at the extensive margin which
would have net values of average product (payment capacities) below
the long-run marginal costs of supplying water, even with subsidized
Bureau water rates being taken at face value. These findings are subject
to about the same interpretation as the rate-of-return findings just cited.

Neither of these samples happens to pick up members of that small

---

[5] This finding is potentially quite consistent with local agencies having realized
benefit-cost ratios (but not marginal benefit-cost ratios) generally in excess of
unity, if buyers' surpluses are included in benefits.

but important group of irrigation districts which operate joint reservoir facilities with Pacific Gas and Electric Company, under contracts whereby the electric utility pays for a dam in return for exploiting it for power yield for a fifty-year period. The character of these contractual arrangements, however, strongly suggests that these districts also probably have excessive water facilities development imputable to irrigation use and excessive interseasonal transfer for this purpose, relative to their own service areas, though the level of facilities development relative to all irrigable land (including that excluded from district service) may not be excessive. Thus, in the sector examined, a generally excessive level of water facilities development is not clearly identified, though its possible existence is not excluded. The major misallocation so far identified is probably more among users than among uses, and no clear indication of excessive over-all interseasonal transfer is found.

Some attention should also be given to water facilities development in the form of single-purpose (though generally dual-function) large reservoirs which are operated on their own accounts by Pacific Gas and Electric Company and Southern California Edison Company. These include sixteen Central Valley reservoirs with individual capacities of more than 40,000 acre-feet and an aggregate capacity comprising about 15 per cent of all major reservoir capacity in the Valley region. All circumstantial evidence suggests that these do not embody overdevelopment or generate excessive interseasonal transfer of water. There is a possibility, but not a clear probability, that their lack of dual- or multi-purpose orientation has led to a deficient level of reservoir development, though the rather abundant development of facilities for irrigation casts some doubt on this hypothesis.

Given the level of water facilities development in the local-agency sector and whatever it implies directly for water allocation, we may also consider other allocational impacts of local development. The following stand out: As regards the interseasonal pattern of releases from storage, utility-owned reservoirs evidently deviate significantly from an ideal multipurpose pattern of releases; reservoirs jointly controlled by utilities and irrigation districts probably do not; reservoirs controlled by irrigation districts and not supporting power generation, as well as the few reservoirs controlled by urban agencies, evidently tend to deviate from an optimal multipurpose operation and, in particular, to give insufficient weight in allocation to recreational in-stream uses and to fish habitat. Interferences by the state Fish and Game Department or through Federal Power Commission hearings apparently have not been sufficient to secure adequate attention to in-stream recreational uses in water allocations and in reservoir release patterns, except in those categories where these uses are pretty well served as a by-product of commercial development. Such commercial development clearly does not include that which is heavily oriented toward supporting diversions for irrigation. The only significant interbasin or long-distance transfers of water encountered in the local-agency sector involve the transfer of relatively trivial amounts of water (perhaps 2 per cent of Central Valley surface diversions) from the Sierra to the San Francisco Bay region, and no appreciable misallocation is ascertainable here.

DEVELOPMENT AND ALLOCATION IN
THE BIG AGENCY SPHERE

The solidest evidence we have on federal and state development in and for the Central Valley consists of two benefit-cost analyses that we have made since 1961: one of the basic features of the Central Valley Project of the Bureau, and one of the Feather River Project of the California Department of Water Resources. Since the Bureau has by now gone beyond the basic features of CVP and plans to go further, and since the Feather River Project is viewed as only the first unit in a much larger California Water Plan, some might argue that an evaluation of the accomplishment of the agencies on the basis of these two appraisals is premature. Yet preliminary analysis of the information that is available on more recently constructed and proposed features of the CVP suggests that any amalgamated benefit-cost ratio for a fuller CVP is going to get worse rather than better. And as to the California Water Plan, a careful reading makes it unmistakably clear that the Feather River Project offers by far its least expensive feature for getting water from Northern California to the southern San Joaquin Valley, the Los Angeles area, and the Mojave and Colorado deserts. Thus it seems evident that the basic features of CVP and FRP represent the Bureau and the California department each at its best in terms of economic efficiency of accomplishment.

The basic features of the CVP include Shasta Dam on the Sacramento River at the north end of its valley, connected hydro facilities that supply power for pumping water south from the Delta as well as power for sale, a major pumping plant at the Delta, and the Delta-Mendota Canal which carries water from the Delta to the San Joaquin River below Friant Dam to replace river water cut off by Friant from rights-holders on the lower San Joaquin (and incidentally delivers some water en route). They include also Friant Dam, the Friant-Kern Canal which carries most of the flow of the San Joaquin southward to the east valley slope of the Tulare Basin area, the lesser Madera Canal which carries water northward from

Friant to augment irrigation water supplies in another service area, and a Contra Costa Canal running from the Delta to the northeast corner of the San Francisco Bay area. For this complex of interrelated facilities, we have calculated[6] two benefit-cost ratios, each for 50- and 100-year time horizons and each at several discount rates. These ratios include:

1) A "standard" ratio of primary benefits to costs, B'/C, where benefits are measured at average values inclusive of buyers' surpluses (payment capacities in the case of irrigation water).[7]

2) The same ratio where agricultural benefits are based on adjusted[8] world prices for price-supported crops (especially cotton), rather than on support prices, on the theory that support prices clearly overstate any addition to national income. These ratios are shown in Table 2.

TABLE 2.

Benefit-Cost Ratios (B'/C) for Basic Features of the Central Valley Project in Terms of Discounted Present Values as of 1953

Time period	Interest rate			
	3%	4%	5%	6%
B'/C without adjustment for surplus crops				
50 years	1.21	1.03	0.89	0.77
100 years	1.45	1.16	0.96	0.81
B'/C using adjusted world prices for surplus crops				
50 years	0.72	0.61	0.53	0.47
100 years	0.85	0.69	0.57	0.49

The basic features of the CVP appear to be marginally efficient at discount rates of 3 or 4 per cent, and inefficient at higher rates even if surplus crops are valued at support prices in calculating benefits. Except for those who believe that a rate as low as 4 per cent is appropriate in calculating the efficient allocation of investible funds among all uses, public and private, the CVP is a non-feasible project, embodying uneconomic development of water facilities and misallocations in the form of excessive interseasonal transfer, excessive long-distance transfer, and excessive allocation of water to irrigation as opposed to other commercial and non-commercial uses. If the value of the surplus crops grown

[6] The benefit-cost analysis of CVP has been made almost entirely by Professor Caves.

[7] We add the prime sign to the B to designate inclusion in benefits of buyers' surpluses, and to distinguish this B' from a different measure of benefits referred to below.

[8] Adjusted for storage costs and losses.

with CVP water is measured realistically from a national-welfare stand-point, the project is a loser at any faintly plausible interest rate.

There are rather clear indications, moreover, that the basic features are of excessive scale, so that $\Delta B'/\Delta C$ for the project falls below unity at any interest rate from 4 per cent up. The ratio of revenues to cost for fifty years at 5 per cent is about 0.3. Reading up from this to the probability that the ratio of benefits priced at marginal values to costs is slightly higher, and making a liberal allowance for increasing returns to scale, we conclude that $\Delta B'/\Delta C$ must be below unity. This suggests the possibility that the basic features of the CVP might have been economically feasible at an appreciably smaller scale, but it doesn't suggest it very strongly. The only ground for showing that an excessive level of water facilities development was not embodied in the basic features of CVP would be a demonstration that its irrigation water was irrationally allocated among service areas, and there is little to support this hypothesis.

The major features of the Feather River Project of the California Department of Water Resources are shown in Tables 3 and 4. Our benefit-cost analysis of this project[9] has been prospective, since the project is still building even though practically all of its ultimate deliveries are under contractual commitments. As the tables show, over half of its deliveries will go to Southern California in a very long aqueduct and pumping system, and most of the remainder to the southern San Joaquin Valley. Delivery schedules, costs, and revenues have been taken directly from state estimates. Irrigation water benefits have been taken, both as marginal (B) and average (B') values, from detailed studies made for the purchasing agencies, with no deductions being made for surplus crops. Urban water benefits have also been calculated both as quantity times marginal value and as quantity times average value inclusive of consumers' surplus $(B$ and $B')$. This calculation follows the principle that marginal value is in any year in any service area the lower of two magnitudes: (1) marginal value in use (liberally equated to the FRP contract price to purchasers), and (2) cost from the marginal alternative source of water (calculated area by area in some detail). A correlative principle is that average value cannot exceed cost from the marginal alternative source, but where this alternative cost is above marginal value, average value lies between them as calculated on the supposition of a price elasticity of demand for urban water of -0.25. The most important alternative cost is that of demineralized ocean water in Southern California after 1984 (when lower-cost alternatives would be exhausted

[9] The benefit-cost analysis of the FRP has been made primarily by Professor Margolis.

TABLE 3.

Major Facilities of the Feather River Project, as Planned in 1964

Facilities	Location	Capacity (reservoir storage or aqueduct head flow)	Length in miles
On stream storage and regulation facilities			
Oroville dam and reservoir[1]	Lower Feather River	3,484,000 af.	—
Five Feather River reservoirs above Oroville	Forks of Feather River	187,900 af.	
Spencer and Dos Rios reservoirs and conveyance facilities	Middle Fork of Eel River	800,000 a.[2]	
Delta facilities			
Barriers, control works, and canals	Lower Delta	—	—
Delta pumping plant	Tracy	10,330 cfs.	—
Aqueducts			
North Bay aqueduct	Delta west to Napa Valley	138 cfs.	32
South Bay aqueduct	Delta[3] south to Santa Clara Valley	363 cfs.	44
Main Southern California aqueduct[4]	Delta south to Tehachapi division point	10,000 cfs.[3]	322
West branch of Southern California aqueduct	Division point south to Castaic reservoir	1,500 cfs.	13
East branch of Southern California aqueduct	Division point east and south to Perris reservoir	1,842 cfs.	118
Central Coastal aqueduct	Main Southern California aqueduct west to Santa Maria River	329 cfs.	110
San Joaquin drainage facilities[6]	South of Bakersfield north to Delta	1,100 cfs.[7]	288

[1] With connected power plant and other facilities.
[2] Estimated annual yield of water; storage capacity n.a.
[3] Strictly from elevated reservoir above the Delta pumping plant.
[4] 103 miles of this aqueduct, from San Luis reservoir south to Kettleman City, is a joint facility of the FRP and the Bureau of Reclamation, having a head capacity of 13,100 cfs. of which the FRP share is 7,100 cfs.
[5] Capacity tapers to 3,800 cfs. at the south end of the San Joaquin Valley.
[6] Joint facility of FRP and Bureau of Reclamation.
[7] Terminal capacity near Delta.

Source: California Department of Water Resources, *The California State Water Project in 1964*, Bulletin No. 132–64 (Sacramento, 1964), Ch. III.

TABLE 4.

Estimated Ultimate Annual Deliveries of Feather River Project Water by Service Area

Service area	Aqueduct source	Ultimate annual deliveries in thousands of acre-feet	Year deliveries are scheduled to begin
Feather River area	Local canals	38.5	1967
San Francisco Bay area, northeast	North Bay aqueduct	73.0	1980
San Francisco Bay area, south	South Bay aqueduct	194.0	1962
San Luis Obispo and Santa Barbara	Central Coastal aqueduct	75.0	1980
Southern San Joaquin Valley	Main Southern California aqueduct	1,362.0	1968
South Coastal Basin	West and east branches of Southern California aqueduct	1,925.0	1971
Antelope Valley–Mojave Desert	East branch of Southern California aqueduct[1]	264.0	1971
Coachella Valley–Palm Springs	Purchasers' spur aqueduct from East branch	68.0	1972
Total deliveries		4,000.0	

[1] And southern end of main Southern California aqueduct just north of Tehachapi division point.

Source: California Department of Water Resources, *The California State Water Project in 1964, Bulletin No. 132–64* (Sacramento, 1964), Table 7.

in meeting scheduled FRP deliveries); we have set this at $100 per acre-foot, on the basis of best projections of current evidence.

Table 5 shows the variety of ratios we have calculated at various discount rates, all for a fifty-year and an eighty-year period. The latter ends in 2039 and is the payout period of the project and the reference period for most state data. These ratios include revenue-cost, benefit-cost with benefits priced at marginal values, and conventional benefit-cost with benefits including buyers' surpluses, with all values discounted to the beginning of 1960.

TABLE 5.

Benefit-Cost and Revenue-Cost Ratios for the Feather River Project, Calculated from 1964 Estimates of 1960 Present Values of Project Benefits, Revenues, and Costs

Rate of discount per annum	.03	.04	.05	.06
I. R/C—Revenue-Cost Ratios[1]				
50 years	0.95	0.83	0.72	0.63
80 years	1.12	0.99	0.80	0.68
II. B/C—Benefit-Cost Ratios with Benefits Based on Marginal Values				
50 years	0.78	0.68	0.54	0.51
80 years	0.95	0.86	0.62	0.56
III. B'/C—Benefit-Cost Ratios with Benefits Based on Average Values				
50 years	1.09	0.94	0.80	0.69
80 years	1.32	1.11	0.90	0.75

[1] The revenues entering these ratios are calculated from uniform average annual equivalent contract prices. If cash-flow revenues reflecting anticipated prepayments and deferred payments are used instead, the R/C ratios are altered slightly, as follows for eighty years:

.03	.04	.05	.06
1.07	0.97	0.82	0.72

Source: See text.

This project rates slightly worse, in terms of efficiency, than the basic features of the Central Valley Project. In view of the rather optimistic population forecasts which underlie estimates of urban water benefits, no discount rate lower than 5 or 6 per cent should be considered realistic, and at these or higher rates it is not economically feasible at its designed scale, embodies excessive or distinctly premature water facilities development, and implements misallocations on the frontiers of interseasonal and interbasin transfers. It may readily be inferred from the B/C ratios that it is overscaled (with $\Delta B'/\Delta C$ below unity); detailed examination suggests that it could have been brought into the range of economic feasibility by down-scaling basic features, eliminating costly and wasteful features like the long East Branch aqueduct across the Mojave Desert, and reducing irrigation water deliveries to the south San Joaquin.

On the basis of these analyses plus preliminary surveys of actual and proposed additions to the projects analyzed, we conclude that in the federal-state sphere of Central Valley water development the first best project opportunities were submarginal as exploited, involving the over-investment and misallocations mentioned, and that the future of progressive development does not look as bright.

CONCLUSION

Recognizing the fact that a number of the findings presented above are unlikely to gain 100 per cent acceptance without challenge or argument, we return to the hypothesis implied above that a late-arriving federal or state agency which attempts multipurpose river basin development in a basin which is already pretty well settled and developed encounters multiple legal and physical disabilities which deter it from approximating its theoretical potential. In addition, it finds a good deal of the cream skimmed from water development opportunities, so that it is induced to undertake suboptimal and frequently submarginal additions to an existing water facilities system. A corollary of this hypothesis is that by far the best case for comprehensive river basin development by a central agency is made in a vacuum—a vacuum in particular of appreciable settlement and prior water development—where it can fully exploit a virgin opportunity, internalizing externalities to the hilt and coordinating all elements. But local interests are unlikely to leave attractive vacuums lying around.

This hypothesis seems to draw some sustenance from the Bureau's experience in the Central Valley, wherein the "disabilities" argument can be documented in considerable detail. It also draws sustenance from any dispassionate preliminary appraisal of those scheduled future features of the California Water Plan which emphasize a large augmentation of irrigation water supply in the Central Valley, not to mention the separate appraisal of the irrigation features of the Feather River Project. As to the other major features of the FRP, they do not serve to test the hypothesis mentioned, but raise extremely serious questions—exaggerated manyfold when pulling Columbia River water into Arizona is seriously suggested—concerning an ongoing tendency toward uneconomic real-estate promotion in arid regions.

It has been suggested that flood-control benefits should be appraised with reference not only to averted losses to people inhabiting highly floodable lands, but also with reference to the net benefits of having people inhabit those lands at all. Any firm believer in the non-existence of secondary and tertiary benefits may ask a comparable question about the wisdom of subsidizing the development or growth of urban centers in the midst of deserts.

REFERENCES

[1] Bain, Joe S., Caves, Richard E., and Margolis, Julius. *Northern California's Water Industry*. Baltimore: Johns Hopkins Press, 1967.
[2] California Department of Water Resources. *Dams Within Jurisdiction of the State of California, January 1962,* Bulletin No. 17. Sacramento, 1963.

The International Columbia River Treaty: An Economic Evaluation

*John V. Krutilla**

$\mathbf{I}$n September 1964, the United States and Canada exchanged ratification of the Columbia River Treaty at ceremonies in British Columbia and the Pacific Northwest. This marked the conclusion of all preliminaries to the implementation of a co-operative plan of development on the Columbia River, initiated by a reference from the two countries to the International Joint Commission (IJC) two decades earlier [ref. 1]. The reason for the long lapse of time between the decision to investigate possibilities of development of mutual value and the conclusion of preparatory work can be explained by the enormous complexities—engineering-economic, political, and administrative—involved in putting together a plan of development which attempts to be at once technically sound, economically justified, and politically acceptable to all those able to promote or impede the development. Obtaining agreement for co-ordinated development and operation of the Columbia River system is a signal achievement, the importance of which may be too obvious to dwell upon. The following brief observations bear making, however.

The Columbia River Treaty represents one of the few cases in which two countries sharing a river system were able to negotiate an understanding concerning an undertaking which involved bothersome political, economic, and financing as well as difficult technical problems. In doing so, the two countries through the IJC made a significant advance in international co-operation through the formulation of a set of principles

* Senior Research Associate, Resources for the Future, Inc.

which would provide the framework for an efficient design of the Treaty system and for division of the gains obtained from the undertaking. We find here recognition of mutual responsibility between riparians in their conduct of affairs on the international stream. There is accepted, if only implicitly, the principle that when a project in one country adversely affects the other, or pre-empts complementary resources as in the case of a transboundary reservoir, the liability incurred by the project to the upstream riparian consists of a share of its net yield in addition to normal compensation for damages. Finally, we see acceptance of a principle that compensation is due one riparian for services provided the other, even if such services are partly of direct benefit to the former.

In physical terms what does the Columbia Treaty provide? Canada is obligated to provide 15.5 million acre-feet of storage in the High Arrow Lakes, Duncan Lake, and Mica Creek reservoirs to be operated predominantly to meet flood-management and power objectives in the United States. The flowage rights in Canada required for the headwaters of the Libby reservoir, with damsite located in the United States, are to be provided by Canada as well, should the United States elect to build the Libby project.[1] In exchange for the stream regulation provided by the Canadian storages, the United States agreed to share equally the increase in dependable capacity and average energy at United States head plants on the U.S. reaches of the Columbia downstream, and to advance payment in amount equal to one-half the estimated damage reduction in the flood plain of the lower Columbia. This sum discounted to the year 1964 was estimated to be approximately $54 million. Although Canada initially elected to have its downstream power share returned for use in British Columbia, it ultimately opted to sell such power entitlement, parts of which commence in 1968, 1969, and 1973, for $254 million (U.S. 1964 worth). In addition, according to the terms of the Treaty, the United States will provide stream regulation having a net present value of approximately $60 million from its Libby project for Canadian head plants downstream on the lower Kootenay in Canada.

In the larger perspective, the Columbia Treaty represents a notable achievement. However, the value of the experience for the development of other potential international undertakings can only be gauged if the Treaty is analyzed in technical detail and from many perspectives. The perspective of this paper is solely economic. Nevertheless, despite the limitations that this implies, I believe that an economic evaluation of an undertaking of the scope of the Columbia Treaty can contribute an im-

---

[1] A decision supported by the executive branch recommendation for appropriations in the 89th Congress, 1st Session.

portant class of information for informed decision making. Consequently, we shall be addressing two broad questions: First, what was the basis for the selection of projects in the Treaty system and how closely did the selection adhere to economic criteria? Second, how does the division of benefits from the co-operative venture affect each party to the Treaty?

THE ECONOMICS OF THE TREATY SYSTEM
PROJECT SELECTION

The task of evaluating the Treaty system from the economic viewpoint is substantially eased, and its relevance established, by the principles formulated by the IJC [ref. 2]. General Principle No. 1 states:

> Cooperative development of the water resources of the Columbia River Basin, designed to provide optimum benefits to each country, requires that the storage facilities and downstream power production facilities proposed by the respective countries will, to the extent it is practicable and feasible to do so, be added in the order of the most favorable benefit-cost ratio, with due consideration of factors not reflected in the ratio.

The first principle thus establishes the basis for selection of economically efficient projects. If applied with fidelity General Principle No. 1 would eliminate from the efficient program all projects for which there is a more economic alternative (whether hydro or thermal for power objectives, and local non-storage and/or non-structural measures in the case of flood management objectives). Moreover, it reflects the significance of the sequence of project construction: namely, that if all of the projects demonstrated to be economic in the ultimate development of the system are designated for construction in the order of their yields (highest yield project first, etc.), the present worth of the net benefits of the Treaty system will be maximized. Thus the gains from the co-operative undertaking available for mutual sharing will be the greatest.

What then were the prospective project sites for selection and what sequence of project construction meets the economic criterion reflected in the IJC principle? There are several options which might be (or have been) evaluated. The physical features of the various combinations of projects, illustrated in Figure 1, represent the basic alternatives identified by the International Columbia River Engineering Board (ICREB) [ref. 3]. That the upper Columbia and Kootenay rivers were logical foci for the international system is apparent, not only because these reaches of the Columbia system affect the flow across the boundary, but also because storage development in these reaches had lagged relative to other portions of the Columbia system pending an international understanding

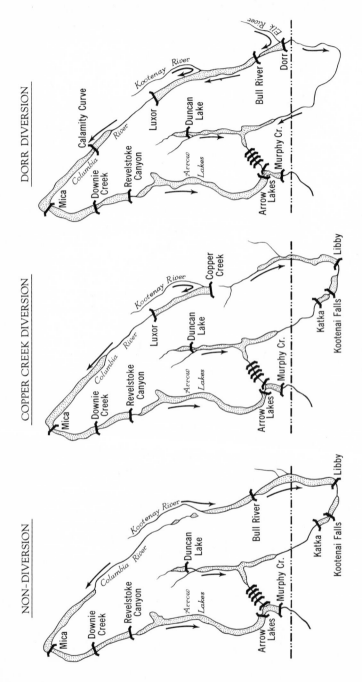

Figure 1. Alternative Upper Columbia development possibilities.

regarding the development of the Upper Columbia system. (See [ref. 4] for background on the state of development of the system.)

From the ICREB investigations we observe not only alternative projects[2] for a plan of development, but also basically two alternative plans of development: a diversion scheme involving the Kootenay and the non-diversion plan. The inferences that can be made from the ICREB and relevant agency staff studies suggest that the most efficient plan[3] would involve the diversion of the Kootenay into the Columbia. This follows because the non-diversion alternative produces 32 megawatts of capacity and 20 megawatts of energy less than the Dorr Diversion, yet represents an increased expenditure of around a third of a billion dollars. A similar observation is pertinent with respect to the Copper Creek Diversion. Although a small increase in power results from the Copper Creek alternative to the Dorr Diversion, the additional investment is increased to $386.4 million. In both instances the increased cost is accounted for by the physical compatibility of the Libby and related Kootenay River developments in the United States[4] with the economic projects in Canada.

One qualification must be made regarding the superiority of the Dorr Diversion. To justify economically the construction of facilities for this plan, it would be necessary to have the head developed all along the Columbia River in Canada and would require a market for such power. A domestic market in British Columbia did not exist for so large a block of power representing, in fact, a multiple of the total market in British Columbia. Moreover, the market in the United States did not provide a relevant alternative, as the existing policy in Canada prevented the export of energy or, in fact, the receipt of capital funds from the United States. Accordingly, while from the standpoint of system efficiency the Dorr Diversion would represent the most efficient development from an overall view, it would be efficient only if a market existed for the output of all of the interdependent projects on the Columbia River in Canada. The only market which would meet this requirement, the export market in the Pacific Northwest, was ruled outside the range of feasible courses of action by the policy governing at the time of negotiations of the Treaty of 1961.

What were the relevant alternatives, then, in the light of the policy con-

---

[2] While in the case of the alternative plans there are physical incompatibilities between two or more projects, there can be also economic incompatibilities, as when the storage function can be performed adequately by either one of two possibilities. In short, physical incompatibility, while sufficient, will not be necessary for mutual exclusiveness among projects.

[3] Subject to the qualifications below.

[4] U. S. spelling, Kootenai.

straints? The negotiations centered about Arrow Lakes, Duncan Lake, Mica Creek, Libby, and Dorr–Bull River, the latter considered not as functioning in a diversion scheme, but rather as an alternative to the mutually exclusive Libby project for regulating stream flows in the natural channel of the Kootenay. While General Principle No. 1 called for addition of projects in the order of their economic yields, consideration had to be given to the lead time for construction and the expected time of need of major new energy sources. For this reason, the Mica project, largest and requiring the longest time for construction, could not be considered for the first addition to the system, as the load development in the Northwest was expected to require a major new source of supply prior to the time the Mica project could be completed.

Table 1 gives the estimated power contribution of the several projects considered in different sequences. Table 2 gives the corresponding benefits and costs[5] and provides an estimate of the present worth of the net benefit of each project or project complex where direct interdependencies exist.[6] From Table 2 it is apparent that the High Arrow–Duncan storage project is marginally better ($20–$30 million) than the Bull River–Dorr storage and would qualify as first to be added in the Treaty system. Considering next the remaining storages along with Mica for second addition, it is quite clear that the Mica project would qualify as early as it can be built, and would thus qualify for second addition in the Treaty system. When we consider the projects for third addition, Bull River–Dorr appears clearly superior to Libby and, other things being equal, would qualify for third addition under the IJC principles.

Although from the system viewpoint the most economical storage on the upper Kootenay was located in British Columbia, the province was not willing to offer the site for construction of a storage project. Several factors were involved. It can be observed that the value of the storage comparable to the Bull River–Dorr or Libby projects is very greatly diminished following the introduction of the High Arrow–Duncan and Mica storages, and did not promise to provide a large, quick, net return commensurate with what British Columbia felt it would be sacrificing to permit the inundation of the East Kootenays. Secondly, British Columbia

---

[5] Costs and benefits were based on alternative assumptions regarding the level of discount rates (4–5.5 per cent), cost of thermal capacity ($130/kw. to $150/kw.), fuel costs (20¢/million Btu to 30¢/million Btu) all selected so as to bracket the range which the value of the variables could be expected reasonably to take. (For source of project construction costs see [ref. 3, 13].)

[6] The complexes involve the East Kootenay storages and the Canal plant in West Kootenay on the lower Kootenay River, and the Mica Creek storage in combination with the Downie Creek and Revelstoke Canyon head plants. Without the storages upstream these head plants would not be feasible.

did not view lightly the problem of financing storages in addition to the main stem storages it would be committing itself to provide. Finally, it felt reasonably secure that the pressures in the United States for the construction of Libby would be such as to permit the inclusion of Libby on terms sufficiently favorable to Canada to justify the rejection of the Bull River–Dorr project in British Columbia's own pecuniary interest. Whether, in fact, the expectation was realized is beyond the scope of this paper. It is sufficient to say that as a result of the negotiations leading to the Treaty of 1961, Canada committed itself to provide storage in the amount of 15.5 million acre-feet in the Arrow Lakes, Duncan Lake, and Mica Creek reservoirs, and permitted the United States to build the Libby project, the headwaters of which would cross the international boundary into Canada.

How does this system correspond to the one which General Principle No. 1 seems to require? First, it appears as though a substantial part of the potential economy from the co-ordinated development of the Columbia River system will be dissipated by the substitution of Libby for the Bull River–Dorr project.[7] The difference in the realized net gain will be on the order of $100 to $150 million less, as a result of the inclusion of the Libby project. Second, with a substantial block of storage provided on the upper Kootenay, the justification of the Duncan Lake project may be questioned. The incremental contribution of the Duncan Lake storage after the Mica, High Arrow, and Libby is very small and raises questions regarding its net contribution to system output and its value to the operation of the system. On the other hand, the Libby project's cost-benefit relationship presents an ambiguous case. Since the Treaty is permissive with respect to its construction rather than mandatory, it is possible to conceive of a system which excludes Libby as well as the Bull River–Dorr storages, substituting local flood protection measures in the Bonners Ferry area to meet local flood hazard problems [ref. 5]. If the Libby project were omitted, the Duncan project would, of course, serve a useful stream-regulating purpose over head plants on the lower Kootenay and Columbia, and its economic position would be affected favorably. In summary, storage on the Kootenay would doubtless be useful, although it is unlikely that both the Libby and Duncan projects can be justified, given the local flood protection measures available for the Kootenai Flats area.

---

[7] While there is little evidence that consideration of the management needs for the unique herds of wildlife influenced the decision, it does appear that the flooding of the East Kootenay Valley consistent with the Bull River–Dorr project would have adversely affected this resource in Canada to a greater degree than would the Libby project.

TABLE 1.

Estimated Power Contribution of Selected Projects Added Sequentially to United States Base System

(Megawatts)

Project	1970–1980 Dependable capacity	1970–1980 Annual energy	1980–1990 Dependable capacity	1980–1990 Annual energy	1990–2000 Dependable capacity	1990–2000 Annual energy	2000–2010 Dependable capacity	2000–2010 Annual energy
First added to U.S. base system[1]								
High Arrow–Duncan								
at site	-0-	-0-	-0-	-0-	-0-	-0-	-0-	-0-
at W. Kootenay plants[2]	111	73	111	73	119	73	119	73
at U.S. base system	1,832	1,118	1,557	845	1,520	780	-0-	290
Total	1,943	1,191	1,668	918	1,639	853	119	363
Libby								
at site	258	188	258	188	320	188	791	228
at W. Kootenay plants[3]	344	212	344	212	451	212	451	212
at U.S. base system	1,380	860	1,040	750	1,000	755	-0-	200
Total	1,982	1,260	1,642	1,150	1,771	1,155	1,242	640
Bull River–Dorr								
at site	158	116	158	116	196	116	630	125
at W. Kootenay plants[3]	344	212	344	212	451	212	451	212
at U.S. base system	1,380	860	1,040	750	1,000	755	-0-	200
Total	1,882	1,188	1,542	1,078	1,647	1,083	1,081	537
Second added after High Arrow–Duncan								
Mica								
at site	1,045	785	1,080	785	1,340	785	2,784	785
at Downie & Revelstoke[4]	-0-	-0-	1,125	838	1,704	838	1,704	838
at U.S. base system	1,168	600	1,175	360	980	295	-0-	160
Total	2,214	1,385	3,380	1,983	4,024	1,918	4,488	1,783

Libby								
at site	259	189	258	188	320	188	791	228
at W. Kootenay plants[3]	266	185	266	185	332	185	332	185
at U.S. base system	588	300	595	175	500	140	–0–	90
Total	1,113	674	1,119	548	1,152	513	1,123	503
Bull River–Dorr								
at site	158	116	158	116	196	116	630	125
at W. Kootenay plants[3]	266	185	266	185	332	185	332	185
at U.S. base system	588	300	595	175	500	140	–0–	90
Total	1,012	601	1,019	476	1,028	441	962	400
Third added after High Arrow–Duncan and Mica								
Libby								
at site	254	207	258	207	320	207	791	228
at W. Kootenay plants[3]	266	185	266	185	332	185	332	185
at U.S. base system	307	170	205	125	170	114	–0–	50
Total	827	562	517	822	822	506	1,123	463
Bull River–Dorr								
at site	154	128	158	128	196	128	630	125
at W. Kootenay plants[2]	266	185	266	185	332	185	332	185
at U.S. base system	307	170	205	125	170	114	–0–	50
Total	727	483	629	438	698	427	962	360

[1] Projects appearing as "Base System" in Annex B, Columbia River Treaty. These consist of projects existing or under construction during 1959–60.

[2] Includes additional units at Brilliant and Waneta plants and integration benefits in the Canadian system.

[3] Includes additional units at Brilliant and Waneta and complete Canal plant.

[4] Downie Creek and Revelstoke Canyon plants are estimated to begin operation about 1980; accordingly, the benefits are lagged a decade behind initial occurrence at site and downstream benefits associated with Mica Creek operations.

TABLE 2.

Estimated Value of Power Output of Selected Projects Added Sequentially to the United States Base System

Project	Capacity energy at	Estimated present worth of benefits		Estimated present value of costs	Estimated present value of net benefits
		$10.34/kw. 15.77/kw. ($ × 10⁶)	$13.80/kw. 27.59/kw. ($ × 10⁹)	($ × 10⁶)	($ × 10⁶)
First added					
High Arrow–Duncan discount rate	4.0%	630.8	—	112.2[1]	$518.6
	5.5%	—	810.3	111.3[1]	699.0
Libby discount rate	4.0%	756.3	—	415.2[2]	344.2
	5.5%	—	944.7	421.7[2]	523.0
Bull River–Dorr discount rate	4.0%	702.2	—	219.6[2]	482.6
	5.5%	—	880.0	220.5[2]	659.5
Second added					
Mica Creek Complex discount rate	4.0%	1,303.9	—	536.0[3]	767.9
	5.5%	—	1,512.2	510.9[3]	1,001.3
Libby discount rate	4.0%	451.3	—	408.6[2]	42.4
	5.5%	—	546.3	415.1[2]	131.1
Bull River–Dorr discount rate	4.0%	397.1	—	213.0[2]	181.1
	5.5%	—	481.4	213.8[2]	267.6
Third added					
Libby discount rate	4.0%	367.5	—	408.6[2]	−41.1
	5.5%	—	443.4	415.1[2]	28.3
Bull River–Dorr discount rate	4.0%	313.3	—	213.0[2]	100.3
	5.5%	—	378.7	213.8[2]	164.9

[1] Includes cost of additional units at Brilliant and Waneta plants.
[2] Includes cost of additional units at Brilliant and Waneta plants and complete new Canal plant.
[3] The Downie Creek and Revelstoke Canyon projects benefits and costs are both lagged ten years to correspond to the time at which they are assumed to be operating.

The foregoing summarizes the state of things as of January 1961, when the Columbia River Treaty was signed.

Although the Treaty was ratified by the United States Senate within a few months in the spring of 1961, its ratification by the Canadian Parliament was delayed three years pending resolution of some issues internal to Canada and the renegotiation of some terms of the Treaty of 1961, found impracticable by British Columbia.

Concurrent with the latter stages of negotiations of the Columbia River Treaty in 1960, the province of British Columbia had become actively interested in the development of the Peace River in north central British Columbia. The Peace Power Project was looked upon with favor as the instrument for the stimulation of economic development of the interior north, and as a means of distributing more uniformly throughout the province the economic advances being realized on the lower mainland. Pursuant to this objective, the province of British Columbia "took over" the previously investor-owned electric utility, the British Columbia Electric Company, and related holdings. The expropriation made possible an integrated operation and secured the one large diversified market in British Columbia, essential to the viability of any large-scale hydroelectric development at that juncture in the economic development of British Columbia (in the absence of access to export markets for power).

With this turn of events it was obvious that if the Columbia development were to proceed in Canada, access to the United States markets was essential. Thus, in the British Columbia view, the export ban on energy and prohibition of capital advances required reconsideration and revision. This became the substance of the Victoria-Ottawa negotiations culminating in the British Columbia–Canada Accord of 1963. Among other matters covered in the agreement was the sanction to sell in the United States Canada's downstream power entitlement, and to use the proceeds of such sale for financing Canadian storage projects called for under the Columbia Treaty. The agreement also provided for Canada's undertaking formal negotiations with the United States toward this end, along with certain modifications and/or clarification of the terms of the Treaty of 1961.

The negotiations to which Canada was now committed were for the purpose of achieving objectives which had been ruled outside the feasible range under policies of the government of Canada during the negotiations preliminary to the Treaty of 1961. Rejection at that time of the invitation to make power from Canadian developments available to the United States, and of the proffer of financial assistance in the construction of Treaty projects, precluded serious consideration of some of the alternatives relevant to the Columbia River in Canada. It should be noted that the prospect of accelerated development appropriate to the schedule of U.S. power requirements, attended by an inevitable power surplus in British Columbia—and, hence, financial infeasibility—was a dominant consideration in the British Columbia choice of strategy for the Kootenays. However, through the expropriation and launching of the Peace River development, the province gained possession of technical information developed by the B.C. Engineering Company, which further enlarged the range of technical alternatives the Columbia development should take into account. In short, during the two-and-a-half years between the signing of the Treaty and the Canada–British Columbia agreement of July 1963, the course of events had produced some fundamental changes in circumstances which differed markedly from the assumptions underlying the negotiation of the Treaty of 1961.

Similarly, in the United States, the circumstances dominating the negotiation of the Treaty had changed appreciably. The projected growth in load in the Pacific Northwest failed to develop. This eliminated the need for an early block of low-cost energy originally thought to be required by the mid-sixties. Moreover, a change in administration in Washington had brought a more sympathetic attitude toward the development of domestic resources by the federal government in the Pacific Northwest. The Dworshak storage project was authorized and its construction begun. The Federal Power Commission was preparing to license a major development at either Nez Perce or High Mountain Sheep for non-federal development. Arrangements for the construction of the Hanford New Production Reactor were completed, adding a substantial source of new power to the regional power supply of the Pacific Northwest. And partly as a result of the stimuli provided by the Federal Power Commission's National Power Survey and by advances in extra-high voltage transmission, interest was heightened in electrical interconnection among the nation's power regions and with Canadian systems, thus improving the prospect for interconnecting the Northwest with the systems in the Southwest and California. An intertie of this sort is technically capable of substituting in large measure for storage in the Columbia Basin in order to make use of the large amounts of otherwise unusable secondary energy, as well as improving prospects for marketing the surplus peaking capability in the Columbia hydro system.

With the commitment to negotiate further in 1963, what were the potential implications of a "fresh start"? Among the many implications, there are some worth exploring here—some, that is, that are connected with the economics of the co-operative undertaking as it was outlined in IJC General Principle No. 1.

In British Columbia, a decision to withhold storage sites from development in the East Kootenays was based on several factors. One factor was especially significant as judged by the staff work devoted to its analysis. An option to substitute Bull River–Dorr for the Libby project, in exchange for providing the United States with power equivalent to the displaced Libby project's at-site generation, would require a diversion of the Kootenay and the full development of head on the Columbia below the point of diversion, if it were to enable British Columbia to retain, ultimately, as much power after sales to the United States as it would by foregoing the development of Bull River–Dorr. The financial implications of this larger, accelerated program of development were oppressive in the British Columbia circumstances.

With the change in policy permitting export of power and receipt of funds from the United States in the construction of Treaty projects, a question arises whether British Columbia officials might have viewed the choice differently if the matter had been opened to reconsideration.[8] In a somewhat related sense this change in policy had economic implications for the Peace, and in turn for the design of the Columbia Treaty system. The decision to proceed with the Peace River Power Project was preceded by a study of comparative costs by the British Columbia Energy Board [ref. 6]. Under assumptions adopted for the comparative evaluation, the Board concluded that power costs from the two sources would be approximately equal and, if a choice had to be made between the Columbia and the Peace, it would need to be governed by considerations other than costs. On the other hand, with the prospect of selling the Canadian downstream power entitlement in exchange for a lump sum capital advance, the Canadian outlays for the Columbia exclusive of the advance would be approximately equal to the Peace construction outlays, with close to 400 megawatts of power for British Columbia use in excess of the amount obtainable for similar outlays on the Peace.

If the Peace were considered apart from any decision on the Columbia for policy reasons internal to British Columbia, its independent existence with enormous storage capacity would raise a question about the storage design capacity on the Columbia. Interconnection of the Peace and Columbia hydro systems through transmission facilities to the load center on the lower mainland would permit the sale of secondary energy from the Columbia whenever available during good water years, the storing of energy in the Peace at such times, and releases from the Peace to firm up

---

[8] The decision to build a high dam at the lower Arrow Lakes and forbear development of the East Kootenay storage and diversion sites had become such a controversial issue and was so vigorously defended by the government of the day, that it seems rather unlikely that the government would have reconsidered the problem at that stage even in the light of the changes in circumstances.

such secondary energy when deliveries from the Columbia would be interrupted during years of adverse stream flows.[9]

This technical possibility, together with retardation in the rate of growth of load in the Pacific Northwest and alternative arrangements for a supply of power scheduled for the mid-sixties which High Arrow was initially intended to meet, will affect the justification of the Arrow project as an integral part of the efficient power system. The value of the Arrow Lakes storage considered incremental to Mica Creek and Libby storage is not very large either with respect to power production or the value of flood damage reduction. The function of the Arrow Lakes and Duncan storage, in fact, could be discharged by Mica and the East Kootenay storage coupled with the integration of the Columbia and the Peace on the one hand, and the Columbia and the Southwest systems on the other. (See testimony of Deane [ref. 8].)

It should be quite clear from the foregoing that the basic assumptions regarding policy-relevant alternatives which governed the selection of the Treaty projects in the negotiations of 1960 were superseded by a different set in 1963. The change in conditions affecting an efficient system was significant and doubtless would have resulted in a different set of projects in the Treaty system if IJC General Principle No. 1 had been applied in 1963. At the same time, because of the long and arduous effort to negotiate an understanding regarding the Treaty projects, neither side appeared eager to reopen the whole range of issues involved; nor is there assurance that new negotiations to update the Treaty system would have been attended by success before the policy-related parameters of the day were again subject to obsolescence. Accordingly, the Columbia River Treaty system retains some awkward elements originally justified by policy, informational, and technical constraints which became obsolete substantially before implementation of the Columbia River Treaty.

THE EQUITY OF THE COLUMBIA TREATY
BENEFIT DIVISION

In addition to formulating a principle relating to efficiency aspects of the Treaty system, the IJC provided a general principle related to equity considerations, i.e., the division of the benefits from co-operative development. To quote IJC General Principle No. 2 [ref. 2]:

[9] With only the Mica complex (i.e., Mica plus Downie Creek, and Revelstoke Canyon) added to the Columbia system existing and/or under construction, the firm load-carrying capability of the Columbia and Peace combined would be increased by a million kilowatts. (See Chantrill and Stevens [ref. 7].)

Cooperative development of the water resources of the Columbia River basin should result in advantages in power supply, flood control, or other benefits, or savings in cost to each country as compared with alternatives available to that country.

At first glance this principle seems to call for symmetrical treatment of the two countries, an inference that is reinforced by some of the principles specific to each function of the multiple-purpose Columbia development. For example, we have for Power Principle No. 6 [ref. 2]:

The power benefits determined to result in the downstream country from regulation of flow by storage in the upstream country should be shared on a basis such that the benefit, in power, to each country will be substantially equal, provided that such sharing would result in an advantage to each country as compared with alternatives available to that country as contemplated in General Principle No. 2. Each country should assume responsibility for providing that part of the facilities needed for the cooperative development that is located within its own territory. Where such sharing would not result in an advantage to each country as contemplated in General Principle No. 2, there should be negotiated and agreed upon such other division of benefits or other adjustments as would be equitable to both countries and would make the cooperative development feasible.

In reality, however, because of the peculiarities of the Columbia case the principles formulated by the IJC do not provide for symmetrical treatment of the two countries. In this special case the principles are completely consonant with permitting one of the participating countries to claim the preponderant share of the jointly produced *net* gain, provided only that the other participant is left no less well off than he would be by relying on an independent domestic alternative. That this should obtain will be clear if we think a moment about some of the relationships involved.

It has by this time become commonplace that the addition of storage to a river system, other things being held constant, is attended by diminishing returns. That is, a given block of storage will yield a great deal more if added at an early point in the sequence of storage development than if added at a later point, provided that the length of the critical period is thereby increased.[10] Accordingly, if in the absence of a cooperative development all of one riparian's storage projects, say, would be added first in the sequence of development they would yield higher returns than were they all to be added in a co-operative scheme following the inclusion of the other riparian's storage. The supramarginality

[10] This is illustrated by inspecting the capacity and energy benefits of Libby or Bull River–Dorr in the three sequences in Table 1.

of such projects would be substantially reduced in the latter case, and in some cases could be entirely eliminated by retarding their inclusion in the system. From this it follows that there will be displacement effects among storage projects in a system.

In the IJC principles there is recognition that the most economic projects be included and in the order of their net benefits. Since the cost per acre-foot of storage is substantially less for Canadian sites than for U.S. sites, all of the Canadian sites qualified for addition ahead of any of the United States storage sites.

This result of General Principle No. 1, coupled with the special principles relating to power and flood control for the purpose of dividing equally the *gross* gains from storage, would assure to Canada a substantially greater amount of power and share of the value of flood-damage reduction than is consonant with U.S. Treaty advantage. (Table 3 indicates the magnitude of the displacement effects under an assumed 1985 system and related conditions.) While supplementary rules governing the situation are provided,[11] no statement indicates that the *net* benefits should be divided equally. Accordingly, it might be expected that the benefits from the Columbia Treaty would not be divided equally, but only that some net advantage could accrue to the United States.

This section, then, will address the question raised by General Principle No. 2: Did both countries, in fact, obtain savings in cost as compared with domestic alternatives available to each?

Benefits to British Columbia

At the time of the decisions leading to the Treaty of 1961, a number of studies existed in Canada which were useful in determining how the co-operative development would measure up as compared with purely domestic alternatives. The province of British Columbia retained the services of Crippen Wright Engineering to investigate the varied means by which the power requirements of British Columbia could be met. The resulting studies showed the most economical means for a purely domestic independent development to be the construction of comparatively small-scaled projects at sites on the Clearwater tributary of the Fraser and Columbia with electrical integration of the two river sources of supply. An alternative means, involving co-operative development of the Columbia and approximating the actual Treaty system, called for construction of the Arrow Lakes and Libby projects with storage up-

---

[11] Such as General Principle No. 2 and the language in Power Principle No. 6 which permit adjustments in order to make a co-operative endeavor feasible.

TABLE 3.

Summary of Economic Comparisons, 1985

Project	Flood control benefits ($000)		Thermal power savings ($000)		Other benefits	Total accomplishments ($000)	
	Without Canadian storage	With Canadian storage	Without Canadian storage	With Canadian storage		Without Canadian storage	With Canadian storage
Flathead Lake Outlet Impr.	656[1]	147[2]	—	114[3]	—	656	261
Knowles	2,991[1]	447[2]	19,866	11,292	58	22,915	11,797
Garden Valley	534[1]	143[2]	9,406[4]	9,236[4]	−34	9,906	9,345
High Mountain Sheep	1,819[1]	239[2]	25,733	23,312	16	27,568	23,567
Lower Canyon	285[2]	285[2]	19,768	17,858	75	20,128	18,218
Penny Cliffs	911[2]	911[2]	11,409	9,483	282	12,602	10,676
Bruces Eddy	2,277[1]	552[2]	8,043	6,801	553	10,873	7,906
Kootenai Falls	—	—	5,646	5,000	—	5,646	5,000
Asotin (W. O. Lock)	—	—	9,095	9,033	32	9,127	9,065
China Gardens (910)	—	—	5,440	5,423	13	5,453	5,436
China Gardens (895)	—	—	4,341	4,308	13	4,354	4,321
Totals	9,473	2,724	118,747	101,860		129,228	105,592
	Δ6,749		Δ16,887			Δ23,636	

[1] Based on project operating in basic flood control plan for control to 800,000 cfs. at The Dalles.
[2] Based on project being placed in operation subsequent to attainment of basic flood control objective.
[3] Power benefit recognized but not evaluated in basic report.
[4] Power benefits.

Source: Columbia River and Tributaries, House Document No. 403 87th Congress, 2nd Session, Supplement to Report on Water Resources Development, Columbia River Basin, North Pacific Division, U.S. Army Corps of Engineers, Portland, Ore., February 24, 1961, Table 10, p. 41.

stream at Kinbasket in lieu of the Mica project. (The output and costs relevant to each are given in Table 4.)

While the Crippen Wright co-operative plan did not correspond exactly to the Treaty projects, the comparison shown in Table 4 does give one an idea at least of the size of benefit British Columbia anticipated from the conclusion of an agreement for the joint undertaking. We observe that an increase of 1.9 billion kilowatt-hours annually attends the co-operative development at an outlay of $56 million less than for the independent alternative. Assuming a value for the power at 4.5 mills per kilowatt-hour at the load center, and a discount alternatively at 5.5

TABLE 4.

Output and Cost of Independent Canadian Development Compared with Co-operative Plan, Crippen Wright Studies

	Independent development	Co-operative development
	Clearwater–Calamity Curve scheme	High Arrow, Kinbasket, and Libby storage scheme
Estimated total generation and transmission costs:		
Investment ($ million)	1,628.5	1,572.5
Annual costs ($ million)	92.3	89.2
Estimated increased annual firm power at B.C. load centers (billion kw-h.)	29.3	31.2

Source: Crippen Wright Engineering, Ltd., *Upper Columbia Hydro-Electric Developments, Interim Report No. 7,* November 1958, chap. 4, pp. IV–10.

per cent and 4.0 per cent, the present worth of this annual stream would capitalize respectively at $144 million and $184 million. Adding the $56 million savings in cost and the share of the flood-damage reduction benefits, the advantage to Canada based on the Crippen Wright studies would total between $250 million and $300 million as a crude estimate.

Parallel studies by the Water Resources Branch of the Canadian Department of Northern Affairs and National Resources in effect support the estimates given above.[12] When the output and cost of the Treaty and complementary projects are compared with those of the most efficient independent Canadian development of the Columbia River in Canada, savings in cost are shown to be between $300 million and $400 million. Since both sets of engineering investigations were conducted without reference to each other, the results may well represent an estimate of the

[12] This is obtainable from a comparison of Study No. 24/1 and Study No. 32/2 in [ref. 9].

appropriate order of magnitude. Moreover, following the negotiation resulting in the Protocol Note and Sales Agreement of 1964, the United States made payment to Canada for downstream power entitlement which, with the payment of flood control benefits and the windfall gains from Libby, would approximate U.S. $400 million reckoned as of the time the scheduled storage services would begin, in 1968–69, 1969–70, and 1973–74.

One additional matter should be noted. During the interval between the signing of the Treaty of 1961 and the final arrangements in 1964, the British Columbia power planners and related decision makers obtained additional information concerning alternative power sources as a result of the expropriation of the British Columbia Electric Company and its engineering subsidiary and related holdings. On the basis of this information, two points were evident: First, in the absence of a co-operative undertaking on the Columbia, independent development of the Columbia would not be the immediate alternative domestic source of power; the Peace River project, and perhaps the development of a large thermal station based on the Hat Creek coal deposits, would almost certainly precede it. Second, if the province of British Columbia were ever to need the Columbia as a source of power, the Columbia Treaty had made provision for the reservation of a large block of power as low in costs as any which exists, in lieu of a marginal resource, which the Columbia in Canada would undoubtedly be if it were developed without United States co-operation.

Benefits to the United States—Phase I

In the course of the negotiations the U.S. negotiating team and supporting staff undertook some studies with the object of checking for correspondence between the results of various combinations of Canadian storage projects and General Principle No. 2 [ref. 10]. The first study attempted to determine what would be the effect of adding High Arrow, Mica, and Dorr–Bull River projects first to the U.S. base system (existing or under construction as of late 1959) and dividing the gain in power equally. It was determined that the cost of such an arrangement exceeded the cost of an independent U.S. alternative by about $290 million,[13] a result consistent with the displacement effects illustrated in Table 3.

The study demonstrated that Canadian storage on the order of 25

---

[13] The system power resources at each of five points in time were identified and the annual cost for the United States of meeting the same load with and without the Canadian storage evaluated. Annual costs were discounted at 2.5 per cent consistent with the interest cost attributable to the system in computing annual costs.

million acre-feet included as first added, with the gross gain in system output divided equally, would not meet the conditions given in IJC Principle No. 2. Therefore, several adjustments were considered. It was agreed that the United States would be permitted to deduct from the downstream storage benefits the secondary energy which was estimated to be salable in any event, *subject to the restriction that no more than 40 per cent of the secondary energy not used for thermal energy displacement in the Pacific Northwest be considered salable.* Second, it was agreed to consider a reduction in the amount of storage to be provided by Canada. Prior to the actual decision on the volume of Canadian storage, the U.S. technical staff analyzed four alternative possibilities, ranging in amount from 8.5 million acre-feet (High Arrow–Duncan) to 16.7 million acre-feet (Mica and Dorr–Bull River) of Canadian storage first added, to test the effects of (a) the reduction in amount of storage and (b) the adjustment to compensate for loss of U.S. salable secondary energy.

These "co-operative systems," each with one of the Canadian storage complements, were compared in turn with the United States domestic system. The results indicated that, by removing the permitted amount of U.S. salable secondary energy from the Canadian entitlement and varying the amounts of reduced Canadian storage, the deficit from the co-operative undertaking for the United States ranged between $72.5 million and $147 million, depending on the storage complement assumed to be provided by the Canadian resources.[14]

Ultimately, of course, the amount of storage provided by Canada was limited to 15.5 million acre-feet, Libby was substituted for Bull River–Dorr, and several other features departing from the assumptions of the above studies became the terms of the Treaty of 1961 governing this aspect of the agreement. No study in terms equivalent to the studies cited was undertaken by the U.S. staff to test the correspondence of the actual Treaty terms with IJC Principle No. 2. The only indication of potential results is given by the Corps of Engineers in studies [ref. 11] designed to re-evaluate the economics of the Major Water Plan projects in the light of prior addition of Canadian storage. (See Table 3.)

This gap in information was filled during the spring of 1965 by an analysis undertaken by Resources for the Future, with the technical assistance of H. Zinder and Associates in co-operation with the Bonneville Power Administration. It was based upon simulations of a domestic system in terms comparable with the Treaty system, identified by an

---

[14] Discounted at 2.5 per cent as in the case of previous study; with a higher discount applied, the deficiency, of course, would be smaller.

international work group in the course of estimating the Canadian power entitlement [ref. 12].

The analysis showed that the excess cost of the Treaty system as compared with the domestic alternative, given circumstances and Treaty terms appropriate to 1961, increased to more than $250 million, as shown below:[15]

	($000)
Present value of excess cost of Treaty system	241,862
Flood control adjustments	
Excess present cost of Treaty flood control measures	+ 62,184
Excess present value of Treaty flood control benefits	− 50,725
Total excess cost of Treaty system	253,321

Several factors account for this: Use of a consistent interest rate in the RFF studies for both hydro and thermal power, more realistic estimates of the thermal costs, and thermal energy displacement by secondary hydro energy reflected in annual fuel costs—all these factors tended to have somewhat different implications for evaluation than the cruder methods employed by the U.S. staff during the negotiations. But perhaps equally important, the additional concessions offered by Canada were substantially dissipated by the excessive cost of the Libby project in relation to U.S. benefits. While the inclusion of Libby in the system may be justified when the benefits of Libby to both countries are compared with the costs, almost all of the costs of the project are borne by the United States while it realizes only about two-thirds of the downstream benefits of the Libby project; the remainder accrue in British Columbia and, under terms of the Treaty, are not subject to sharing with the United States.

The above observations reflect an evaluation of the Treaty for the United States in terms of General Principle No. 2 under conditions prevailing in 1961. Before the exchange of ratification, however, the terms of the Treaty of 1961 were altered to require the disposal of Canada's downstream power entitlement in the United States, which had implication both for the amount of hydropower from the Columbia available to the United States and for the cost of meeting power loads in the Pacific Northwest. In the interim, the groundwork had been laid for an agreement to implement the Pacific Northwest–California-Southwest intertie. This latter change in conditions affects the value of Canadian

---

[15] Detailed tables comparing (1) the projected peaking capacity and critical-period average generation for the U.S. domestic systems and the Treaty system, and (2) the projected cost of the systems, are included in the full-scale study on which this paper is based. See [ref. 14].

storage to the U.S. power systems. The intertie can be used to substitute in part for storage by firming up a block of secondary energy; moreover, by connecting the Northwest hydro region with the Southwest's predominantly thermal power regions, it provides a market for the use of any residual secondary energy that is surplus to the needs of the Northwest, as thermal displacement energy. Accordingly, a proper evaluation of the Treaty in terms of IJC General Principle No. 2 would need to incorporate the retention of Canadian power entitlement for use in the United States at a lump sum cost equivalent to $254 million (1964 worth), and evaluation of the intertie functioning in the Northwest power region.

A Digression on the North-South Extra-high-voltage Interconnection

There are a number of interesting economic aspects of the intertie between the Northwest and the Southwest, and if our purpose were to determine whether or not intertie benefits exceed costs, it would be necessary to evaluate them. However, our concern here is to determine how the intertie might be used in the Treaty and the domestic systems, and to consider the difference in costs of meeting similar objectives when the intertie is assumed to be operating in both systems. The two uses of the intertie that are likely to show differing results as between the Treaty and the domestic systems relate, first, to the firm power which will be available from secondary hydro energy in the Northwest complemented by economy energy imported from the Southwest, and, second, to the receipts from sales of residual surplus secondary in the Southwest for thermal energy displacement.

How much firm energy will it be economical to obtain with Northwest secondary and imported complementary economy energy? This will depend on: (1) amount of excess hydro capacity in the system, (2) amount of secondary energy, (3) price of energy sold as secondary, (4) price of energy sold as firm, (5) amount and cost of imported economy energy, and (6) efficiency with which imported economy energy can be used in response to anticipated adverse stream flow conditions.

We can set up a model which will incorporate these factors in operational relations.

Let

Z_{ijk} = Megawatts of secondary energy in year i and month j of system condition k ($k = 1, \ldots, 6$),

T_k = Optimal megawatts of increased firm power from intertie ($0 \leq T \leq \beta_k$), ($k = 1, \ldots, 6$),

K_s = Value per megawatt-month of energy sold as secondary,

K_c = Cost per megawatt-month of imported economy energy,

K_p = Value per megawatt-month of firm power,

$1/\alpha$ = Per cent efficiency with which imported energy is used,

B_k = Megawatts of excess hydro capacity during system condition k,

R_{ijk} = Net gain in dollars in year i and month j of firming secondary energy with intertie imports during system condition k,

$\bar{R}_k$ = Average annual net gain from firming secondary energy with intertie during system condition k;

then

$$\bar{R}_k = \sum_i^{30} \sum_j^{12} R_{ijk}/30$$

where

$$\bar{R}_{ijk} = \begin{cases} K_p T_k - K_s T_k & Z_{ijk} \geq T_k \\ K_p T_k - K_s Z_{ijk} - [\alpha(T_k - Z_{ijk})] + (\alpha - 1)(T_k - Z_{ijk})K_s & Z_{ijk} < T_k \end{cases}$$

Given the data, the range of firm power increments from zero to an appropriate constraint level can be investigated. The optimal level of increased firm power from the intertie is given by the condition that $\bar{R}_k$ be a maximum.

The data of the model were obtained as follows. The monthly megawatts of secondary energy were obtained from the system simulations for each level of development employing a thirty-year hydrologic trace. These hydropower studies also provided the information on amount of excess hydro capacity, which was useful in determining how much energy in fact would need to be imported and the price range it was likely to fall into. The prices are given as follows:[16]

K_c = 3.25 mills/kw-h. plus 10% line loss, or \$2,609.75/mw-month

K_s = \$17.50 kw. less 5% line loss, or \$1,385/mw-month

K_p = 3.75 mills/kw-h. at 65% load factor, or \$2,737.50/mw-month.

One additional parameter requires specification, i.e., the efficiency with which imported economy energy is utilized is assumed to be 67 per cent. That is, 50 per cent more energy is assumed to be imported for firming than is found in retrospect to be required owing to errors of forecasting runoff. All excess imported energy, however, is assumed to be resold subsequently at the general secondary energy rate.

[16] The Federal Power Commission's *Steam Electric Plant Construction Cost and Annual Production Expenses* (Sixteenth Annual Supplement, 1963) was reviewed to determine what fuel costs were incurred for production of electricity in the southwest. It seemed quite clear that an adequate amount of energy at 3.25 mills/kw.-h. or less would be available to firm up power to the level of excess hydro capacity in the system. The secondary energy rate was taken as given by Bonneville Power Administration policy, while the prime power rate was taken to reflect what is thought to be the lowest cost alternative source of firm power.

Table 5 gives the estimated amount of firm power which it is economic to obtain from the intertie.

Since there is substantially more storage in the Treaty system than in the domestic system at any comparable point in time, there will be less secondary energy to combine with imported energy. Accordingly, the cost of equivalent blocks of intertie firm power would be greater for the Treaty system, since a larger proportion of the block would have to be imported than in the domestic system. For this reason, subject only to there being adequate hydro capacity in the system, the domestic system

TABLE 5.

Intertie Firm Power and Corresponding Net Gain from Intertie Operation

Level of development and system identification	k	I_k Intertie firm power (mw.)	$\bar{R}_k$ Average annual gain from intertie operations ($000)
1968–69	1		
Treaty system		900	10,000
Domestic system		1,200	13,491
1969–70	2		
Treaty system		300	3,528
Domestic system		1,300	14,725
1976–77	3		
Treaty system		200	1,358
Domestic system		1,300	11,389
1983–84	4		
Treaty system		800	5,066
Domestic system		0	0
1988–89	5		
Treaty system		400	2,620
Domestic system		634	6,026
2010–11	6	——	——

typically will be able to firm up a greater amount of secondary energy than the Treaty system, and at a substantially larger average net gain.

Aside from the use of the intertie to convert secondary into firm power, the intertie will be used also for transmitting surplus secondary energy to California and the Southwest. In the legislation setting up the intertie, preference was accorded the Northwest for use of power generated on the Columbia, permitting the export only of power surplus to the needs of the Pacific Northwest. Use of secondary energy in the Northwest, in addition to that converted to firm via the intertie, will consist of sales of high-grade interruptible power (about 552 mw. in the early years) and fuel displacement for the initially small amount of thermal power in the Northwest. To estimate the average annual surplus secondary (S_k) net of Northwest requirements we have:

$$S_k = \sum_{i}^{30} \sum_{j}^{12} [Z_{ijk} - (T_k + I_{ijk} + D_k)]/360$$

$$\text{except } Z_{ijk} - (T_k + I_{ijk} + D_k) \begin{cases} = 0 \text{ when } Z_{ijk} < (T_k + I_{ijk} + D_k) \\ = 4,400 \text{ when } Z_{ijk} = (T_k + I_{ijk} + D_k) > \\ \quad 4,400, \end{cases}$$

where Z_{ijk} = megawatts of secondary energy in year i and month j of
system condition k

T_k = megawatts of firm power from intertie operations during
system condition k

I_{ijk} = megawatts of high-grade interruptible power in year i and
month j of condition k

D_k = megawatts of secondary energy required for fuel displacement under condition k.

The data employed and the computed results are given in Table 6.

TABLE 6.

Estimates of Surplus Secondary Energy Available for Sale to Southwest

(*Megawatts*)

Levels of development and system identification	k	Value of T_k	Value of D_k	Value of I_k	Average annual surplus secondary
1968–69	1				
Treaty system		900	393	552	1,181
Domestic system		1,200	393	552	1,375
1969–70	2				
Treaty system		300	397	552	1,168
Domestic system		1,300	397	552	1,592
1976–77	3				
Treaty system		200	345	0	2,404
Domestic system		1,300	345	0	2,369
1983–84	4				
Treaty system		800	4,199	0	686
Domestic system		0	5,310	0	938
1988–89	5				
Treaty system		400	8,118	0	94
Domestic system		634	8,081	0	297
2010–11	6	All secondary energy can be used for thermal displacement in Northwest.			

Benefits to the United States—Phase II

With estimates of the additional firm power which the intertie can provide economically for each system, a comparison can be made of the cost performance of the Treaty and domestic systems. First, however, it will be useful to provide the model for estimating fossil fuel requirements and costs for the two systems, as this has not been done previously.

We wish to determine the difference in the fossil fuel displacement by secondary energy corresponding to each of the two systems at each level of development. What we wish to know for purposes of comparing the cost behavior of the two systems is the amount of fossil fuel required (C_k) that is net of displacement by secondary energy surplus to the needs of conversion to firm, and net also of provision during the early years of high-grade interruptible power. This is computed for each system and level of development as follows:

$$C_k = \sum_i^{30} \sum_j^{12} (F_k - Y_{ijk}) /360 \text{ except } F_k - Y_{ijk} \begin{cases} = 0 \text{ when } Y_{ijk} > F_k \\ = F_k \text{ when } Y_{ijk} < 0 \end{cases}$$

where all terms are defined as previously and,

F_k = critical period average thermal generation for system condition k

$Y_{ijk} = Z_{ijk} - (T_k + I_{ijk})$.

The results of these computations are given for reference in Table 7.

Given the Pacific Northwest power region's load estimates, the hydropower output from the Columbia power system simulation,[17] the firm

TABLE 7.

Average Megawatts of Fossil Fuel Requirements for Each System and the Several Levels of Development

(Megawatts)

Level of development and system identification	k	Values of F_k	Values of Y_{ijk}	Average annual generation with fossil fuel
1968–69	1			
Treaty system		393	$Z_{ij1} - 1,452$	138.7
Domestic system		393	$Z_{ij1} - 1,752$	157.2
1969–70	2			
Treaty system		397	$Z_{ij2} - 852$	250.5
Domestic system		397	$Z_{ij2} - 1,852$	159.8
1970–77	3			
Treaty system		345	$Z_{ij3} - 200$	154.2
Domestic system		345	$Z_{ij3} - 1,300$	143.9
1983–84	4			
Treaty system		4,199	$Z_{ij4} - 800$	2,617.9
Domestic system		5,310	$Z_{ij4} - 0$	3,034.1
1988–89	5			
Treaty system		8,118	$Z_{ij5} - 400$	5,727.8
Domestic system		8,081	$Z_{ij5} - 634$	5,531.7
2010–11	6			
Treaty system		40,210	$Z_{ij6} - 0$	37,502.0
Domestic system		40,307	$Z_{ij6} - 0$	37,092.8

[17] See footnote 15.

power available from the intertie operation (Table 5), the net fuel requirement for the thermal component of the system (Table 7), and the residual secondary surplus for sale (Table 6), we can put together the cost performance of the two systems as follows:

	($000)
Present value of excess cost of Treaty system	354,758
Flood control adjustments:	
Excess present cost of Treaty flood control measures	+ 62,184
Excess present value of Treaty flood control benefits	− 40,500
Total excess cost of Treaty system	376,444 + added

cost of Canadian energy $y\, t + 30\, -$.

From the cost comparisons it appears that the amount of funds advanced to Canada as prepayment for the downstream nominal gain from storage greatly exceeds the amount of real (net of displacement of U.S. supramarginality in storage and intertie) or net gain from the Canadian storage. With the intertie in operation the excess cost of the Treaty system (1968–69 worth) is increased about $100 million above the total estimated to apply under the 1961 Treaty terms and conditions. The deficiency in the arrangements for the United States, therefore, as measured by the test of IJC General Principle No. 2 under the terms of the Treaty of 1961, was substantially enlarged by the terms of the Protocol Note and Sales Agreement of 1964 and the coincident availability of the North-South intertie.

CONCLUDING OBSERVATIONS

Based on the results of the analysis above, it appears that the Columbia River Treaty of 1961 resulted in a system design which is less economic than was technically possible, and in this respect the Treaty system departed from the spirit of IJC General Principle No. 1. Moreover, three years elapsed between the ratification of the Treaty in the United States Senate and the ratification by the Canadian Parliament. During this interval developments occurred of major significance for the economical design of the Columbia hydro system. The polycentric machinery for reaching decisions on the international features of the Columbia River system, however, were cumbersome. Thus it was not necessarily prudent to reopen the Treaty of 1961 for renegotiation to take into account the new possibilities for economizing in the production of the region's power supplies. Implicit in this position is the feeling that there is an inherent value in agreement *per se* between two riparians such as the United States and Canada, irrespective of the particular economic outcome for the United States. Those who do not take this position would be willing to risk failure to reach agreement of any sort in an effort to renegotiate new terms which would take into account the Peace River, the North-South intertie, and other factors in the interest of economy and pursuit of advantage to both riparians.

The ultimate division of the gains appears to be inequitable. Given the cost of the excess baggage in the Treaty system, the gains to Canada were provided for, not by the increase in efficiency stemming from joint development, but by the United States' loss in relation to available alternatives. However, as I have indicated, such a viewpoint may be too restricted. Suppose that the Columbia Treaty is regarded not as an isolated affair between Canada and the United States in which the benefits to either party are tied to the outcome of the specific negotiations, but rather as one of many matters on which the two countries must come to mutual accommodation: in that event, it is not at all clear that the division of the nominal gains is inequitable. The vital interests of the United States were in no way affected in the Columbia matter. It was an area in which the United States could make an attractive arrangement in exchange for concessions perhaps involving North American continental defense or perhaps other areas in which the vital interests of the United States are at stake. Unless one knows all the elements of the broader background, therefore, one cannot properly judge the equity of the Columbia Treaty terms. One can say only that the arrangement for the division of benefits, as evaluated in terms of IJC Principle No. 2, did not result in a saving in cost to the United States as compared with alternatives available to it.

REFERENCES

[1] Reference from the Canadian and the United States Governments to the International Joint Commission. Ottawa and Washington, March 9, 1944.

[2] *Report of the International Joint Commission on Principles for Determining and Apportioning Benefits from Cooperative Use of Storage of Waters and Electrical Interconnection within the Columbia River System.* Ottawa and Washington, December 29, 1959.

[3] International Columbia River Engineering Board. *Water Resources of*

the *Columbia River Basin*. Report to the International Joint Commission, United States and Canada, Ottawa and Washington, 1959.

[4] Krutilla, John V. "Columbia River Development: Some Problems of International Cooperation," in *Land and Water: Planning for Economic Growth*. Boulder: University of Colorado Press, 1961.

[5] *Report on Survey for Flood Control of Kootenai River in Kootenai Flats Area, Idaho*. U.S. Army Engineer District, Seattle, December 1, 1958.

[6] British Columbia Energy Board. *Report of the Columbia and Peace Power Projects*. Victoria, B.C., July 31, 1961.

[7] Chantrill, R. J., and Stevens, Jack D. *Power Capabilities and Operating Aspects of the Peace River Project and a Pacific International Power Pool*. Vancouver, B.C.: Peace River Power Development Co., Ltd., May 1960.

[8] Testimony of Richard Deane. *Standing Committee on External Affairs, Minutes of Proceedings and Evidence*, No. 21. Ottawa, May 7, 1964, pp. 1042, 1049, 1053–54.

[9] *Summary of Water Resources Branch Power Output Studies of Columbia River*. Ottawa: Department of Northern Affairs and National Resources, February 1964.

[10] *International Columbia River Studies: Costs of [sic] Analysis of a Canadian–U.S. System vs. an Alternative U.S. System*. North Pacific Division, U.S. Army Corps of Engineers, Portland, Ore., April 25, 1960; and *Alternative System Studies: U.S.–Canadian Development of the Columbia River*. Bonneville Power Administration and North Pacific Division, U.S. Army Corps of Engineers, Portland, Ore., July 8, 1960.

[11] *Columbia River and Tributaries*. House Doc. No. 403, 87th Congress, 2nd Session—"Supplement to Report on Water Resources Development, Columbia River Basin." North Pacific Division, U.S. Army Corps of Engineers, Portland, Ore., February 24, 1961.

[12] *Columbia River Development: Determination of Canadian Downstream Power Entitlement*. Technical Report, Work Group No. 1, November 1963.

[13] *Water Resource Development, Columbia River Basin*, Vol. 1. North Pacific Division, U.S. Army Corps of Engineers, June 1958; and correspondence with the Department of Northern Affairs and National Resources, Ottawa.

[14] Krutilla, John V. *The Columbia River Treaty: A Study in the Economics of International River Basin Development*. Baltimore: Johns Hopkins Press, in press.

Planning a Water Quality Management System: The Case of the Potomac Estuary

Robert K. Davis*

T his is a study of the cost of alternative systems for dissolved oxygen management in the Potomac River estuary. The study uses case materials of a water quality planning study prepared by the U.S. Army Corps of Engineers, which identified and analyzed the pollution problem in the Potomac estuary [ref. 1]. These materials are supplemented by engineering information drawn from the advanced waste treatment program of the U.S. Public Health Service, from engineers representing manufacturers, and from consulting engineers engaged by Resources for the Future. The technologic functions developed in this study are believed comparable in reliability to the cost functions used by the Corps of Engineers. Nevertheless, because of the experimental nature of some of the processes analyzed, the results reported here cannot be viewed as a technical revision of the Engineers' proposal for the Potomac, but rather as a consequence of some strategic modifications in the water resource planning process.

The plan for the Potomac represents the first major proposal to incorporate low-flow augmentation for quality control into a multiple-purpose river basin plan. The proposal for sixteen major flow augmentation reservoirs in the Potomac basin reflects the findings of a preliminary

* Research Associate, Resources for the Future, Inc. This paper reports on current findings of a continuing RFF study of the Potomac estuary.

99

study of the prospects for water supply and demand in 1980 and 2000, which was prepared by Nathaniel Wollman for the U.S. Senate Select Committee on National Water Resources [ref. 2]. Wollman's conclusions that in the eastern United States water quality would become the dominant water resource problem in the next twenty to fifty years are consistent with the proposal of the Corps of Engineers in their Potomac study: that the low-flow augmentation for maintaining water quality should be twice that needed for municipal and industrial water supplies.

The Federal Water Pollution Control Act, as amended July 20, 1961, established low-flow augmentation for water quality control as a nonreimbursable purpose of federal multipurpose water resource systems, and thereby focused attention on low-flow augmentation as a measure for water quality management. The Corps of Engineers recently estimated that by 1980 it should provide about 320 million acre-feet of additional reservoir storage capacity, much of which is based on presumed requirements for water quality control [ref. 3]. The fact that this is about double the storage in the 214 reservoir projects operated by the Corps in 1962, gives some idea of the magnitude of the problem.

The comprehensive river basin surveys now being undertaken by the Public Health Service in eight basins[1] can be expected to add considerably to our understanding of the water quality management problem and its dimensions. In the meantime, the Corps' Potomac report offers us the first of what will probably be a number of efforts to cope with water quality problems through the water resources planning process as it is currently practiced.

Economics can provide useful tools for examining the adequacy of water resources planning. Allen V. Kneese's recent work in this field has pointed out the gains to be realized from more systematic approaches to planning for water quality management [ref. 4, 5]. Possible approaches range from finding efficient solutions to technical problems, to creating appropriate institutional arrangements for making effective planning and management decisions. Two major questions arise in systematic planning: (1) What is the optimal scale of expenditure for water quality improvement: that is, how much are we willing to pay for it? (2) What is the least-cost solution among alternatives for achieving a given scale of output: that is, what is the most efficient technical means of accomplishing a given level of quality improvement?

---

[1] The list of comprehensive projects includes Arkansas-Red Rivers (completed), Chesapeake Bay–Susquehanna River, Columbia River, Great Lakes–Illinois River, Delaware Estuary, Ohio River, Southeastern Rivers, and Hudson River–Lake Champlain. Eleven more projects are scheduled to start between fiscal years 1966 and 1969.

ROBERT K. DAVIS

THE PLANNING PROCESS

The major elements in a planning process which seeks to satisfy as fully as possible an expressed desire of a community are: (1) a set of objectives, and (2) technological information on the costs of producing desirable sets of results. In the conventional water resources planning process, performance in attaining objectives is measured by quantitative criteria such as "value of flood damages avoided," or "costs of alternatives to hydroelectric generation facilities." Benefits thus measured are compared with the costs of the "best," that is, the least-cost method for achieving a particular scale of output. The benefit-cost rules for optimizing with and without constraints have been formally specified in a number of economic studies.[2]

There are a number of shortcomings in the conventional water resources planning process, whether it is applied generally or specifically to water quality management. The Harvard Water Studies Group, for example, has demonstrated that the complex task of locating the optimum point on the response surface of a water resource system is not likely to be successfully discharged without the aid of relatively new analytic tools such as computer simulation, synthetic hydrologic traces, and sophisticated algorithms [ref. 7].

No matter how impeccable the methodology may be, however, it may be subject to systematic bias by excluding from the analysis certain kinds of alternatives. For example, White's work on adjustment to floods [ref. 8, 9] has revealed several possible alternatives to structural measures for dealing with floods; and Fox [ref. 9] has argued that in any planning situation equity considerations and incommensurable effects can be satisfactorily handled only by developing fuller public discussion of the alternative courses of action. Hence, there appears to be justification for asking if the low-flow augmentation proposed by the Corps is the best solution to the Potomac basin's pollution problems.

In dealing with water quality planning efforts in the Potomac estuary we are confronted with some problems that are characteristic of the situation in many eastern river basins. In this densely populated area, demand for recreation is a large component, but as yet methods for measuring the benefits to be derived from water made fit for recreation are still experimental. They are much less easily come by than those commonly used to quantify the benefits from flood control, hydroelectric power, and navigation projects. These benefits have a meaningful relationship to society's willingness to pay for the services produced by a project. By contrast, the benefits deriving from reservoirs planned for water quality

[2] For classical treatment of benefit-cost analysis, see Eckstein [ref. 6].

101

management in the Potomac were calculated not on the basis of willingness to pay, but of alternative cost, where single-purpose projects constructed by local jurisdictions to meet defined local requirements were assumed to be the relevant alternative.

Not surprisingly, the total cost of all the single-purpose, non-integrated, locally financed reservoir projects assumed as alternatives greatly exceeds the cost of an integrated, multipurpose, federally sponsored system. There are three reasons for this result. First, the single-purpose, non-integrated system is costed on the assumption that local governments would pay higher interest rates than the federal government. Second, the non-integrated system is based on the assumption that each need center will act without regard to the possibility that flow augmentation upstream may also be useful downstream. Third, the multipurpose system shows a benefit over the single-purpose system for any storage purpose principally because recreation assumes a share of the storage costs under the separable costs-remaining benefits allocation method used, even though no incremental storage is added for the recreation purpose. Consequently, since the estimates for recreation benefits in the Potomac plan essentially are composed of arbitrary numbers, they can tell us nothing about the desirability of the proposed investment.

There is hope that benefit-estimating procedures can be improved. Even so, limitations in the measurability of system costs may be even more intractable. One is made aware of this by the heated public discussion aroused over the choice of several of the reservoir sites in the Corps of Engineers' proposal for the Potomac. The problem is especially serious where scenic and recreational considerations are important in different ways to various groups in society. Because such difficult-to-measure values must be taken into account, it may not be possible for the planner, in the role of technical expert without political responsibility, to define the "best" plan for water development and use. In the eastern United States this is an increasingly serious obstacle to the application of systematic water resources planning techniques.

One might conclude from this brief review of water quality planning in the Potomac basin that the most that can be achieved toward optimization under present limitations is to demonstrate that a recommended plan is the minimum-cost solution for achieving a particular water quality standard and to provide information on the sensitivity of system costs to changes in the standards. However, there may be substantial ambiguities as to what constitutes a least-cost solution—for example, when equity considerations between different types of outdoor recreationists are examined. These are sufficient reasons to reopen the case of the Potomac estuary with an expanded array of alternatives and analytic tools. Is the

Corps' plan the most efficient solution, and is it the most equitable solution for the money?

In making this case study we shall set aside some of the institutional and technical constraints now affecting the planning process. In particular, we wish to know if the 1961 amendment, which identified low-flow augmentation as the sole water quality management device available to multipurpose river-basin planners on a non-reimbursable basis, has introduced serious inefficiencies into federal expenditure programs for interquality improvement.

Another question concerns the assumption that plans must be based on known and accepted technologies. This may be a defensible assumption for short-range planning, but a plan which attempts to deal with a fifty-year time horizon must surely take account of possible effects of technological advances on the ranking of alternative systems.

We shall examine several questions concerning the analysis of alternatives. One concerns the incomplete or inappropriate analysis of certain kinds of processes. This can involve inappropriate comparisons of costs and incomplete analyses of costs. Because some waste treatment processes involve high operating costs relative to capital costs, it makes a great difference in cost comparisons whether the processes are operated continuously or for only that fraction of the time when, because of hydrology, temperature, and other conditions, they are actually needed.

Another potential source of error is worth exploring. Certain alternatives may have been examined in the Potomac study on the assumption that they and other processes were mutually exclusive, when in fact incremental examination of tradeoffs might prove that a process rejected as too costly on an either/or basis is attractive in a mixed system.

Finally, we shall illustrate how the planning process can be used to generate information on alternatives that may be equally costly but substantially different in other respects, and how information can be generated on the question of selecting the most desirable water quality standard.

STRATEGY OF THE STUDY

The strategic elements of the study are: (1) characterizing the set of input-output relationships in the physical system in a way that leads logically to the development of a set of instruments for managing the system; (2) devising a strategy for sampling the cost surface in order to reduce the problem to finite proportions; (3) developing an algorithm for defining the alternative systems and locating the least-cost system in the sample set of systems.

Input-Output Relationships

The set of input-output relationships pertaining to dissolved oxygen management in the estuary is represented in Figure 1. The output, or objective of the system in this case, is maintaining a minimum monthly mean dissolved oxygen in a particular reach of the estuary. The objective adopted by the Corps and consequently for this study is a minimum monthly mean value of 5 parts per million (ppm). The forces which act upon dissolved oxygen are of two kinds: forces over which we have some control, or "instruments," and forces over which we do not exercise control—call them "data." The instruments and data affect dissolved oxygen through a set of structural relations that have been specified by T. A. Wastler in a study of the estuary [ref. 10]. Wastler's model is the basis

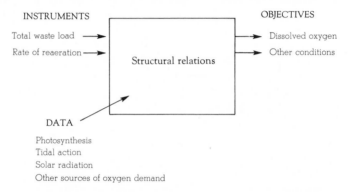

Figure 1. Model of dissolved oxygen management system in the Potomac estuary.

for the present study even though it may soon be superseded by a current Public Health Service study.

The two instruments in the system scheme are regulation of the waste load and reaeration. The waste load in the estuary comes from the sewage treatment plants of the metropolitan area of Washington, D. C., and from the residual wastes in the river. The size of the oxygen-demanding waste load in the critical reach of the estuary may be controlled by increasing sewage treatment above the level of 90 per cent removal of biochemical oxygen demand (BOD) assumed by the Corps, or by directing treatment plant discharge to other locations. The latter is effective because treatment plant discharge is now concentrated in the upper estuary—one four-mile reach in an estuary that is 115 miles long. (See Figure 2.)

Low-flow augmentation affects dissolved oxygen by displacing some of the waste load farther downstream and also by inducing higher rates

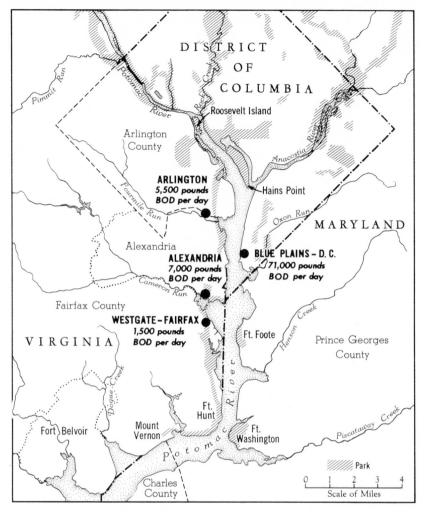

Figure 2. Upper Potomac River estuary, with projected waste loads for the year 2010.

of reaeration in the estuary. Reaeration is the process of transferring oxygen from the atmosphere to a body of water. The oxygen problem in the estuary arises because natural reaeration will not be sufficient at times of low flow and high temperatures to enable the estuary to meet the oxygen demand of the waste load present and simultaneously to maintain a mean dissolved oxygen level of 5 ppm. While only a limited portion of the estuary would be affected severely by oxygen depletion, if that portion became completely and persistently depleted of oxygen, it would

become malodorous and would suffocate many fish. At very low dissolved oxygen content, but short of complete depletion, the estuary
would cease to be attractive for boating and fishing. Besides the reaeration effect of low-flow augmentation, reaeration can be accomplished by
devices which reoxygenate the water.

We have, then, two sets of instruments for study: One, consisting of
waste treatment and waste diversion, affects the total size of the waste
load discharged into the problem stretch of the estuary; the other consists of reaeration techniques which treat the estuary itself.

The uncontrolled or exogenous inputs in the system are principally
those natural processes which the analysis does not presume to control.
These are principally photosynthesis, tidal action, and solar radiation.
The demand of benthic sludge may also be important.[3] Thus, no account
is taken of the prospects for controlling tidal action with engineering
works, or for controlling photosynthesis in aquatic plants (chiefly algae)
through hormones or through influencing the nutrient content and turbidity of the estuary.[4]

Cost Minimization Strategy

The cost minimization problem presents both a conceptual and a computational problem. Figure 3 portrays a constant output function representing an infinite number of combinations of the processes A and B
that are capable of producing output Q. Q in this case is the target of 5

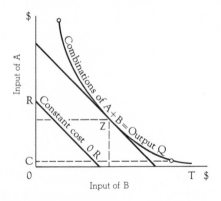

Figure 3. Process combinations to produce output Q.

[3] In this study all exogenous inputs are either collapsed into a temperature
variable which takes on monthly values corresponding to the mean of the maximum monthly temperatures, or else are obscured by the use of monthly average
performance data.
[4] In some views, it is necessary to control photosynthetic activity by algae in
order to achieve a desired amount of control over dissolved oxygen [ref. 11].

ppm dissolved oxygen in the estuary. The minimum cost point for the production of Q is given by the tangency of a constant cost line such as OR with the constant output line. This tangency is represented in the figure by the point Z. Defining the problem in these terms, we first must accomplish a mathematical derivation of the cost function and then solve a problem in the calculus of constrained minimization.[5]

The mathematical derivation of the cost function may be impossible because of the large burden that complete specification of input-output functions places on the process engineers and because of the mathematics of a complicated function of variables. Obviously the problem must be simplified.

The strategy for simplifying the analysis and description of the function is to sample the multivariate cost function at a limited number of points.[6] This entails three steps: (1) selection of points to be sampled and their translation to performance levels; (2) collection of information on costs and performance of the basic processes to be included for the levels of performance to be sampled; (3) combination of the processes at these discrete levels of activity in order to describe all feasible mixes of the basic processes.

Sampling the Cost Function

The sampling strategy consists of systematically sampling the trade-off relation conveniently visualized as existing between low-flow augmentation and any set of the alternative processes for reducing or offsetting the waste load in the estuary. We assume from the Public Health Service estimates that by the year 2010 the daily oxygen demand (BOD_5) in the estuary will be about 100,000 pounds. If we reduce the low-flow augmentation input, we must counter by reducing the waste discharge or offsetting it by an equivalent amount. Each point on the trade-off function represents a combination of waste reduction or offset and a low-flow augmentation capacity to accommodate the 100,000-pound waste load. To obtain a set of such points we examine points at 20,000-, 40,000-, 60,000-, and 80,000-pound capacity for waste reduction or offset

[5] The formal solution to a constrained cost minimization is found in Henderson and Quandt [ref. 12, p. 51]. The solution states that the marginal product, per dollar's worth of each of the inputs or processes, must be equal over all inputs, subject to satisfaction of the conditions that the marginal products be diminishing and that the minimum is not a local minimum. It may not be possible to satisfy the condition of equivalence in the marginal products of the processes; in which case, some process or set of processes will dominate the optimal solution to the problem over some range of scale.

[6] For a discussion of alternative sampling strategies in a problem of this sort, see Maass et al. [ref. 7, ch. 10].

by the alternative instruments. These points expressed in performance units correspond to steps I-IV, respectively, in Table 1.

In order to develop the specific processes for reducing or offsetting the waste load, we must study waste treatment in terms of the percentage reduction in BOD, redistribution of the effluent in volume of effluent handled, and reaeration devices in terms of pounds of oxygen transferred to the estuary daily.

In all, we will look at five waste treatment processes, one process for effluent distribution, and two processes for reaeration, or a total of eight basic processes in addition to low-flow augmentation.[7] (Table 2)

The cost information developed in the alternative processes falls into

TABLE 1.

General Processes and Level of Activity

Process	Activity level in daily performance units			
	Step I	Step II	Step III	Step IV
Waste treatment; at D.C. plant only (%)	92.8	95.3	98.6	....[1]
Effluent distribution (mgd)	170	340	510	680
Artificial reaeration (lb.)[2]	30,000	60,000	90,000	120,000
Performance in terms of BOD$_5$ reduction or offset (lb.)	20,000	40,000	60,000	80,000

[1] The 80,000-lb. performance level of waste treatment would involve incorporating all waste treatment plants in the metropolitan area into the analysis.

[2] Pounds of oxygen transferred daily.

TABLE 2.

Present Value of All Costs for 50-Year Period of Analysis at 3.5 Months Annual Operation and 4 per cent Discount Rate

(Millions of dollars)

Process	Level[1]			
	20,000	40,000	60,000	80,000
Microstraining[2]	12	38	—	—
Step aeration[3]	13	32	—	—
Chemical precipitation	18	32	—	—
Powdered adsorption	43	72	102	—
Granular adsorption	95	156	216	—
Effluent distribution	19	39	50	87
Diffused reaeration	2.2	3.3	4.6	5.8
Mechanical reaeration	1.7	2.8	3.8	4.7

[1] Level in pounds BOD$_5$ removed or offset daily.

[2] Second level of microstraining is preceded by step aeration.

[3] Second level of step aeration consists of chemical precipitation following step aeration.

[7] See [ref. 13] for a technical discussion of technologies and sources of information on the alternative processes.

three categories: the capital costs, or costs of creating the capacity; the annual standby costs, or costs that must be incurred each year for maintenance, standby crews and the like, regardless of whether operating or not; operating costs, incurred only when the process is used. Operating costs are broken down into power costs and other costs so that the sensitivity of the results to reductions in power rates can be explored. It is necessary to specify the life of the capital equipment so that allowances for replacement can conform to the Corps' fifty-year period of analysis.

Some differences exist among processes in all the categories of cost. Effluent distribution, the two carbon adsorption processes, and the combination of step aeration followed by microstraining are extremely capital intensive (as is low-flow augmentation). Chemical precipitation consists almost solely of operating costs. Devices for reaeration fall between the two extremes. Both effluent distribution and carbon adsorption have large power requirements (20 million kilowatt-hours monthly are required to distribute 680 million gallons daily of effluent).

In order to proceed with the analysis it is desirable to summarize the cost data so that we may work with one number for cost as a function of scale. We shall adopt a static framework in order to simplify the problem. Therefore, the task is to reduce these mixtures of costs to a summary number representing the present value of fifty years of operation for each process at some level of intensity, at some expected annual period of operation, at some power rate, and at some rate of discount.[8]

From inspection of the cost data, it is obvious that the reaeration devices are the least costly of the alternative processes for reducing or offsetting the waste load and that the two carbon adsorption processes are the most costly means. These relations hold at all levels of operation.

---

[8] The basic notion of cost computation is the following: For each process and each level we desire a present value, call it cij, for the ith process and jth level which will be composed of initial capital costs, K, annual standby costs, S, monthly operating cost, O, and power costs to be derived from monthly power requirements, V. The computation of present value is:

$$C_{ij} = F_i(r) K_{ij} + a_{50}(r) \left[S_{ij} + d_k \frac{Vij}{730} + m(O_{ij} + P_k V_{ij}) \right]; i = 1, 8; j = 1, 4$$

where K, S, V, and O have been identified and where $F_i(r)$ is an interest-sensitive conversion of short-lived capital to the period of analysis.

$a_{50}(r)$ is the present value of an annuity at some discount rate, r.
d_k is the demand charge for power.
m is the expected annual operating period in months.
p_k is the energy charge for power.

This formulation permits interest, operating period, and power rate to vary as input parameters and can be generalized to handle other than fifty-year periods of analysis. (The annual expected operating period is derived by simulating the operation of the reservoir system for the historic hydrologic trace. Reservoir simulation is discussed later.)

As between microstraining, step aeration, chemical precipitation, and effluent distribution, the cost differences do not appear to be significant. Process costs proved to be mostly insensitive in ordering to variations in power rates, interest rates, and length of annual operating period. This general result may be attributed to the relatively uniform unimportance of power costs and other operating costs vis-à-vis capital costs in most processes. Chemical precipitation is the one exception to this generality, its costs varying strikingly with operating period and discount rate.[9] Virtually all costs of chemical precipitation are operating costs.

The chief importance of this sensitivity analysis is to illustrate the large advantages accruing to processes requiring high operating costs, when such processes are used for only brief periods at infrequent intervals. The differences are great enough to make worthwhile a search for waste treatment processes that are substantially less capital intensive than the conventional waste treatment process.[10]

The novelty of intermittent operation of high performance waste treatment facilities, or of any devices intended to alleviate transient water quality problems, deserves a word of emphasis. Because the environment of most receiving waters is variable, both seasonally and diurnally, and also as a result of the stochastic nature of hydrologic and meteorologic variation, the practice of operating treatment plants at constant levels produces a varying quality of water. As we move above conventional levels of treatment, particularly to high-cost processes, it becomes uneconomic to operate continuously at high levels if there are periods when those high levels of treatment do not improve water quality sufficiently to justify the large operating costs.

In this problem the standard of a 5 ppm minimum monthly mean carries the implication that raising the level of dissolved oxygen above 5 ppm has no value. Adopting the rule that none of the waste treatment or offset facilities will be operated unless needed to prevent the dissolved oxygen content from falling below the target, it is then a matter of simulating the operation of any of the reservoir systems for the thirty-year hydrologic record to discover the number of months in which operation of the reaeration, diversion, or advanced waste treatment processes would have been needed. During the thirty-year record there were about 105 months in which dissolved oxygen would have been deficient if the waste load had been 100,000 pounds BOD. Thus, the need to operate

---

[9] For example, if operated continuously (12 months each year), and if operating costs vary linearly with operating period, the present value of all costs of chemical precipitation discounted at 4 per cent rises to $110 million, or more than 3 times the costs of operating only 3.5 months each year.

[10] For the general logic of this idea, see Kneese [ref. 5, pp. 138–40].

remedial devices averaged 3.5 months annually. Simulating reservoir systems also helped to develop a cost function for low-flow augmentation. We turn now to that aspect of the study.

ANALYSIS OF THE LOW-FLOW AUGMENTATION SYSTEM

The low-flow augmentation system developed by the Corps of Engineers includes storage for water supply and water quality demands at various points in the basin, storage for flood control in several structures, and the purchase and development of reservoir lands for reservoir-based recreation. Figure 4 shows the locations of major reservoirs in the Corps' recommended plan. Table 3 lists these reservoirs by yield and construction costs. Here the reservoir system is divided into river basin and estuary components. The river basin component of ten reservoirs is capable of satisfying all water withdrawal demands in the basin, including the demands at Washington, D. C., as projected for the year 2010. The same ten reservoirs also satisfy the flow augmentation requirements for water quality purposes at all points in the basin upstream of the District of Columbia. Because of this, it is possible to identify an increment in the reservoir system that is associated only with low-flow augmentation requirements in the estuary.

The incremental importance of the estuary portion of the system is suggested by the relative importance of the water supply and water quality requirements defined for the Washington metropolitan area. The water withdrawal requirements of the Washington metropolitan area for the year 2010, projected to average 1,590 cubic feet per second, are equal to the total amount of flow augmentation planned for the rest of the basin for both water quality and water supply purposes. The additional flow requirements to meet the oxygen targets in the estuary are equivalent to an annual yield of 2,340 cfs from the six reservoirs listed separately in Table 3.

Two problems in the incremental separation of the costs of any integrated multipurpose system revolve around the questions of joint product relations and the sequence in which the purposes are to be added or separated. After careful study of both these issues, it can be stated with confidence that the incremental separation of the costs of the Potomac estuary system from the costs of the rest of the system[11] is not affected by

---

[11] The somewhat complicated reasons why neither the joint product relations nor the sequential question interferes with the incremental analysis of the system are instructive for the usefulness of incremental analysis in other multipurpose systems. They are dealt with in detail in the RFF case study, now in preparation, on which this paper is based.

111

questions of joint product relations nor by the order in which the estuary purpose is added or subtracted from the reservoir system.

A COST FUNCTION FOR LOW-FLOW AUGMENTATION

The costs of low-flow augmentation for the points on the cost surface to be sampled were derived by scaling down the Corps low-flow augmentation system for the estuary. The scaled-down systems were arrived at by trial and error simulations of alternative reservoir systems by using a simulation program originally devised by the Corps for its system design work on the Potomac. Criteria for accepting a modified system required comparability with the performance of the Corps' original system over the thirty-year hydrology for which simulation runs were made. In all modified systems the ten reservoirs serving upstream needs (see Table 3 and Figure 4) were retained. The cost function exhibits some discontinuities because the individual reservoirs were dealt with as indivisible inputs, but the discontinuities are not severe because a range of reservoir sizes with comparable cost/yield performances was available.

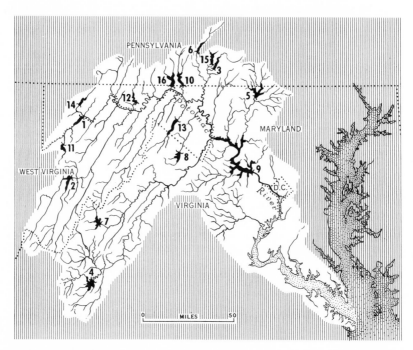

Figure 4. Major reservoirs in recommended plan. Numbers are identified in **Table** 3. (Source: *PRB Report*, Vol. 1, p. 30 [ref. 1].)

TABLE 3.

Proposed Reservoir Yields and Costs

Systems and reservoirs[1]	Yield (cfs)	Construction costs (*Millions of dollars*)
A. Upstream System		
Headwater reservoirs	650	104.75
1. Bloomington	212	51.06
3. Chambersburg	64	13.35
4. Staunton	163	25.80
5. Six Bridge	104	15.49
6. West Branch	65	13.83
7. Brock's Gap	147	18.16
8. Winchester	45	12.09
11. Mount Storm	55	10.39
14. Savage II	58	13.46
15. Back Creek	28	8.85
Total	1,591	287.23
B. Estuary System		
Reservoirs		
2. Royal Glen	484	32.51
9. Seneca	1,400	116.93
10. Licking Creek	138	13.30
12. Town Creek	97	12.57
13. North Mountain	137	19.78
16. Tonoloway Creek	84	15.70
Total	2,340	210.79
Grand total cost		498.02

[1] Numbers are keyed to the map, Figure 4.

Source: PRB Report, Vol. 1, p. 38, and Vol. 2 [ref. 1]. Reservoir yields were determined from available hydrologic records, using mass curve analysis.

The scaling of reservoir systems was based on the relationship between river discharge and assimilative capacity of the estuary developed from Wastler's study of the estuary [ref. 10]. The performance requirement for a reservoir system can be translated readily from this relationship to a schedule of monthly flow targets that must be delivered to the estuary in order to meet a particular assimilative capacity.

In computing costs for the respective reservoir systems, account must be taken of the differences in flood damage reduction and recreation services realized by any scaled-down system in comparison with the reservoir system proposed by the Corps. The model for computation of net reservoir system costs for the jth system is:

$C_j = i[CS_i - BF_i - CFP_i + BFP_i - (BR_i - CR_i)]$ where i varies over the set of included reservoirs and:

CS_i is the initial cost of storage in the ith reservoir plus operation and maintenance

BF_i is flood benefits obtained in ith reservoir

CFP_i is cost of alternate flood projection works for ith reservoir

BFP_i is benefits of alternate flood protection works for ith reservoir

CR_i is cost of recreation facilities in ith reservoir

BR_i is benefits of recreation obtained in ith reservoir.

All costs are expressed as present values to conform to the costs in Table 2.

The costs of the jth reservoir system are therefore the cost of the storage structures net of any gains from including flood storage in the reservoirs over alternative flood protection works, such as levees and flood walls, and net of the gains from recreation opportunities created.[12]

The costs of low-flow augmentation at specified levels of operation are as shown in Table 4.

TABLE 4.

Cost of Low-Flow Augmentation

Waste load (Pounds BOD₅)	Cost of low-flow system (*Millions of dollars*)
20,000	46
40,000	77
60,000	96
80,000	114
100,000	139

All costs are present values for fifty years discounted at 4 per cent.

ALTERNATIVE SYSTEMS

We may now proceed to study systems involving various combinations of the four types of measures which might be taken to solve the water quality problem in the estuary: flow augmentation, higher levels of waste treatment, distribution of the waste to other parts of the estuary, and reaeration of the estuary. The objective of the analysis is to discover the minimum-cost combination of processes that will achieve the oxygen objective established for the estuary.

In the previous analysis all costs of nine alternative processes at four discrete levels of operation have been collapsed to one number, C_{ij}, the cost of the ith process operated at the jth level of intensity.[13] The next

[12] In the first analysis recreation benefits are treated as equal to costs of recreation facilities and lands, so that net recreation advantage of the different flow augmentation systems is ignored. This treatment of recreation benefits asserts that expenditures on recreation lands and facilities can be made as beneficially for other recreation opportunities as for the reservoirs in the estuary system. The National Park Service has said as much for the two largest reservoirs (Seneca and Royal Glen).

[13] See Tables 2 and 4.

114

step is to find the minimum sum of the C_{ij}'s which constitutes a feasible solution for attaining the 100,000-pound level of waste reduction or offset. The feasibility constraint is simply that the combination of processes used does not operate on more than the maximum gallonage of sewage available for treatment or distribution. That is, it would be redundant in terms of our technical information to treat 600 million gallons of sewage daily by a tertiary process and also distribute it to the lower part of the estuary. However, it would be feasible to partition the sewage, treating half of it and distributing the other half, if this would achieve the desired level of waste reduction.

The search for the minimum-cost solution in this case, where we have discrete levels of the activities, can be handled "as a combinatorial problem" or "by combining various processes at various levels subject to the requirement and the feasibility constraint." The nine discrete process cost functions together with the feasibility constraint give us a sample of about 300 alternative systems from the infinite number of possible systems.

The least-cost system consists of any combination of the two reaeration processes, its cost being about $7 million (present value). The cost advantage of reaeration devices over the alternatives is surprisingly large. If they are precluded from the analysis, then the next least costly system consists of low-flow augmentation and either effluent diversion or one of the waste treatment processes: microstraining, step aeration or chemical precipitation at a system cost of $128 million over low-flow augmentation. This set of results suggests that the gains of casting a wider net over the alternatives for solving water quality problems can pay large dividends in cost savings. In particular, there are some novel technologies that bear further investigation.

The carbon adsorption processes do not lend a cost advantage to any system. The relatively high costs of even powdered carbon adsorption, as seen in the process matrix, make it necessary to look for other advantages in the process if its application is to be justified. One such advantage is the fact that its performance is instantaneous, a characteristic also of the other physical-chemical processes, microstraining and chemical precipitation. Since the carbon adsorption processes are in the developmental stage, further studies may show ways of designing these processes for intermittent use which will substantially cut the total costs of using them.

When we allow other than directly measurable costs to influence the ranking of alternative systems, we are confronted with the inadequacies of the criteria for choice available to the system planner. One of the issues that has arisen in the case of the Potomac is the relative value of the Seneca reservoir for water storage versus the existing recreational

115

uses of the area.[14] Leaving aside the possibilities for using reaeration devices, there are difficulties in comparing the different bundles of costs and benefits in alternative systems with and without the Seneca reservoir. Without reaeration devices there must be some low-flow augmentation to offset the fraction of the waste load that is not affected by techniques for reducing the waste load. Only the first step in the low-flow augmentation cost function precludes Seneca. A system incorporating the minimum of low-flow augmentation with distribution of all of the metropolitan sewage effluents to the area below Mount Vernon has a system cost of $133 million. It is likely that a proposal to divert sewage effluents to the middle estuary would encounter downstream opposition, even though the effluents could be rendered bacteriologically harmless. Preservation of Seneca might be purchased at real downstream costs.

Another substitute for Seneca might be the installation of the powdered carbon adsorption process at all major metropolitan sewage treatment plants (in addition to the main plant as previously assumed). Coupled with a minimum of low-flow augmentation, such a system might be adequate to achieve the 5 ppm oxygen objective. The system cost would probably be $180 million. The choice now lies between inundation of Seneca or its preservation either at the cost of some disadvantages below Washington or at an expenditure of an additional $40 million or $50 million. The criteria for making such a planning choice are not likely to be clearly specified in the authorizing resolution of Congress under which the study of a basin is undertaken. Therefore, it is necessary for proper social decision making that the planner keep such alternatives viable until he has sufficient guidance from some appropriate decision-making power for making the choice.

The waste treatment alternative to Seneca also raises some practical questions of financing and operating portions of municipal treatment plants as a part of a regional water quality management plan. Under present financial policies, local governments would pay none of the costs of low-flow augmentation for quality management and all of the costs of tertiary waste treatment. From the local viewpoint, waste treatment as an alternative to low-flow augmentation can have little if any merit. Equal difficulties arise when consideration is given to intermittent operation of a tertiary waste treatment process in a locally operated plant, where the tertiary process is an integral part of a regional or basin-wide management system. The regional operating authority capable of this sort of management does not exist in the Washington metropolitan area today.

[14] Located about fifteen miles above Washington on the mainstream of the river, Seneca reservoir would inundate about thirty miles of the river and the C & O Canal towpath between Seneca, Maryland, and Harpers Ferry.

The attractive prospect of using reaeration devices to maintain oxygen levels, in addition to presenting the problems of operating and financing mentioned above, illustrates another set of issues applying to most of the processes we have investigated. While none of the technological information is purely speculative, there is no doubt that in varying degrees learning-by-doing would be involved in its adaptation and application.

To a large extent the amount of knowledge that must be acquired before either type of reaeration device studied could be applied to the Potomac estuary with reasonably satisfactory results can be translated into costs. Two kinds of cost would be involved: costs of field trials and other preliminary means of perfecting the method; and the cost of adapting action in anticipation of perfecting superior reaeration technologies. In making appropriate decisions, the increased risk of serious dissolved oxygen depletion attending delays in taking any sort of action must be balanced against the costs of flexible systems that can accommodate anticipated technological developments such as the perfection of reaeration processes. It is clear that actions involving small or short-lived capital investments are to be preferred over large or long-lived capital investments. It is also clear that flexibility is difficult to achieve in the absence of a continuing planning organization.

SOME ADDITIONAL DIMENSIONS OF THE PROBLEM

This discussion omits full treatment of some additional dimensions of choice that underlie the assumptions and technical decisions of the *Potomac River Basin Report*. The RFF study from which this paper is derived has proceeded to a stage where the nature and significance of these additional matters have begun to clarify. They include the optimal level of dissolved oxygen, the variance and other statistical features of the dissolved oxygen performance produced by any combination of target and system, the choice of strategies for dealing with ignorance and uncertainty, and the choice of variables other than dissolved oxygen to be managed in the maintenance of water quality.

The optimal oxygen target can be a matter of some consequence. Dropping the target from a minimum mean of 5 ppm to a minimum of 3 ppm amounts to about a $44 million decrease in the costs of the low-flow augmentation system. This is a sufficient difference in costs to raise some question as to the desirability of meeting particular oxygen targets. The question separates into two parts: What are the consequences of different oxygen performances, and what are we willing to pay to achieve or to avoid these consequences?

Reservoir system simulation has produced some information concerning differences in oxygen performance at the 5 ppm and 3 ppm targets. The principal finding concerns the frequency with which monthly mean oxygen values dropped below the 5 ppm value when the performance target was lowered from 5 ppm to 3 ppm. Adopting the lower target meant that a lower level of dissolved oxygen was reached during some months in about 40 per cent of the years in the thirty-year hydrology. The months of occurrence were usually the summer months, when lower dissolved oxygen content might be most damaging. On the other hand, the spring and fall months, when migratory fish might be affected by the lower content, were rarely a problem.

This small beginning at specifying the statistical behavior of dissolved oxygen points to a major deficiency in the present analysis. The mean, variance, and perhaps the higher moments of distribution of dissolved oxygen levels are important parameters affecting the selection of optimal performance targets as well as optimal systems. In assessing losses, not only is the expected distribution of performance important, but the mean value selected as a target and the collection of measures designated to achieve it are also factors to be considered. There are deficiencies in the model of dissolved oxygen behavior incorporated in our simulation program with respect to its deterministic treatment of temperature, solar radiation, and photosynthetic behavior. Finally, variations in short-period oxygen performance may be important but cannot be evaluated in the present model because they are obliterated in the monthly time unit used in the simulation program.

These inadequacies mean that we face in our study the same inability to discriminate between the performances of alternative targets and systems as must have confronted the Corps of Engineers and the Public Health Service in their determination of the optimal set of flow requirements and reservoir storage for maintaining dissolved oxygen in the estuary. The means they used for dealing with this lack of information is instructive for what it reveals about the costs of inadequate information.

The strategy consisted of boosting flow requirements in a manner which recognized only part of the temperature sensitivity ascribed to the monthly flow requirements by Wastler [ref. 10] and in the *PRB Report* [ref. 1, Vol. 5, p. 571]. This can be interpreted as providing enough extra storage in the reservoir system to meet adverse contingencies of considerable magnitude. This adjustment added 324,000 acre-feet of storage to the estuary system at an incremental cost of about $42 million (present value). Thus, 30 per cent of the total cost of the estuary system is a hedge against uncertainty. At these costs it is appropriate to search for less costly means of insuring against adversity or else to know the magnitude of the losses avoided by this strategy. Unfortunately, the models we have so far developed are incapable of giving us information on the reduced probability of adversity which this $42 million purchases.

Thus far in this study we have followed the example of the *PRB Report* in adopting dissolved oxygen as the sole criterion of water quality, and on the bases of the results obtained we have suggested the importance of choices made concerning the minimum level of dissolved oxygen, as well as the importance of probabilistic behavior both in oxygen balance and in the system meeting the mean requirements. In evaluating a wide range of alternative systems for managing dissolved oxygen in the estuary, another major problem is encountered. Dissolved oxygen performance alone is not a satisfactory criterion for evaluating the effects of alternative systems. Color and turbidity are perhaps incrementally more important than dissolved oxygen when the level of dissolved oxygen is above that needed to keep the estuary safely aerobic. Concentrations of coliform bacteria affect the value of the estuary for water contact sports. Different systems are likely to have different effects on the amounts of suspended silts and clays in the estuary and on the density of the plankton crop—hence, on color and turbidity—but the direction and magnitude of the differences remain to be investigated. Similarly, the concentration of coliform bacteria in the waters may be affected by river flow or by the distribution of effluents. The effects of spatial and time distribution of oxygen in the estuary, together with these other effects, are likely to be influenced by the timing and amount of low-flow augmentation, whereas reaeration devices, for example, probably would produce a different and perhaps more flexible spatial and time distribution of oxygen concentration.

Without elaborating further on aspects of the study that are in need of further analysis, it is obvious that widening the basis for choice of technical alternatives necessarily forces a widening of the criteria for evaluating systems. There is a need to specify those aspects of water quality, other than dissolved oxygen content, that can assist in evaluating the performance of alternative systems, and also to analyze the statistics which may distinguish different levels of the criteria and the performance of different systems.

CONCLUSIONS

This paper demonstrates the nature of the gains to be realized from expanding the analysis of alternatives in the water resources planning process. Some productive dimensions of an expanded analysis are:

1) To extend the analysis to more than one kind of objective and to more than one set of objectives so that we can at least begin to ask some questions about willingness to pay for results. In the process, we should be able to improve our ability to describe the results we seek in terms and with criteria that the planner can work from.

2) To extend the analysis to payoffs from possible changes in technology, because technology to a large extent is controlled by the direction and magnitude of research effort and because adaptability over time in a system may be a means to efficient system design, if technical change is expected to change substantially the nature of the optimal system.

3) To extend the analysis to possibilities which may be precluded by current institutional arrangements, in order to know something of the gains derived from rearranging institutions bearing on the design and operation of water quality management systems.

REFERENCES

[1] *Potomac River Basin Report* (PRB Report). U.S. Army Engineer District, Basin Studies Branch, Baltimore, February 1963.

[2] U.S. Senate Select Committee on National Water Resources. *Water Resources Activities in the United States: Water Supply and Demand.* Committee Print No. 32. Washington: U.S. Government Printing Office, 1960.

[3] Weber, Eugene W. "Relation of Regulation for Quality Control to Activities of the Corps of Engineers," *Symposium on Stream Flow Regulation for Water Quality Control.* Cincinnati: Robert A. Taft Sanitary Engineering Center, 1963.

[4] Kneese, Allen V. *Water Pollution: Economic Aspects in Research Needs.* Washington: Resources for the Future, Inc., 1962.

[5] ———. *The Economics of Regional Water Quality Management.* Baltimore: Johns Hopkins Press, 1964.

[6] Eckstein, Otto. *Water Resources Development.* Cambridge: Harvard University Press, 1958.

[7] Maass, Arthur, *et al. Design of Water Resource Systems.* Cambridge: Harvard University Press, 1962.

[8] White, Gilbert F. *Choice of Adjustment to Floods.* Research Paper No. 93. Chicago: University of Chicago, Department of Geography, 1964.

[9] Fox, Irving K. "The Potomac Puzzle: Is There a Reasonable Solution?", *Atlantic Naturalist,* Vol. 17, No. 2 (1962).

[10] U.S. Public Health Service. *Report on the Potomac River Basin.* Technical Appendix to Part VII, by T. A. Wastler. Cincinnati: Robert A. Taft Sanitary Engineering Center, August 1962.

[11] Wolman, Abel, and Geyer, John Charles, with William Colony. *Report on Sanitary Sewers and Waste Water Disposal in the Washington Metropolitan Region.* Baltimore, 1962.

[12] Henderson, James, and Quandt, Richard. *Microeconomic Theory, A Mathematical Approach.* New York: McGraw-Hill, 1958.

[13] Davis, Robert K. "Some Economic Aspects of Advanced Waste Treatment," *Journal Water Pollution Control Federation,* December 1965.

RESEARCH ON EVALUATION PROBLEMS

Comparisons of Methods for Recreation Evaluation

Jack L. Knetsch and *Robert K. Davis**

Evaluation of recreation benefits has made significant headway in the past few years. It appears that concern is increasingly focusing on the hard core of relevant issues concerning the economic benefits of recreation and how we can go about making some useful estimates.

The underlying reasons for this sharpening of focus are largely pragmatic. The rapidly increasing demand for recreation, stemming from the often-cited factors of increasing population, leisure, incomes, mobility, and urbanization, calls for continuing adjustments in resource allocations. This is the case with respect to our land and water resources in general; but more specifically it bears on such matters as the establishment of national recreation areas, setting aside or preserving areas for parks and open spaces in and near expanding urban areas, and clearly on questions of justification, location, and operation of water development projects.

Recreation services have only recently been recognized as products of land and water resource use. As such, they offer problems that do not occur when resolving the conflicting uses of most goods and services—for example, steel and lumber. Conflicting demands for commodities such as these are resolved largely in the market places of the private economy, where users bid against each other for the limited supplies.

Outdoor recreation, however, has developed largely as a non-market commodity. The reasons for this are quite elaborate, but in essence out-

* Research Associates, Resources for the Future, Inc.

door recreation for the most part is produced and distributed in the absence of a market mechanism, partly because we prefer it that way and have rejected various market outcomes, and partly because many kinds of outdoor recreation experience cannot be packaged and sold by private producers to private consumers. This absence of a market necessitates imputing values to the production of recreation services. Such economic benefits can be taken into account in decisions affecting our use of resources.

MISUNDERSTANDINGS OF RECREATION VALUES

Discussions of values of outdoor recreation have been beset by many misunderstandings. One of these stems from a lack of appreciation that the use of outdoor recreation facilities differs only in kind, but not in principle, from consumption patterns of other goods and services. Another is that the market process takes account of personal and varied consumer satisfactions.

It is, furthermore, the incremental values that are important in making decisions relative to resource allocations. The incremental values of recreation developments of various kinds are a manageable concept which can be used for comparisons, in spite of the very great aggregate value that some may want to attribute to recreation. Nothing is gained—and no doubt a great deal has been lost—by what amounts to ascribing the importance of a total supply of recreation to an added increment, rather than concentrating on the added costs and the added benefits.

A similar difficulty arises with respect to questions of water supply. That man is entirely dependent upon the existence of water is repeatedly emphasized. While true, the point does not matter. Decisions necessarily focus on increments and therefore on the added costs and the added benefits that stem from adding small amounts to the existing total.

Further, no goods or services are priceless in the sense of an infinite price. There is an individual and collective limit to how much we will give up to enjoy the services of any outdoor recreation facility or to preserve any scenic resource. The most relevant economic measure of recreation values, therefore, is willingness on the part of consumers to pay for outdoor recreation services. This set of values is comparable to economic values established for other commodities, for it is the willingness to give up on the part of consumers that establishes values throughout the economy.

Failure to understand these value characteristics results in two types of error. The first is the belief that the only values that are worth considering are those accounted for commercially. A second and related source of error is a belief that outdoor recreation experience is outside the framework of economics, that the relevant values have an aesthetic, deeply personal, and even mystical nature. We believe both of these to be incorrect. In particular, the notion that economic values do not account for aesthetic or personal values is fallacious and misleading. Economically, the use of resources for recreation is fully equivalent to other uses, and the values which are relevant do not necessarily need to be determined in the market place. This last condition does indicate that indirect means of supplying relevant measures of the values produced may be necessary. But this is an empirical problem, albeit one of some considerable dimension, and the primary concern of this paper.

The problem of using imputed values for value determination has been met with a considerable degree of success for some products of water resource development. Procedures have been developed to assess the value of the flood protection, irrigation, and power services produced by the projects, even though in many cases a market does not in fact exist or is inadequate for the actual benefit calculations. Without commenting on the adequacy of these methods, it is generally agreed that such measures are useful in evaluating the output of project services.

NATIONAL AND LOCAL BENEFITS

Discussions of these topics have often been further confused by failure to separate two types of economic consequences or benefit. This has led to improper recognition of relevant and legitimate economic interests, and to inferior planning and policy choices.

There are, first, what we may call primary benefits, or national benefits. Second, there are benefits we may refer to as local benefits, or impact benefits. Both sets of values resulting from investment in recreation have economic relevance, but they differ, and they bear differently on decision.

The primary recreation benefits, or values, are in general taken to be expressions of the consumers' willingness to pay for recreation services. These values may or may not register in the commerce of the region or in the commerce of the nation, but this does not make them less real. When appropriately measured, they are useful for guiding social choices at the national level. The other set of accounts is concerned with local expenditure of money for local services associated with recreation. While outdoor recreation is not marketed—in the sense that the services of parks, as such, are not sold to any great extent in any organized market—money does indeed become involved in the form of expenditures for travel, equipment, lodging, and so forth. The amount of money spent in connection with outdoor recreation and tourism is large and growing, making outdoor recreation expenditures of prime concern to localities and regions which may stand to benefit. Our concern is with measuring the more difficult of the two types of benefit just mentioned—national recreation benefits. While these are measured essentially by the consumers' willingness to pay, in some cases the benefits extend to the non-using general public.

ALTERNATIVE MEASUREMENT METHODS

There are obvious advantages to evaluating recreation benefits by market prices in the same manner as their most important resource competitors. However, as we have indicated, past applications have been hampered by disagreement on what are the meaningful values. In spite of growing recognition that recreation has an important economic value, economists and public administrators have been ill-prepared to include it in the social or public calculus in ways that lead to better allocations of resources.

The benefits of recreation from the social or community viewpoint are alleged to be many and varied. Some of the descriptions of public good externalities arising from recreation consumption are gross overstatements of the real values derived from the production of recreation services. But recreation benefits do in fact exist. Where externalities are real—as in cases of recreation in connection with visits to various historic areas or educational facilities, or where preservaton of unique ecological units has cultural and scientific values—they should be recognized in assigning values to the development or preservation of the areas. However, it is our view that, by and large, recreation is a consumption good rather than a factor of production, and the benefits to be enjoyed are largely those accruing to the individual consumer participating. This is even more likely to be the case with recreation provided by water projects. The large bulk of primary recreation benefits can be viewed as the value of the output of the project to those who use them. This view stems from the concept that recreation resources produce an economic product. In this sense they are scarce and capable of yielding satisfaction for which people are willing to pay. Finally, some accounting can be made of this economic demand.

As the desirability of establishing values for recreation use of resources has become more apparent over the past few years, a number of methods for measuring or estimating them have been proposed and to some extent used. Some of the measures are clearly incorrect; others attempt to measure appropriate values, but fall short on empirical grounds [ref. 1, 2, 3].

Gross Expenditures Method

The gross expenditures method attempts to measure the value of recreation to the recreationist in terms of the total amount spent on recreation by the user. These expenditures usually include travel expenses, equipment costs, and expenses incurred while in the recreation area. Estimates of gross recreation expenditures are very popular in some quarters; for one thing, they are likely to produce large figures. It is argued that persons making such expenditures must have received commensurate value or they would not have made them. The usual contention is that the value of a day's recreation is worth at least the amount of money spent by a person for the use of that recreation.

These values have some usefulness in indicating the amount of money that is spent on a particular type of outdoor recreation, but as justification for public expenditure on recreation, or for determining the worth or benefit of the recreation opportunity afforded, they are of little consequence.

The values we seek are those which show not some gross value, but the net increase in value over and above what would occur in the absence of a particular recreation opportunity. Gross expenditures do not indicate the value of the losses sustained if the particular recreation opportunity were to disappear, nor do they show the net gain in value from an increase in a particular recreation opportunity.

Market Value of Fish Method

A proposed method for estimating the recreation benefits afforded by fishing imputes to sport fishing a market value of the fish caught. The main objection to this procedure is the implied definition that the fish alone are the primary objective of the activity.

Cost Method

The cost method assumes that the value of outdoor recreation resource use is equal to the cost of generating it or, in some extreme applications, that it is a multiple of these costs. This has the effect of justifying any contemplated recreation project. However, the method offers no guide in the case of contemplated loss of recreation opportunities, and allows little or no discrimination between relative values of alternative additions.

Market Value Method

Basic to the market value method measure is a schedule of charges judged to be the market value of the recreation services produced. These charges are multiplied by the actual or expected attendance figures to arrive at a recreation value for the services.

The method is on sound ground in its emphasis on the willingness of users to incur expenses to make choices. However, the market for outdoor recreation is not a commercial one, certainly not for much of the recreation provided publicly and only to a limited extent for private recreation. It is in part because private areas are not fully comparable with public areas that users are willing to pay the fees or charges. It seems, therefore, inappropriate to use charges paid on a private area to estimate the value of recreation on public areas. Also a single value figure or some range of values will be inappropriate for many recreation areas. Physical units of goods and services are not everywhere equally valuable, whether the commodity be sawtimber, grazing, or recreation. Location in the case of recreation affects value greatly. Moreover, differences of quality and attractiveness of recreation areas are not fully comparable or recognized by the unit values.

There are other methods, but few have received much attention. Where does this leave us? The only methods to which we give high marks are based on the concept of willingness to pay for services provided.

METHODS BASED ON WILLINGNESS TO PAY

We have alluded to two kinds of problems we face in measuring the benefits of outdoor recreation: the conceptual problems and the measurement problems.

Conceptually, we wish to measure the willingness to pay by consumers of outdoor recreation services as though these consumers were purchasing the services in an open market. The total willingness of consumers to pay for a given amount and quality of outdoor recreation (that is, the area under the demand curve) is the relevant measure we seek. Our conceptual problems are essentially that any measurement of effective demand in the current time period, or even an attempt to project effective demand in future time periods, must necessarily omit from the computation two kinds of demand which may or may not be important. These are option demand and demand generated by the opportunity effect.[1]

[1] These concepts are developed by Davidson, Adams, and Seneca in "The Social Value of Water Recreational Facilities Resulting from an Improvement in Water Quality: The Delaware Estuary," published in this volume.

Option demand is that demand from individuals who are not now consumers or are not now consuming as much as they anticipate consuming, and who therefore would be willing to pay to perpetuate the availability of the commodities. Such a demand is not likely to be measured by observance or simulation of market phenomena. The opportunity effect derives from those unanticipated increases in demand caused by improving the opportunities to engage in a recreational activity and thereby acquainting consumers with new and different sets of opportunities to which they adapt through learning processes. To our knowledge no methods have been proposed which might be used to measure these two kinds of demand for a good.

Notwithstanding the undoubted reality of these kinds of demand, our presumption is that effective demand is likely to be the predominant component of the aggregate demand for outdoor recreation of the abundant and reproducible sorts we have in mind. We further presume that this quantity can be estimated in a useful way, although by fairly indirect means, for we have no market guide of the usual sort. Two methods—a direct interview, and an imputation of a demand curve from travel cost data—currently appear to offer reasonable means of obtaining meaningful estimates.

Interview Methods

The essence of the interview method of measuring recreation benefits is that through a properly constructed interview approach one can elicit from recreationists information concerning the maximum price they would pay in order to avoid being deprived of the use of a particular area for whatever use they may make of it. The argument for the existence of something to be measured rests on the conception that the recreationist is engaged in the utility maximizing process and has made a rational series of allocations of time and money in order to participate in the recreation being evaluated. Since the opportunity itself is available at zero or nominal price, the interview provides the means for discovering the price the person would pay if this opportunity were marketed, other things being equal.

The chief problem to be reckoned with in evaluating interview responses is the degree of reliability that can be attached to the information the respondent provides the interviewer. Particularly on questions dealing with matters of opinion, the responses are subject to many kinds of bias.

One such bias of particular interest to economists stems from the gaming strategy that a consumer of a public good may pursue on the theory that, if he understates his preference for the good, he will escape being charged as much as he is wiling to pay without being deprived of the amount of the good he now desires. This may be a false issue, particularly when it comes to pursuing recreation on private lands or waters, because the consumer may be well aware that the owner could, through the exercise of his private property rights, exclude the user from the areas now occupied. An equally good case can be made that, on state and national park lands to which there is limited access, particularly when at the access points the authority of the state is represented by uniformed park patrolmen, recreationists would have no trouble visualizing the existence of the power to exclude them. This being the case, it is not unreasonable to expect the recreationist to be aware of some willingness to pay on his part in order to avoid being excluded from the area he now uses.

Counterbalancing the possibility that the recreationist may purposely understate his willingness to pay in order to escape charges is the possibility that he may wish to bid up his apparent benefits in order to make a case for preserving the area in its current use, a case equally appropriate on private or public lands and waters.

The problem, to continue the argument, is narrowed to one of phrasing the question in such a way that the recreationist is not asked to give his opinion on the propriety of charging for the use of recreation areas.

It has become something of a principle in survey methodology that the less hypothetical the question, the more stable and reliable the response. By this principle, the respondent ought to be a consumer of the product rather than a potential consumer, thus distinguishing the data collected as pertaining to effective demand rather than to option or potential demand. It may also be preferable to impose the conditions on the interview that it occur at a time when the respondent is engaged in the activity. This may contribute to the accuracy of the responses by reducing the requirement that he project from one situation to another. (Admittedly, it is desirable to experiment with the methodology on this question, as well as others, in order to determine its sensitivity to such variations.)

In sum then, we expect to discover the consumer's willingness to pay through a properly constructed interview, and further, we expect that this measure will be the same quantity as would be registered in an organized market for the commodity consumed by the respondent. In other words, we hold a deterministic view that something exists to be measured, and is a sufficiently real and stable phenomenon that the measurement is useful.

The Interview Procedure. The wilingness to pay of a sample of users of a forest recreation area in northern Maine was determined in interviews on the site [ref. 4]. The interviews included a bidding game in which respondents could react to increased costs of visiting the area. Bids were systematically raised or lowered until the user switched his reaction from inclusion to exclusion or vice versa. At the beginning of the interview rapport was established with the respondents largely through objective questions inquiring into their recreation activities on the area, on other areas, and the details of their trips. The bidding questions were interspersed with a series of propositions for which the respondent was to indicate his opinion in the form of a positive, negative, or neutral reaction. His reactions to increased expenses connected with the visit constituted the essence of the bidding game. Personal questions regarding income, education, and the like were confined to the end of the interview.

The sampling procedure amounted to cluster sampling, since the procedure followed was to locate areas of use such as campgrounds and to systematically sample from the available clusters of users. The interviews were conducted from June through November by visiting areas in the privately owned forests of northern Maine and in Baxter State Park.

The data from the interviews is pooled to include hunters, fishermen, and summer campers. This pooling is defended largely on the grounds that no structural differences between identifiable strata were detected in a multiple regression analysis of the responses.

The procedure imputes a discontinuous demand curve to the individual household which may be realistic under the time constraints faced particularly by vacation visitors and other non-repeating visitors. This rectangular demand curve (Figure 1) reflects a disposition either to come at the current level of use or not to come at all if costs rise above a limiting value. Its realism is supported by a number of respondents whose reaction to the excluding bid was precisely that they would not come at all. It seems reasonable to view the use of remote areas such as northern Maine as lumpy commodities which must be consumed in five- or six-day lumps or not at all. Deriving an aggregate demand function from the

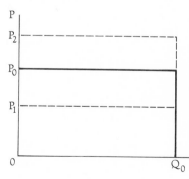

Figure 1. At prices in the range $0 - P_0$ the constant amount Q_0 will be demanded. Above P_0 demand will fall to zero. The individual may be in one of three states depending on the reigning price. Consider three individual cases with market price at P_0: The user paying P_1 is excluded; P_0 is associated with the marginal user; and P_2 is the willingness to pay of the third user who is included at the reigning price, P_0.

133

individual responses so characterized is simply a matter of taking the distribution function of willingness to pay cumulated on a less-than basis. This results in a continuous demand schedule which can be interpreted for the aggregate user population as a conventional demand schedule.

For the sample of 185 interviews, willingness-to-pay-per-household-day ranges from zero to $16.66. Zero willingness to pay was encountered in only three interviews. At the other extreme, one or two respondents were unable to place an upper limit on their willingness to pay. The distribution of willingness to pay shows a marked skewness toward the high values. The modal willingness to pay occurs between $1.00 and $2.00 per day per household.

Sixty per cent of the variance of willingness to pay among the interviews is explained in a multiple regression equation with willingness-to-pay-per-household-visit a function of income of the household, years of experience by the household in visiting the area, and the length of the stay in the area. (See Equation 1.) While the large negative intercept of this equation necessitated by its linear form causes some difficulties of interpretation, the exhibited relation between willingness to pay, and income, experience, and length of stay appears reasonable. The household income not only reflects an ability to pay, but a positive income elasticity of demand for outdoor recreation as found in other studies. It is also significant that an internal consistency was found in the responses to income-related questions.

$$W = -48.57 + 2.85Y + 2.88E + 4.76L \qquad\qquad R^2 = .5925 \qquad (1)$$
$$ (1.52)\quad (0.58)\quad (1.03)$$

$$W = \overset{.76}{} \overset{.20}{} \overset{.60}{} \qquad\qquad\qquad .3591^* \qquad (2)$$
$$W = .74L \quad E \quad Y$$
$$ (.13)\ (.07)\ (.17)$$

Standard errors of regression equations: (1) 39.7957; (2) 2.2007
Standard errors of coefficients are shown in parentheses.
W = household willingness to pay for a visit.
E = years of acquaintance with the area visited.
Y = income of the household in thousands of dollars.
L = length of visit in days.
F = ratios of both equations are highly significant.
* Obtained from arithmetic values of residual and total variances. (R^2 of the logarithmic transformation is .4309.)

The significance of years of experience in returning to the area may be interpreted as the effect of an accumulated consumer capital consisting of knowledge of the area, acquisition of skills which enhance the enjoyment of the area, and in some cases use of permanent or mobile housing on the area.

The significance of length of stay in the regression equations is that it both measures the quantity of goods consumed and also reflects a quality dimension suggesting that longer stays probably reflect a greater degree of preference for the area.

Colinearity among explanatory variables was very low. The general economic consistency and rationality of the responses appear to be high. Respondents' comments indicated they were turning over in their minds the alternatives available in much the same way that a rational shopper considers the price and desirability of different cuts or kinds of meat. Both the success in finding acceptable and significant explanatory variables and a certain amount of internal consistency in the responses suggest that considerable weight can be attached to the interview method.

The Simulated Demand Schedule. While providing an adequate equation for predicting the willingness to pay of any user, the results of the interviews do not serve as direct estimates of willingness to pay of the user population, because the income, length of stay, and years' experience of the interviewed sample do not accurately represent the characteristics of the population of users. Fortunately, it was possible to obtain a reliable sample of the users by administering a questionnaire to systematically selected samples of users stopped at the traffic checking stations on the private forest lands. A logarithmic estimating equation, although not as well fitting, but free of a negative range, was used to compute the willingness to pay for each household in the sample. (See Equation 2.) The observations were then expanded by the sampling fraction to account for the total number of users during the recreation season.

The next step in the analysis consists of arraying the user population by willingness to pay, and building a cumulative distribution downward from the upper limit of the distribution. Table 1 shows the resulting demand and benefit schedule. The schedule accounts for the total of about 10,300 user households estimated to be the user population in a 450,000-acre area of the Maine woods near Moosehead Lake, known as the Pittston area.

The demand schedule is noticeably elastic from the upper limit of $60.00 to about $6.00, at which point total revenues are maximized. The interval from $60.00 to $6.00 accounts for the estimated willingness to pay of nearly half of the using households. Total benefits at $6.00 are

TABLE 1.

Demand and Benefit Schedules for Pittston Area Based on Alternative
Estimates of Willingness to Pay

Price	Interview results		Willingness to drive (interview method)		Willingness to drive (travel cost method)	
	House- hold visits	Benefits[1]	House- hold visits	Benefits[1]	House- hold visits	Bene- fits[1]
$70.00	0	0				
60.00	11.36	$ 747.77				
50.00	15.35	983.56				
40.00	44.31	2,281.46				
30.00	150.22	6,003.19	11.36	$ 384.79	165	$ 3,800
26.00	215.80	7,829.71				
22.00	391.07	12,027.89				
20.00	536.51	15,099.31	76.96	1,890.12	422	12,134
18.00	757.86	19,275.95				
16.00	1,069.01	24,607.81				
14.00	1,497.75	31,027.17	392.29	7,287.06		
12.00	1,866.41	35,802.70				
10.00	2,459.70	42,289.68	2,157.91	28,921.93	1,328	26,202
8.00	3,100.99	48,135.01				
6.00	4,171.89	55,794.64				
4.00	5,926.94	64,436.36	5,721.06	53,531.68	3,459	44,760
2.00	7,866.02	70,222.66				
0.00	10,333.22	71,460.94	10,339.45	63,689.99	10,333	69,450

[1] Benefits are computed as the integral of the demand schedule from price maximum to price indicated. Willingness to drive computations are based on an assumed charge of 5¢ per mile for the one-way mileage.

$56,000. The price range below $6.00 accounts for the other half of the using households, but only for $15,000 in additional benefits. Benefits are estimated as the cumulative willingness to pay or the revenues available to a discriminating monopolist.

Willingness to Drive vs. Willingness to Pay. An alternative expression of the willingness of recreationists to incur additional costs in order to continue using an area may be found in their willingness to drive additional distances. This measure was first proposed by Ullman and Volk [ref. 5] although in a different version than is used here. (See also [ref. 6].)

Willingness to drive additional distances was elicited from respondents by the same technique used to elicit willingness to pay. If there are biases involving strategies to avoid paying for these recreation areas, then certainly willingness to drive is to be preferred over willingness to pay as an expression of value. Analysis of the willingness to drive responses shows that a partly different set of variables must be used to explain the responses. Equation 3 shows willingness to drive extra miles to be a function of length of stay and miles driven to reach the area.

$$Wm = 41.85 + 20.56L + .15M \tag{3}$$
$$ (3.03) \quad (.04) (R^2 = .3928)$$

Wm = willingness to drive additional miles.
L = length of visit in days.
M = miles traveled to area.

The respondents thus expressed a willingness to exert an additional driving effort, just as they expressed a willingness to make an additional money outlay if this became a requisite to using the area. Moreover, there is a significant correspondence between willingness to pay and willingness to drive. The simple correlation coefficient between these two variables is .5. Because of the correlation with length of stay, the reduction in unexplained variance produced by adding either variable to the equation in which the other variable is the dependent one is not very high. However, willingness to pay was found to increase about 5¢ per mile as a function of willingness to drive additional miles. This result gives us a basis for transforming willingness to drive into willingness to pay.

We may now construct a demand schedule for the Pittston area on the basis of willingness to drive, and compute a willingness to pay at 5¢ per mile. The resulting demand and benefit schedules appear in Table 1. The estimated $64,000 of total benefits is very close to that developed from the willingness to pay interview. While one may quibble about the evaluation of a mile of extra driving and about the treatment of one-way versus round-trip distance, the first approximation using the obvious value of 5¢ and one-way mileage as reported by the respondents produces a result so close to the first result that we need look no further for marginal adjustments. The initial result strongly suggests that mileage measures and expenditure measures have equal validity as a measure of benefits in this particular case at least.

There are some differences between the respective demand schedules worth noting. The much lower price intercept on the willingness to drive schedule reflects the effect of the time constraint in traveling as well as our possibly erroneous constant transformation of miles to dollars when an increasing cost per mile would be more reasonable. The travel schedule is also elastic over more of its range than the dollar schedule— also perhaps a result of the constant transformation employed.

This initial success with alternative derivations of the benefits schedule now leads us to examine an alternative method for estimating the willingness to drive schedule.

137

Travel-Cost Method of Estimating User-Demand Curve

The direct interview approach to the estimate of a true price-quantity relationship, or demand curve, for the recreation experience is one approach to the benefit calculations based on willingness to pay. An alternative approach has received some recognition and has been applied in a number of limited instances with at least a fair degree of success. This uses travel-cost data as a proxy for price in imputing a demand curve for recreation facilities. [Ref. 7, 8, 9, 10.] As with the direct interview approach, we believe that estimates derived from this approach are relevant and useful for measuring user benefits of outdoor recreation.

The travel-cost method imputes the price-quantity reactions of consumers by examining their actual current spending behavior with respect to travel cost. The method can be shown by using a simple, hypothetical example. Assume a free recreation or park area at varying distances from three centers of population given in Table 2.

TABLE 2.

Visits to a Hypothetical Recreation Area

City	Population	Cost of visit	Visits made	Visits/1,000 pop.
A	1,000	$1.00	400	400
B	2,000	3.00	400	200
C	4,000	4.00	400	100

The cost of visiting the area is of major concern and would include such items as transportation, lodging, and food cost above those incurred if the trip were not made. Each cost would vary with the distance from the park to the city involved. Consequently, the number of visits, or rather the rate of visits per unit of total population of each city, would also vary.

The visits per unit of population, in this case per thousand population, may then be plotted against the cost per visit. A line drawn through the three points of such a plot would have the relationship given by the equation of $C = 5 - V$, or perhaps more conveniently $V = 5 - C$, where C is cost of a visit and V is the rate of visits in hundreds per thousand population. This information is taken directly from the tabulation of consumer behavior. The linear relationship assumed here is for convenience. Actual data may very well show, for example, that $1.00 change in cost might have only a slight effect on visit rate where the visit is already high in cost, and a large effect on low-cost visits.

The construction of a demand curve to the recreation area, relating number of visits to varying cost, involves a second step. Essentially, it derives the demand curve from the equation relating visit rates to cost, by relating visit rates of each zone to simulated increases in cost and multiplying by the relative populations in each zone. Thus we might first assume a price of $1.00, which is an added cost of $1.00 for visits to the area from each of the three different centers used in our hypothetical example. This would have the expected result of reducing the number of visitors coming from each of the centers. The expected reduction is estimated from the visit-cost relationship. The total visits suggested by these calculations for different prices or differing added cost are given as:

Price (added cost)	Quantity (total visits)
$0.00	1,200
1.00	500
2.00	200
3.00	100
4.00	0

These results may then be taken as the demand curve relating price to visits to the recreation area. While this analysis takes visits as a simple function of cost, in principle there is no difficulty in extending the analysis to other factors important in recreation demand, such as alternative sites available, the inherent attractiveness of the area in question or at least its characteristics in this regard, and possibly even some measure of congestion.

A difficulty with this method of benefit approximation is a consistent bias in the imputed demand curve resulting from the basic assumption that the disutility of overcoming distance is a function only of money cost. Clearly this is not so. The disutility is most likely to be the sum of at least three factors: money cost, time cost, and the utility (plus or minus) of driving, or traveling. The total of these three factors is demonstrably negative, but we do not know enough about the significance of the last two components. In all likelihood their sum—that is, of the utility or disutility of driving and the time cost—imposes costs in addition to money. To the extent that this is true the benefit estimate will be conservatively biased, for, as has been indicated, it is assumed that the only thing causing differences in attendance rates for cities located at different distances to a recreation area will be the differences in money cost. The method then postulates that if money cost changes are affected, the changes in rates will be proportional. What this bias amounts to is, essentially, a failure to establish a complete transformation function relating the three components of overcoming distance to the total effect on visitation rates. The resulting conservative bias must be regarded as an understatement of the recreation benefits which the approach is designed to measure.

Application to Pittston Area. The travel-cost method was applied to the same area as that used to illustrate the interview method of recreation benefit estimation. The same data were utilized to allow at least a crude comparison of the methods. In all, 6,678 respondents who said the Pittston area was the main destination of their trip were used in the analysis.

Visit rates of visitors from groups of counties near the area and from some states at greater distances were plotted against distance. The results were fairly consistent considering the rough nature of the approximations used in estimating distance. A curve was drawn through the points, giving a relationship between visit rates and distance. The demand curve was then calculated, giving a price-quantity relationship based on added distance (or added toll cost) and total visits. It was assumed initially that travel cost would be 5¢ per mile, using one-way distance to conform with our earlier analysis of travel cost by the interview method.

The results at this point were not comparable to the interview method because of a difference in the number of users accounted for. It will be recalled that in the analysis we are now describing only those respondents were used who had specifically stated that the visit to the Pittston area was the main destination of the trip. In order to make this number comparable to the total number of users accounted for in the interview estimate, we counted at half weight the 1,327 respondents who said that Pittston was *not* the primary destination of the trip, and also included in this group the non-response questionnaires and others with incomplete information. In this way we accounted for the same number of users as in the interview estimate. This very crude approximation points out the problems of the multiple-destination visit, but perhaps adequately serves the present purpose.

On the basis of these approximations, the benefit estimates on an annual basis were $70,000, assuming 5¢ per mile one-way distance. While the assumptions made throughout this analysis are subject to refinement, the exercise does seem to illustrate that the procedure is feasible from a practical standpoint and does produce results that are economically meaningful.

COMPARISON BETWEEN TRAVEL-COST AND INTERVIEW METHODS

Having demonstrated that fairly close results are obtained from both the interview and imputation methods of estimating recreation benefits on the basis of reactions to travel costs, and further that the interview method of directly estimating willingness to pay agrees closely with both estimates based on travel costs, we can now begin to assess the meaning of these results. In some ways the task would be easier if the results had not agreed so closely, for the three methodologies may imply different things about the users' reactions to increased costs. At least, it is not obvious without further probing as to why the agreement is so close.

The interview and imputation methods of estimating benefits on the basis of willingness to incur additional travel costs do not, for example, neatly imply the same relationship between distance traveled and willingness to incur additional travel costs. The estimating equation derived from the interviews (Equation 3) suggests that the farther one has traveled, the greater additional distance he will travel. Yet the imputation procedure implies that the willingness to drive by populations in the respective zones does not vary consistently with distance. Furthermore, according to the interviews, responses to the monetary measure of willingness to pay do not attribute any variance in willingness to pay to the distance factor, nor is an indirect relationship obvious. It seems relevant to inquire into the implied effects of these factors to discover why the alternative procedures appear to imply substantially different determinants of willingness to pay.

The superficial agreement in results may be upheld by this kind of further probing, but there are also some methodological issues which should not be overlooked. The travel-cost methods are obviously sensitive to such matters as the weighting given to multiple-destination visits and to the transformation used to derive costs from mileage values. Both methods are sensitive to the usual problems of choosing an appropriately fitting equation for the derivation of the demand schedule. The interview method has a poorly understood sensitivity to the various methodologies that might be employed in its use. Moreover, even the minimal use of interviews in studies of recreation benefits makes the method far more costly than the imputation method based on travel costs.

There are, however, complementarities in the two basic methods which may prove highly useful. In the first place, the two methods may serve as checks on each other in applied situations. One is certainly in a better position from having two methods produce nearly identical answers than if he has to depend on only one. There are also interesting possibilities that interviews may be the best way of resolving the ambiguities in the travel-cost method concerning the treatment of multiple-destination cases and for finding the appropriate valuation for converting distance into dollars. Much can be said for letting the recreationist tell us how to handle these problems.

In sum, we have examined three methods of measuring recreation benefits. All three measure recreationists' willingness to pay. This, we argue, is the appropriate measure of primary, or national, benefits. Furthermore, the measures are in rough agreement as to the benefits ascribable to an area of the Maine woods. This may be taken as evidence that we are on the right track. There are, however, some rough spots to be ironed out of each of the methods—an endeavor we believe to be worthy of major research effort if benefit-cost analysis is to contribute its full potential in planning decisions affecting recreation investments in land and water resources.

REFERENCES

[1] Lerner, Lionel. "Quantitative Indices of Recreational Values," in *Water Resources and Economic Development of the West.* Report No. 11. Proceedings, Conference of Committee on the Economics of Water Resources Development of Western Agricultural Economics Research Council with Western Farm Economics Association. Reno: University of Nevada, 1962.

[2] Merewitz, Leonard. "Recreational Benefits of Water-Resource Development." Unpublished paper of Harvard Water Program, 1965.

[3] Crutchfield, James. "Valuation of Fishery Resources," *Land Economics,* Vol. 38, No. 2 (1962).

[4] Davis, Robert K. "The Value of Outdoor Recreation: An Economic Study of the Maine Woods." Ph.D. thesis, Harvard University, 1963.

[5] Ullman, Edward, and Volk, Donald. "An Operational Model for Predicting Reservoir Attendance and Benefits: Implications of a Location Approach to Water Recreation," *Proceedings Michigan Academy of Sciences,* 1961.

[6] Meramec Basin Research Project. "Recreation," Chap. 5 in *The Meramec Basin,* Vol. 3. St. Louis: Washington University, December 1961.

[7] Clawson, Marion. *Methods of Measuring the Demand for and Value of Outdoor Recreation.* RFF Reprint No. 10. Washington: Resources for the Future, Inc., 1959.

[8] Knetsch, Jack L. "Outdoor Recreation Demands and Benefits," *Land Economics,* Vol. 39, No. 4 (1963).

[9] ——. "Economics of Including Recreation as a Purpose of Water Resources Projects," *Journal of Farm Economics,* December 1964. Also RFF Reprint No. 50. Washington: Resources for the Future, Inc.

[10] Brown, William G., Singh, Ajner, and Castle, Emery N. *An Economic Evaluation of the Oregon Salmon and Steelhead Sport Fishery.* Technical Bulletin 78. Corvallis: Oregon Experiment Station, 1964.

The Economics of Industrial Water Utilization

Blair T. Bower*

Industry has become the largest withdrawer of water in the United States, and projections suggest that its share of total water withdrawals will increase. At the same time it should be emphasized that the consumptive use, or net depletion, of water in industry, unlike in irrigated agriculture, is a relatively small proportion of the gross water applied. Industry in addition is a major producer of liquid wastes, with all that this implies for problems of waste disposal. Given the anticipated growth of the U.S. economy, both the absolute magnitude of the quantity of water withdrawn and used and the liquid wastes produced by industry will increase substantially. Therefore, an understanding of the nature of industrial water utilization and the factors that affect it is important to future water resources planning, development, and management.

Traditionally, projections of industrial "needs" or "requirements" for water have been made solely on the basis of physical quantities. The most common method has been to extrapolate past trends of water intake per unit of product or per employee, without analyzing the factors affecting industrial water utilization. Generally, little consideration has been given to: (1) substitution possibilities among the components of industrial water utilization systems;[1] (2) the relationship of water to other

* Associate Director, Quality of the Environment Program, Resources for the Future, Inc. Research for this paper was made possible by a grant from the National Science Foundation, made prior to the author's appointment to the RFF staff.

[1] For a discussion of substitutions in industrial water utilization, see Bower [ref. 1].

factor inputs to the production process; and (3) the impact of technological changes on industrial water utilization. An easily foreseeable result has been that even short-run projections of industrial water "needs"
have often been considerably in error. To illustrate, what factors explain
the 26 per cent increase in pulp and paper production between 1954
and 1959, with an increase in water intake of only about 8.5 per cent?
[Ref. 2.] To what can be attributed the performance of 104 petroleum
refineries in the period 1949 to 1959, when their refining capacity increased by over 51 per cent while their fresh water intake increased by
only 5 per cent? [Ref. 3.]

It is apparent that there are factors affecting industrial water utilization
that are not reflected in simple aggregate figures of water intake per unit
of product or per employee. To develop a more rational picture of water
demand and supply relationships in industry, it is necessary to define
specifically the relevant variables affecting industrial water utilization and
to attempt to determine the interrelationships among them.

SOME PROBLEMS OF DEFINITION

The first problem of definition involves the term "industrial water
utilization." Specifically, industrial water utilization means the totality of
water and steam flows—including intake water and waste water treatment—for all water uses within a production unit, from one or more
points of intake through the one or more points of discharge of the final
effluents. As a common basis for discussion, a generalized diagram of an
industrial water utilization system is shown in Figure 1. The system can
usefully be divided into the following constituent subsystems: (1) intake
subsystem including source development and transmission facilities to the
water treatment subsystem and/or directly to the points of input to or
use in the production process; (2) the water treatment subsystem, with
the degree of treatment applied to various water streams being a function
of the quality of intake water and of the quality of water required for
different uses within the production unit; (3) the water and steam
circulation subsystem associated with the actual production process itself,
i.e., the facilities for conveying water and steam to and from the points
of use within the production process; (4) waste treatment subsystem
including facilities for collecting and conveying waste flows; and (5)
final discharge subsystem.[2] It should be emphasized that there may be

[2] The problem of the disposal of solid wastes from an industrial process has a
direct impact on the water utilization system. The treatment and final discharge or
disposal of liquid wastes are affected by the nature and magnitude of the solid
wastes from the production process. No consideration is given herein to solid
wastes.

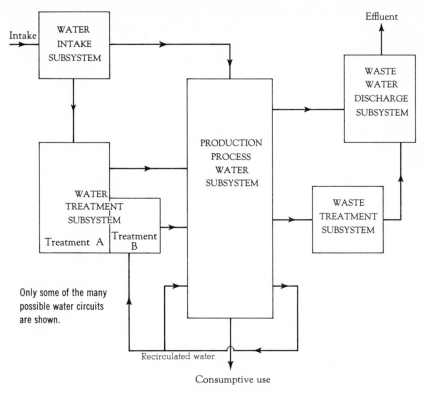

Figure 1. Generalized industrial water utilization system.

several components of each subsystem, i.e., several different water intake facilities or a number of different waste treatment facilities.

A second problem of definition also involves terminology. Over the years various terms have been applied to water utilization in general, and particularly to industrial water utilization. Terms found in the professional and lay literature include water use, water consumption, water need, water requirement, water demand, water withdrawal, water intake, makeup water, consumptive use of water, net depletion of water, discharge, waste water discharge, blowdown, effluent, recirculated water, degree or extent of recirculation, per cent recirculation, per cent reuse, recirculation ratio, and reuse ratio. This listing may well not be complete, but it suggests the range of terminology involved and the consequent problem of communication.

To illustrate: much has been made of the reduction in water usage in various heavy water-using industries over the past ten to fifteen years. For the pulp and paper industry, Knowlton [ref. 4] cites a reduction in "water usage" over a five-year period of from 66,400 to 57,000 gallons per ton of product. As Table 1 shows, it is the water *intake* per ton that decreased. In contrast, the gross water applied per ton—i.e., the total amount of water used to produce a unit of product in the industry— increased by almost 13 per cent from about 160,000 to about 180,000 gallons per ton.

TABLE 1.

Water Utilization in the Pulp and Paper Industry

	1954	1959
1. Annual production (million tons)	26.9	34.0
2. Annual intake of water from all sources (billion gal.) [I]	1,786	1,937
3. Water intake per unit (gal/ton)	66,400	57,000
4. Annual quantity of water recirculated (billion gal.) [R]	2,456	4,109
5. Water recirculated per unit (gal/ton)	91,300	120,900
6. Annual gross application of water (billion gal.) [G] [2 + 4]	4,242	6,046
7. Gross application of water per unit (gal/ton)	157,700	177,900
8. Annual quantity of waste water discharged (billion gal.) [D]	1,620	1,824
9. Waste water discharge per unit (gal/ton)	60,200	53,700
10. Annual consumptive use of water (billion gal.) [C] [2 − 8]	166	113
11. Consumptive use of water per unit (gal/ton)	6,200	3,300
12. Waste load per unit from the production process (pounds of BOD/ton)	——	194 [1]
13. Waste load of final effluent per unit (pounds of BOD/ton)	180 [2]	68 [3]
14. C/G × 100%	3.9	1.9
15. C/I × 100%	9.3	5.8
16. I/G × 100%	42.1	32.0
17. R/G × 100%	57.9	68.0

[1] Based on an industry average 65% reduction in biochemical oxygen demand in waste treatment; for 1962.
[2] 1943.
[3] 1962.
Source: National Council for Stream Improvement, New York.

Figure 2 charts the definitions of terms that will be used in my discussion of industrial water utilization. The total quantity of water necessary to process a unit of raw material, such as a ton of raw tomatoes or a barrel of crude, or to produce a unit of output, such as a ton of pulp or a ton of steel, is denoted as the "gross water applied." This includes water for all in-plant uses such as boiler feedwater, process water, cooling water, and domestic-sanitary water. It is obtained from some combination of intake water and recirculated water. The intake water may be fresh, brackish, or sea water, reclaimed sewage effluent, or water obtained from another user.

The term "water demand" is often used to imply a specific *physical* quantity of water needed, in terms either of intake water or gross water applied. Such usage obscures the economic implications associated with the term "demand." Demand for water is similar to demand for any

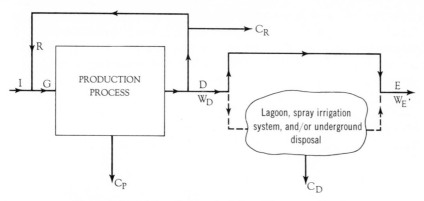

Figure 2. Definition of terms in industrial water utilization.

I = Intake water.

R = Recirculated water.

G = Gross water applied for all in-plant uses.

C = Consumptive use or net depletion of water, = $C_p + C_D + C_R$, where C_p = consumptive use in the production process, C_D = consumptive use in the waste water disposal system, and C_R = consumptive use in the recirculation system.

D = Waste water discharge from the production process.

E = Final effluent from the production unit (available for reuse). Where a lagoon or spray irrigation system is involved, it consists of lagoon outflow seepage, and/or surface runoff, if any.

W_D = Waste load in the waste water discharge, for example, pounds of BOD.

W_E = Waste load in the final effluent, pounds of BOD.

Degree of recirculation = R/G 100%.

factor input to an industrial production process. As used in this paper, water intake is equivalent to the economic concept of water demand. It is not a fixed, immutable figure, but is meaningful only in relation to a number of factors.

Recirculated water may be obtained from one or more water circuits within the plant. The quantity of recirculated water should be measured at the input side of the production process. This merely emphasizes that where water is recirculated through a cooling tower, a portion of the water is lost by evaporation and does not reach the input to the water circuit where it is to be reused. The degree of recirculation, as defined, is a measure of the *proportion* of the gross water applied which is obtained from recirculated water. This proportion may vary from zero to over 90 per cent.

In the process of production some portion of the gross water applied is almost always consumed or depleted—i.e., evaporated into the atmosphere and/or incorporated into the product itself. The consumptive use includes steam loss, which in some cases may be a major portion of the total consumptive use. The consumptive use of water for the production unit as a whole is the sum of the consumptive use in the production process itself, that in waste water disposal, and that in water recirculation.

The waste water discharge from the production process may or may not be equivalent to the final effluent from the production unit. Where the waste water discharge is conveyed either to a non-evaporative waste treatment facility and thence to a receiving water course, or directly to the receiving water body, the waste water discharge usually is the same as the final effluent. But where some portion or all of the waste water discharge is conveyed to a lagoon, stabilization pond, earthen basin, spray irrigation system, and/or to underground disposal, some or all of the waste water does not reach the final effluent. This water is not available for reuse downstream, except where there is seepage or surface outflow from the lagoons, ponds, and spray irrigation systems. The important point is that there may be a significant difference between the waste water discharge from the production process itself and the final effluent from the production unit.

The waste loads in the discharge from the production process and in the final effluent are designated as W_D and W_E, respectively. They are measured in pounds of biochemical oxygen demand (BOD), chemical oxygen demand (COD), suspended solids, or some other water quality parameter. The separation of the waste load resulting from the production process from that in the final effluent is essential in order to identify the effects on waste loads of various factors related to the production process and the effects of waste treatment measures. When, as is usual, data on waste loads are compiled only in terms of quantities in the final effluent, any determination of the impacts of various factors on the waste loads is prevented. The situation is illustrated in the sketch below:

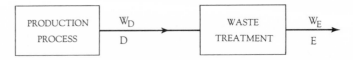

How do changes in the production process affect W_D (and D) and, for any given W_D, how do changes in waste treatment affect W_E (and E)?

The terms given in Figure 2 refer to total volumes for the production unit. On a unit basis, each of the terms is expressed as gallons, liters, acre-feet, or cubic feet, per unit of raw product processed (e.g., barrel of crude petroleum), or per unit of final product output (e.g., ton of pulp, case of canned green beans), and as pounds or grams of waste load (e.g., BOD) per barrel or per ton.

One final definition: total water utilization costs are comprised of all costs of obtaining, handling, and disposing of water from intake to outlet.

These costs involve both payments to external agencies and the capital and operation, maintenance, and replacement (OMR) costs of all in-plant water facilities. Included are, for example, the capital and OMR costs of wells, piping, pumps, valves, chlorinators, cooling towers, and stabilization ponds, pumping costs, and amounts paid for purchased water and for sewer charges.

A problem associated with definition is that of the availability and accuracy of data on industrial water utilization, including water quantities, water qualities, and related factors. To my knowledge, no report dealing with industrial water utilization discusses the accuracy and adequacy of the data. This includes reports by the U.S. Bureau of the Census and the U.S. Bureau of Mines, reports by individual industry associations, and the often-cited *Water in Industry* surveys by the National Association of Manufacturers. For example, all figures in the latest NAM *Water in Industry* report [ref. 5] are tabulated in such a manner as to imply equivalent accuracy for the data from all industries. In reality, the accuracy of water data varies widely from industry to industry, from plant to plant within any given industry, and in relation to the different factors involved—e.g., quantity of intake compared with quantity of recirculated water, amount paid for water compared with in-plant costs of pumping water, and quality of boiler feedwater compared with quality of waste discharge. Any systematic investigation of the available data will reveal obvious inconsistencies, large data gaps, and the crudity of many estimates.

SOME BASIC OBSERVATIONS ON INDUSTRIAL WATER UTILIZATION

One way of organizing a discussion of the economics of industrial water utilization is to offer what might be termed some basic observations, or propositions, which serve to emphasize various considerations relating to the area of study.

My first observation is that water is simply one factor input to the production process; as such it should be analyzed in economic terms in the same manner as other factor inputs. For example, if labor costs increase, the rational entrepreneur seeks ways and means of saving on labor; the response of industry to water costs should be the same [ref. 6].

One slight modification of this observation is necessary. Where water has been plentiful with respect to quantity and quality at both the intake and effluent ends of the production unit, little consideration has been given in the past—and to some extent today—to total water utilization costs. It is not necessary to point out that the situation of relative plenty in connection with water is decreasing in many areas. Although management attitudes may sometimes lag in their approach to water costs, this lag is rapidly diminishing under the impetus of the changed water environment.

To some extent the relatively little consideration which has been given to water costs in the past is explained by the relatively small proportion of total production costs represented by total water utilization costs. This is true even for the heavy water-using and/or heavy water-polluting industries. Chemical manufacturing—an industry characterized by complex water utilization and multiple wastes—is a case in point according to statements by representatives of the industry. Data are sparse on just how small this proportion is. According to Gurnham [ref. 7, p. 204], annual expenditures by ten chemical companies for pollution control over several years ranged from 0.06 per cent to 1.4 per cent of net plant and equipment evaluation, averaging about 0.33 per cent. Stated differently, pollution control expenditures by these companies averaged about 0.2 per cent of net sales, ranging from 0.04 to 1.6 per cent. The percentage of total production costs is, of course, some higher. Waste treatment and disposal costs for the heavy water-using and water-polluting industries are generally several times intake water costs, the ratio being on the order of 3:1 to 6:1. Thus, the order of magnitude of the proportion of total production costs represented by total water utilization costs for these firms ranged perhaps from about 0.1 per cent to about 3 per cent.

Testimony presented by a paper industry representative before a U.S. Senate Committee indicated that waste treatment costs represented about 4 per cent of the sale price [ref. 8]. But it is not clear from the statement whether or not the costs mentioned are *net* of internal savings, for example, from materials recovery. The capital cost of waste treatment facilities in a recently constructed paper plant represented about 3 per cent of the total capital investment in the plant [ref. 9]. The data from the thirty plants with complete reports appearing in the "14th Steam Station Cost Survey" of *Electrical World* [ref. 10] showed an average cost of about 0.1 mill per net kilowatt-hour for "water, lubrication, supplies." This represented about 3 per cent of the average production cost of 3.5 mills per net kilowatt-hour.

I do not intend to imply that these costs are insignificant, but the point remains that total water utilization costs apparently are not a major portion of total production costs, even for heavy water-using and/or water-polluting industries.

My second observation is that water utilization in industry cannot validly be analyzed without reference to other factor inputs to the production process. Consider the filling operation in canning vegetables. The installation of a brine overflow recovery system will reduce the spill of brine, with a consequent saving of water and salt. Even so, savings are not likely to be high enough to justify investment in a recovery system. On the other hand, when the fuel required to heat the brine is considered also, the combination of fuel, salt, and water savings may be sufficient to justify the installation.

A different situation obtains when the objective is to increase the speed with which containers are filled in order to achieve savings in labor costs. High-speed filling often results in an increase in spills with consequent increases in waste load, gross water applied, and total water utilization costs. A reduction in labor costs outweighs the added costs represented by the increased water utilization and waste handling.

The interrelated nature of factor inputs in industrial operations can be exemplified by water and heat. In many cases, investment in a recirculation system cannot be justified solely on the basis of savings in water costs. But where the water has been heated, a saving of water can also mean a significant saving of heat. The joint savings often economically justify investment in a changed water utilization system [ref. 11].

My third observation is that the criterion used by industry in evaluating possible investments in water utilization systems is, in general, the rate of return on the investment. This is particularly true of an existing plant where possible modifications are many. Modifications in the water utilization system—for example, the brine recovery system mentioned above—are compared with other possible investments for reducing total production costs. Water saving in industrial operations is instituted not merely to save water (compare [ref. 12]), and it should be noted that suboptimization—i.e., minimizing total water utilization costs—does not always yield minimum total production costs.

The criterion for analyzing investments in water utilization systems is applied by a production unit within whatever constraints may exist. These are internal—budget limitations, product output quality requirements, available technology and the like—and external, such as the finite availability of physical quantities of water and specific physical limitations, whether quantitative, qualitative, or both, imposed on effluents.

My fourth observation is that industrial water utilization systems are usually designed after most of the parameters fixing the production process—the product mix, level of output, and raw material availability—have already been determined. In petroleum refining, for example, the type of crude to be used has a major impact on process equipment selection, because of the different characteristics of various crudes. Given the

151

crude to be used and the output mix, the production processes are selected, from which the temperatures and pressures at which the operations will take place are known. Given the temperatures and pressures, the water utilization system is then designed to minimize total water utilization costs or total production costs.

In some cases the design of the water utilization system may result in modifications of the production process itself, the raw materials to be used, or both. For example, because the nature and magnitude of waste loads are a function of the type of crude, a shift in process equipment or other inputs may be the most efficient means of handling waste problems, given whatever external constraints may exist on the effluent. However, modifications of production processes solely because of water problems appear to have been exceptions rather than the rule.

My fifth observation is that technological changes have substantial and varied impacts on industrial water utilization. Although this observation will be discussed in conjunction with the next, it merits separate mention. Often technological changes in industry have not been recognized or explicitly considered for their impact on water utilization. In canning, for example, increasing the efficiency of syrup filling machines has been stimulated by the objective of saving syrup. The fact that reduced spill of syrup also means a reduced waste load in terms of pounds of BOD per unit of raw product processed or per unit of product, has not been considered. The introduction of mechanical harvesting of tomatoes offers a different example of the impact of technology on water utilization. Although some of the consequences of its use had been partially foreseen, its impact on water utilization was not directly examined, nor was any move made to defer the use of mechanical harvesters because of water problems.

Thus, technological changes affecting water utilization have usually been stimulated by factors not directly related to water—for example, rising labor costs, rising raw material costs, and/or industry competition. Although such developments may have had substantial positive impacts on water utilization, the rationale for introduction was not the saving in total water utilization costs. Similarly, where the impacts have been negative (i.e., increasing total water utilization costs), the developments have been introduced regardless.

My sixth observation is that the water utilization pattern for a given production unit is affected by many factors, some of which are related to the external water environment and others that are not. The quantity and time pattern of plant water intake, Q_{It}, plant waste water discharge, Q_{Dt}, plant consumptive use of water, C_t, plant effluent, Q_{Et}, and the waste loads in the waste water discharge, W_{Dt}, and in the plant effluent,

W_{Et}, are joint functions of such factors as: the quantity and quality and their respective time patterns of the water available at the plant intakes, including both surface and ground water; the water and waste treatment processes within the plant; the technology of the production process, including the output mix (since the production processes selected are in part a function of the desired final outputs); the physical layout of the plant; the operating rate; product output quality requirements; the degree and cost of water recirculation within the plant; the nature and quantity of solid wastes from the production process; the limitations or controls on the final liquid effluent from the production unit; controls on gaseous effluents; the quantity and quality and their respective time patterns of water available for dilution at the final effluent points; the availability of places for final disposal of waste discharges, including underground storage; and the ratio of total water utilization costs to total production costs.[3] Conceptually, this joint function can be expressed as follows:

$$Q_{It}, Q_{Dt}, C_t, Q_{Et}, W_{Dt}, W_{Et} =$$
$$f[Q_t, q_t, T, PP, L, OR, poqr, R, S, E_c, A_c, Q_{dt}, q_{dt}, D, c_w/c_t],$$

where

Q_t and q_t	= the quantity and quality and their corresponding time patterns of water available at the intake;
T	= the water and waste treatment processes within the production unit;
PP	= the technology of the production process;
L	= the physical layout of the plant;
OR	= the operating rate;
$poqr$	= the product output quality requirements;
R	= the degree of recirculation;
S	= the solid wastes from the production process;
E_c	= the limitations on the final liquid effluent;
A_c	= the limitations on the final gaseous effluent;
Q_{dt} and q_{dt}	= the quantity and quality and their corresponding time patterns of water available for dilution at the effluent point;
D	= availability of places for final disposal of wastes; and
c_w/c_t	= the ratio of total water utilization costs to total production costs.

[3] The quantity and quality of the air available for dilution of the gaseous effluents conceptually should also be included in the equation, in addition to controls on air pollution, because of the interrelationships between methods for handling liquid and gaseous wastes. For a short discussion of these interrelationships, see [ref. 7, p. 192] and [ref. 13].

153

Obviously, not all of the variables on the righthand side of the equation are independent. For example, the quality of water at the intake in terms of total dissolved solids is a function of the quantity of water at the intake. The extent of recirculation is a function of the effluent controls, the technology of the production process, and the cost of recirculation. The waste treatment processes adopted are a function of the effluent controls, the technology of the production process, and the nature and magnitude of solid wastes. And so on.

The impact of various factors on industrial water utilization can be measured by changes in the unit values of water intake, gross water application, consumptive use, and waste loads of the discharge and the final effluent, i.e., I per unit, G per unit, C per unit, W_D per unit, and W_E per unit, respectively. The difficulty is in separating the effects of various factors. The interactions among the factors probably preclude definitive delineation of the effects of any one factor on industrial water utilization. However, data available from various industries can serve to illustrate some of the apparent effects, as well as to illuminate some economic implications.

My seventh and final observation is that to a large extent industrial water utilization problems are unique to each particular plant and to each plant site. Only gross generalizations are possible. Each situation involving plant site, production process, product mix, and the water environment tends to be unique. At least, this is the expressed viewpoint of many people in industry. For example, experienced designers of petroleum refineries have stated that variations from one refinery to another are so great—even when the refineries are in the same general area and process the same general crudes—that developing meaningful generalizations is virtually impossible. (On this point see [ref. 14].) Although this point of view is probably valid with respect to specific data, i.e., pounds of BOD per barrel of crude, it is not valid with respect to generalizations about the nature and direction of *responses* of industrial water users to various factors. The view does serve to emphasize the complexities involved in attempting to define the factors, their interrelationships, and their impacts on industrial water utilization.

FACTORS AFFECTING INDUSTRIAL WATER UTILIZATION

The following discussion will attempt to provide some details on the above observations, primarily by focusing on the impacts on industrial water utilization of technological changes, product output quality requirements, quality of raw product inputs, and factors in the external water

154

environment. Examples are taken from various industries. Because of space limitations, one important factor affecting water utilization, namely, plant operating rate, is not considered here. It is dealt with in detail in a study of the canning industry, now in preparation. That the operating rate, defined as the quantity of raw product processed or the quantity of product output per unit of time, has a direct and major impact on water utilization is reasonably well established. In general, higher operating rates are associated with lower gross application of water per unit and lower waste water discharge per unit. To the extent that the average operating rate for a plant can be increased, the efficiency of water utilization per unit will increase. The impacts of operating rate on water utilization should be kept in mind during perusal of the following sections.

Technology of the Production Process and Final Product Quality Requirements

Because of the impossibility of segregating the technology of the production process from the quality requirements for the final product outputs, the impacts of these factors will be discussed together. Petroleum refining provides some useful examples. The nature of refineries has changed significantly in the last twenty years. Not only has the average size increased, but there has been a definite trend toward the production of a wider range of products in any single installation. Instead of a relatively simple distillation-cracking operation typical of refineries twenty years ago, present-day refineries may have hydrogen treating units, reforming units, alkylation units, and units for the production of the entire range of lubricants. To characterize refineries, Nelson [ref. 15] has developed an index of refinery complexity, basically related to product mix. The trend in refinery complexity over the past forty-five years and projected over the next twenty-five years is shown in Figure 3.

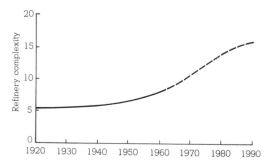

Figure 3. Trends in refinery complexity in the United States. (Source: Nelson. W. L., in *Oil and Gas Journal,* Vol. 61, No. 37 [1963], Figure 1, p. 118.)

Increasing refining complexity appears to result in increases in both the cooling load and the gross water applied per barrel of crude processed, and probably also an increase in the magnitude and complexity of the waste load per barrel. The relationship between refinery complexity and what Nelson terms "total clean-water" needs is shown in Figure 4. A similar relationship exists between refinery complexity and refinery waste load.

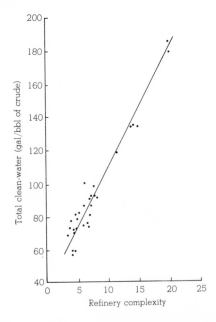

Figure 4. Relationship between refinery complexity and clean-water needs. (Based on Nelson, W. L., in *Oil and Gas Journal,* Vol. 61, No. 3 [1963], Table 1, p. 80.)

Although some developments both in the production process and in product output requirements in petroleum refining have tended to increase the gross water application per unit of crude processed, at least one technological development in the industry has tended in the opposite direction. Integration is a factor reducing gross water application per unit. A conventional refinery is one in which the typical refinery units are separated by intermediate storage. In an integrated refinery the refining facilities are located adjacent to one another, essentially as one big unit. Stock is run directly from one unit as the charge to the next unit. The adoption of integration at the Sohio Toledo refinery saved about 10,000 gallons per minute of cooling water capacity [ref. 16].

In the pulp and paper industry, both technological changes and final product quality requirements have had important impacts on water utilization. As shown in Table 1, the gross water applied per unit of product increased during the 1954–59 period. Industry sources indicate that this trend has continued. The increase in gross water applied per unit is a result of higher quality standards for the final products, the introduction and growth in production of colored paper products, and an increase in the production of speciality papers. At the same time that the unit gross water applied has increased, the consumptive use per unit appears to have decreased. Why this is so is not clear, but it is conceivable that process changes have enabled installation of more closed cooling systems with a consequent reduction in evaporative losses.

With respect to impact on unit waste load in the final effluent, Table 1 shows a reduction from 180 pounds of BOD per ton to 68 pounds over the period 1943–62. To some unknown extent this reduction was a result of a shift in the production process. Of the approximate 10.5 million tons of wood pulp produced in 1942, about 35 per cent were produced by the sulfate process. Twenty years later, of an industry output of 29 million tons, over 60 per cent were produced by the sulfate process. Evidence suggests that the shift in the proportion of total output produced by the sulfate process did not occur primarily because of waste disposal problems in the industry.

The increased efficiency of kraft liquor recovery systems and the installation of sulfite by-product and recovery facilities have resulted in a major reduction in the organic load per unit of product [ref. 17]. Reduction in waste load per unit of product has also resulted from reduced solids losses through recirculation of process water and the use of solids removal equipment, the retention of increased percentages of wood substances in the wood product, more efficient recovery of chemicals and heat from spent pulping liquors, and the recovery of by-products. Depending on the method of pulping used—mechanical, semichemical, chemical—the waste load in pounds of BOD per ton can vary from less than 50 to more than 500 [ref. 18]. Efficient heat and recovery systems, such as those employed in many chemical pulp mills, can reduce the pulp losses as much as 95 per cent.

Reduction of the unit waste load in the final effluent has also been achieved in the pulp and paper industry through extensive installation of waste treatment facilities. In analyzing the factors affecting industrial water utilization in the industry, the problem, as noted previously, is to determine the proportion of the reduction attributable to process changes and the proportion resulting from waste treatment. For example, one kraft mill reduced its average effluent waste load from 57 pounds of BOD per ton in 1955, to 25 pounds per ton in 1960 [ref. 19]. This was accomplished by means of tighter plant operation, reuse of process water, constant observation of waste production, and waste treatment. It is not possible, from the data available for this plant, or for the industry as a whole, to separate the impacts of the various factors.

In the steel industry, major technological changes in recent years have been introduction of the basic oxygen process, continuous casting, and automation, including computer-controlled production. The basic oxygen process appears to reduce the gross water applied per unit but to increase slightly the consumptive use per unit. This is because, although less water is needed for equipment cooling, water is required for gas cooling and conditioning. The quantities involved for the latter two operations are small, but the water is entirely consumed in contrast to open-hearth operations where only indirect cooling is required [ref. 20].

With respect to the impact of continuous casting on water utilization, there are varying opinions. Some industry representatives believe there will be no change; others think that there will be a reduction in both the gross water applied and the consumptive use per ton of product output. Continuous casting appears to enable enclosure of the cooling system so that the cooling water applied and the resulting steam can be confined and condensed, rather than be lost by evaporation [ref. 21].

Automation of steel production also engenders different opinions in the industry. Automatic control presumably will result in an over-all improvement in production efficiency, which in turn should reduce the gross water applied per unit. There probably will be little or no impact on unit consumptive use and unit waste load. In some industries, however, automation has a definitely positive impact on water utilization. For example, the introduction of automation in milk processing and cheese plants has resulted in a reduction in the waste load per unit of product processed. A similar result has been achieved in dairy plants by the installation of automatic cleaning systems.[4]

Automation, both automatic control of production and automatic control of water flows, has not progressed very far in some industries. Canning is an example. As the cost of water as a factor input increases, more extensive investment in automatic controls of water will become justified, thereby reducing gross water applied per unit.

In the canning industry, final product quality requirements as well as technological developments have had major impacts on water utilization. In the last two decades, standards for the quality of the final canned product, and hence for the quality of the input raw product, have become increasingly stringent. If all other factors had remained the same, the

[4] For a description of these two results, see [ref. 22].

result would have been an approximate doubling of the gross water applied per case [ref. 23].

Concern for product quality has led to the development of new methods for cleaning raw products prior to the cooking and filling steps in the canning process. In the last two seasons tests in actual canning operations have shown that dipping tomatoes in a hot lye solution can achieve virtually complete elimination of fly eggs [ref. 24]. However, the procedure requires a significant increase in the gross water applied per unit because of the additional washing necessary to insure removal of the lye. Product quality in canning is also improved by utilizing wet conveying of products inside the plant (i.e., in flumes), instead of dry conveying on belts. This procedure also increases the gross water applied per unit. The likely trend in the future toward even higher final product quality requirements will result in continued pressure for larger unit gross water application.

A measure of the increasing efficiency of processing equipment in the canning industry is the upward trend in case yield—i.e., cans of final product output per ton of raw product processed. Case yield is directly related to the type of processing equipment, as well as to the quality of the raw product input. Over the last twenty years, the average case yield in the industry for peaches has increased from about forty cases per ton to about fifty-five cases per ton. A similar trend has occurred in canning pears, where the case yield has increased from about forty to about fifty cases per ton. One significant result is that as the case yield increases, more of the raw product is actually incorporated in the final product output, thereby reducing the waste load per ton of raw product processed.

A related effect on waste load in the canning industry stems from increasing the efficiency of filling operations. The syrup spilled in the canning of fruit products, such as peaches, although small in absolute volume, contributes highly concentrated waste in terms of BOD load. Even a small increase in the filling efficiency will achieve a significant reduction in the waste load per unit of raw product processed.

One of the major developments in canning has been the hydrostatic sterilizer or cooker. Although such units have been used in Europe for at least twenty years, the first installations in the United States were made only within the last few years. Data suggest that, compared with conventional still retorts, hydrostatic sterilizers significantly decrease the gross water applied per unit of product processed [ref. 25].

In terms of developments in the canning industry over the last fifteen years, it appears that water utilization, as measured by gross water applied and waste load per unit, has been affected more by technological developments and product quality requirements than by developments in methods for handling water within the plant, such as improved washing systems, improved cleanup operations, and automatic control of water flows. As far as the evolution of processing equipment is concerned, however, it is the opinion of equipment manufacturers that the ultimate in case yield has essentially been reached, at least for peaches and pears. Short-run future increases in the efficiency of water utilization in canning (i.e., reduction in gallons applied per unit and/or waste load per unit) are likely to stem more from developments in methods for in-plant handling of water and improvements in raw product quality, than from developments in processing equipment.

Quality of Raw Product Inputs

The characteristics of raw product inputs to the production process have significant impacts on industrial water utilization. In petroleum refining, the characteristics of raw crude vary significantly depending on the source of the crude—for example, in terms of the sulfur content. Hence, water utilization, particularly waste loads, for a given product output mix will vary significantly depending on the type of crude used.

In canning, impacts on water utilization associated with developments in raw product input stem from two sources: (1) methods of harvesting, and (2) quality of the raw product. Mechanical harvesting is increasing for vegetable products such as tomatoes and green beans. The proportion of raw product tomato input that is mechanically harvested is over 50 per cent for some canneries in California and is increasing rapidly. For many canneries packing green beans, all of the raw product input is already mechanically harvested. To date, mechanically harvested crops have considerably more dirt and debris on the raw product input at the cannery and a larger proportion of damaged raw product than the same raw products handpicked. The result has been a sizable increase in the gross water applied per unit of raw product processed and in the waste load per unit of product, in terms of both pounds of BOD and suspended solids per ton.

At the same time, developments in the quality of the raw product itself are steadily taking place. They include: new varieties more amenable to mechanical harvesting; more disease-resistant varieties which reduce cullage at the cannery, thereby improving case yield and reducing waste load; achievement of greater uniformity in the raw product, enabling more efficient utilization and increasing case yield; and new varieties which ripen earlier in the canning season and others which ripen more uniformly over the season, thereby enabling higher mean operating rates. All of these developments improve the efficiency of water utilization and

160

reduce the gross water applied and/or the waste load per unit of raw product processed.

Effluent Controls

Effluent controls, which may be either in the form of sewer charges (effluent charges) or in the form of physical limitations, have important impacts on industrial water utilization. The effluent charges or standards imposed provide constraints within which modifications of the water utilization system of an industrial plant are made. A variety of responses can occur. It should be emphasized that the response of an industrial plant to the imposition of effluent controls cannot be divorced from the total water utilization system of the plant from intake to outlet. For example, recirculation of water may be stimulated more by problems of waste disposal than by problems of intake water quantity and quality.

Two basic points in relation to waste disposal problems require emphasis. First, the nature and character of the waste products—liquid, solid, and gaseous—resulting from a production unit are determined primarily by three factors: (1) the raw materials used; (2) the final product mix; and (3) the manufacturing or production processes used. These factors can vary widely from plant to plant within the same industry. Second, reducing the quantity and increasing the concentration of pollutants in the effluent enable more economic treatment of wastes to yield the required effluent quality level or to yield the maximum reduction in effluent charges. It is easier and more economical to treat a small volume of highly concentrated waste than to treat a large volume of dilute waste [ref. 26].

In addition to the various mechanical, chemical, and biological waste treatment processes available to reduce the waste load in the final effluent, other alternatives can be adopted in response to imposed effluent controls. These include: (1) by-product or factor input recovery, (2) process modification, (3) recirculation of water, and (4) the use of stabilization ponds or lagoons. The economics of by-product recovery is a function of the concentration of the pollutant in the effluent and of the size of the operation, the latter because of the economies of scale which generally exist in by-product recovery processes. For example, in the Blaw-Knox Ruthner sulfuric acid recovery process, the treatment cost of pickle liquor on the basis of 8.5 per cent free acid in the liquor decreases from about $3\frac{1}{2}$ cents/gallon to about 3 mills/gallon as the quantity of pickle liquor processed increases from 30,000 gallons/day to 160,000 gallons/day [ref. 27]. Another example of by-product recovery is the conversion of cottage-cheese whey into salable protein food supplements, thereby eliminating a particularly difficult waste disposal problem [ref. 28].

Process modification is a second possible response to imposed effluent controls. An excellent example is provided by the accomplishments of a large chemical plant, where the dollar volume of output doubled over a fifteen-year period while the waste loads in terms of pounds of BOD and phenolics per day were both reduced by over 90 per cent. Process modification—for example, changing the polymerization catalyst in one process and increasing the reaction temperature in another—was an important factor in these reductions.[5]

A third major response to effluent controls is the adoption or the increase of water recirculation within the plant. It is obvious that as the quantity of water intake increases, the quantity of effluent and the waste disposal costs rise correspondingly. Thus, faced with effluent charges and/or the necessity for meeting specified effluent quality standards and/or limitations on the quantity of effluent, the most general reaction by industry is to curtail the intake of water in order to reduce waste disposal costs [ref. 30]. By recirculation, the volume of effluent can be reduced substantially, which in turn reduces the size and cost of effluent treatment and handling facilities.

There is generally a limit to the extent of recirculation. For example, in pulp and paper production the extent of recirculation can reach the point where the production process is hindered by such conditions as increased rates of corrosion, foaming, freeness and sheet formation troubles, felt plugging, and product quality deterioration [ref. 31]. The savings in effluent charges and waste disposal costs must be balanced against the increased costs of water recirculation and the incremental production costs resulting from the other problems.

In the canning industry, recirculation of water in order to reduce the quantity of effluent is a common response to the imposition of sewer charges on canneries discharging to municipal sewerage facilities. But there are other results which have not always been anticipated. In many canneries, increasing the extent of recirculation has resulted in increases in both the gross water applied and the in-plant consumptive use per unit of raw product processed. The general relationships between unit water recirculation and (a) unit gross water application and (b) unit consumptive use are illustrated in Figure 5. The savings from reduced waste disposal costs, including effluent charges, must be at least sufficient to compensate for the costs of recirculation and the costs associated with the incremental increase in the gross water applied.

---

[5] For a description of the various changes, see [ref. 29].

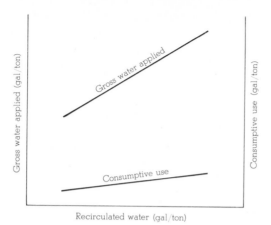

Figure 5. Unit recirculation vs. unit gross water applied and unit consumptive use of water in canning.

Some of the increase in unit gross water applied as recirculation increases can be explained by the deteriorating quality of the water as it is recirculated. However, it appears that the most common cause is the practice of recirculating the same amount of water regardless of the volume of raw product being processed. Recirculating water systems in canning are generally operated at full capacity. The pumping rate is not varied with the rate of product flow. As a consequence, when the inflow of raw product decreases, the gross water applied per unit of raw product processed or per unit of output increases significantly.

Recirculation of water cannot be accomplished without incurring costs. The primary factors affecting cost appear to be: (1) the complexity of the production process in terms of the number of component processes and units involved, (2) the spatial layout of the production process, (3) the range of products produced in the plant, and (4) the extent of water quality degradation in the production process. These four factors are interrelated.

Generally, the first water to be recirculated in a plant is that which is easiest to collect and to convey to the point or points in the production process where it can be used without treatment. As more water is recirculated, the distances between points of collection and points of use are likely to increase, and some treatment of the recirculated water will probably be necessary. As the degree of recirculation approaches the physically feasible maximum—i.e., limited by the in-plant consumptive use—the last gallons of water are being recirculated and the cost of each is high.

This general trend toward increasing marginal costs as the degree of

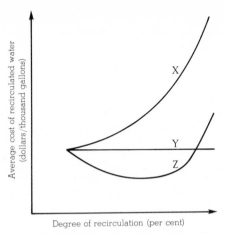

Figure 6a. Water recirculation cost functions.

recirculation increases is illustrated by X in Figure 6a. Such a relationship appears particularly relevant to installations characterized by high levels of the four factors enumerated above. In a relatively simple production process where there is basically only one operation, for example in the concentration of copper ore, the cost of recirculated water may well be virtually constant throughout the range of feasible recirculation. This case is illustrated by Y in Figure 6a. Where most of the water used in the production process is for cooling, there are likely to be economies of scale in recirculating water, with the resulting recirculation cost function as shown by Z in the diagram. If the various factors affecting recirculation could be combined in some sort of index of plant complexity, the relationship between complexity and cost of recirculated water could be represented as in Figure 6b.

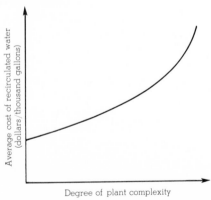

Figure 6b. Relationship between plant complexity and water recirculation cost.

That the canning industry is probably not unique with respect to the impacts of recirculation on water utilization is demonstrated by Figures 7 and 8. Figure 7 shows the relationship between unit water recirculated and unit consumptive use in petroleum refining, based on data for 138 refineries. Figure 8 shows the relationship between unit recirculation and gross water applied, based on data for 159 refineries. The increase in consumptive use per barrel as recirculation increases is relatively small in absolute magnitude, but is in the expected direction. In petroleum refining, the major use of water is for cooling, and the easiest circuit in which to adopt recirculation is the cooling water circuit. Usually, this involves the use of cooling towers or ponds, for which the in-plant consumptive use is larger than for once-through cooling systems.

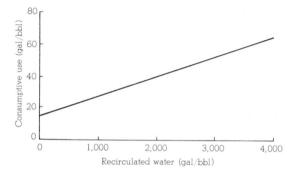

Figure 7. Relationship between unit recirculation of water and unit consumptive use in petroleum refining.

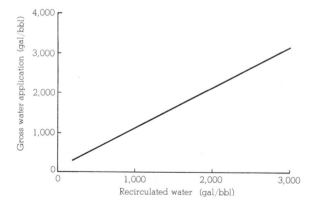

Figure 8. Relationship between unit recirculation of water and unit gross water application in petroleum refining.

All of the increase in gross water applied per barrel of crude as the extent of recirculation increases probably should not be attributed to recirculation. Other factors are likely to affect the apparent result. For example, the larger the refinery the greater is the likelihood that the refinery represents a complete refinery producing a large range of petroleum products with a multiplicity of different types of processing units. In such refineries the gross application of water per barrel of crude processed, as indicated previously, is larger than in refineries of less complexity. Such refineries also offer more opportunities for recirculation. Nevertheless, the data suggest that recirculating more water does result in an increase in gross water applied per barrel of crude processed.

A fourth possible response to effluent disposal problems is the utilization of stabilization ponds or lagoons, spray irrigation systems, and underground disposal. Although these are accepted methods of waste handling, they merit separate mention because of their impact on the consumptive use of water. Given a level of effluent charges and/or specific effluent quality requirements, and given the availability of land, the use of stabilization lagoons can be a relatively inexpensive method for handling wastes and is, in fact, quite commonly used by the canning industry.

Each of these methods of effluent disposal results in a substantial increase in the consumptive use of water per unit of raw product processed or per unit of product output. For example, available data on water utilization by petroleum refineries in 1959 show a mean consumptive use of forty-seven gallons per barrel for seventy-four refineries using stabilization ponds, spray irrigation, and/or underground disposal, in contrast to a mean consumptive use of thirty-three gallons per barrel for sixty-four refineries not employing these methods. Underground disposal of an effluent logically can be considered as resulting in a consumptive use of water, because the water so handled is not available for reuse downstream. Thus, the imposition of effluent controls can have a significant impact on consumptive use of water in industry.

Cost of Intake Water

Just as effluent controls have an impact on industrial water utilization, so the cost of intake water, including necessary water treatment costs because of intake water quality, also has a significant impact. One would expect that as the cost of intake water increases, the quantity of intake per unit would be reduced, primarily by increased in-plant recirculation of water. Even where intake water costs are increasing, whether or not recirculation will be adopted or increased is a function of the relative costs of recirculation versus all costs of intake water—i.e., supply, pumping, and conveying.[6]

Data from a study by Gilkey and Beckman of copper operations in Arizona [ref. 33] suggest that as the cost of intake water increases, there is a decrease in the proportion of gross water applied that is obtained from new intake water. Although the cost figures submitted by the individual operations are probably not comparable, the trend is reasonably clear. For these operations the cost of recirculated water ranged from about equal to about 10 per cent of new intake water. There are, of course, factors other than cost that have an influence on the extent of recirculation: physical limitations on the available supply and the type of operation, for example.

As noted, the most common industry response to an increase in intake water costs is to increase the extent of recirculation. According to Clarke, ". . . industrial waters generally cost from 2 to 25 cents per 1,000 gallons compared with 1 to 5 cents for recycled cooling water and 2 to 13 cents per 1,000 for treated sewage effluent." [Ref. 34, p. 25.] Recirculation will often merit consideration when intake water, although adequate in quantity, is inadequate in quality, thereby requiring treatment to meet the quality necessary for in-plant use. This is true even for cooling water. In the economic comparison of once-through and recirculation systems, the factors to be evaluated include the costs of pumping, pretreatment, sterilization, inhibition of corrosion, prevention of scale, and disposing of water—all in terms of capital as well as operation, maintenance and replacement costs [ref. 35].

In addition to reduction in intake water costs, in-plant recirculation of water has other advantages. These include: (1) reduction in chemical, thermal, and biological pollution; (2) increased flexibility for plant expansion without the necessity of providing larger water mains and sewers; (3) relative simplicity in treating and handling the concentrated waste water; (4) maximum freedom from water pollution by upstream users because the quantity of intake water is reduced; and (5) reduced cost of corrosion control in a closed system [ref. 34, p. 26].

It should be noted that in many cases rate structures for industrial water users encourage high water intake per unit of product. Generally, large consumers receive lower rates for using more water—i.e., the more water used, the lower the price per 1,000 gallons. In such situations it often becomes less expensive for the industrial user to discharge once-used water than to adopt recirculation.

[6] For a description of a specific case, see Howell [ref. 32].

CONCLUDING REMARKS: INDUSTRIAL WATER UTILIZATION, MANAGEMENT PERCEPTIONS AND PUBLIC POLICY DECISIONS

The preceding discussion has attempted to demonstrate that industry, in the main, does respond to economic factors in considering water utilization. Although there is no uniformity, accepted investment criteria are applied in industry to investment decisions with respect to water utilization systems within whatever constraints may exist, such as physical controls on effluents, technology, product output quality requirements, and input raw product quality. As the cost of water to industries increases, either or both through increased intake water costs and increased waste disposal costs, the general reaction is to increase the extent of water recirculation. When the sum of waste treatment and intake water costs becomes larger than the costs of closed cycle operation, the latter will be adopted. It should be noted that in some cases, closed cycle operation is the minimum cost solution even where water intake and waste disposal costs are low.

The preceding discussion has also, it is hoped, demonstrated the major impacts that technological changes, product output quality requirements, and raw product input quality can have on industrial water utilization. Technological changes have often occurred with little consideration for their impact on water utilization; conversely, most technological changes have not been made because of water problems.

Management Perceptions[7]

Three principal stimuli to management perception of water problems seem to exist: two internal to the firm, the third external. The two internal stimuli are (1) regular consideration of various alternatives for investing the funds of a firm or a plant budgeted for improvements, and (2) fixed physical limitations relating to plant capacity and/or industrial water utilization systems.

With respect to the first, possible investments in water utilization system changes are compared with other alternative investment possibilities for reducing total production costs. Various possible investments are formulated, the savings determined, and a ranking established. The results are then presented to higher management. Those investments

[7] I am indebted to Gilbert White and Robert Kates for raising the question about management perceptions of industrial water utilization problems. Responsibility for the adequacy of the characterization of the stimuli of management perceptions is mine.

having the greatest payoffs are adopted until the available funds are exhausted. Some of those adopted may involve water utilization systems.

With respect to the second, industrial water utilization problems may thrust themselves on management's consciousness when plant expansion or modification is decided upon, and the capacity of the existing industrial water utilization system is inadequate to enable the expansion or modification. At this point various changes in the industrial water utilization system may be considered, such as modification of the system to reduce water utilization per unit of product, particularly water intake, effluent, and waste load; and process changes which will reduce unit water utilization. Note that the stimulus here derives from the internal incapacity of the water utilization system, not from limitations in external supply.

The external stimulus comprises one or more of the following: imposition of effluent charges or standards, significantly increased costs of intake water, and fixed physical limitations on intake water supply and/or permitted effluent. Management perception is often first aroused by the imposition of effluent charges where none previously existed, or by a drastic increase in intake water costs as, for example, when a plant purchases water from a municipal system and the system at some point in time must be enlarged by capital investment. Fixed physical limits on the available supply of water, as in areas of limited ground-water yield, and/or fixed physical limits on effluent quantity established by local or regional agencies, can similarly bring to management a sudden awareness of water problems. Usually this will occur when plant changes are being considered in connection with expansion, new products, or changed production schedules.

Public Policy Decisions

The observations, or propositions, I have made about the nature of industrial water utilization and the response of industry to the "water environment" have important implications for public policy decisions concerned with water resources planning, development, and management.

First, because industry has become the major water withdrawer in the United States and is likely to increase its predominance in the future, the extent of water resources development—in terms of surface- and ground-water storage facilities, water and waste treatment facilities, and the operation of water resources systems in general—will depend on patterns of industrial water utilization. Estimates of future storage requirements, of quantities of water necessary for dilution, and of the extent of public treatment measures necessary to maintain or achieve specified water

169

quality objectives will be a function of the intake, consumptive use, waste discharge, and waste loads of the various industrial users. Planning that does not consider the economics of industrial water utilization in relation to the responses to water costs, effluent controls, and technological changes will result in inefficient allocation of resources to public water resources development.

Second, recent proposals have been made for legislation on a national level to provide incentives for industrial plants to construct waste treatment facilities (for example, see [ref. 36]), and similar proposals have been made in various states. The economic efficiency of such proposals is questionable. Because industrial firms analyze water utilization problems wherever possible in terms of the greatest return per dollar invested, if costs of waste treatment measures to the individual plant are substantially reduced by tax incentives, grants, or increased depreciation allowances, waste treatment facilities may well be adopted more readily than alternatives such as water recirculation and process changes. From society's viewpoint, the most efficient pattern of water utilization may not be achieved by the former [ref. 37].

Third, increasing attention is being paid to the possible use of effluent charges in water resources management.[8] The evidence indicates that where sewer charges have been levied, they have been effective in stimulating industries to modify either production processes or waste treatment methods or both [ref. 39]. What is known of the impact of sewer charges on water utilization in the canning industry substantiates this.

In contrast, Kinney [ref. 40] argues that the imposition of effluent charges would not necessarily result in the reduction of pollution. Some companies, he claims, would favor a continuing operating expense (i.e., effluent charge) in preference to the capital and OMR expenses involved in constructing and operating company waste treatment facilities. The argument does have some validity because industrial firms, in general, would prefer not to be in the waste disposal "business"—but it overlooks the rationale for effluent charges: i.e., that the charges should be increased until modifications are in fact incorporated into industrial water utilization systems. On the whole, the evidence to date does not support Kinney's contention. An excellent example of the effectiveness of the application of a system of water supply and waste disposal charges within a single industrial operation is described by Sercu [ref. 41]. When the utilities division of the company in question levied intake water and waste disposal charges against each department of the operation, it stimu-

---

[8] For a detailed exposition relating to such charges, see [ref. 38].

lated modifications of water utilization systems as well as process changes within the departments.

Finally, the imposition of charges on both intake and effluent should not be undertaken without considering other possible impacts on water utilization in addition to absolute reductions in water intakes and waste loads. As has been indicated, one of the most efficient methods for reducing waste loads in the final effluent can be the use of stabilization ponds, spray irrigation systems, and/or underground disposal. One result, however, is an increase in the consumptive use of water, which may be on the order of 50 per cent in terms of water per unit of raw product processed or per unit of final product. Although small in absolute quantity, such increases may be significant in areas that are relatively short of water. Because the consumptive use of water is the factor limiting the level of economic activity in any area, there can be a conflict between the objective of reducing waste loads and the objective of minimizing consumptive use.

Consequently, it may be that what should be considered instead of a water intake charge and/or an effluent charge is a "water utilization charge." Such a charge would take account of aspects of industrial water utilization in addition to water intake and final effluent and, where water is relatively short, it might encourage industry to reduce its consumptive use. Credits against water utilization charges could be given to those users who accomplish such a reduction in their production units. As an example: In the manufacture of tomato products such as paste and catsup, instead of permitting the water extracted from the tomatoes to escape into the atmosphere, facilities would be encouraged which would capture and condense the water for further use.

The water utilization charge might therefore be based on the four factors: quantity of water intake, Q_I; consumptive use of water C; quantity of effluent, Q_E; and the waste load in the effluent, W_E. Expressed symbolically:

$$\text{Water utilization charge} = f\,[Q_I,\, C,\, Q_E,\, W_E]\,.$$

Just how such a charge would be formulated in quantitative terms and what relative weights should be given to the various factors, remain matters for further investigation and consideration.

REFERENCES

[1] Bower, B. T. "Industrial Water Utilization: Substitution Possibilities and Regional Water Resources Development," *Proceedings of the Regional Science Association, Western Section.* Urban Systems Report No. 1. Tempe: Arizona State University (1964).

[2] National Council for Stream Improvement of the Pulp, Paper and Paperboard Industries, New York.

[3] Stormont, D. H. "Refiners Make Good Use of Fresh-water Supplies," *Oil and Gas Journal,* Vol. 61, No. 8 (1963), p. 90.

[4] Knowlton, D. C. "Progress in Pollution Abatement and Water Conservation," *Tappi,* Vol. 47, No. 11 (1964), p. 16A.

[5] National Association of Manufacturers. *Water in Industry.* New York, 1965.

[6] Hazen, R. "The Years Ahead—Resources, Plant, and Planning," *Journal American Waterworks Association,* Vol. 54, No. 10 (1962), p. 1173.

[7] Gurnham, C. F. "Control of Water Pollution," *Chemical Engineering,* Vol. 70, No. 12 (1963).

[8] *Hearings Before a Special Committee on Air and Water Pollution of the Committee on Public Works,* U.S. Senate, 88th Congress, 1st Session (1963), p. 549.

[9] *Research and Development News,* Water Information Center, Vol. 6, No. 7 (1965), p. 2.

[10] Olmsted, L. M. "14th Steam Station Cost Survey," *Electrical World,* Vol. 164, No. 16 (1965), p. 109.

[11] McKie, W. K. "Wasted Water: Profits Down the Drain," *Industrial Water Engineering,* Vol. 2, No. 4 (1965).

[12] Watson, K. S. "Elements of Water Management," in *Industrial Water Conservation.* Continued Education Series No. 83. Ann Arbor: University of Michigan School of Public Health, 1959, p. 23.

[13] Brown, K. M., and Kurtis, S. "Solved—Difficult Waste Disposal Problem," *Petroleum Refiner,* Vol. 29, No. 8 (1950).

[14] Elkin, H. F., and Austin, R. J. "Petroleum," in Gurnham (ed.), *Industrial Wastewater Control.* New York: Academic Press, 1965, p. 289.

[15] Nelson, W. L. "Future Water Requirements of Refineries," *Oil and Gas Journal,* Vol. 61, No. 37 (1963), p. 118; and "Clean-Water Needs of Refineries," *Oil and Gas Journal,* Vol. 61, No. 3, p. 80.

[16] Cross, J. R. "Water Conservation Efforts in the Oil Refining Industry," in *Industrial Water Conservation.* Continued Education Series No. 83. Ann Arbor: University of Michigan School of Public Health, 1959, p. 106.

[17] Amberg, H. R. "By-product Recovery and Methods of Handling Spent Sulfite Liquor," *Journal Water Pollution Control Federation,* Vol. 37, No. 2 (1965).

[18] Gehm, H. W. "Pulp and Paper," in Gurnham (ed.), *Industrial Wastewater Control.* New York: Academic Press, 1965, p. 362.

[19] Morgan, O. P. "A Summary of the Air and Water Pollution Abatement Efforts of Weyerhaeuser Kraft Mill at Springfield, Oregon," *Proceedings Tenth Pacific Northwest Industrial Waste Conference.* Pullman: Institute of Technology, Washington State University, 1961, p. 124.

[20] Cannon, D. W. "Industrial Re-use of Water: An Opportunity for the West," *Water and Sewage Works,* Vol. 3, No. 5 (1964).

[21] "Continuous Casting in Operation," *Mechanical Engineering,* Vol. 85, No. 8 (1963), p. 51.

[22] Hibbs, R. A. "Effect of Automation and Circulation Cleaning on the Waste Disposal Load of Dairy Processing Plants," *Proceedings Tenth*

Pacific Northwest Industrial Waste Conference. Pullman: Institute of Technology, Washington State University, 1961.

[23] Statement of the National Canners Association before the National Resources and Power Subcommittee of the House Committee on Government Operations, June 11, 1963, D1212.

[24] "Lye Bath Perfected for Ridding Tomatoes of Fly Eggs," *Canner-Packer,* Vol. 134, No. 2 (1965).

[25] Nair, J. H. "Hydrostatic Sterilizers," *Food Engineering,* Vol. 36, No. 12 (1964).

[26] Hewson, J. L. "Economic Use of Water and the Solution of Effluent Disposal Problems in the Heavy Chemical Industry," in *Re-use of Water in Industry.* Butterworths: International Union of Pure and Applied Chemistry, 1963, p. 185.

[27] National Technical Task Committee on Industrial Wastes. "Blaw-Knox Ruthner Sulfuric Acid Recovery Process." Process Sheet No. 3.

[28] "Upgrades Cheese Whey, Solves Disposal Problem," *Food Engineering,* Vol. 37, No. 11 (1965).

[29] von Frank, A. J. "Process Change in a Major Chemical Plant." Paper presented at the National Meeting, Water Pollution Control Federation, Atlantic City, N.J., 1965.

[30] Riegel, H. I. "Industry's Water Problems and Their Solution," *Iron and Steel Engineering,* Vol. 34, No. 11 (1957).

[31] Gehm, H. W. "Pulp and Paper," in Gurnham (ed.), *Industrial Wastewater Control.* New York: Academic Press, 1965, p. 359.

[32] Howell, G. A. "Re-use of Water in the Steel Industry," *Proceedings Fourth Pittsburgh Sanitary Engineering Conference.* Pittsburgh: University of Pittsburgh, 1963.

[33] Gilkey, M. M., and Beckman, R. T. *Water Requirements and Uses in Arizona Mineral Industries.* Bureau of Mines Information Circular 8162, 1963.

[34] Clarke, F. E. "Industrial Re-use of Water," *Industrial and Engineering Chemistry,* Vol. 54, No. 2 (1962), p. 25.

[35] Partridge, E. E., and Paulson, E. G. "Supply, Design and Operate for Water Economy," *Chemical Engineering,* Vol. 70, No. 12 (1963), p. 127.

[36] Mantel, H. W., *et al. Industrial Incentives for Water Pollution Abatement.* New York: Institute of Public Administration, 1965.

[37] Kneese, A. V. "Economic Challenges Must Be Met," *Chemical Engineering Progress,* Vol. 59, No. 11 (1963), p. 23.

[38] Kneese, A. V. *The Economics of Regional Water Quality Management.* Baltimore: Johns Hopkins Press, 1964.

[39] Poston, H. W., *et al.* "A Water Quality Control Program for the Illinois River Basin." Paper presented at the Annual Meeting of the Central States Water Pollution Control Association, Urbana, Illinois, 1964, p. 14.

[40] Kinney, J. E. "Blind Spots in Pollution Control," *Industrial Water Engineering,* Vol. 2, No. 5 (1965).

[41] Sercu, C. L. "How a Chemical Company Solved a Water Crisis," *Effluent and Water Treatment Magazine* (London), Vol. 2, No. 10 (1962).

The Social Value of Water Recreational Facilities Resulting from an Improvement in Water Quality: The Delaware Estuary

Paul Davidson, F. Gerard Adams, and *Joseph Seneca**

In many rural areas, outdoor recreational facilities may still be, both conceptually and in practice, free goods. In large, growing, urban regions, however, water recreational facilities are economic goods (at least conceptually even if in practice there is no market price), that are becoming increasingly scarce relative to demand. The rapidly growing urban population in the United States has put increasing pressure on the demand for water recreational facilities, while the growth of industry has reduced the supply either by diverting the water to industrial uses or by lowering the quality of the water to a level that does not permit recreational activities.

Two requirements are necessary for water recreational activities: (1) the quality of the water (oxygen content, purity, absence of odors, etc.) must be high enough to permit such activities as fishing, swimming, and other water sports; and (2) various accessory commodities used in these activities must be readily available. The rapidly rising sales of pleasure boats, and equipment for fishing, picnicking, and water sports are indica-

* Respectively: Professor of Economics, Rutgers—The State University; Associate Professor of Economics, and Research Fellow in Economics, University of Pennsylvania. The research was supported by a grant from Resources for the Future, Inc. The work was done at the Economics Research Services Unit of the Wharton School of Finance and Commerce, University of Pennsylvania. The Survey Research Center of the University of Michigan provided the data on which the empirical study of recreational activity is based; the authors would like particularly to thank Professors George Katona and Eva Mueller. The cost data were provided by the Delaware Estuary Comprehensive Study of the U.S. Public Health Service; in this connection, the authors would like to thank Dr. Robert V. Thomann.

tive of the growth in demand for outdoor water recreational facilities. In response to this demand, it appears that a reasonably efficient private market has developed to allocate resources into economic activities that provide consumers with the necessary recreational accessories. It is also apparent from the decrease of fish life in most estuaries, the increase of water pollution, and the frequent need for governmental agencies to restock existing fishing preserves, that the private sector has failed to allocate a similar quantity of resources for maintaining the quality of water facilities.[1] This market failure implies a divergence between social and private benefits and costs.

The purposes of this paper are to identify the major causes of market failure in outdoor water recreational facilities, and to attempt to develop a method of estimating social benefits and costs of such facilities. The method is demonstrated in a case study of the Delaware estuary. It is hoped that this study will provide guidelines useful in making similar estimates for other estuaries near large urban areas. The empirical aspects of the paper are mainly of a reconnaissance nature.

CAUSES OF MARKET FAILURE[2]

Bator has defined market failure in terms of allocation theory as "the failure of a more or less idealized system of price-market institutions to sustain 'desirable' activities or to estop 'undesirable' activities" [ref. 1, p. 351]. He suggests five ways in which market failure may be exhibited: *by existence*—that is, if there is no set of relative market prices that will accurately reflect the maximization of a welfare function by being equated to a set of marginal rates of substitution; *by signal*—when the price system guides profit-maximizing entrepreneurs into a position of profit minimum or local profit-maximums rather than the maximum maximorum; *by incentive*—when the price system allows negative profits in some desired industries; *by structure*—if self-policing perfect competition is not present, then prices will not lead to Pareto optimality; and *by enforcement*—that is, if there is some arbitrary legal or organizational imperfection in the market which prevents introduction of proper ac-

---

[1] This does not imply that a private market in water recreational facilities has not been developed; the increasing popularity of the home swimming pool and the private mountain lake resort attests to the existence of a private market. Given the obvious larger scale economies of providing water recreational facilities, however, it would appear that, for example, the home swimming pool market is a poor "second-best" alternative.

[2] This section is based primarily on Bator's excellent taxonomic paper [ref. 1].

counting prices for inputs or outputs into profit-maximizing production decisions or utility-maximizing consumption decisions.

Bator has suggested that these modes, listed in Table 1, are due to three possible, but not mutually exclusive, causes of market failure: ownership externalities, technical externalities, and public goods externalities.[3]

In the case of ownership externalities, the basic cause of market failure is non-appropriation or the inability of the owner of a factor of production (because of legal or other reasons) to charge for the value of its services. This is failure by enforcement. Ownership externalities play an important part in the failure of the private market to provide a sufficient quality of water for outdoor recreational facilities.

Technical externalities are due either to indivisibilities or to increasing returns to scale. With indivisibilities, there are kinks in the firm's cost curves. Although production may occur when price (P) equals marginal cost (MC) and exceeds average cost (AC), this position may represent a local profit maximum rather than the profit maximum maximorum. Thus, we have failure by signal.

Alternatively, even in the absence of indivisibilities, there may be increasing returns to scale, so that with marginal cost-pricing, $P = MC < AC$, losses would be incurred, and we have failure by incentive. The neo-classical economists recognized, of course, that perfect competition and increasing returns to scale were incompatible. Increasing returns normally lead to monopoly, resulting in market failure by structure.

A combination of indivisibilities and increasing returns to scale are important elements in the production of outdoor water recreational facilities, and an unfettered private sector will not properly allocate resources to this activity.

Public goods externalities occur when an individual's consumption of a good "leads to no subtractions from any other individual's consumption of that good" [ref. 2, p. 387]. Accordingly, there is no need to ration public goods between individuals, and no set of market prices for public goods is useful for individual production and/or consumption decisions.[4]

Since there is no set of market prices which "will efficiently ration any fixed bill of [public] goods" [ref. 1, p. 371] a private market for public goods will fail by existence.

---

[3] An externality is defined as any situation where some Paretian costs and/or benefits are not taken into individuals' (decentralized) production and/or consumption decisions which are based solely on market costs and prices.

[4] Thus if public good X is offered for sale at a price that equals its marginal production costs, each satisfaction-maximizing buyer will equate his marginal rate of substitution between X and private good Y to the ratio of the prices of X and Y (where $P_y = MC_y$); consequently X will be underutilized.

TABLE 1.

Causes and Modes of Market Failure

Mode \ Cause	Ownership externality	Technical externality (indivisibilities in the source of supply or economies of scale)	Public goods externality
Existence			No set of market prices can properly reflect benefits, e.g., national defense, lighthouses, knowledge, non-peak demand
Signal		With kinks in cost curves $P = MC \geq AC$ but not maximum maximorum	
Incentive		$P = MC < AC$ due to increasing returns to scale	
Structure		$P > AC \geq MC$ in the case of monopoly pricing	
Enforcement	Legal or organizational imperfection, e.g., shared natural resources, investment spillovers		

This non-rationing aspect of public goods externalities has a significant implication. It suggests that for non-storable goods, whenever there are indivisibilities in the production process and simultaneously the total quantity demanded at a zero price is less than capacity production at that price, the quantity demanded by buyer A will not reduce the amount available to satisfy the demand of buyer B, i.e., there is a public goods externality. (If a commodity is storable, on the other hand, the fact that the total quantity demanded at a zero price is less than capacity production does not necessarily lead to a public good externality, since the excess supply can be held over to accommodate demand in future periods.) Thus, in periods of off-peak demand when the marginal production costs of non-storable goods are near zero, both technical and public goods externalities may come into play at the same time.[5] We find this situation is relevant for outdoor water recreational facilities.

Externalities and the Estuary

It is not difficult to show why the provision of water recreational facilities in an estuary will exhibit market failure because of a blend of the three types of externality conditions.

An estuary by its very nature leads to externalities. An estuary, such as the Delaware, covers a large geographical area and passes through the property of many individuals, firms, and governmental units. Therefore, "water use and waste disposal by one unit can have a direct effect on the operations of others." [Ref. 3, p. 3.] The fact that upstream users cannot, in a free market, be forced to pay for reducing the quality of the water that is passed on downstream (mainly by adding pollutants) indicates an important market failure by enforcement due to an ownership externality. It is the fugacious nature of water quality which prevents market incentives from properly allocating resources [ref. 4, pp. 70–71].

There is sufficient evidence that upstream users have reduced the quality of the water in the Delaware River from Trenton to the sea to such a degree that it has been made almost unusable for water recreational activities. In order for sport fish to survive and flourish a certain minimum level of dissolved oxygen must be present in the surrounding

---

[5] The classical case of bridge crossings at off-peak hours is an ideal example of a production process of a non-storable good which exhibits both technological and public goods externalities. (Bator, however, is not clear on this point and consequently he worries whether bridge crossings—at less than capacity—are technical or public goods externalities [ref. 1, p. 377].) Moreover, there may be a number of non-storable goods whose production processes exhibit indivisibilities and simultaneously have no physical capacity limitations (e.g., TV and radio broadcasts, lighthouses). A private market for such goods will fail because of a blend of technical and public goods externalities.

water. The upper Delaware River, above Trenton, still contains some of the best sport-fishing waters in the area. The dissolved oxygen level has remained high as the natural bacterial processes have been able to cope with the relatively small amounts of organic waste entering the river. The estuary region, however, has seen a continual deterioration of water quality and a decline in the level of fish life.

Statistics collected by the Delaware Board of Fish and Game Commissioners show that the catches of shad in parts of the estuary adjacent to the state of Delaware have decreased by 96.4 per cent between 1880 and 1960. This decline has occurred despite repeated attempts to bolster the shad population by artificial means and it

> . . . is now generally accepted that such stockings were useless, and that the shad runs have decreased due to the failure of the juvenile fish to survive the low oxygen water of the upper Delaware River on their return from the spawning grounds. This condition has been brought about by the continual increase in domestic and industrial pollution from Trenton to Marcus Hook. . . . [Ref. 5, p. 14.][6]

The level of dissolved oxygen depends on many factors.[7] When organic wastes enter a stream they are converted into inorganic salts by the bacteria normally present in the water. If the waste level is not too high, this purification process utilizes oxygen and does not produce offensive odors. If, however, the concentration of organic wastes exceeds a certain level, then the conversion process occurs anaerobically (by bacteria not using free oxygen) and offensive odors are emitted. The presence of wastes normally leads to some biochemical oxygen demand (BOD). The rate at which oxygen is demanded from the water depends not only on waste levels but also on such factors as temperature, rate of aeration, flow of the stream, and chemical characteristics of the water.

On the other hand, certain factors restore dissolved oxygen to the water. This reaeration process depends on such factors as velocity of stream flow, area of air-water interface, and photosynthesis.

Of course, the level of dissolved oxygen is not the only parameter of water quality.[8] In the empirical section we use varying dissolved oxygen (D.O.) levels as indexes of threshold conditions necessary for various water activities. The associated costs for each D.O. level are used to con-

[6] The Delaware River Basin Commission has also noted that a zone of near oxygenless water in a portion of the tidal estuary has nearly wiped out the Delaware Basin's anadromous fish population [ref. 6, p. 54].

[7] The following technical information is based primarily on Kneese's work [ref. 3, ch. 2].

[8] Obviously the presence of such pollutants as cyanide salts or certain pathogens will make the water unfit for recreational activities, no matter what the dissolved oxygen level.

struct a "supply" schedule. It is recognized that many other conditions affect water quality: for example, turbidity, temperature, and flow variations. Although we are aware of these pertinent considerations, consistent cost data are presently only available for oxygen levels; thus, for pragmatic reasons dissolved oxygen is used here as a first approximation of an index of water quality for recreation purposes.

The level of dissolved oxygen in the water of downstream users depends in large measure on the activity and uses of the water made by the upstream users. This ownership externality is based on the fugacious nature of water quality, and does not depend in any way upon recreational activity per se being one of the specified activities.[9]

In a free market, of course, the upstream community could not collect payment from the downstream beneficiaries of water quality improvement nor would it compensate them for the effects of pollution.

The most usual corrective policy for an ownership externality is to integrate the independent users of the factor or facilities [ref. 1, p. 375; ref. 7, pp. 97–98]. In the case of an estuary, this implies putting the entire estuary under a single management[10] so as to internalize all benefits and costs. But although integration would eliminate market failure by enforcement, technical externalities would remain in the production of water recreational facilities. Consequently, control of water quality by integration is not sufficient to assure the proper allocation of resources into recreational facilities by means of an otherwise free market.

The estuary is basically a natural indivisible source of water recreational facilities. There are, of course, some alternative sources within geographical proximity, such as fresh water lakes for fishing, the New Jersey and Delaware ocean coastline for swimming and boating, as well as 3,500 acres of public water recreational areas. From a quantitative point of view, however, were fishing possible in the estuary, the supply of fishing water there would far exceed that available from surrounding lakes. Even more important, however, is the fact that the lakes, the upper Delaware River, and the ocean shore are all more distant from the centers of population than the estuary[11] and consequently, if equal supply

---

[9] Kneese prefers to call this a "technical link" between economic units [ref. 3, p. 12], but we shall restrict the concept of technical externalities to the definition provided by Bator.

[10] In the Delaware estuary, some degree of integration has been accomplished by establishment of the Delaware River Basin Commission whose function is to provide a comprehensive multipurpose water resources plan which "will bring the greatest benefits and produce the most efficient service in the public welfare."

[11] In 1963, approximately 5½ million people lived in the Delaware Basin from the Trenton-Morrisville area to the Pennsylvania-Delaware state line (on both sides of the river), while less than 900,000 lived on the Basin area above Trenton and 360,000 in the two ocean counties bordering the mouth of the estuary.

facilities were available in the estuary, other things being equal, they would be more desirable than the existing more distant facilities.

Accordingly, the estuary would be the major source of water recreational facilities, and a free market would fail by structure (i.e., because of monopoly pricing) as well as by signal and incentive due to increasing returns to scale and indivisibilities[12] in the production of water recreational facilities.

Since the source of this externality is basically the indivisibility of the source of supply, it might be assumed that efficient allocation could be accomplished by some sort of integrated public utility arrangement with private ownership and a marginal cost-pricing policy with subsidies to make up any deficits. Although such a policy would eliminate market failure due to technical externalities, the optimum solution in the market still would not be obtained because of failure by existence, as shown in the following discussion.

Public Goods Externality and Water Recreation. There are three interrelated factors which lead to failure by existence (due to public goods externality) in the market for outdoor water recreation facilities in an estuary. These factors are inherent in (a) the time variability on the demand side of water recreation and involve questions of off-peak demand, the option demand for water recreational facilities, and a phenomenon here called "learning by doing"; and in (b) the lack of storability of the commodity on the supply side.

1. Off-Peak Demand and Public Goods. When indivisibilities exist in the production of any non-storable commodity, such that X units per period of the good (where $X > 1$) must be produced, if any at all are to be produced, then the marginal cost of all the units between 1 and X is zero (or negligible). If the demand for that commodity during any period is such that less than the quantity X is desired at a zero price, then we may state that we have a period of "off-peak" demand. In the off-peak period, what individual A consumes does not in any way restrict the amount that is left for B to consume as long as the total quantity that would be consumed by all the individuals is equal to or less than X (at a zero price). In such a period of off-peak demand, therefore, any good which has the aforementioned type of indivisibility in production and is not storable exhibits the characteristics of a public good. Accordingly,

---

[12] Kneese suggests that: "Economies of scale in the production and distribution of a standard quality are such that the costs of separately controlling quality for each individual household are prohibitive" [ref. 3, p. 27].

there is no set of prices which would efficiently ration these goods during off-peak periods.[13]

In the case of outdoor water recreational facilities, for example, the production of a level of water quality necessary to bring back enough fish life to attract people to sport fishing in the Delaware estuary would exhibit sufficient indivisibilities so that most days of the year will have "off-peak" fishing demands.

Water recreational facilities in the Delaware estuary have the same characteristics as a bridge over the Delaware between Philadelphia and Camden. It is the very nature of the bridge that there are indivisibilities in the production of its services and that its services are non-storable; therefore, any positive toll (user charge) during the off-peak period is economically inefficient. Outdoor water recreational facilities are a blend of "technical" and "public goods" externalities and the "correct" price for an extra fisherman or swimmer (below capacity of the facility) is zero— the same as for an extra boat using the facilities of a lighthouse or an extra stroller on a bridge. A zero price, however, cannot properly allocate scarce resources in a free market, and so government must accept an allocative role.

The public good externality due to off-peak demand for water recreational facilities is basically due to a combination of two forces: the time variability of demand for the good, and the non-storability of the good (e.g., fishing activity days) over time so that excess supply quantities cannot be carried over to periods of peak demand. It is this time dimension on both the demand (variability) side and the supply (storability) side which leads to a failure of the water recreational facilities market by existence.

Moreover, because of the inherent time variability of demand, two other factors may contribute to failure by existence on the demand side— failure due to option demand, and failure due to learning-by-doing.

2. Option Demand for Water Recreational Facilities.[14]   Individual consumption commodities apparently possess characteristics that give them a public-good nature. The principal characteristics of such goods are: infrequency and uncertainty of consumption by individual consumers; costliness of reactivating or increasing production that has been curtailed; and non-storability of product [ref. 8, pp. 471–72].

---

[13] This is particularly true because of the leisure nature of sport fishing (as well as other water recreational activities) which implies that weekdays will almost always be off-peak.

[14] This discussion is based on Weisbrod's work [ref. 8].

Many goods, of course, possess the characteristics of infrequency and uncertainty of purchase by consumers and indivisibilities in production, but do not have a public-good nature—for example, the demand for durables such as automobiles. In these cases, marginal cost calculations would take into consideration the possibility of carrying at relatively low economic costs the excess production from slack to peak demand periods plus the user-cost of capital facilities, and would, therefore, in a world of perfect knowledge about the future, provide sufficient guidelines for the proper allocation of production and sales over time. The additional characteristic of non-storability—a characteristic that infrequently purchased durable goods usually do not have—makes water recreation a public good.[15]

At any point of time, only a small proportion of the population may be purchasing the product (e.g., be engaging in fishing activity). Many others may plan to use the product (or facilities) some time in the future. In order to guarantee that the facility will be available in the future, some of the potential users would be willing to pay a price, that is, they should be willing to purchase an option on the product for future use. In the case of outdoor recreational facilities in an estuary, there is no normal market mechanism where this demand for future facilities can be exercised. Normally, only charges against present users can be made.

In the case of water recreation in the Delaware estuary, if new facilities are actually made available, the utilization by present consumers would not reduce the quantity of facilities available for future potential users, so that the latter group may have the option on future use without having to pay for it. Marginal cost-pricing for present users would involve only present marginal costs of production and, because of the physical impossibility of storing, these costs would not include any carrying charges. Consequently, when someone exercises his option demand, the price he pays will not include a charge for having the facilities available when wanted.[16]

---

[15] There will still remain some categories of infrequently purchased durable goods which are not easily categorized as either public or private goods only, e.g., fashion-oriented durable goods. In the case of fashion-oriented goods, obsolescence because of fashion changes may increase the user costs of inventory sufficiently to make the carrying of inventory economically undesirable even if physically possible. (An obvious example is the daily newspaper.) Can such goods be left to a private market? Fuller analysis of the time dimension of product markets is essential in welfare economics. For an interesting discussion of the time dimension aspects see [ref. 9, ch. 17].

[16] In private (monopoly) swim clubs, for example, this option often takes the form of purchasing a subscription bond for entering members, which may later be resold. Those who do not purchase such bonds are excluded from using the facilities.

184

Thus, as Weisbrod concludes, the

> . . . provision of the option is a pure collective good . . . it (the option to consume in the future) may be "consumed" (enjoyed) by all persons simultaneously, and the consumption by one person does not subtract from the consumption opportunities for others. . . . Of course, it must be reiterated that the option value is important for resource-allocation only to the extent that when added to user demand it would affect the level of supply—that is, would make the difference between remaining open and closing, or between providing a given increment in service or not. . . . [Ref. 8, p. 473.]

Obviously, the option demand can exist to a greater or less degree for many goods. Whether this option demand is a public good demand and whether it is a significantly important factor depends upon the lack of storability of the product, the infrequency of purchase, and the costliness of expanding production in response to fluctuations in demand. It would appear that all these factors are significant in outdoor water recreational activities. First, fishing, swimming, or boating activity days cannot be stored. Second, as is indicated in the empirical portion of this paper, capital costs for providing increments in the quality of the water in an estuary are substantial. Third, the demand for outdoor recreational activity days is closely related to erratic fluctuations in weather conditions as well as to normal seasonal variations in climate. This adds an uncertain and variable frequency of use to the daily and seasonal variability of demand for such activities.

Data collected by the Michigan Survey Research Center indicate the infrequency with which a majority of the population engage in such activities. During the twelve months prior to the survey, the percentages of the sample population that did not engage in swimming, fishing, and boating were 57.3 per cent, 61.0 per cent, and 71.0 per cent, respectively. At any point of time, only a minority of the population is engaging in these activities. Among the non-participants, however, a significant proportion (over 10 per cent of each group) indicated a desire to engage in these activities in the future. This suggests a significant public good externality because of option demand.

Furthermore, the data indicate a large proportion of participants in each activity would like to engage in more activity days in the future than they have in the past. This desire for increased future activity by those already participating is suggestive of the public good externality described as the "learning-by-doing" concept, and provides additional evidence of the importance of the option demand.

185

3. Learning-by-doing. The relationship between present and future potential use of outdoor water recreational facilities leads to a third possible cause of a public good externality.

Closely related to the option demand factor is the learning-by-doing relationship. If water recreational facilities are neither available nor easily accessible, people tend not to engage in these activities. Should they participate, however, their realized enjoyment often exceeds their expectations, and as a result they will tend to increase their demand for facilities. Moreover, skill is often essential for the enjoyment of these activities. When facilities are not readily available, skills will not be developed and, consequently, there may be little desire to participate in these activities. If facilities are made available, opportunities to acquire skill increase, and user demand tends to rise rapidly over time as individuals learn to enjoy these activities. Thus, participation in and enjoyment of water recreational activities by the present generation will stimulate future demand without diminishing the supply presently available.[17] Learning-by-doing, to the extent it increases future demand, suggests an interaction between present and future demand functions, which will result in a public good externality, as present demand enters into the utility function of future users.[18]

Moreover, since there is at present a paucity of water recreational facilities readily available in the Delaware estuary area, the impact of adding facilities on both the option demand and learning-by-doing external effects is an important consideration. To gain some understanding of the effect of adding to facilities in this region, a frequency distribution of fishing participation rates in relation to the available sport-fishing water-acres per capita in the region was made for the respondents of the Michigan survey. This distribution indicates that, as the quantity (and to some extent the quality as the probability of overcrowding diminishes) of facilities increases, the proportion of non-participants who have no desire to go fishing in the future declines from 54.9 to 41.3 per cent; while the proportion of non-participants who indicate a desire to engage in the activity in the future progressively decreases from 11.3 to 2.2 per cent as more of this group of non-participants shift to fishing. Thus, it would appear that as facilities become more readily available, groups of non-

[17] In fact, as suggested above, sufficient present demand for the facilities in question may be the only way a future source of supply can be assured.

[18] Throughout this analysis we have ignored an obvious public good by-product externality associated with improved water quality—reduced odors and/or a pleasant-looking river—which is available to all consumers on a non-rationable basis [ref. 15, p. 12]. Furthermore, the provision of recreational facilities may also reduce the incidence of juvenile delinquency. The importance of such externalities, however, can be exaggerated and they are particularly difficult to quantify.

participants tend to exercise their option demand and become active fishermen. Accordingly, one might infer that the option demand for fishing facilities is quite high in the Delaware estuary area because of the relative lack of fishing waters.

Furthermore, as facilities improve, not only does the proportion of fishing participants rise, but the proportion of the participants who would like to engage in the activity even more in the future tends to increase. This suggests that the learning-by-doing externality increases when additional facilities are provided.

Theoretical Conclusions

This analysis indicates that all three types of externalities—ownership, technical, and public goods—are involved in the market for outdoor water recreational activities in an estuary. No wonder that the private sector has failed to properly allocate resources in this market. Even if this market were organized under an active policy of integrating the potential facilities under a single private management and subjecting the management to public utility price controls, it would still exhibit failure by existence due to the public goods nature of the product over time.

The inevitable conclusion is that, if an approach to economic efficiency is desired, water recreational activities in an estuary cannot be left to the private sector. Even if the activities are placed under the public sector, *positive user charges will be inefficient.*[19]

Public authorities are left with two exceedingly difficult problems: the quality of the facilities, if any, to be provided, and financing the construction and maintenance of these facilities. The remainder of this paper is concerned primarily with an approach to solving the first issue.

A COST-BENEFIT ANALYSIS OF THE RECREATIONAL VALUE OF AN IMPROVEMENT IN WATER QUALITY IN THE DELAWARE ESTUARY

Cost-benefit methodology has been developed as the basic tool for deciding the economic desirability of specific water projects.[20] In general, unless there is a budgetary constraint, economists agree that a project should be undertaken whenever the present value of the associated

---

[19] In the short run, a positive user charge may be made during peak-load periods in order to achieve optimality-in-exchange. However, see below for a further discussion of capacity.

[20] The use of cost-benefit analysis in water resources projects has been amply discussed elsewhere [ref. 3, 4, 10, 11, 12, 13, 14, 15].

stream of net benefits discounted at the appropriate social rate of discount is greater than present cost of the facilities. This is the guiding rule in the analysis which follows.

The major problem in cost-benefit analysis of a water resource project is how to correctly identify and quantify the benefits and costs. The latter are the opportunity costs of resources at full employment. They are usually assumed to be approximately equal to the money outlays on capital construction.

The measurement of benefits is much more complex. First, the presence of ownership externalities suggests that not all the beneficiaries can be identified by observing market transactions. One must identify by other means all the beneficiaries, including those who gain by means of spillovers, while being careful at all times not to double-count the benefits.

Second, and perhaps more important, because of the public goods externality aspect, market prices, even if they exist, are not likely to be indexes of benefits. As Bator emphasized:

> . . . a pricing game will not induce consumers truthfully to reveal their preferences. It pays each consumer to understate his desire for X relative to Y, since his enjoyment of X is a function only of total X, rather than, as is true of a pure private good, just as that fraction of X he pays for. [Ref. 1, p. 370.]

Thus, even if a market price for water recreational facilities is available, it will be an underestimate of benefits.[21] Moreover, to the extent that public authorities are already providing some water recreational facilities as a public good at a zero price, the market price in the rest of the market cannot easily be interpreted. Consequently, a method of measuring benefits without appealing to market prices must be adopted.[22]

An attempt at such a method has been developed for this study. Schematically, our method can be described as follows:

An estimate of the relationship between total capital costs and the resulting improvement in the quality of water (as measured by dissolved oxygen) is obtained. This relationship can be graphed as an upward

---

[21] Some investigators have attempted to use interviewing techniques (in a pricing game) in order to estimate benefits by obtaining a measure of the consumers' willingness to pay for the use of the facilities. For example, see [ref. 16].

[22] Many ingenious attempts to build a demand curve for recreational activities (in the absence of observable market prices) have been made. (See, for example, [ref. 17].) No critical discussion of these methods will be presented here, since most of them involve the demand for already existing facilities, while we are interested in analyzing the benefits that will accrue from proposed facilities. For a concise, lucid discussion of these other methods, see [ref. 18].

sloping curve such as *TC* in Figure 1a. From this total cost function, an upward sloping marginal cost function can be derived (*MC* in Figure 1b).

A certain minimum quality level of water must be maintained if consumers are to engage in a particular recreational activity. Relying on dissolved oxygen only as a measure of water quality, we may postulate that at least 3 milligrams per liter (Mg/L) of oxygen are necessary to eliminate offensive odors and therefore to allow boating, 4 Mg/L for sport fishing and 5 Mg/L for swimming. On the quality axis these threshold values for the different activities can be indicated as in Figure 1c. Once a threshold value is obtained or surpassed, consumers can engage in the corresponding water-oriented activity.

If we can plot the present value of total activity days (of all water recreational activity) in units of calendar days—i.e., the future prospective stream of days of activity discounted back to a current day basis—on the ordinate axis against different levels of water quality on the abscissa, then, for a given community, we should obtain an upward

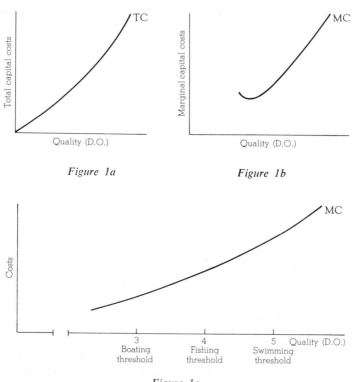

Figure 1a

Figure 1b

Figure 1c

sloping curve such as TAD in Figure 2a.[23] This TAD schedule depicts the present value (in days) of recreational activity for each level of water quality. From this total-days curve, we can obtain a downward sloping marginal activities days curve (MAD) as in Figure 2b.[24] The latter schedule indicates increments in the present value of calendar activity days for each increment in water quality as a result of facility and water improvement.

These TAD and MAD curves can be converted to present value of total net benefits and marginal net benefits functions (i.e., net of operating costs), respectively, if an appropriate factor can be established for converting units of calendar days into units of benefits (satisfactions in terms of dollars). Assume a scalar conversion factor exists (call it X dollars per day). The points on the TAD and MAD schedules can be multiplied by X to obtain the present value (in dollars) of total and marginal benefits for water recreational activities associated with various levels of water quality. If we then place this derived marginal benefit (MB) schedule on the same axes as the MC schedule of Figure 1b, welfare would be maximized if the quality of the water is improved up to the point where the MB and MC schedules intersect (at point Q_1 in Figure 2c).

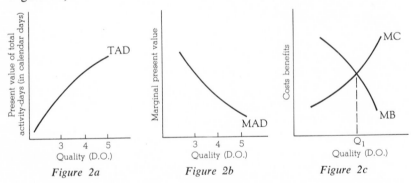

| Figure 2a | Figure 2b | Figure 2c |

[23] For example, for fishing this is obtained by discounting the total activity days that the population would engage in each year. Thus, if f_1 is total fishing activity days demanded in year 1, and f_2 is total fishing activity days in year 2, etc., and r is the appropriate social rate of discount, then the present value (in units of calendar days) of total fishing activity days (TAD_f) can be computed from the equation:

$$TAD_f = \frac{f_1}{(1+r)} + \frac{f_2}{(1+r)^2} + \cdots + \frac{f_n}{(1+r)^n}.$$

To simplify the discussion, we assume at this point that the TAD curve is smooth and continuous rather than the step function implied by the threshold D.O. value for each activity.

[24] It is not necessary that the MAD curve be downward sloping throughout its entire length. Actually the MAD curve need only cut the MC curve from above.

Consequently, if as a first assumption we postulate that the only beneficiaries of improvement in the quality of the water in the Delaware
estuary are consumers of water recreational activities,[25] then for any
given value of X there will be a unique marginal benefits curve. Thus in
Figure 3, a family of marginal benefits curves (one curve for each postulated value of X, where $X_1 < X_2 \cdots < X_n$) are superimposed on the
MC curve. This family of curves suggests that the optimal quality level
depends on the propensity of the community to engage in recreational
activity days and the appropriate value of X. Given the costs of improving water quality and consumers' demand for recreational activities based

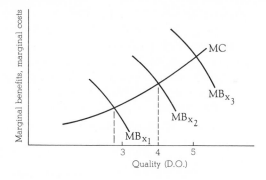

Figure 3

on certain socioeconomic characteristics such as income, race, age, etc.,
then the value of X (which might be termed the average benefit or value
per activity-day for the representative consumer) determines the optimal
level of water quality. Thus if X_1 is the relevant value, then, according
to Figure 3, it would not be desirable to improve the water quality to
the threshold level necessary to permit even sport boating on the estuary.
If X_2 were the relevant parameter, then quality should be improved to a
level which would permit boating and fishing but not swimming. Consequently, "we are not confronted with a question of absolutes—of clean
water versus dirty water or of fish versus factories—but one of efficient

---

In fact, in some regions increasing marginal present values are likely. Ultimately,
however, the slope of the MAD curve will decrease and eventually there will be
diminishing marginal recreational activities with improvements in quality. Similarly, it is not necessary for the MC curve to be upward sloping throughout its
length. Ultimately, however, there will be increasing marginal costs for further
improvements in water quality.

[25] If there are other beneficiaries, welfare maximization would require adding
the benefits accruing to the non-recreational group into the total benefits function
before deriving the appropriate marginal benefits curve.

adjustment to water reuse." [Ref. 12, p. vii.] As long as the improvement in water quality can be viewed as a continuum of possibilities the problem "reduces to setting the marginal cost of another degree of enhancement of quality equal to the marginal value to consumers of that enhancement." [Ref. 4, p. 159.]

In summary, our mode of attack is as follows: First, we utilize preliminary (unpublished) estimates of a Public Health Service study to produce the total cost curve; second, we use data from a survey conducted by the Michigan Survey Research Center to estimate empirical relationships between activity days and certain socioeconomic characteristics of the participants, and some rough measures of available facilities. Using population projections made by the Penn-Jersey Transportation Study, it will be possible to estimate the demand for fishing, swimming, and boating activity days for the Delaware estuary for each year through 1990. These estimates are prepared in two versions—with and without improvement in the water quality of the Delaware. Using these estimates for each activity[26] we are able to fit a TAD function. From the latter we obtain a MAD function for the relevant region of water quality and using the conversion factor X, the family of MB curves as in Figure 3 can be established.

Finally, the MC curve derived from the Public Health Service cost estimates in conjunction with a chosen MB curve can be used to suggest, as a first approximation, the optimum level of water quality in the Delaware estuary. Alternatively, the level of the conversion factor X which will justify a chosen degree of water quality improvement can be determined.

EMPIRICAL ANALYSIS OF WATER RECREATION ACTIVITY

The basic source of information was a survey of 1,352 households carried out by the University of Michigan Survey Research Center in the fall of 1959.[27] Among the many socioeconomic and attitudinal questions asked of each household, were inquiries into the frequency of engaging in swimming, fishing, and boating over the preceding twelve months.

A multivariate regression analysis of the data was undertaken to isolate the variables that influence participation in boating, fishing, and swimming as a recreational activity. Initially, regression analysis was used to determine the probability of participation in each of these sports by

[26] See equation in footnote 23.

[27] For a discussion of the data and for other statistical studies on them, see [ref. 19].

means of dummy dependent variables with an 0–1 code for "no partici-pation" during the previous twelve months versus "participation" (re-gardless of amount). As a second stage in the analysis, the amount of participation in days was studied, considering only those individuals who had actually participated. The independent variables consisted of two types: socioeconomic variables, e.g., age, income, sex, etc.; and locational or physical factors, i.e., variables related to region of the coun-try, facilities available, and urban–non-urban considerations.

In general, the socioeconomic variables were found to be more impor-tant in determining whether individuals participate or not in a water recreational activity, while the locational factors were significant in only a few instances. Yet, interestingly, the socioeconomic variables differed in importance among the activities, and occasionally the physical factors played an important role. A subsequent analysis of several variables measuring the presence of water facilities was added. The results of this addition follow the discussion of the socioeconomic and locational variables.

The following are the variables used in our empirical analysis:

Variable	Symbol	Description
Age	A	discrete midpoint values of class intervals
Income	Y	discrete midpoint values of class intervals
Sex	S	0 if female 1 if male
Education	E	1 if grade school highest attainment 2 if high school highest attainment 3 if college highest attainment
Race	R	0 if non-white 1 if white
Life cycle	L_1	0 if no children in household 1 if children in household
	L_2	0 if no children over 5 years old 1 if children over 5 years old
Urbanization (belt)	U	0 if urban location 1 if suburban or outlying location
Occupation	O	0 if blue collar 1 if white collar
Region	G	0 if Northeast or North Central 1 if West or South
Participates in fishing	FP	0 if non-participant 1 if participant
Participates in swimming	SP	0 if non-participant 1 if participant
Participates in boating	BP	0 if non-participant 1 if participant
Water per capita	W	area of sport fishing water per capita by state, 1960
Expert rating of swimming facili-ties in primary sampling unit	SPS	discrete values of 1 through 5
Expert rating of fishing facilities in primary sampling unit	FPS	discrete values of 1 through 5
Coastal area presence	C	0 inland area 1 coastline or Great Lakes present

193

Probability of Swimming Participation. In the probability of participation analysis, the best results were obtained for swimming. In this case almost all of the socioeconomic variables tested proved significant and together they explained 28 per cent of the observed variation. The basic equation for the probability of swimming participation is:

$$SP = .4298 - .0112A + .1929Y + .0559S + .1248E + .1761R$$
$$(.0644) \quad (.0008) \quad (.0407) \quad (.0244) \quad (.0184) \quad (.0397)$$

This basic equation yielded an R^2 (adjusted for degrees of freedom) of .280.

As one would expect, age is of considerable importance in a physically oriented activity such as swimming. In fact, age alone accounts for 18 per cent of the observed variation. Moreover, a frequency distribution of swimming activity by age showed a rise during younger ages, a peak in the 18–24 group, and then a marked decline.

The income variable, though yielding a small regression coefficient, is highly significant for swimming participation and is responsible for explaining an additional 5 per cent of the variation. The sex of the respondent is only marginally significant and adds little to increasing the explanation of the observed variation. Education and race maintain their statistical significance throughout the swimming analysis.

Two other socioeconomic variables, life-cycle (i.e., the presence or absence of children in the household) and occupation (white collar or blue collar), when added individually or simultaneously to the basic equation, yielded at best a marginal improvement. The life-cycle variable gives a negative value implying that the absence of children is a factor making for participation, but the regression coefficient is only marginally significant, and the result for the occupation variable is statistically non-significant.

The locational factors were added to the basic equation, first one at a time then all together. The region variable shows a negative but non-significant coefficient. The urban–non-urban coefficient is negative and almost significant at the 5 per cent level. The negative sign implies that (while urban–non-urban considerations are of minimal importance for swimming) urban populations may be slightly more inclined to engage in recreational swimming. This is not as surprising as it may first appear, since, of the three water sports, participation in swimming requires the least amount of natural facilities. For urban populations, swimming pools and swim clubs as well as nearby lakes and beaches may partly offset the advantage of the greater natural facilities of non-urban areas. Moreover, the greater natural facilities of rural areas may encourage people to engage in alternative water and non-water recreational activities (such as fishing, hiking, camping), while the paucity of such facilities in urban regions may concentrate participation on swimming.

The non-significance of the regional variables seems to imply the universality of the sport throughout the country, so that no region shows a markedly higher participation rate, although tabular results show a slightly higher participation rate in the west and northeast. When the region and urban variables are added simultaneously to the basic equation, they both appear non-significant.

The availability of water recreational facilities in each of the primary sampling units of the Michigan sample has been rated by a panel of experts on a 5-point scale ranging from "no facilities" to "very good facilities." The addition of this rating variable to the basic equation added very little, its coefficient being negative and non-significant. The negative sign might, if the coefficient were significant, imply that experts' judgments about the availability of facilities were inversely related to the decision on whether to participate or not, but this does not imply that the rating might not be important in indicating the number of times a participant engages in the activity in a twelve-month period.

In summary, the probability of swimming participation analysis suggests that the socioeconomic characteristics of age, income, education, and race are the most influential factors determining whether an individual swims. Physical and location factors are not important in the swim–no swim decision, i.e., if a person likes to swim he will do so, at least once during the year, apparently regardless of the facility and area factors. Of course, this conclusion is only in reference to the "all or nothing" idea of participation; one may still expect location and physical factors to be relevant in influencing the actual number of days engaged in the activity among those who do participate.

Attempts to improve the fit of the basic equation by changing the form of the independent variables were unsuccessful. Use of a parabolic age variable and an adjustment for the age of children over and under five yielded non-significant results. It would appear that the presence of children is more important than the age of the children in deciding whether or not to participate in swimming, while locational factors are secondary in importance to the basic socioeconomic characteristics.

Probability of Fishing Participation. Although the dominance of the socioeconomic variables remains in explaining the probability of fishing participation, a slightly different set of variables is involved. The basic fishing equation is

$$FP = .0073 - .0033A + .1845Y + .0943S + .0707E + .1679R$$
$$ (.0650) \quad (.0082) \quad (.0410) \quad (.0246) \quad (.0186) \quad (.0400)$$

which yielded an R^2 of .109. The life-cycle variable (children–no children) was not significant for fishing. A parabolic age variable and occupational variables were non-significant in all cases and do not seem relevant to the question of fishing participation.

Physical factors do not appear to be significant in the fishing participation regression. On the whole, the same arguments that suggest the unimportant role of locational and physical factors in relation to swimming appear to be applicable to fishing as well, though this may not appear as intuitively obvious. One might believe that, for example, urban versus non-urban location would influence fishing participation, but the statistical analysis provides no evidence to support this supposition.

Probability of Boating Participation.   Boating, more than the other two water-oriented recreational activities, requires the availability of large natural facilities if it is to be engaged in at all. The swimmer and the fisherman, once they have decided to participate, can usually find some facilities if only the local YMCA pool or nearby mud-bottom catfish creek. For the boating participant, on the other hand, the availability of adequate sized facilities is likely to be an overriding factor in whether he can participate or not. Thus, while we may still expect the availability of facilities to be an important factor in influencing the number of days of participation for fishing and/or swimming, in the case of boating, the facilities variable should be pertinent in affecting the probability of participation per se. The inconvenience and cost of boat maintenance plus the high initial capital expense for boating necessitates the availability of sufficiently good facilities in a nearby area.

In the regression analysis of the probability of boating participation, the importance of physical facilities is easily seen. Moreover, socioeconomic characteristics which are significant for fishing and swimming are insignificant for boating, i.e., the regression coefficients for income, education, and occupation are all non-significant, while race and age squared have only marginally significant coefficients.

The basic equation for boating participation is

$$BP = .26596 - .00649A + .06253Y + .19746S$$
$$(.07859) \quad (.00106) \quad (.04278) \quad (.02700)$$
$$+ .01606R - .16785L_1 + .07182L_2$$
$$(.04453) \quad (.07279) \quad (.03710)$$
$$+ .1003G + .07737U + .38485W + .05514C$$
$$(.0273) \quad (.03016) \quad (.07800) \quad (.03261)$$
$$+ .03142FPS$$
$$(.01001)$$

which has an adjusted R^2 of .107.

Boating appears to be more popular with the non-urban population. The region of the country also proves significant and implies that people in the South and West are more likely to participate in boating than in the Northeast or North Central states. Since an expert rating of the quality of boating facilities in each sampling area is not available, the rating of fishing facilities (*FPS*) was used as a proxy. Since the ratings are based on the availability and development of natural water facilities, the use of the *FPS* variable was not entirely arbitrary. The *FPS* rating had a significant coefficient, when added with region, to the basic socio-economic variables.

Water Area Variables.   Finally, an attempt was made to use a measure of recreational water per capita as a proxy for the quantity of water facilities available for each recreational activity. The most accessible statistic was acres of recreational fishing water in each state in 1960. This statistic was divided by the population of the state in 1960 to yield a water per capita variable (*W*). A further variable allowing for the presence of a coastline or Great Lakes frontage for each state was introduced. This coastal variable (*C*) attempts to account for the water facilities not included under the acres per capita statistic. These are rough measurements at best, since among different parts of the same state the effective availability of water may differ greatly.

Neither of these variables proved significant for swimming participation. This is not too surprising since both the *W* and *C* variables measure an index of quantity of water, and artificial and private facilities rather than natural areas may be more relevant for swimming. However, the water variable did prove significant in the fishing equation, and both the coastal and water variables were relevant for boating participation. This last result tends to support the argument that of the three sports, boating requires as a necessary condition the presence of substantial water area as a factor influencing participation per se. The final equations used for actual probability estimates including these variables appear under the heading "Estimated Benefits from Water Improvement," below.

Amount of Participation.   Analysis of the amount of participation (i.e., by those individuals who had reported at least one day's participation) is the next stage of the study. It would have been desirable to explain amount of participation in terms of number of days, but considerable experimentation revealed that it is difficult to distinguish among individuals who participated two, three, and four days, and the Survey Research Center data classify all those with greater participation into an open-ended "more often" class. Attempts to reconcile the data with the

197

National Recreation Survey met with little success, and it was decided to assign a value of 1 to respondents with little participation, i.e., 1–4 days during the year, and a code of 2 to those who indicated "more often."[28] Also, a change was made in the age variable with the 18–35-year-old group, assuming a value of one, and those above zero.

The best fit ($R^2 = .408$) for swimming follows:

$$SWP = 2.13957 + .13259A + .54881S - .93444R$$
$$(.30491) \quad (.09566) \quad (.06733) \quad (.28423)$$

Not surprisingly, sex and age affect the amount of participation in the same way as in the probability analysis. The locational and facilities variables did not have significant effects, but the negative coefficient of the race variable, in contrast to our prior results, has interesting implications. Non-white status may reduce the probability of participation, perhaps through unequal availability of facilities or discrimination, this being so especially for swimming. Yet for those non-whites who do participate— presumably those with access to facilities—the participation rate is relatively high. In the Delaware estuary area, which contains a significant non-white population and a relative lack of facilities, it is reasonable to conclude, therefore, that with accessible facilities the amount of participation would exceed our probability projections.

The results of the boating and fishing analysis proved disappointing although several manipulations of the dependent variable were tried. However, further analysis may be expected to show that availability and accessibility of facilities are relevant to the amount of participation in both activities.

Potential Demand. The presence of substantial "option demand" by respondents who "would like to do more" of an activity has been noted previously in the discussion of option demand. Possible causes are income, age, race, lack of time, and other relevant considerations. The failure to attain a desired rate of participation can be attributed, in part, to the lack of facilities. This enables us to consider the implications in terms of potential demand. In regression equations, coding the "unsatisfied" group with a value of one and the satisfied group with zero, we looked for negative coefficients on the facility variables. Such coefficients would suggest that the "would like to do more" categories contain poten-

---

[28] The importance of careful collection and scaling of participation data should be stressed. On the one hand, an indeterminate open-end "more often" class is not sufficiently precise over a period as long as one year. On the other hand, more frequent sampling with detailed numerical accounts of number of days' participation risks error, because the respondent may report days he has reported previously or may miss days through fear of duplication.

tial demand which would be realized with the creation of additional facilities. While only some of the regression coefficients are statistically significant, the signs are generally in the expected direction.

From the signs of the coefficients in the following equations (where *PSP, PBP,* and *PFP* indicate potential recreational use in swimming, boating, and fishing, respectively), we can infer that lack of facilities is a deterrent to participation, and that with available facilities we would get a higher participation probability and participation rate than our initial probability analysis projections yield.[29] It is interesting to note that the

$$PSP = .1801 - .0662W - .0072SPS,$$
$$(.0255) \quad (.0601) \quad\quad (.0071)$$

$$PBP = .1697 - .0117FPS,$$
$$(.0214) \quad (.0067)$$

$$PFP = .2959 - .0213FPS$$
$$(.0264) \quad (.0083)$$

effect of the facility index, the *FPS* and *SPS* ratings, are negative in all three cases and imply that extent and quality of facilities may be of greater influence than the size of potential usage area. That is, a lake with access areas, boat ramps, dockage space, and associated services would encourage achievement of the desired rate of participation more than the same water area without the developed ancillary facilities.

Estimated Benefits from Water Improvement

The final empirical work attempted to obtain projections of participation probability and days' use estimates for the eleven-county estuary area and to integrate these with the theoretical cost-benefit analysis.

Using the best probability equations and inserting appropriate values of the relevant exogenous characteristics, an estimate of the dependent variable, probability of participation, can be computed. This value applied to the population estimates, along with an estimate of the mean-days' participation per participant, yields days' usage value. The net effect of improvement in water facilities can also be established.

From the equations below, the probability of participation for each age group, by race, was computed for each sport.

---

[29] A further analysis comparing the two cases for fishing participation, "zero, would like to participate" and "would like to more often," also pointed out the negative relationship of the desire to engage further with the facility variables, e.g.:

$$PFP = .8524 + .00096G - .1655U - .5490W - .0708FPS$$
$$(.0921) \quad (.06314) \quad (.06642) \quad (.1518) \quad (.0218)$$

$$SP = .42981 - .01124A + .19293Y + .05599S \quad\quad (1)$$
$$(.06444) \; (.00081) \quad (.04074) \quad (.02440)$$
$$+ .12475E + .17605R$$
$$(.01844) \quad (.03965)$$

$$FP = -.06360 - .00493A + .18654Y + .09247S \quad\quad (2)$$
$$(.06840) \; (.00098) \quad (.04157) \quad (.02463)$$
$$+ .07052E + .17359R + .23456W + .04931C$$
$$(.01858) \quad (.04002) \quad (.06984) \quad (.02726)$$

$$BP = .26596 - .00649A + .06259Y + .19746S \quad\quad (3)$$
$$(.07854) \; (.00106) \quad (.04278) \quad (.02700)$$
$$+ .01606R - .16785L_1 + .07182L_2 + .10034G$$
$$(.04453) \quad (.07279) \quad (.03710) \quad (.02732)$$
$$+ .07736U + .38485W + .05513C + .03142FPS$$
$$(.03011) \quad (.07800) \quad (.03268) \quad (.01001)$$

Values for the exogenous variables were computed and placed in the probability equations. Age assumed discrete midpoint values of the age classes. Males as a per cent of total population for each age group became the sex variable and race entered as 0 or 1. Income per spending unit in 1957–59 dollars was obtained from the 1960 census [ref. 20], and educational attainment from the Current Population Reports series [ref. 21]. Life-cycle averages came directly from the sample population with similar values applied to both races. The facility indexes reflected the present relative absence of opportunities to engage in outdoor water recreation sports.[30] The FPS rating was 2.0 with a small W value accounting for an eleven-county water acreage area excluding the Delaware River. A weighted population average by county was computed for the belt code.

With this completed, the probability of participation for the eleven-county area could be estimated and the resulting values for each sport in 1960 appear in Table 2. Not surprisingly, the values indicate that of the three sports swimming is likely to be the activity most engaged in for both the white and non-white population (excepting the older non-white groups). The decline in participation probability with age is most marked for swimming, falling from .76 to .08 for whites and from .52 to 0 for non-whites. Neither of the other two activities show such a rapid fall, again reflecting the strong negative effect of age in the case of swimming.

Educational attainment is an important element for both swimming and fishing, with the pronounced differences between the race groups

[30] The coastal variable was given a value of 1 to reflect the area's proximity to the Delaware Bay and Atlantic Coast.

TABLE 2.

Probability of Participation and Total Participants
(Prior to Delaware River water improvement)

Age	Swimming 1960		1975		1990	
	White	Non-white	White	Non-white	White	Non-white
18–24	.7661	.5243	.7854	.5761	.8297	.5947
25–34	.7144	.4435	.7718	.4712	.7958	.5348
35–44	.6203	.2983	.6774	.3801	.7354	.4258
45–54	.5036	.1568	.5756	.2640	.6369	.3034
55–64	.2953	0	.4156	.0834	.4790	.1616
65 >	.0886	0	.2081	0	.2543	0
Participants	1,461,387	131,783	1,943,156	231,100	2,547,304	373,986
Total participants	1,593,170		2,174,256		2,921,290	
Days/part.	6.78		6.78		6.78	
Total days participation	10,801,693		14,741,456		19,806,346	

Age	Fishing 1960		1975		1990	
	White	Non-white	White	Non-white	White	Non-white
18–24	.4050	.1815	.4265	.2164	.4613	.2342
25–34	.4053	.1565	.4395	.1870	.4837	.2268
35–44	.3785	.0961	.4285	.1523	.4845	.1907
48–54	.3302	.0309	.3897	.1020	.4486	.1382
55–64	.2152	0	.2988	.0076	.3548	.0629
65 >	.0949	0	.1727	0	.2122	0
Participants	895,458	43,217	1,207,520	87,894	1,647,184	157,530
Total participants	938,675		1,295,414		1,804,714	
Days/part.	4.12		4.12		4.12	
Total days participation	3,867,341		5,337,106		7,435,422	

Age	Boating 1960		1975		1990	
	White	Non-white	White	Non-white	White	Non-white
18–24	.3444	.3271	.3601	.3273	.3661	.3280
25–34	.2850	.2468	.2900	.2471	.3015	.2265
35–44	.2087	.1689	.2163	.1707	.2317	.1781
45–54	.1727	.1302	.1810	.1321	.1974	.1398
55–64	.1497	.1172	.1555	.1177	.1686	.1235
65 >	.0749	.0555	.0768	.0544	.0844	.0579
Participants	587,071	88,796	728,637	129,670	927,295	184,849
Total participants	675,867		858,307		1,112,144	
Days/part.	3.82		3.82		3.82	
Total days participation	2,581,812		3,278,733		4,248,390	

causing the large discrepancies for any given age group probability. For example, the 35–44 age group in the swimming equations accounts for .08 of the difference in the respective race group probabilities. This observation also applies to the other groups and raises interesting implications for the future probability estimates when the educational differential may be expected to narrow, if not converge. Income provides the other main cause of differences of probability estimates between the races, with the prospect that this too may narrow as non-white income rises relative to white.

In fishing and boating, the values of the relevant variables of water per capita, *FPS*, and coastal considerations raise problems that are of importance. Future projections are made on the assumption of constant facilities. Improvements in availability and facilities may significantly raise participation, or neglect and deterioration may prove to be deterrents. This question is, of course, central to the idea of natural resource improvement, and later, in the section headed "A Clean River," we will attempt to measure the increase in usage and satisfaction resulting from the availability of clean water. The measurements will compare the effects of static conditions in water resources with those of improved conditions, and will present the resulting cost-benefit implications.

In addition to relevant values, Table 2 also shows actual days' usage, figures for which were available, and numbers of participants for each sport in 1960. In the latter case, our probability values were applied to the appropriate age and race breakdowns of population figures for the eleven-county area, to obtain estimates of the number of participants for each group. These figures were then multiplied by the average number of days' use per participant in the three activities.

To obtain projections for 1975 and 1990, the same procedure as is described above was used, and changes in the values for population, education, income, and belt code were calculated over the thirty-year span. Population figures for 1960 and projections for 1975 and 1990 were obtained from the Penn-Jersey Transportation Study [ref. 22] and adjusted to conform to the desired breakdowns. An annual growth rate of 1.75 per cent in personal income per spending unit was assumed in line with past trends of personal income.[31] Education projections by the Bureau of Census [ref. 21] were used; these are available through 1980 but as with population, they are composite estimates. Our 1960 values could be appropriately "aged" through the period, and the problem remains only to obtain values for the younger groups. We followed the reasoning that by 1975, and surely by 1990, the young age groups for both races will attain approximately the same educational level, thus

---

[31] The same growth rate was applied to whites and non-whites. Recent figures show a relatively higher non-white value (1.89 per cent) yet this is for employed individuals and does not account for the higher non-white unemployment rate. In the future the income differential between the groups will narrow, yet this is difficult to project.

allowing the use of composite projections, although deference was given to a persisting race differential.

With population growth, a change in belt code values is mandatory as the eleven-county area becomes increasingly urban. We used weighted averages reflecting population by county (0–1), coded with respect to its urban–non-urban conditions based on estimates of population per square mile. Delaware and Mercer counties join New Castle, Camden, and Philadelphia in their urban characteristic over the period and the belt value decreases. Finally, the water area was not allowed to experience any growth, and hence water per capita fell as population rose. No improvement was postulated in facilities, leaving the *FPS* rating unchanged. The remaining sociological factors were assumed to hold to their former values for want of information, and perhaps justification, to alter them. The number of days' use by participants was assumed fixed at the 1960 level. With these changes and assumptions, we were able to obtain the 1975 and 1990 estimates of probability of participation and days' use shown in Table 2.

In all cases and in all age groups, probability increases, with the race differentials narrowing somewhat reflecting income and education gains, and yielding large increases in total days' usage figures.[32] The effect of education on non-white participation is especially strong and is the single most important factor in its increase. The white gains are related more to income growth, reflecting a much larger value for that variable than for any other for any given income group over the thirty years. The drags upon participation probability growth are the belt value, *W*, and *FPS*, each declining or staying unchanged. The total usage figures for the three years are summarized below. It is apparent that the large values shown have implications for the area's economy, the welfare of its inhabitants, and courses of action for its local governments.

Days' Usage per Year
(Assuming no improvement in the Delaware)

	1960	1975	1990
Swimming	10,801,693	14,741,456	19,806,346
Fishing	3,867,341	5,337,106	7,435,422
Boating	2,581,812	3,278,733	4,248,390
Total	17,251,146	23,357,295	31,490,158

[32] Looking at the probability figures, it is interesting to note the relatively higher increases in participation probability of the older age groups. This can be traced to the population becoming more homogenous, e.g., education levels are fairly uniform in 1990 for all age groups in comparison with their 1960 values. Thus, a trend towards recreation being general throughout the population, in contrast to the present dominance by the relatively young, is a fair conclusion. This is especially true for swimming, and to a lesser degree for fishing, as evidenced by the tables.

Consideration is not given here to certain long-term trends. The growth and spread of leisure time will undoubtedly bring increasing attention and participation to all types of recreation. Although present to some degree in the income variable, this factor may change both the number of participants and the mean participation rate over time. The estimates also understate actual participation through their failure to include the participation of children—a significant lack, especially as applied to swimming.[33]

A Clean River

One of the primary concerns of this study is to obtain an empirical estimate of the effects of a usable Delaware River on recreational activity. Two exogenous variables, water per capita and the *FPS* rating, provide measures of the recreational resources of any given area and were used to obtain an estimate. In the calculations above, eleven-county water-per-capita value excluding the area of the Delaware River[34] was used in the probability equations, along with the relatively low *FPS* value (2.0) of the area. In this section, we estimate the usage which would occur with improvement in the river.

The Delaware River from Trenton to Liston Point covers 57,600 acres, a substantial body of water, and although boating and fishing do occur they are negligible when compared to their potential occurrence if the river's water quality were improved. Figures of water per capita, including and excluding the river, appear below.

Total Area of Water Excluding the Delaware River

Pennsylvania (5 counties)	3,219 water-acres
New Jersey (5 counties)	4,800 water-acres
Delaware (1 county)	3,598 water-acres
Total	11,617

Fishing Water-Acres Per Capita (W)

	1960	1975	1990
Without Delaware	.0034976	.0029466	.0023779
With Delaware	.0208400	.0175566	.0141684

[33] The failure of the survey to record participation of children and other family members understates our estimates of the number of participants. It is likely that the amount of "family or household" participation exceeds the survey analysis of individuals. If each individual also represents a spouse and children who engage concurrently in the activity, the days' usage figures would increase substantially.

[34] Values of surface water areas were obtained from the Delaware River Commission, New Jersey Department of Agriculture, and the Delaware and Pennsylvania Fish and Game commissions.

Below Liston Point, where the tidal diffusion is predominant, the Delaware enlarges into the Delaware Bay, an area of approximately 880 square miles. None of the Bay water was included in our estimates, as it is now recreationally usable. Nevertheless, one might argue that a decline in pollution would improve the quality and quantity of recreation in this area and directly benefit commercial fisheries, particularly the shad- and shell-fishing industries, which have long been suffering.

Adding the Delaware River's acreage and computing the water variable along with a resulting improvement in the *FPS* rating (to 3.0), new probabilities and usage results were obtained. The effects of the *W* and *FPS* variables could only be computed for those sports where they proved significant in our earlier calculations, i.e., fishing and boating. This is not to say that, if improved, the river would not be used for swimming nor that it would not provide better facilities than other bodies of water, but simply that our data do not show that improvement would result in greater swimming participation.

Comparing the new estimates (Table 3) with the results, shown in Table 2, without the river, a significant increase in participation, particularly for boating, is apparent. Contrasting the sports for the projected years, a half-million days' usage growth in boating is observed along with a 50,000-day increase in fishing for any given projection year. These figures are substantial, yet they may be underestimates. Fishermen are attracted by fish: the river below Trenton has a coarse fish population, but with water quality improvement and a resulting return of game fish, particularly shad, fishing activity is certain to increase.

The argument of option demand is applicable here, as is the "learning-by-doing" idea. A clean river will attract the activity of people who were not previously participants, thus our estimates, particularly for fishing, are downward biased. The boating usage figures are quite substantial, largely as a result of assuming an improved "facilities index," and, with the tendency of boating and fishing participation to coincide, a further increase in activity days can be expected.

On the basis of our statistical evidence, swimming, the most popular activity, would not alter in amount. Yet, although it would be difficult to establish swimming facilities in certain parts of the river even if the water were made clean—for example, around the harbor and commercial dockage areas of Philadelphia and Camden—it is feasible that swimming could occur between Trenton and upper Philadelphia and also below both Philadelphia and Camden. The cost of raising water quality to a level acceptable for swimming would be high, but not out of the question if swimming were confined, for example, solely to the stretch above Philadelphia. A cleaned-up river might still have differences in water

TABLE 3.

Probability of Participation and Total Participants
(Assuming improvement of Delaware River water quality)

| | *Fishing* | | | | | |
| | 1960 | | 1975 | | 1990 | |
Age	White	Non-white	White	Non-white	White	Non-white
18–24	.4091	.1856	.4299	.2198	.4641	.2370
25–34	.4094	.1606	.4429	.1904	.4865	.2296
35–44	.3826	.1002	.4320	.1557	.4873	.1935
45–54	.3343	.0350	.3931	.1054	.4514	.1410
55–64	.2193	0	.3022	.0110	.3575	.0657
65 >	.0990	0	.1761	0	.2150	0
Participants	907,135	44,797	1,218,737	89,913	1,658,229	159,857
Total participants	951,932		1,308,650		1,818,086	
Days/part.	4.12		4.12		4.12	
Total days participation	3,921,960		5,391,638		7,490,514	
Differential[1]	54,619		54,532		58,092	

| | *Boating* | | | | | |
| | 1960 | | 1975 | | 1990 | |
Age	White	Non-white	White	Non-white	White	Non-white
18–24	.3926	.3653	.3973	.3625	.4022	.3641
25–34	.3232	.2850	.3272	.2843	.3376	.2626
35–44	.2465	.2071	.2535	.2079	.2678	.2142
45–54	.2105	.1684	.2182	.1694	.2335	.1759
55–64	.1875	.1554	.1927	.1549	.2047	.1596
65 >	.1131	.0937	.1140	.0916	.1205	.0940
Participants	698,843	106,868	850,813	154,167	1,070,264	218,238
Total participants	805,711		1,004,980		1,288,502	
Days/part.	3.82		3.82		3.82	
Total days participation	3,077,816		3,839,024		4,922,078	
Differential[1]	497,155		560,291		673,688	

[1] Effect of Delaware River water quality improvement: difference between total days' participation in Table 2 and Table 3.

quality, making fishing and boating attractive from Philadelphia south and participation in all three sports between Trenton and Philadelphia. The use of the river for swimming in certain areas is another source of potential usage not accounted for by our analysis.

Summing up, the estimates indicate a large increase in activity resulting from an improved river. Combining the sports, the figures run close to 600,000 days for any year and, as we have noted, there are several strong reasons why the figures must be regarded as underestimates.

Empirical Cost-Benefit Estimates

The final phase of the empirical work done for this study deals with an illustrative application of the theoretical cost-benefit analysis presented in the first part of the paper. Referring to that discussion, we are interested in the present value of days' activity resulting from a water quality improvement and in comparisons of this with costs after a conversion of days into dollars has been made. Note that the following figures are only illustrative and preliminary and do not imply policy actions.

Using the days' activity projections for each sport with and without a clean river and interpolating, the days' activity values for each year from 1960 to 1990 can be computed. Discounting these to the year 1965[35] by 5 per cent annually and summing, we can obtain the present value in days for each sport (Table 4) and plot these against their respective dissolved oxygen requirements to obtain the *TAD* curve (Figure 4a). The present values as calculated here for each sport assume that recreational benefits are the sole result of the quality improvement. But undoubtedly there would be certain "spillover" effects from the clean-river program— such additional benefits, for example, as reduced cost of the areas' potable water treatment facilities, industrial benefits, aesthetic considerations, and increased commercial fisheries revenue. In any theoretical analysis these should be valued and included in the calculation of present value. On an empirical basis, however, these values are not available. Thus, the present value of each sport reflects only recreational usage of the clean water.

From the differentials of the *TAD* curves with and without the clean river an estimate of the *MAD* curve can be made (Figure 4b). This schedule indicates the net present value of days' activity as a consequence of water and facility improvement. Applying a series of arbitrary dollar values (from $1 to $5) of a day's activity, we may convert the *MAD* schedule into a family of marginal benefit functions (Figure 4c).

The Public Health Service's Delaware Estuary Comprehensive Study

TABLE 4.

Present Value in Days (1965–1990)

		Without River	With River	Differential
Boating		50,208,471	58,974,571	8,766,100
Fishing		81,611,727	82,492,451	880,724
Swimming		222,416,214		

MB_x Schedules

Boating	$(x = \$1)$	\$ 8,766,100	Fishing	$(x = \$1)$	\$ 880,724
	$(x = \$2)$	17,532,200		$(x = \$2)$	1,761,448
	$(x = \$3)$	26,298,300		$(x = \$3)$	2,642,172
	$(x = \$4)$	35,064,400		$(x = \$4)$	3,522,896
	$(x = \$5)$	43,830,500		$(x = \$5)$	4,403,620

[35] See footnote 23.

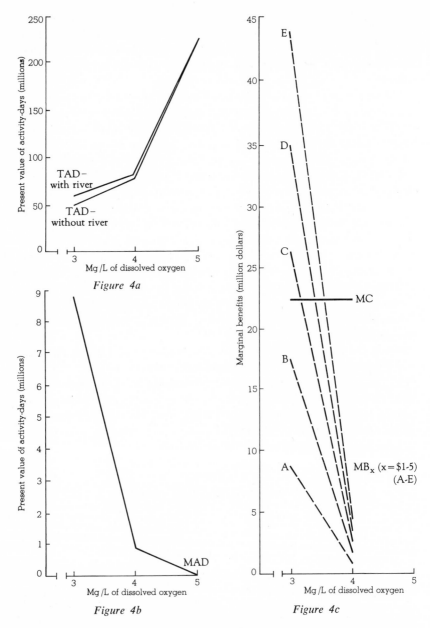

Figure 4a

Figure 4b

Figure 4c

presents preliminary cost estimates of varying water conditions for levels of 2 and 4 Mg/L of dissolved oxygen; these were used to obtain a marginal cost curve. Since the boating-fishing step is between the 3 and 4 dissolved oxygen level, a linear relation of the 2–4 Mg/L D.O. cost estimates was assumed to obtain a cost value for a level of 3 Mg/L. The cost estimates for both levels of dissolved oxygen were made from the following postulated river conditions: a 3000 cfs flow at Trenton, a diffusion rate of 2 mi^2/day, a decay rate of 0.2 day^{-1} and a reaeration rate of .15 from Trenton to below the Philadelphia-Camden area and .22 from there south. Taking the marginal cost estimate (here constant from the linear assumption) and placing it upon the marginal benefit schedules, we note intersections of the cost curve with the $3, $4, and $5 conversion curves. The demand schedules have been drawn here as continuous curves; however, our assumption of threshold dissolved oxygen values implies they are step functions, with the activity commencing only at the discrete three, four, and five dissolved oxygen values and the circled points on the MB_X curves then are the relevant values. For example, the increased usage of the river for boating, if valued at about $2.55 per day, would cover the costs to obtain the 3 Mg/L dissolved oxygen level. Again, these values are meant to be illustrative although they may not be unreasonable.

A word on the exclusion of the present value of swimming is appropriate. In the case of our study, due to the lack of significance of the facility variables in the initial probability analysis, the amount of swimming would not be affected by the water quality improvement. Yet it is not improbable that swimming will increase with water quality improvement in some areas, but this would presumably represent a shift from other facilities. On the other hand, we make no allowance for the qualitative aspects of swimming in the open water. This might raise the value of the MB_X curves at the 5 Mg/L point. Finally, the argument of potential demand, "learning-by-doing," and the exclusion of children's participation would also raise the MB_X curve at each level.

CONCLUSION

In a society that increasingly concerns itself with "ease of life" and "leisure time" goods and services, greater attention must be given to recreation. To a large extent recreation involves water. While some of the equipment and facilities such as boats, fishing rods, and even swimming pools are privately consumed, open clear water is difficult to obtain by a market process. The failure of the private market to adjust this important supply aspect is becoming increasingly apparent, especially in the eastern metropolitan areas.

This paper has examined the reasons for market failure in the case of water recreational facilities and has concluded that the water recreational potential of a river estuary cannot be left to the private sector. We have explored an analytical approach to compare the benefits and costs of water recreational facilities. This approach involves empirical estimation of the actual and potential use of facilities at various levels of water purity; it does not, however, solve the important question of valuation. Using consumer survey data, we have carried out an empirical investigation of the determinants of water recreational activity. The results serve as the basis for an illustration of a benefit and cost analysis of water quality improvement for the Delaware River estuary.

The study has been exploratory in nature and the empirical conclusions must be considered tentative. The data point out the large volume of activity in water sports and the tendency for this activity to grow substantially over the next thirty years. The relation of certain social and economic population characteristics and their influence on recreational activity has been discussed. The impact of improvement of water recreational facilities has been measured, though our tentative estimates probably err in the downward direction. Empirical problems were encountered from the survey data, which fail to record with sufficient precision the extent of activity and the factors that encourage and discourage use—for example, availability, accessibility, and quality of facilities. These are important questions which deserve further study. There is also need for more understanding and information on participation by children, potential demand, "learning-by-doing," and the spillovers between various activities.

While the approach in terms of actual and potential days' use of facilities is feasible, this does not mean that these are the only considerations that might govern the development of water recreational facilities and/or the preservation of the natural watershed. To some extent, it is possible to "produce" clean water and a clean river system. However, it is not possible to reproduce the natural ecological system of the river basin once it has been destroyed. The finality of the destruction of a natural environment places the question in a somewhat different light; it is an important aspect that has not been considered here.

REFERENCES

[1] Bator, F. "The Anatomy of Market Failure," *Quarterly Journal of Economics,* Vol. 72 (August 1, 1958).
[2] Samuelson, P. A. "The Pure Theory of Public Expenditures," *Review of Economics and Statistics,* Vol. 36 (November 1954).

[3] Kneese, A. V. *Water Pollution: Economic Aspects and Research Needs.* Washington: Resources for the Future, Inc., 1962.

[4] Hirshleifer, J., De Haven, J. C., and Milliman, J. W. *Water Supply: Economics, Technology and Policy.* Chicago: Chicago University Press, 1960.

[5] Delaware Board of Fish and Game Commissioners. *The Delaware Conservationist.* Dover, Del., Spring 1963.

[6] Delaware River Basin Commission. *First Annual Water Resources Program.* Trenton, February 1965.

[7] Davidson, P. "Public Policy Problems of the Domestic Crude Oil Industry," *American Economic Review,* Vol. 53 (March 1963).

[8] Weisbrod, B. A. "Collective-Consumption Services of Individual-Consumption Goods," *Quarterly Journal of Economics,* Vol. 78 (August 1964).

[9] Weintraub, S. *Price Theory.* New York: Pitman Publishing Co., 1949.

[10] Outdoor Recreation Resources Review Commission. *ORRRC Study Reports,* Nos. 1–27. Washington: U.S. Government Printing Office, 1962.

[11] Eckstein, O. *Water Resource Development, The Economics of Project Evaluation.* Cambridge: Harvard University Press, 1958.

[12] Kneese, A. V. *The Economics of Regional Water Quality Management.* Baltimore: Johns Hopkins Press, 1964.

[13] Maass, A., Hufschmidt, M. M., Dorfman, R., Thomas, H. A., Jr., Marglin, S. A., and Fair, G. M. *Design of Water Resource Systems.* Cambridge: Harvard University Press, 1962.

[14] McKean, R. *Efficiency in Government through Systems Analysis with Emphasis on Water Resources Development.* New York: John Wiley and Sons, 1958.

[15] Merewitz, L. *Recreational Benefits of Water Resource Development.* Unpublished Harvard dissertation, June 1964.

[16] Davis, R. K. "Recreation Planning as an Economic Problem," *Natural Resources Journal,* Vol. 3 (October 1963).

[17] Clawson, M. *Methods of Measuring Demand for and Value of Outdoor Recreation.* RFF Reprint No. 10. Washington: Resources for the Future, Inc., February 1959.

[18] Lerner, L. J. "Quantitative Indices of Recreational Values," in *Water Resources and Economic Development of the West,* Report No. 11, *Economics in Outdoor Recreation Policy.* Conference proceedings of the Committee on the Economics of Water Resources Development of the Western Agricultural Economics Research Council and the Western Farm Economics Association. Nevada, 1962.

[19] Mueller, Eva, and Gurin, Gerald, assisted by Margaret Wood. *Participation in Outdoor Recreation: Factors Affecting Demand among American Adults,* ORRRC Study Report 20. Washingon, U.S. Government Printing Office, 1962.

[20] U.S. Bureau of Census. *1960 Census,* Pennsylvania, New Jersey, Delaware volumes.

[21] U.S. Bureau of Census. *Current Population Reports,* Series P-20, No. 121, 1963, and Series P-20, No. 91, 1959.

[22] Penn-Jersey Transportation Agency. *Foreground of the Future,* Vol. 2, Penn-Jersey Reports. Philadelphia, 1964.

STUDIES OF WATER REALLOCATION

Regional Economic Interdependencies and Water Use

L. M. Hartman and *D. A. Seastone**

This paper presents some selected aspects of a larger study concerned with an economic analysis of allocation procedures for developed supplies of water. Physical and economic interdependencies associated with water use have given rise to various legal and organizational procedures which modify the usual market allocation process. The objectives of our study are to analyze the economic aspects of these interdependencies and identify those effects which have welfare implications. This analysis then suggests procedures which would allow the "water market" to operate in a more efficient manner.

Efficiency criteria have been used for analyzing transfer procedures, which involves mostly a consideration of external effects. Thus, identifying conditions for an efficient transfer requires a comparison not only of the direct effects on income from the transfer, i.e., between the buyer and seller, but also costs and benefits brought about by indirect or external effects.[1] Physical effects occur which may alter the quantity and quality of

* Associate Professors of Economics, Colorado State University. This is a report of a study funded by a grant from Resources for the Future. John V. Krutilla, Irving K. Fox, and Allen V. Kneese of Resources for the Future contributed to the development of the original problem area and have given valuable assistance as the study progressed. Professors Rufus B. Hughes, Stephen C. Smith, and David W. Seckler, of the Department of Economics, Colorado State University, have contributed immeasurably to the development of ideas presented in this paper.

[1] There are undoubtedly many indirect effects from any transaction. Mishan [ref. 1] makes the statement, "An all-pervading interdependence is what makes economics so intractable a subject." In water use some of these effects are quite obvious and can in principle be measured by market indicators. These are the kinds of effects referred to here.

the supply to other users. These effects have given rise to many of the legal restrictions against water transfers and have some interesting economic aspects in terms of efficient use. Income effects from community economic interdependence may influence allocation decisions and are relevant for an efficient use of resources. The effects are discussed in this paper.[2]

One of the results of a transfer of water resources from one use to another or from one area to another is a change in economic activity, causing adjustments in those sectors of a local economy which are related to the basic water-using activity through purchase or sale of inputs and outputs. In this respect the problem is not unique to water use, but is a general result inherent in any situation where a change in basic economic activity occurs. Theoretically, a transfer of water from one region to another would be no different from a decision of a large firm to relocate a manufacturing plant. The income effect from a water transfer becomes a more important problem because the public affected may be included in the decision-making organization and block any and all transfers. Since some planned control is exercised over water use, the question arises whether these control arrangements are permissive of efficient allocation, and if not, what modifications would lead to greater efficiency, in view of the nature of the external effects.

One aspect of the problem as conceived in the following analysis arises because of resource immobilities, indivisibilities in factor services, and overhead costs in the water-selling region or water use. Another aspect of the problem is due to general unemployment or to unemployment in the water-buying region or water use. These kinds of problems have evidently not been treated in the welfare literature because of a tendency among economists to assume a high degree of mobility and full employment, and a public faith in the free-market mechanism. This faith is evidently not held by professionals and practitioners associated with water use, since there is a widespread presumption that a market system will not operate to allocate water.

In Section I we shall discuss the general problem of transfers that may increase national income under conditions where immobilities and unemployment exist. The nature of interdependency effects are examined in Section II and conclusions presented as to whether the effects are externalities in a welfare sense. Northern Colorado regional input-output model measures of some of the interdependency income effects are presented in Section III as illustrative data.

---

[2] Three articles by the authors present an analysis of various aspects of allocation procedures and organizational arrangements. [Ref. 2, 3, 4.]

I

TRANSFERS THAT MAY INCREASE NATIONAL INCOME

In order to formulate the problem as simply and explicitly as possible, we will consider a three-region model encompassing the national economy. Regions A and B are relatively small and accessible to each other in terms of a water transfer; the third region is C, the "rest of the world." A and B may also be interpreted in some cases as different uses within the same region. It is assumed that the transfer goes from A to B and releases resources from A, which may or may not move into employment in B or the "rest of the world," and may pull resources from the "rest of the world" into B. Possible resource movements are depicted in Figure 1.

In this diagram we have indicated a transfer of water, ΔW, from region A to region B. Depending upon the magnitude of the water transfer, possibilities of factor substitutions, demand elasticities, etc., there will be incremental quantities of labor and capital unemployed in region A. Mobile labor and capital, denoted by ΔN and ΔC, may move into region B or C as indicated. Also, it is presumed the use of the transferred water in region B will entail pulling other resources out of region C or region A, as indicated by the ΔN and ΔC coming into B. The diagram also is pertinent if A and B are interpreted as different uses within the same region. That is, movements of resources may be between uses rather than necessarily involving a spatial movement.

Looking at national income as one relevant measure of welfare, we can consider the effects of a water transfer on national income. Obvi-

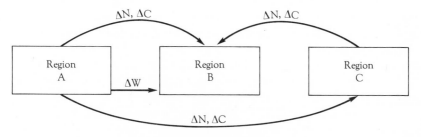

ΔN = incremental quantities of labor
ΔC = incremental quantities of capital (facilities)
ΔW = incremental quantities of water

Figure 1. Possible resource movements.

217

ously, the transfer of water into region B increases income there, otherwise the transfer would not take place, and the transfer of water out of region A decreases income there, other things equal. Whether the transfer affects the income in region C depends upon mobility and the existing state of capital and labor employment. It seems rather straightforward that, if labor and capital resources were perfectly mobile, and if the economy were in a state of full employment, the simple criteria of the marginal value product of water in B being greater than that in A would assure a transfer that would increase national income. A problem arises when in reality resources are not perfectly mobile and when less than full employment exists.

Would the more or less free-market ideal of traditional economic theory necessarily operate to effect a transfer increasing national income under conditions of immobility and unemployment? The answer seems straightforward enough—it would not. Private sellers of water *do not* count as costs the loss of income to immobile labor and capital in secondary sectors, whereas it is a loss in national income. Also, buyers of water *do* count as costs employment of unemployed labor and capital, whereas it is not a cost to the community, except for loss of leisure time enjoyment by labor. Whether the deviations from national income increasing transfers by a free-market transaction are serious would be a matter for community judgment in specific situations. Empirical research could estimate the effects, and the decision to permit or stop free-market transfers would be a political one. If no compensation were paid to income losers and the community decided on the basis of votes, it would probably be that no transfers would take place. However, if the transfer decision were made by a central planning agency, then obviously the thing to do would be to carefully calculate income gains against losses. In any case, recognition of the nature of income gains and losses attendant upon a transfer is of interest either to assess the functioning of free-market forces or as a conceptual background for an empirically estimated planning model.

The institutional aspects of the problem are similar to those of other kinds of economic activities. Unrestricted free-market forces ignore the externalities. Regional political arbitration tends to lead to a stalemate and maintenance of the status quo unless political pressure is brought to bear by an extra-regional power. And central planning and control, besides being antithetical to widely held values, has certain organizational features which may not be desirable from the purely management point of view. The current scene in the Colorado River basin attests to the strength of economic interests which prevail in settling the interstate allocation of water in this basin. We make no attempt in this paper to go into the institutional aspects of the problem, but merely point out there are institutional implications from the analysis.

Without going into the details of the nature of the external effects and of immobilities and unemployment, criteria for transfers increasing national income can be specified under various sets of assumptions. They are derived from production-function concepts and are presented in the Appendix. Here, they are discussed briefly on an intuitive basis. The existence of immobilities would appear to be a rather general phenomena consistent with a normal state of economic affairs, whereas unemployment strikes one as an aberration from a normal state of affairs. However, for symmetry of treatment the two have the same kinds of effects on transfer criteria except that they work in opposite directions, so we will consider both kinds of phenomena on an equal basis.

Assuming full employment equilibrium in A, B, and C, and perfect mobility of all resources, this implies that the transaction price for water must be equal to or greater than the marginal value product of water in its present use in area, or use A, in order to assure a national income increasing transfer. If there is a transfer cost for the resources, then the price must be enough greater that the discounted value of the difference exceeds the transfer cost. In general, this kind of criterion can be stated for any imperfections in the market process. If immobilities exist, then the transfer price of water must be enough greater than the present marginal value product of water to offset the loss of income due to the immobilities. On the other hand, if unemployment or underemployment exists in the buying area or use, then the transfer price could be correspondingly lower than the marginal value product of water in its present use, since the transfer would result in additional income to that attributable to water alone.

Under conditions of general unemployment the rather obvious criterion would be to compare the total decrease in area income in A to the total increase in area B. Assessment of income effects for any one of the conditions regarding immobilities and unemployment involves economic interdependencies, since income in secondary sectors would also be affected by the water transfer. If we can conclude that the existence of immobile capital facilities is a general phenomenon, then the loss of income to these facilities is in the nature of an externality, since the owners of the facilities would not be involved in the water-selling transaction under free-market institutions. We have devoted the next section of the paper to a discussion of these effects. Many of the interdependency-income effects are encompassed in the Leontief-type input-output model and some illustrative input-output estimates will be presented in a later section.

II

THE NATURE OF INTERDEPENDENCY EFFECTS

Several different kinds of interdependency effects are identifiable, as follows: type (1) effect—a household income consumption multiplier effect; type (2) effect—a business multiplier effect on suppliers of production inputs and related sectors; type (3) effect—a cost-increasing effect on firms processing output from the water-using activity; and type (4) effect—an accumulative effect on the public sector through loss of tax revenues and reduction in use of public facilities. Effects (2) and (3) would be peculiar to the kind of water-using activity and effects (1) and (4) would be general for any use. For an intraregional transfer, effects (1) and (4) would be matched by compensating effects stemming from the buying use, so effects (2) and (3) would be the ones of major concern. There may also be some compensating results for type (2) and (3) effects, depending on the nature of the changed uses.

The effect on profits of a decline in sales for a trade firm (wholesale or retail) is depicted in Figure 2. This effect would stem from a decline in household-income consumption and from a decline in demand for production inputs from the water-using sector, type (1) and (2) effects. Point S_1 represents some local equilibrium level of sales and corresponding profits of $R-C$. Some costs are perfectly variable as indicated by the slope of the total cost function; some are discretely variable as indicated at sales of S_2 and S_3, and some are fixed for all levels of sales. Thus, as

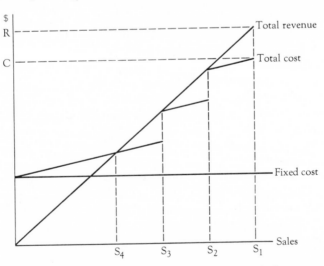

Figure 2. Cost-revenue relationships for a trade firm.

sales volume declines, the firm will experience profits falling and going to zero at point S_2; thereupon it will release from employment a discretely variable input, a clerical employee for example, and move to sales volume S_3 and so forth. At sales less than S_4 the firm would be out of business and the income effect would be $R-C$. However, any reduction in sales would result in a loss of profit income as indicated. In a multi-firm sector one would expect all firms to experience some reduction in sales as demand declined, and marginal firms would go out of business.

This loss of profit income is an externality, if there is no compensating re-employment of the capital facility, and if the market does not provide a mechanism for the profits, which are of the nature of economic rents to be capitalized into the value of water. If this were possible, it would assure that the income of the new use would be sufficiently high to balance this loss. It would appear to be implausible that profits would be transferred to the water-using activity via a lower price on the input sales because of lack of incentives. This would be true, inasmuch as demand for variable inputs is inelastic due to a lack of substitutability of them for capital and labor in the basic water-using sector.

There are theoretical grounds for thinking that the income effect on type (3) firms would give rise to a response through the market system to effect a transfer of income from that sector to the water-using sector, so the end result would be a redistribution of income rather than an effect on allocative efficiency.

We can suppose that firms in type (3) category would be selling in a competitive national market and would be initially in a price-cost equilibrium as depicted in Figure 3. That is, they would be producing at output Q with price P sufficient to cover average total cost given by the curve ATC_1. Initially, as water was sold from the basic water-using sector, these firms would bid up the price of the raw material output from the water-using activity until their cost curve was shifted to ATC_2 in Figure 3, i.e., average total cost equals S while price equals P. In the figure, $PT = SP$, so at ATC_2 the firms are not recovering their capital costs, and income equal to these costs have been redistributed to the water-using firms via the price mechanism. The higher price on the basic sector output would result in a greater return to water and a consequent higher price, reflecting the transferred profits from the processing sector. The type (3) firms would continue to operate until their capital facilities wore out or until water transfers reduced their supply of raw materials and increased their costs past a point on ATC_2.

The market could feasibly operate to phase out the type (3) firms, if buying of water were not done immediately. That is, the entire basic water-using sector could sell out at one time and at a price which did not

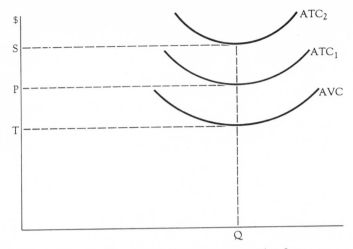

Figure 3. Price-cost relationship for processing firms.

cover the loss of income to capital in the type (3) firms. Thus, the existence of an external effect for these type firms would depend upon a timing element.

A question insufficiently investigated in current literature concerns the performance of non-market activities in areas of economic decline occasioned by resource movements [ref. 5]. The specific sequence of events contemplated in the previous discussion involves the transfer of water resources from area A and the subsequent loss of other resources in area A. Although capital and labor immobilities may exist, there will be an appreciable loss of these resources as they seek productive employment in areas B and C.

The use of public capital facilities such as roads, school buildings, etc., would decline and loss of the value of the service provided would, also, be a national income loss. As with the type (1) and type (2) effects, there appears to be no mechanism for the value of this service to be capitalized into the value of water. Thus, in the market process the transfer would take place without recognition of this loss of income. While it is conceptually clear that a loss of income occurs, it is not clear how the magnitude of the income loss could be measured.

Also, the demand for certain public services is inelastic and requires provision of a minimal service. With persisting overhead costs of maintaining facilities and with declining use, the per capita cost of providing the minimal service would increase at least in the short run. Thus, interregional transfers would face the declining area with a declining tax base and an increasing cost of providing public services.

TABLE 1.

Per Capita Expenditures for Public Services in Selected Counties of Colorado

	Five declining counties	Five growth counties
Per capita expenditures for education	$151	$138
Per capita expenditures for health/hospitals	23	4
Per capita expenditures for welfare	62	29
Total per capita expenditures	355	247

This characteristic of public-sector behavior growing out of a resource shift is illustrated by per capita expenditures on public services between five Colorado counties which have declined rapidly in recent years and five Colorado counties which have dominated Colorado growth. This comparison is presented in Table 1.

The evidence in Table 1 clearly indicates a higher per capita expenditure for public services for declining areas. This does not measure the quality of the service provided and undoubtedly there are some differences. However, much of the difference could be due to short-run cost effects in the declining areas, i.e., spreading an overhead cost over fewer residents, and/or economies of scales in the growth counties.

A case could be made for a new average long-run equilibrium cost at higher level after a transfer. For example, suppose areas A and B before a transfer are both operating at the minimum point on a long-run average cost curve for public services, point N in Figure 4, where population is measured on the horizontal axis and per capita expenditure on the vertical. As the transfer of (water) resources is made between areas A and B, the declining population in area A has the effect of moving area A backward on the horizontal axis and to a higher average per capita cost on the vertical axis, say to point D. Area B gains population but realizes no further economies of scale. In fact, the data suggest that the average cost curve is not flat over an extended range and that diseconomies will exert themselves as population begins to increase beyond some point, R in Figure 4.

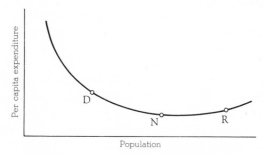

Figure 4. Average cost of public services.

223

This is to suggest that water and attendant population transfers could have the effect of introducing scale diseconomies in one and possibly both areas concerned with the transfer. This means that it will require a higher per capita expenditure in area A to obtain minimal quality standards and there is no offsetting decline in average per capita cost in area B; there is in effect an increase in the resources needed in areas A and B to implement a minimal public service. This implies that some optimum exists for spatial population distribution in terms of providing public services. And since geographic allocation of water to some extent affects population distribution, then it becomes a part of the water allocation problem.

III

MEASURES OF INTERDEPENDENCY INCOME EFFECTS

The Leontief input-output model, when estimated for a water-using economic community, gives estimates of type (2) effects of the previous discussion. When households are included as producing inputs of labor services and consuming outputs from other local sectors, the model also gives estimates of type (1) effects. This model has been quite widely discussed in the literature, so no attempt will be undertaken here to present the model in detail. (See, for example, Isard [ref. 6] for a discussion of the input-output model in regional analysis.) In general, it is a linear model relating flows of goods and services between economic sectors. The solution gives estimates of fractional changes in output for any sector resulting from an exogenous dollar change in the output of any other sector. Flows of goods and services for a seven-sector model were estimated for a northern Colorado area. The solution matrix for this model is presented in Appendix Table 1 and will be discussed as indicative of the relative magnitudes of the type (1) and (2) effects for this type area and use. The magnitude of the agricultural multiplier of this study is comparable to those of other studies, being approximately 2, which indicates that for every dollar change in agriculture output a corresponding dollar change is induced in all other sectors. (See, for example, Lund [ref. 7], Rao and Allee [ref. 8].) Included in the model are the basic water-using sector (agriculture) and the related secondary public (government) and household sectors. The agriculture column in Appendix Table 1 contains the relevant multiplier effects. Added to the matrix are several income rows to permit measurement of income effects. Row (8) coefficients measure the wage and salary payment per dollar of output from each sector, row (9) coefficients measure the profit and rent payments per dollar of output for each sector.

224

The direct and indirect effect on wages and salaries paid per dollar change in basic sector output is $0.318 (= $C_{11} A_{s1} \cdots + C_{71} A_{s7}$, Appendix Table 1). This means that if agricultural output is increased or decreased by one dollar, wages and salaries will increase or decrease by $0.318. Of this amount, $0.190 is agricultural labor income and $0.128 is labor income in the other sectors which are dependent upon agriculture.

The direct and indirect effect on profits and rents is $0.268 (= $C_{11} A_{91} \cdots + C_{71} A_{97}$, Appendix Table 1). Of this amount, $0.239 is agricultural capital income and $0.029 is capital income in dependent sectors.

These per dollar of output figures can be converted to per acre-foot estimates by multiplying them by an estimate of gross return per acre-foot of water use in agriculture. A survey estimate of gross return per acre-foot of water delivered to the farm headgate is $27.00. (See Goode [ref. 9]. The estimate is based on crop adjustments to Colorado's Big Thompson supplemental water on 150 sample farms.) This would give an area estimate of $54.00 for each acre-foot if use is doubled by return flow, i.e., the first use of the acre-foot generates $27.00 in value of gross output and the sum of subsequent return flow uses adds another $27.00 in value of gross output [ref. 10].

Thus an estimate of the effect on area salary and wage income of an increase or decrease of one acre-foot in water supply would be $54.00 × 0.318 = $17.17, of which $10.26 is in the agriculture sector and $6.91 is in dependent sectors. An estimate of the effect on profits and rents is $54 × $.239 = $14.47 per acre-foot, of which $12.91 is in the agriculture sector and $1.57 is in dependent sectors. Using these estimates as illustrative data, then they indicate that the selling price of water in a free-market transaction would be near to a capitalized value of the $12.91, which is the profit and rent income for agriculture. The income externality for capital facilities in other sectors is $1.57, so a national-income-increasing transfer price would need to be near the capitalized value of $14.47 (= $12.91 + $1.57). It should be pointed out that all of the possible effects are not measured in the input-output model estimates. A declining agriculture crops sector would also affect the agriculture processing sector and the livestock sector by increasing the cost of their raw material inputs, type (3) effect. This effect is not estimated in our model. Also, the effect on the public sector type (4) effect is not estimated in this model. The type (3) effects would be of importance, particularly if water transfers out of the region were large and occurred in a relatively short time as discussed in Section II.

One obvious type transfer of importance for which the above estimates are applicable is from irrigation to municipal use. The problem of growing municipal areas, faced with a need to increase their water supply, can be viewed as one of choosing between two alternatives. The city can buy up irrigation rights or build relatively expensive transportation facilities to import water from regions of surplus supplies, or in other ways develop new supplies. For example, Hirshleifer *et al.* [ref. 11] have proposed that the city of Los Angeles buy out the irrigation water from the Imperial Valley. Would the loss of income from this course of action be greater or less than the cost of importing new supplies from the Northwest? Restricting the problem to these two alternatives supposes that population and/or industry demand for location is sufficiently inelastic to justify the cost of either alternative, i.e., that water rates resulting from either alternative would not deter the continued growth of the area.

The welfare calculus of these two alternatives involves comparing the cost of developing the new supplies to the loss of income resulting from buying developed supplies from present uses. If we just capitalize the income figures for each type income, it gives some idea of the varying magnitudes which might be applicable. For example, with a 5 per cent rate the capital value of profits and rents lost in agriculture is $258.00; that for total profits and rents is $288.00 and that for total area income is $633.00. Community leaders and regional planners may tend to look at loss of total income as the relevant consideration since their interest would be towards keeping people and in terms of regional rather than national income.

IV

CONCLUSION

We have indicated that certain income externalities exist in water transfer situations and have pointed out some of the implications of immobilities and unemployment for transfers that can increase national income. This gives a basis for policy considerations in a planning context and, also, for judging the efficiency of free-market institutions. Unemployment in a buying use appears to be potentially of greater significance than immobilities in the losing sector, although one could make a stronger case for the general existence of sunk-capital facilities than for unemployment.

It would appear that the timing of transfers is an important consideration bearing upon the magnitude of sunk-capital facility immobilities and their effect on efficient transfers. Also, the loss of income (utility) and adjustments in the public sector are neglected aspects of the problem. These problems present a challenge for future investigation.

Appendix

In Section I we discussed general considerations for transfer conditions that can increase national income in situations of immobility and unemployment. This argument is presented here in a systematic way using regional production function concepts. Although some of these conditions seem quite obvious, a systematic derivation may help in clarifying the issues involved. The general model is as follows:

$$\text{region A income: } Y_a = f(N, C, W), \tag{1}$$

$$\text{region B income: } Y_b = g(N, C, W), \tag{2}$$

$$\text{region C income: } Y_c = h(N, C), \tag{3}$$

where N = units of labor, C = units of capital, W = units of water, and f, g, and h denote aggregate production functions for regions A, B, and C, respectively. Income and its change in the various regions is:

before transfer national income $Y_1 = Y_a + Y_b + Y_c,$ (4)

after transfer national income $Y_2 =$

$$Y_a - \Delta Y_a + Y_b + \Delta Y_b + Y_c + \Delta Y_c. \tag{5}$$

The condition for $Y_2 > Y_1$ is that $\Delta Y_b - \Delta Y_a + \Delta Y_c > 0$ where:

$$\Delta Y_a = f'(N)\Delta N_a + f'(C)\Delta C_a + f'(W)\Delta W$$
$$\Delta Y_b = g'(N)\Delta N_b + g'(C)\Delta C_b + g'(W)\Delta W$$
$$\Delta Y_c = h'(N)\Delta N'_a + h'(C)\Delta C'_a - h'(N)\Delta N'_b - h'(C)\Delta C'_b,$$

and thus the condition is

$$g'(N)\Delta N_b + g'(C)\Delta C_b + g'(W)\Delta W - f'(N)\Delta N_a - f'(C)\Delta C_a -$$
$$f'(W)\Delta W + h'(N)\Delta N'_a + h'(C)\Delta C_a - h'(N)\Delta N'_b - h'(C)\Delta C'_b > 0. \tag{6}$$

The meaning of symbols is: ΔN_a and ΔC_a are increments of labor and capital facilities unemployed in region A; ΔN_b and ΔC_b are increments of labor and capital newly employed in region B; $\Delta N'_a$ and $\Delta C'_a$ are increments of labor and capital moving into employment in region C, and $\Delta N'_b$ and $\Delta C'_b$ are increments of labor and capital which have left region C to be employed in region B. The notation $f'(N)$, $f'(C)$ and $f'(W)$ represent the marginal value product of labor, capital, and water, respectively. Thus, for example, $f'(N)\Delta N_a$ measures the change in regional income due to the change in the quantity of labor ΔN_a. The sum of the changes for all factors equals the total income change. This follows from a familiar mathematical theorem concerning homogenous functions of degree one or that of production theory concerning constant returns to scale. The assumptions of constant returns is not necessary but it simplifies the presentation.

Assuming that full employment equilibrium exists in regions A, B, and C, and perfect mobility of all resources, the condition for a national income increasing transfer exists when:

$$g'(W)\Delta W > f'(W)\Delta W \tag{7}$$

where from equation (6) by assumption, $f'(N) = g'(N) = h'(N) = P_n =$ equilibrium wage rate; $f'(C) = g'(C) = h'(C) = P_c =$ equilibrium rate of return to capital; $\Delta N_a = \Delta N'_a$, $\Delta C_a = \Delta C'_a$, $\Delta N_b = \Delta N'_b$, and $\Delta C_b = \Delta C'_b$.

Thus, all the components of income changes cancel out except the differential income change to water in the two regions. This is the traditional welfare economics solution for an efficient allocation of a resource, and it would be effected by a market system under the further assumption of profit-maximizing behavior by resource owners. However, if in fact resources are not perfectly mobile and full employment does not exist, then some alteration in the criteria is required. We shall examine relevant criteria under three sets of assumption regarding mobility and employment.

These assumptions are listed below and spelled out in terms of the values of relevant variables. The condition (6) above is specified for each set of assumptions. Assumptions (a) are: full employment equilibrium in A, B, and C, perfect mobility of labor and immobility of capital facilities in A. This implies the values of variables and functions in (6) to be:

$$f'(N) = g'(N) = h'(N) = P_n = \text{wage rate};$$
$$f'(C) = h'(C) = g'(C) = P_n = \text{return to capital};$$
$$\Delta C'_a = 0; \Delta N_b = \Delta N'_b; \Delta N_a = \Delta N'_a; \Delta C_b = \Delta C'_b. \tag{8}$$

And thus (6) reduces to:

$$(6') \quad g'(W)\Delta W > f'(W)\Delta W + P_c\Delta C_a.$$

Under these assumptions the condition for a desirable transfer reduces to a question of whether the *increased* productivity of water (combined with other resources) in B offsets the loss of income from unemployed, immobile capital facilities in A.

Assumptions (b) are: unemployment in A, B, and C implying that:

$h' = 0$ for all factors. And thus condition (6) reads:

$$(6'') \quad g'(N)\Delta N_b + g'(C)\Delta C_b + g'(W)\Delta W > f'(N)\Delta N_a + f'(C)\Delta C_a$$
$$+ f'(W)\Delta W. \tag{9}$$

Under these assumptions the condition for a national income increasing transfer becomes a question of whether the total income generated by the transfer of water into B is greater than the total loss of income in A, i.e., the left side of (6″) is ΔY_b and the right side is ΔY_a.

Assumptions (c) are: full employment in A and C, unemployment or underemployment in B, and immobility of capital in A, implying that:

$\Delta N'_b = \Delta C'_b = \Delta C'_a = 0$. And, thus, condition (6) reads: (10)

(6‴) $f'(N)\Delta N_b + f'(C)\Delta C_b + g'(W)\Delta W > P_c\Delta C_a + f'(W)\Delta W.$

The condition reads that total regional income in B resulting from the transfer be greater than the loss of income to capital and water in A.

It should be emphasized that the production function in this model includes both the water using activity and related sector activities, so that employment effects consist of both a direct and indirect component. The unemployed capital in region A, ΔC_a, may be looked upon as consisting of two components; one, which we will designate $\Delta_1 C_a$ is an unemployed increment of capital owned by the water user and another component, $\Delta_2 C_a$, is an unemployed increment of capital belonging to suppliers of inputs to the water user.[3] Also, the marginal value product of water is one which takes into account consumptive use-return flow relations as we have developed in a previous article [ref. 10]. The model is intended to indicate both the direct and indirect components of regional income changes due to the water transfer.

Suppose, for the moment, that the model exists under conditions where the buyers and sellers of water are also the users, i.e., that no organization or agency has control of water use. What would a free-market solution be under these conditions?

We can suppose that the transfer would not take place unless the following (free-market) condition holds:

$$g'(W)\Delta W > [f'(W)\Delta W + P_c\Delta_1 C_a].$$ (11)

This can be considered a free-market transfer criterion since the right side of the inequality represents the amount the seller would need to cover his loss of income and the left side the amount of income the buyer would earn in the new use. Under assumptions (1), the indirect effect on capital income, $P_c \Delta_2 C_a$, is not considered in the transfer and obviously would not be under free-market institutions. Thus, a free-market transfer could take place which would not be national income increasing if the indirect effect on capital income were of a sufficient magnitude. Condition (11) above is quite different from conditions (6″) and (6‴), which were derived from sets of assumptions (b) and (c).

[3] The component of income $P_c \Delta_2 C_a$ in secondary sectors may be an incremental loss due to an indivisibility and not necessarily due to abandonment of a sunk-capital facility.

APPENDIX TABLE 1.

Inverse Matrix of a Regional Input-Output Model

	Agriculture	Agriculture processing	Trade	Construction	Service and utilities	Government	Household
	(1)	(2)	(3)	(4)	(5)	(6)	(7)
(1)	1.000 (C_{11})	.141 (C_{12})	.003 (C_{13})	.001 (C_{14})	.003 (C_{15})	.002 (C_{16})	.004 (C_{17})
(2)	.033 (C_{21})	1.034 (C_{22})	.023 (C_{23})	.009 (C_{24})	.021 (C_{25})	.017 (C_{26})	.029 (C_{27})
(3)	.869 (C_{31})	.357 (C_{32})	1.245 (C_{33})	.271 (C_{34})	.411 (C_{35})	.366 (C_{36})	.709 (C_{37})
(4)	.016 (C_{41})	.009 (C_{42})	.010 (C_{43})	1.084 (C_{44})	.014 (C_{45})	.018 (C_{46})	.026 (C_{47})
(5)	.133 (C_{51})	.084 (C_{52})	.054 (C_{53})	.081 (C_{54})	1.132 (C_{55})	.220 (C_{56})	.217 (C_{57})
(6)	.165 (C_{61})	.097 (C_{62})	.089 (C_{63})	.073 (C_{64})	.128 (C_{65})	1.232 (C_{66})	.204 (C_{67})
(7)	.591 (C_{71})	.365 (C_{72})	.146 (C_{73})	.270 (C_{74})	.324 (C_{75})	.489 (C_{76})	1.182 (C_{77})
Wages and Salaries	.190 (A_{81})	.060 (A_{82})	.068 (A_{83})	.183 (A_{84})	.123 (A_{85})	.294 (A_{86})	—
Profits and Rent	.239 (A_{91})	.060 (A_{92})	.010 (A_{93})	.006 (A_{94})	.090 (A_{95})	.036 (A_{96})	—

Source: Che Sheng Tsao, "An Input-Output Analysis for an Irrigated Agricultural Area," unpublished Master's thesis, and Frank M, Goode, "An Input-Output Study of a Four-County Area in Northern Colorado," unpublished Master's thesis, Colorado State University, 1964. The input column of the agriculture sector was estimated from individual crop studies. The output of the agriculture processing sector was distributed using data from a complete survey of these firms. Other coefficients and flows were estimated from secondary data and other studies.

Only with specific values of the variables would the transfer be national income increasing. The question this analysis raises concerns mobility and employment assumptions which are questions for empirical determination in specific situations.

REFERENCES

[1] Mishan, E. J. *Welfare Economics*. New York: Random House, 1964, chap. 2.

[2] Hartman, L. M., and Seastone, D. A. "Alternative Institutions for Water Transfers: The Experience in Colorado and New Mexico," *Land Economics,* February 1963.

[3] ———. "Welfare Goals and Organization of Decision Making for the Allocation of Water Resources," *Land Economics,* February 1965.

[4] ———. "Efficiency Criteria for Market Transfers of Water," *Journal of Water Research,* June 1965.

[5] ———. "Resource Transfers and Economic Externalities in the Public Sector." Paper presented at New Orleans, La., November 1965. *Proceedings National Tax Association,* 1966.

[6] Isard, Walter. *Methods of Regional Analysis*. Cambridge: MIT Press, 1960, chap. 8.

[7] Lund, Richard E. *A Study of the Resources, People and Economy of Southeastern Wyoming*. Cheyenne: Wyoming Natural Resources Board, 1962.

[8] Rao, Ananda S., and Allee, David J. *An Application of Inter-industry Analysis Emphasizing Agriculture to San Benito County, California*. Giannini Foundation Research Report No. 278. Berkeley: University of California, 1964.

[9] Goode, Frank M. "An Input-Output Study of a Four-County Area in Northern Colorado." Unpublished Master's thesis, Colorado State University, 1964.

[10] Hartman, L. M., and Seastone, D. A. "Efficiency Criteria for Market Transfers of Water," *Journal of Water Research,* June 1965.

[11] Hirshleifer, J., Milliman, J. W., and De Haven, J. C. *Water Supply: Economics, Technology, and Policy*. Chicago: University of Chicago Press, 1960.

Water Transfer Problems: Law

Willis H. Ellis*

I

n the western United States, water may be a limiting factor of production. Through this limitation, the amount of income which an area or region can generate may also be restricted. As a result, the growth potential of the region may be limited as to the number of people within the region and their standard of living. Most of the country has an ample physical quantity of water, but the West is running short in terms of future growth. As this occurs, one or both of two things must result: population growth must cease, or the standard of living must go down. Since the arid West is experiencing this phenomenon more severely than other regions, one would expect that population growth would slow down or even reverse itself before living standards would fall.

Western communities are understandably reluctant to let either situation happen. There are basically two things a community can do when its growth is threatened by a limited supply of water. It can find new sources of supply, or it can utilize its limited supply more efficiently to maintain area income. This paper will consider the possibilities inherent in the second alternative.

THE IMPORTANCE OF CREATING A WATER RIGHT THAT IS SENSITIVE TO THE MARKET SYSTEM

It is now well established that in western United States income to the region per unit of water consumed is less for agriculture than for either industry or recreation. It has been estimated that in the Rio Grande basin

* Associate Professor of Law, University of New Mexico. This paper is the product of a larger research project in the Department of Economics, Colorado State University. The project is supported by Resources for the Future, Inc. The author wishes to acknowledge the research assistance of Timothy W. Glidden, second-year student, University of New Mexico, College of Law.

in 1975 one acre-foot of water will return $50 per year if used in agriculture, $200 to $300 if used for recreation, and $3,000 to $4,000 if used for industry [ref. 1].

If the West is to share in national growth, it must be able to move water consumption from low-income agricultural uses to high-income industrial uses when the opportunities arise. One would expect that the water market would perform this function automatically; that when an industry wanted to move to a western location it would be able to buy water rights now in agricultural use because it could afford to pay the farmer more than he could make with the same amount of water. In practice, however, water rights have proven difficult to purchase, and there has been surprisingly little transfer of water rights from agriculture to higher economic uses [ref. 2].

DIFFICULTIES IN ALLOCATING APPROPRIATION WATER RIGHTS IN A MARKET SYSTEM

The market system presupposes communication between potential sellers and buyers and a careful examination of the items for sale on the basis of which offers are made. Communication is at the heart of a market system. Buyers cannot know whether they want what is offered and how much it is worth to them unless they can know exactly what they are buying. When we are selling things that have corporeal substance, there is seldom any difficulty in communicating the characteristics of the product to buyers.

A water right, however, does not have corporeal substance. It is solely a creature of law. It is a set of relationships between the person who is said to own the water right and all other persons in the world, relative to a particular source of water. The specificity with which these relationships are defined is a function of the law of various jurisdictions in which the water right is located.[1] If this degree of specificity is high, a water right can be valued in the market in much the same way a physical thing, such as a bushel of corn, would be valued. But if the degree of specificity is low, then a potential buyer will be uncertain about the amount of water available for sale, and will be unlikely to bid.

In most western states there are three reasons why a water right purchaser is unable to determine exactly what quantity of water a given right represents:

---

[1] The location of any given surface water right acquired by appropriation is the location of the point of diversion from the public source. (West End Irr. Co. v. Garvey, 117 Colo. 109, 184 P.2d 476 [1947].)

234

1. Inadequate definition of the amount of water the right entitles the owner to use;
2. Possibility of past abandonments or forfeitures;
3. Steps that have generally been felt necessary to protect junior appropriators when there is a change in the point of diversion.

1. *Inadequate Definition of the Amount of Water the Right Entitles the Owner to Use.* In most appropriation doctrine, states' water rights are defined in such incomplete terms (such a low degree of specificity) that a would-be buyer could not possibly know what he was bidding for. The first and most important thing the buyer wants to know is how much water this right will entitle him to consume. Most western water rights are defined, quantitatively, only in terms of rate of flow, and not in terms of volume.[2] In Colorado, for example, the owner's decree, and the records of the State Engineer, state that farmer X owns a right to take so many cubic feet of water per second from a stated stream to irrigate a stated tract of land.[3] Farmer X does not take this rate of flow twenty-four hours a day for the entire irrigation season. If he did, he would have neither crops nor soil left. He might, for example, put water on his fields four times during the irrigation season [ref. 4, 5]. The amount of water that farmer X consumes in using his water right will depend upon the number of acres he irrigates, the crops he grows, the amount of fertilizer he uses, the yield per acre he attempts to realize, the porosity of his soil, the efficiency of his diversion facilities, his own efficiency as an irrigator, and perhaps the amount of rain his land receives during a given season. Yet all that the water records indicate to the potential buyer is so many second-feet of flow.

[2] The most common rate of flow measurement is the cubic foot per second, abbreviated "second-foot." In measuring the flow of water passing through a given ditch or stream, the area of the cross-section of that ditch or stream is multiplied by the velocity of the water measured in feet per second. The difficulty encountered by most purchasers in attempting to determine what quantity a given water right, defined in terms of second-feet, represents, is that no time period is included in the definition. One is unable to know how much water a given flow measurement represents unless the amount of time that the flow is to last is also given. Most difficulties arise in determining this vital time factor. The "acre-foot" is a much better measurement in that no time factor is necessary. One acre-foot represents the amount of water that will cover one acre of land with water one foot deep (43,560 cubic feet or 325,851 gallons). The rate of flow measurement of one second-foot running for twenty-four hours amounts to a volumetric measurement of 1.98 acre-feet. (See [ref. 3].)

[3] One segment of the Colorado Adjudication Act of 1943, appearing as Colo. Rev. Stat. Ann. § 148–9–13 (1963), provides in part as follows: "The decree to be entered by the court at the conclusion of each adjudication shall determine and establish . . . the amount of water which shall be held to have been appropriated. . . . [That] right to divert water shall be decreed in second feet. . ."

New Mexico, on the other hand, is an example of the same basic inadequacy in a very different setting. Until recently there was no adjudication of water rights in New Mexico at all. Water rights dating prior to 1907 were acquired simply by putting water to beneficial use and are, for the most part, still not defined in any official or reliable way. Since 1907, water-right owners have been required to obtain a permit which does define the right to some extent. Initially the permit defined the right in terms of a rate of flow measurement. Eventually this definition was changed to the volume the right owner was entitled to divert each year. However, it has been estimated that over 60 per cent of the water rights in the state predate 1907, and are thus undefined rights.[4]

The New Mexico State Engineer is now engaged in a project to adjudicate all water rights in the state. At present, however, 90 per cent or more of the state's water rights are not adjudicated, and progress is slow.

One of the interesting results of the adjudication that has been completed is the fact that water-right prices have undergone substantial increases in each basin as soon as the adjudication decree has become final.[5] While this fact certainly supports the thesis of this paper, it cannot be argued as specific proof. Many of the water rights in each adjudicated area have not just been defined more specifically, they have been defined for the first time. An unadjudicated water right for which there was no permit (because it is pre-1907) was not defined at all.[6]

In addition, it is unfortunate that the present New Mexico adjudications are resulting in decrees that are still not as specific as they could

---

[4] The estimation is based on approximations only, received in personal conversation with the New Mexico State Engineer.

[5] Information obtained from the New Mexico State Engineer's office indicates that in the Roswell ground-water basin, ground-water rights prices have gone from approximately $100 per acre-foot, the price before the adjudication of that basin, to over $300 per acre-foot.

[6] It must be apparent to the reader that under these conditions in New Mexico, it would be impossible to enforce priorities throughout most of the state. The existence of a vast number of undefined water rights makes the enforcement of priorities impossible. Fortunately, however, the policy under the state's permit system of prohibiting the creation of new water rights when a stream is fully appropriated, and an historical co-operative attitude between water users, make it possible to allocate water without enforcing priorities. Water is currently shared among most right holders on a pro-rata basis. This New Mexico experience raises the interesting question of whether the economic criteria for a water right are met as well by this system of pro-rata allocation with a limit on the number of rights allowed as they are by the conventional prior appropriation doctrine. There is some indication that a pro-rata system would be more efficient and less harsh than a priority system. The question may be of considerable importance for riparian doctrine states that may at some time in the future investigate the possibility of adopting a better system of water law as they approach full use of their available supplies.

and should be. The decree defines the right quantitatively in terms of the volume that may be diverted from the public source. This is a long step ahead of the Colorado decree, but still short of defining the volume *consumed,* which is the figure a potential buyer must have. Thus the buyer must still spend money investigating the right, and bear the risk of being wrong.

This deficiency is all the more perplexing because the state engineer, who makes all of the original determinations of quantity, apparently must calculate the consumptive use in arriving at the volume diverted.[7] But the consumptive use figure is not included in the decree, and the potential buyer must spend his own money to duplicate what the state engineer has already done.

It requires considerable calculation by experts to determine how much water has been put to beneficial use [ref. 6]. And, of course, the water right is limited to that amount. The courts are careful to see that the city or industry that buys a right consumes no more water than its previous owner did with the same right.[8] Thus, in order to know how much water it would get (if it bought the farmer X water right) the purchaser must expend substantial sums of money, after which it often faces equally expensive litigation because others with rights in the same source can often find experts whose analysis is different [ref. 2].

2. *Possibility of Past Abandonments or Forfeitures.*[9] If a buyer must change the point of diversion—as most buyers must—the questions of abandonment and forfeiture may be raised in the change of point of diversion proceeding.[10] Therefore, it is not until this stage of the procure-

---

[7] Personal conversation with the New Mexico State Engineer has revealed that the volume of water entered in each decree is calculated by determining consumptive requirements and return flow figures for an entire area, and then determining each farmer's share of these figures according to the quantitative relation his right bears to the whole area.

[8] Green v. Chaffee Ditch Co., 150 Colo. 91, 371 P.2d 775 (1962); Cantlin v. Carter, 397 P.2d 761 (Idaho, 1964).

[9] Abandonment is a common law concept defined as an intentional relinquishment of a known water right. The controlling element necessary for abandonment to occur, where a water right has been relinquished, is the intent of the right holder to give up the right without intending to repossess it at a later date. (Utt v. Fry, 106 Cal. 392, 39 P. 807 [1895].) Forfeiture is solely a creature of statute, and may be distinguished from abandonment in that it is the involuntary or forced loss of a right after non-use for a statutory period. (In Re Manse Spring and Its Tributaries, 60 Nev. 280, 108 P.2d 311 [1940].)

[10] Generally, a change in point of diversion request will attract allegations of abandonment or forfeiture by parties affected by the change. For statutory provisions allowing these allegations to be considered, see Colo. Rev. Stat. Ann. § 148–9–22 (1963) and Colo. RCP, rule 99 (1963); N.M. Stat. Ann. §§ 75–4–6 and –5–26 (Supp. 1965); Utah Code Ann. § 73–1–4 (1953); Wyo. Stat. Ann. §§ 41–47 to –53 (1959, Supp. 1963).

ment of a water right that a buyer will discover whether or not any portion of the water right he is interested in has been abandoned or forfeited. Not only are all purchasers faced with this uncertainty, but they also face the possibility of expensive litigation in which they must defend the water right in question.

3. *Steps that have Generally been Felt Necessary to Protect Junior Appropriators when there is a Change in the Point of Diversion.* When a water right is sold to a new user, that user must almost always change the point of diversion in order to put it to his own use. All western jurisdictions allow this change only to the extent that existing uses of other appropriators on the stream will not be adversely affected.[11] Owners of water rights that are junior to the one being transferred can be adversely affected if they were in a position to take the return flow before the transfer and will not be in that position after the transfer. The details of the various ways in which this can happen are set out and discussed in the appendix.

SOLUTIONS

1. *Inadequate Definition of the Amount of Water the Right Entitles the Owner to Use.* The most obvious solution is to define, in a public and authoritative way, all water rights in terms of consumptive use by volume measurement. In most states this would require legislation directing the state engineer's office or other appropriate body to determine the volume of water consumed by every water right in the state. The owner of the right, and anyone else owning a right in the same source, could ask for a hearing to contest the accuracy of the engineer's determination. Of course, some public expense is involved, but it seems small when compared with the cost to the state in opportunities lost by keeping water in low economic uses.

If all rights were officially stated in terms of consumptive use by volume, a would-be purchaser would know what he was buying. Most of the uncertainty and needless expense would be taken out of purchasing a water right, and the market system could operate with some degree of efficiency. It is futile to think that water rights will ever be allocated in any but the most inefficient way until the rights themselves have been adequately defined.

Certainly, the program and experience in New Mexico prove that

---

[11] Colo. Rev. Stat. Ann. § 148–9–25 (1963); Calif. Water Code § 1702; Kan. Gen. Stat. Ann. § 82a–708b (Supp. 1961); Utah Code Ann. § 73–3–3 (1953).

redefinition on a statewide basis, if done at a reasonable pace, is feasible. Of course, in Colorado and Montana this solution should also include the additional innovation of providing that the original finding of fact in the adjudication proceeding would be made by the state engineer rather than a trial court. But this step is highly desirable in these states in its own right [ref. 2].

There is a Constitutional objection that can be made to any attempt to redefine water rights. There is authority in some states that an irrigation water right has no absolute limit in volume amount.[12] The owner of the right is able to irrigate the same acreage on which the right was created and maintained, growing the crops ordinarily grown in that area using amounts of water reasonably required for good husbandry. In other words, the limiting factor is not a quantity of water but rather the demands of good husbandry on a stated number of acres in a stated area.

As a result of this somewhat elastic quantitative definition of a water right, it is at least theoretically possible that a good water right will entitle its owner to more water in a year of little rain than in a year of plentiful rain. If rights are redefined in absolute quantitative terms, the owners of good (old) rights can complain that they have been deprived of the right to take more water in a year in which they need more because there is less than average rainfall. It can be argued that taking this possibility is taking property without compensation.

At one time there was a need for this elastic definition of water rights, but today's requirements are just the opposite. An appropriation right was originally defined in a time when it was possible to acquire a good new water right, and the need was to leave all the water in the stream except that which was being put to beneficial use. The courts emphasized that the rights were limited by reasonable needs of the land, and did not give "a monopoly of the water."

Today the needs of the West are a good deal different. As it becomes impossible to acquire new water rights it is increasingly necessary to transfer old rights from the uses for which they were created to new, more valuable uses. Thus, the needs that suggested a flexible right have completely reversed themselves, and a firm, transferable right is now called for.

In addition, we need to know from the agricultural engineers how much variation there is from year to year in the amount of irrigation water needed for good husbandry because of the variation in rainfall. It may be that the contribution of rainfall to the total water intake of irrigated crops in this area is so small as to be *de minimus*. If this should

---

[12] E.g., Union Mill & Mining Co. v. Dougberg, 81 Fed. 73 (C.C.D. Nev. 1897).

prove to be the case, then senior rights would not actually lose anything of value when redefined into more absolute terms. If, on the other hand, investigation should indicate that there actually is substantial variation in the water needs of irrigated crops because of fluctuation in rainfall from one season to another, then the courts will have to face squarely the Constitutional objections. However, it would be a mistake to assume that there will be a loss to the owners of senior rights without undertaking some quantitative research to determine whether or not this is the case.

It does not seem to have occurred to anyone in New Mexico to make such an objection to the statewide adjudication process now going on. Most adjudications in New Mexico are based upon consent decrees signed by the owner of the right. Presumably such an owner waives this objection by consenting to specific limitation.

It could also be argued that redefinition is regulation under the police power rather than condemnation.[13]

Should a right be defined as the smallest, the largest, or the average amount it has consumed over the years? One might be tempted to avoid the Constitutional question by using the largest amount the right has ever used. But this would prove wasteful in years when the amount was not needed, since there would be no way to prevent the owner from taking and wasting it. The average amount consumed is perhaps the figure most likely to be agreed upon. But, if the farmer is limited to this, he may be deprived of property in dry years.

It would be technically possible to leave the water right as it is by redefining it on the basis of an average or even minimum amount, and then requiring the state engineer to adjust all rights upward each season if the rainfall is less than normal. The only salable right would be the minimum, but in years when its agricultural owner could have taken more its new owner should be able to do the same.

The New Mexico experience, described above, indicates that it is neither a hardship upon farmers, nor unacceptable to them, to define their water rights in more or less rigid, quantitative terms. The experience of some states with statutes setting a maximum amount of water that may be put on one acre of land[14] is further evidence on the same point.

---

[13] Several states have in effect made agricultural water rights inelastic by either enacting statutes which limit the amount of water that may be applied to a given amount of land, e.g., Wyoming, or by defining water rights in permits or decrees in terms of the exact volume which may be diverted throughout an entire year under that right, e.g., New Mexico rights have been adjudicated to date. The fact that these legislative acts have not been effectively challenged on Constitutional grounds may be some indication that redefinition will not be so challenged. Cf [ref. 7].

[14] See note 13 and [ref. 7].

After all, once the right is transferred for the first time it is then and for-ever more rigidly defined as to the quantity of water that may be consumed.[15]

The basic difficulty behind these problems is the dual standard the law is trying to apply today. On the one hand we gave the farmer an elastic right because that seemed the natural thing to do when the creation of new rights, and not purchase of old, was the way to get water. But we insist that the purchaser's right be inelastic in order to protect other, junior rights on the same source.

2. *Possibility of Past Abandonments for Forfeitures.* Redefinition will also solve most of the abandonment problem. In redefining rights, the state engineer and the courts will have to determine whether any portion of a right has been abandoned or forfeited. After a short limitation period this adjudicated redefinition should be unassailable. The record in the engineer's office should be the conclusive definition of the right in much the same way that a Torrens Certificate defines title to registered land.[16] Thus, the big problem of possible past abandonment would be ended once and for all. Only the problem of abandonment after the redefinition would remain, and this would not be substantial, since actual abandonment of water rights today is extremely rare. However, future abandonment or forfeiture could cause economic waste in isolated cases. The doctrines of abandonment and forfeiture as applied to water rights also grew up in an era in which the emphasis was upon saving the water in the streams for the acquisition of new rights. This is no longer possible, and our present "water wealth" consists of the good (old) rights that exist on our streams. Abandonment and forfeiture of water rights are not like abandonment of land. When land is abandoned it still exists to be occupied and put to use by someone else. When a water right is abandoned or forfeited it is destroyed, and the water which it could have received is given away free in small amounts to all the users on the same source. Thus abandonment and forfeiture are uneconomic allocations of water, and furthermore destroy a right which might have been sold to a user who could have made better economic use of it. How much better if the legislature would provide that abandoned or forfeited water right would escheat to the state for the purpose of its public sale at auction. In this way the right would be used by the highest bidder, who presumably could make the most money with it.

[15] See Green v. Chaffee Ditch Co., note 8.

[16] For a comprehensive analysis of the Torrens system of real property title registration, its historical background, and its application in the United States, see either 5 Tiffany, Tiffany on Real Property, §§ 1314–21 (3rd ed. 1939) or 6 Powell, Powell on Real Property, §§ 919–23 (1958).

3. *Steps that have Generally been Felt Necessary to Protect Junior Appropriators when there is a Change in the Point of Diversion.* I have been unable to find an appellate court opinion that discusses the return-flow problem as such. The statements that one finds are like that in the often cited case of Farmer's Highline Canal and Reservoir Co. v. City of Golden:[17] "All elements of loss to a stream by virtue of a proposed change should be considered and accounted for." The texts writers consider (no doubt rightly) that one of these "elements of loss" may be the lost return flow from the transferred use [ref. 8].

Whether or not this kind of loss will result from the transfer is a question of fact to be determined by the trier of fact[18] on the basis of evidence. If such loss is found, the court or administrative agency will condition the transfer upon the giving up of enough of the right to replace the loss.[19] These determinations are presumably buried in transcripts of cases that have not been appealed. One of the problems is that no general principles have been worked out to guide courts and state engineers in deciding that a particular transfer does or does not injure junior appropriators because of the loss of return flow. Because of the complexity of these problems, one suspects that there has been a tendency in the past to ignore the possibility of these problems.[20] The appendix following this paper is an attempt to fill this need.

The device the courts must presumably have adopted to protect junior rights where there is loss of return flow is to limit the purchaser of the senior right to a diversion of the amount of water which the original owner had *consumed,* i.e., subtracting from the right an amount equal to the return flow at the old point of diversion. By reducing the senior right in this manner after it has been moved downstream, the court allows the junior right to take an amount of water out of the stream before it gets to the senior right, which is equal to the return flow which they had enjoyed when the senior right was above them.

[17] 129 Colo. 575, 272 P.2d 629 (1954).

[18] In a few western states the trier of fact will be a state trial court (e.g., Colorado); in most western states it will be the state engineer's office or other designated administrative body.

[19] City of Colorado Springs v. Yust, 126 Colo. 289, 249 P.2d 151 (1952).

[20] The author is not really entitled to say this because he has not combed through the records of transfer proceedings in county courthouses and administrative files. At this point this is no more than a suspicion because of the remarkable fact that in case after case involving changes in point of diversion over long distances, no mention at all is made of possible loss of return flow resulting solely from the change in physical position on the stream. For example, in Green v. Chaffee Ditch Company, 150 Colo. 91, 371 P.2d 775 (1962), the change in point of diversion is *13 miles* upstream, and yet (as usual) there is not one word in the opinion about the return flow problem. The appendix to this paper shows that loss of return flow may result in transfers upstream as well as downstream.

Although the junior rights are protected by this device, the result upon the efficiency of the water market can be disastrous. The purchaser must pay for substantially more than he gets. Add to this the fact that the purchaser does not know how much his right will be reduced to protect junior appropriators until the court has spoken, and you have a market situation not conducive to transfer.

Hartman and Seastone [ref. 8] have identified the inefficiencies of this situation and suggested that the solution is to allow purchasers to sell the additional return flow that they pay for but do not receive. In working out the implications of this idea, several different opportunities present themselves. As a basis for the following discussion the reader should clearly understand what the rights of the junior appropriators are.

The guarantee that the prior appropriation system of water law makes to all water-right owners is that no acts of man will ever reduce their chances to obtain water with the priority they have established according to the time they (or their predecessors in title) first put water to beneficial use. It is felt that arid portions of the country must extend such a guarantee in order to induce reliance by those whom it hopes will invest their lives and their capital in those areas. This is a big guarantee and appropriators are entitled to it, but to no more. They have no *right* to the windfalls which the courts now bestow upon them by protecting a few junior appropriators in such a rough and oversimplified manner.

It can be demonstrated that the instances in which this kind of protection is needed will be few. The only time there is a return-flow problem in a downstream transfer is when the right being bypassed is the most senior of all those below the original location of the right being transferred. (This is discussed in detail in the appendix.) The problem arises in an upstream transfer only when there are no rights between the right being transferred and the one alleging injury that are senior to the right alleging injury, and the right being transferred is moved above a right senior to the right alleging injury. (This too is discussed in detail in the appendix.)

It is interesting to note that the pro-rata system of water allocation, which is mentioned in footnote 6, would avoid almost all of these return-flow problems.

CONCLUSION

At the present time the water-right market is inefficient because those who would enter it must expend considerable amounts of money just to do so—money entirely separate from any price set on the rights that may be available in the market. This paper has tried to show how a state could, if it chooses, pay these costs in advance so that potential buyers could enter the water-right market and pay (in the vast majority of cases) only the agreed price for the right purchased. The benefit to the state in greater economic returns from its available supply of water should be great.

APPENDIX

Downstream Transfers

The basic return-flow problem properly so called can be seen in the following diagram if we assume that each water right is entitled to take 10 second-feet and returns 50 per cent of this to the stream. Further assume that there is only 10 second-feet in the stream. The number of each water right represents its place in the priority list.

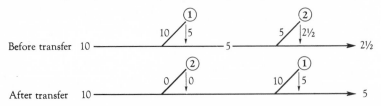

Before the transfer, number two got one-half of its right, or 5 second-feet, because that was the amount of return flow from number one's use. After the downstream transfer of number one, number two gets nothing when there is only 10 second-feet in the stream because number two must let all 10 second-feet go downstream to number one.

Under these conditions the court or agency will presumably reduce the amount number one is entitled to take after transfer until number two is left in exactly the same position it was in before the transfer. It is easy to go astray here because with 10 second-feet in the stream number two will get the same amount (5 second-feet) it would have gotten before transfer if number one is reduced to $7\frac{1}{2}$ second-feet: However, it will

not do to simply reduce number one to a $7\frac{1}{2}$-second-foot right, because if we do number two will suffer when there is less than 10 second-feet in the stream, thus: Number two must leave $7\frac{1}{2}$ second-feet in the stream

244

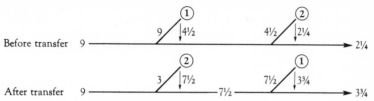

for number one, and therefore can divert only 3 second-feet, leaving 6 which, when combined with number two's return flow of $1\frac{1}{2}$, provides $7\frac{1}{2}$ for number one. It can be seen that number two gets $1\frac{1}{2}$ second-feet less than it would have before the transfer under the same stream conditions. This adverse differential increases as the stream flow diminishes until it reaches $7\frac{1}{2}$ when, of course, number two gets nothing.

It has been assumed that the senior right being transferred, must be reduced to a *diversion* right equal to its *consumptive* right before transfer. It has apparently been thought that this would protect the bypassed junior right since it, in effect, takes away from number one, at the headgate, an amount equal to its return flow at its original location, and it is this return flow that the bypassed junior right is deprived of. However, it can be demonstrated that it is impossible to protect the bypassed right without reducing the transferred right to zero. No matter how much we reduce the transferred right, the bypassed right gets nothing when stream flow gets down to that amount. Whereas before the transfer the junior right would always get half of the amount the senior right diverted (assuming a 50 per cent return flow).

Although there is no final solution possible short of disallowing the transfer (and thereby the sale), the instances of the impact of this problem will amount to a very small per cent of total transfers. The classical situation in which downstream transfer does not create a return-flow problem is the following.

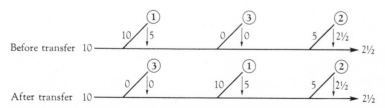

Although number three has been bypassed, and number one's return flow no longer comes into the stream just above its headgate, it is not damaged. This is true because the bypassed right, not being senior of all those below number one, could not enjoy number one's return flow even before the transfer. When the stream was low number three had to let number one's return flow pass by for number two. Most transfers will present a situation like that just diagrammed.

A water law scholar, Professor Sax, has recently questioned the idea that protection should be extended to junior appropriators who are affected by transfers:

> It is interesting to note that the problems created by the absolutist attitude toward protecting junior appropriators are absent in the parallel situation in real property law. The reason is that a landowner has never been thought to have a property right in the maintenance of neighboring uses. For example, a theatre may exist when I open a restaurant down the block, and theatre patrons may be a valuable source of business for me. Nonetheless, I cannot prevent the theatre from converting into a warehouse, though the change is economically disastrous for me. Cf. Reichelderfer v. Quinn, 287 U.S. 315 (1932). Why should juniors on a stream be in a better position than landowners like the restaurateur? [Ref. 9.]

It would be unfair to ascribe any position to Professor Sax since this is a question placed in a teaching book for the purpose of stimulating students. It may also be the case that Professor Sax is not referring to our problem since this question is placed after Green v. Chaffee Ditch Co., 150 Colo. 91, 371 P.2d 775 (1962), a case that does not discuss the return-flow problem properly so called, which we are dealing with here. Nevertheless, the question is appropriate for our problem.

Because of the small percentage of instances in which the return-flow problem will arise in downstream transfers, the fact that it will usually affect only one junior right, and the impossibility of achieving a complete solution where it does arise, it is strongly urged that the junior right not be protected from this contingency.

Allowing the owner of the transferred right to sell either water or a water right downstream, as suggested by Hartman and Seastone [ref. 8], is not a solution for two reasons.

(1) As shown above, the transferred right must be reduced to zero to protect the junior rights under all stream conditions where the problem arises at all.

(2) The amount available downstream by reducing the transferred right constantly changes as stream flow changes. If water *rights* were sold the question of what position in the priority list to give them would be impossible to answer.

Upstream Transfers

The following diagrams show the situation in which an upstream transfer will injure a junior right.

246

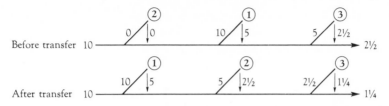

Before transfer the junior right (number three) was assured of number one's return flow because it was the senior right below number one. After the transfer upstream, number three is no longer the senior right below number one, and must give up number one's return flow to number two. If the upstream transfer bypassed junior rights that are senior to any rights downstream, those downstream junior rights will be injured by the transfer. All downstream rights junior to the bypassed right, and close enough to be affected, will be injured, although in diminishing amounts as they are more and more junior to the bypassed right (because they had benefited less and less from the return flow of the senior right as they were farther and farther from it in the priority list). In other words, in the above diagrams number two benefited by the upstream move of number one, and all downstream rights junior to number two must lose correspondingly.

Fortunately, the solution is easier than understanding the problem. The status quo can be maintained in the above diagrams by simply requiring number two to let at least 5 second-feet go down to number three at all times, i.e., number two may never deplete the stream below 5 second-feet. The diagram after transfer then reflects the same figures as does the diagram before transfer:

There is even some authority for this solution. In Cache la Poudre Reservoir Co. v. Water Supply & Storage Co., 25 Colo. 161, 53 Pac. 331 (1898), the senior right on the Cache la Poudre River was a mill with a right to use 60 second-feet for power purposes. Upstream rights had to leave this amount in the stream for the senior mill. Since the mill was not a consumptive use, junior rights below it were assured of 60 second-feet simply because of their physical position on the stream. When the mill right was abandoned, the court held that the then senior upstream rights still had to pass 60 second-feet to the downstream juniors so that they would be in the same position they were in when they perfected their rights. This case is directly analogous to our situation even though it does not involve a change in point of diversion.

Although it is anomalous to see senior rights passing water down to juniors, the senior rights have not been damaged because they are in exactly the same position they were in when they perfected their rights.

REFERENCES

[1] Wollman, Nathaniel. *The Value of Water Alternative Uses.* Albuquerque: The University of New Mexico Press, 1962, p. xvii.

[2] Hartman, L. M., and Seastone, D. A. "Alternative Institutions for Water Transfers: The Experience in Colorado and New Mexico," *Land Economics,* Vol. 34 (February 1963), p. 31.

[3] Trelease, Frank J., Bloomenthal, Harold S., and Geraud, Joseph R. *Cases and Materials on Natural Resources.* St. Paul, Minn.: West Publishing Co., 1965, p. 8.

[4] Houk, Ivan Edgar. *Irrigation Engineering.* New York: John Wiley & Sons, Inc., Vol. 1, 1951, p. 327.

[5] Israelsen, Orson W., and Hansen, Vaughn E. *Irrigation Principles and Practices* (3d ed.). New York: John Wiley & Sons, Inc., 1962, p. 266.

[6] Blaney, Harry F., and Criddle, Wayne D. "Determining Water Requirements for Settling Water Disputes," *Natural Resources Journal,* Vol. 4 (May 1964), p. 29.

[7] "Comment: Control of Access by Frontage Roads—Police Power or Eminent Domain?" *Kansas Law Review,* Vol. 11 (1963), p. 388.

[8] Hartman, L. M., and Seastone, D. A. "Efficiency Criteria for Market Transfers of Water," *Water Resources Research,* Vol. 1, No. 2 (1965), p. 169.

[9] Sax, Joseph L. *Water Law Cases and Commentary.* Boulder, Colo.: Pruett Press, Inc., 1965, pp. 206, 207.

POLITICAL AND ADMINISTRATIVE STUDIES

Optimal Flood Damage Management: Retrospect and Prospect

*Gilbert F. White**

In the worldwide struggle to manage water resources for human good the gap between scientific knowledge of optimal methods and their practical application by farmers, manufacturers, and government officials is large and generally widening. Man's ability to forecast streamflow, to store water and transport it long distances, to alter its quality and extract it from great depths is growing more rapidly than his skill in putting the improved technology to earthy, daily use. This gap between the desirable and the actual is especially dramatic where peasant societies are exposed to new agronomy and water technology, but the contrast is hardly less striking in sectors of United States production where we often think of new techniques as being avidly embraced. Farmers who over-irrigate, manufacturers who neglect tried water conservation devices, and officials who misuse measures of economic efficiency testify to the difficulty.

At times we placidly accept this gap, as when a projection of future national water needs assumes that industry will not increase the adoption of new technology [ref. 1]. At other times we confidently ignore it, as when economic justification for a flood protection scheme assumes all the farmers will change their farming system to take advantage of new conditions [ref. 2]. When the failure to employ economically optimal management practices is frankly confronted, it often is charged off to cultural lag, or ignorance, or inept social organization.

* Professor of Geography, University of Chicago. The author is indebted to Robert W. Kates and W. R. D. Sewell for their helpful criticism of an early draft of the paper.

In a broad sense we are dealing with the basic and immensely intricate problem of how social change takes place non-violently, and we must recognize it has strong and diverse components of customary cultural behavior, organized social action, and natural environment. A soothing and academically safe observation is to say we need more research on why the optimum is not achieved. Clearly this is true, but I feel uncomfortable about even that platitude because some of the research on both technology and analytical methods seems to have widened rather than narrowed the gap in the field of water resources. And the gap promises to widen still further if I read correctly the lessons to be drawn from the American encounter with water resources and the shape of federal programs to come. There is reason to suspect that concentration of analysis on testing for economically efficient solutions may have impeded attainment of the efficiency goal. To modify Voltaire's observation, perhaps the search for the best has been, in these instances, the enemy of the good.

The United States' attempt to manage flood damage over more than three decades illustrates the point. From experience with the planning, construction, and study of the national flood protection efforts, beginning with the massive public works projects of 1933, a few conclusions emerge. That record of natural catastrophe, far-flung surveys, and gigantic expenditures suggests that similar though less grandiose events may well unfold on the flood plains of other developing lands. It also suggests that some portion of the myopic view of remedies, of the failure to understand how choices are made, and of the difficulty in interpreting scientific findings—troubles which have dogged federal flood activities to date—may trip up such growing programs as pollution abatement, water supply, and recreation.

I shall try to review the experience with management of flood losses in several steps. In beginning, a confession must be made of our confusion concerning optimal management. Next, the state of our knowledge about the human use of flood plains is summarized. That is sharpened by pointing out those findings that seem sufficiently valid to warrant recommendation for public policy. The obverse, of course, is admitting what we do not know, thereby outlining major research needs. Both knowledge and ignorance are stated more concretely in reference to the Denver flood of June 1965. Finally, what we have learned that may be of value in other sectors of resources management is the subject of a concluding section.

Were this a review of works of art rather than of engineering construction, public policy, and geographic studies it might be called program notes on a retrospective show. I do not attempt to appraise all the thinking which has bloomed in the muddy wake of U.S. floods. It has been summarized elsewhere [ref. 3, 4, 5, 6]. The emphasis here is on what some of us associated with University of Chicago studies have learned that commends further public action, and on the lessons that may be relevant in distant flood plains or in broader fields of water management.

CONCEPTS OF THE OPTIMUM

If the optimum management of flood damage is taken as that form of flood plain use that is most satisfactory and desirable in yielding the largest net social benefits over an investment period, it must be admitted at the outset that there are pitifully few grounds for judging where it has been achieved. This is because the methods of assessing optimal use are still crude and have been tried in only a few areas. It is difficult to tell whether a given reach of a valley will best serve the needs of the community in one use rather than any other. Rare is the community that is able to define its land needs clearly. Even if methods were established and readily applied, the political task of using the results in urban planning is fraught with complications. When faced with the question, it is common for agencies to follow a greatly simplified process of judgment, such as that embodied in the Milwaukee and Detroit municipal policies of buying up valley bottoms for recreational use without attempting to weigh the alternatives, or the implicit decision in Los Angeles that any land which can be protected from floods at reasonable cost should be used for residential, commercial, and industrial purposes. In some of these cases and in certain clearly warranted protection projects, the present use no doubt is optimal.

If, on the other hand, optimal management is taken as that combination of adjustments to flood hazard for any given use that yields the largest net social benefits, the task is much simpler. At hand are relatively satisfactory methods of comparing the social costs of protection or flood proofing or insurance with the ever available alternative of simply bearing the loss. [Ref. 3, pp. 83–92.] Not that there are no differences of professional judgment; there are, as is shown later, but that major definition and approach seem valid.

The federal policy, freely translated and omitting numerous details, is that flood damage is undesirable, and that the government is prepared to prevent it by feasible engineering or watershed treatment so long as the benefits to whomsoever they may accrue exceed the costs and so long as local interests contribute to the costs of non-reservoir projects. Surveys by the Corps of Engineers and the Soil Conservation Service characteristically assess costs and benefits for one or more engineering schemes for loss reduction. As economic critics have pointed out, these comparisons do not select the optimum: they may ignore incremental analysis, and discount practices are in question [ref. 7, 8]. Thousands of completed survey reports give benefit-cost findings and their implicit forecasts as to what the future will bring.

Inherent in those surveys are a pair of ambiguities. One hinges on the obvious fact that what is optimal for the community may not be optimal for individual managers of flood plain land, depending upon arrangements for sharing costs and benefits. A second is the policy of cost sharing. The Corps sometimes counts benefits from land value enhancement resulting from more intensive use only if necessary to obtain a favorable benefit-cost ratio, and then seeks to recover part as local contribution; the Soil Conservation Service counts them but has no authority to require reimbursement for them. The Corps is not expected to seek reimbursement for the cost of protection from reservoirs. A change in one of these policies by the Congress or a change in the social arrangements for providing technical assistance to individual managers would alter the estimated optimum.

It must be admitted, then, that hortatory declarations as to the proper national policy for making wise use of flood plains can only come to grips at long distance and in a shadowy way with the question of wisest use. They really are addressed, for the most part, to the more limited question of whether or not, given a particular use, the adjustment selected is optimal.

However, there are several bits of evidence that the uses prevailing in United States flood plains in the 1960's are less than optimal. In the more limited goal of federal legislation, we have not been doing well. It is clear that the mean annual toll of flood losses has been rising for half a century [ref. 9]. This in itself would not be evidence of less than optimal use, for it might be that rising total losses would be a characteristic of wise use. Such a conclusion is thrown into doubt by the widespread attempts of flood sufferers to avoid future losses through flood protection works, and by the inability of the federal government, in its expenditure of more than $7 billion since 1936 on protection works, to curb the volume of flood losses. Further scepticism is induced by the readiness of some managers to change their uses of flood plains when presented with new information and opportunities, and by the growing recognition by the Corps of Engineers, itself, that engineering works alone are not fully serving their intended aim.

We know a little about the over-all shift in use of flood plains in the

United States. Corps of Engineers studies show that encroachment continues to be rapid in most sections of the nation. The invasion is predominantly urban, and in many areas consists in enlargement of existing commercial and industrial uses or the expansion of urban uses along new highways [ref. 10]. Loss potential mounts vigorously in reaches where partial protection is offered by dams or levees.

Two aspects of rural flood plain use seem clear from sample studies. One is that the major encroachments of loss potential upon rural flood plains are for new urban use rather than for agriculture [ref. 11]. The second is that in selected places where additional protection against flooding has been provided by watershed protection works there has not been rapid intensification of cropping. (See Burton [ref. 2].) Insofar as the latter relation is true, it challenges the assumption underlying much of the Watershed Protection program that decreases in flood frequency and magnitude will lead to prompt increases in intensity of farm use. It also appears from Burton's work that where parts of a farm are protected, there is a tendency for farmers to gamble on higher risks in unprotected lands [ref. 2, pp. 39–41].

In general, the primarily urban protection programs are running fast to keep up with further encroachments; and the agricultural program is failing to satisfy its promise for farmland use changes, and increasingly is protecting or promoting urban invasion of flood plains. Individual managers of the flood plain are working over large areas at cross-purposes with stated federal aims.

How much do we now know as to why and how these managers—both public and private—behave as they do in the face of floods?

KNOWLEDGE OF FLOOD PLAIN USE

My first preoccupation with American flood problems was with the primitive methods of economic justification practiced by public agencies thirty years ago. When the first national Flood Control Act was passed in 1936, the simple and in many respects more comprehensive comparison of land values that had been used to justify local drainage and Miami Conservancy investments was being replaced by the more complicated but narrowed benefit-cost computations used in the 308 Studies. From my appraisal of the situation came probably the first and certainly the worst paper ever published on the subject in an academic journal [ref. 12]. There also emerged the recognition that engineering protection works are only one of the several adjustments which a flood plain manager may make to flood hazard.

Very slowly it became evident in subsequent years that a benefit-cost calculation has little meaning in seeking optimal solutions unless it predicts with modest reliability the streams of gains and losses that probably will flow from the area in the future. To do this requires sufficient understanding of the behavior of flood plain managers to discern how they may be expected to respond to whatever conditions are postulated for the future. Is a dam likely to reduce net losses downstream? How would a shopkeeper be inclined to use a new map showing his hazard from flooding? Would a change in cost sharing alter a farmer's view of his feasible alternatives? Seeking answers to questions such as these leads to examination of what managers in fact see as their range of choice, how they evaluate the flood hazard, what they regard as available technology for adjusting to floods, what appears to be the economic efficiency of each available technique, and how they are encouraged or constrained by social action. We cannot realistically assume these people to be uniformly well-informed, rational optimizers, nor can we dismiss them cavalierly as stupid, pigheaded, or knaves. More will be said later about models of flood plain behavior.

How Much Choice?

The range of choice open to flood plain users in dealing with flood hazard was outlined systematically in 1942 and has not changed greatly since. [Ref. 13, Table 2.] It was apparent then, as now, that the heavy federal emphasis on full support of reservoir projects and partial support of other engineering protection encouraged both public agencies and individual property managers to think of their choice as being between bearing the loss or enjoying federal protection. The early Tennessee Valley Authority program and the Department of Agriculture Watershed Protection program reinforced this view. Emergency evacuation, while facilitated by Weather Bureau river forecasts, was not specifically organized. Structural adjustments and land elevation were not canvassed in federal studies, and were not promoted by federal or other public agencies. Relief was available principally for extreme hardship. Insurance was lacking in all but a few special cases. Change in land use rarely was considered; a reduction in intensity of use was presumed to meet invariably with local opposition (a presumption later shown to be false). Prediction of enhancement in land value by changing to a more intense use was avoided for a long time, because of fear of open involvement with speculative land development, and the extreme option of relocation of entire communities was so abrupt, radical, and lacking in implementation that it was practical in only a few instances.

It now appears in hindsight that the 1942 typology of human adjustment to floods was misleading and that, while showing principal alternatives, it set back thinking about solutions. The fault lay in two aspects of the classification of adjustment. One was the inclusion of social guides to adjustment as though they were in themselves adjustments. For example, land use regulation was listed as an alternative public measure, whereas we now recognize it as being a possible guide to any adjustment or use. Second, a change in land use was listed as one alternative adjustment. This is true for any given situation of land use, but as stated it carried the implication that a change in use excludes other adjustments. A more accurate way of stating the range of choice would be to show seven different adjustments for each of all possible land uses, as indicated in Table 1, and to omit any mention of the various social actions which might be taken to affect the choice.

The effect of the earlier classification, which still appears in discussions of zoning ordinances or flood plain information studies, is to imply that the range of adjustments applies only to the current use, and that any change in use will mean reduction in intensity. As a result, the possibility of a different use or of use regulation often is ruled out of consideration before it is canvassed: a town rejects zoning on the ground it would automatically prevent commercial uses; a property owner opposes land use studies because he thinks they surely will lead to his relocation or to downgrading of land value. They may, but they do not necessarily have that effect.

Moreover, we have come to recognize that the process of choice is dynamic rather than static. To think of there being a decision only when a major project is under consideration is to ignore the variety of paths along which adjustments move. [Ref. 3, pp. 18–21.] When attention is focused on these diverse paths, then more importance is attached to critical times of decision and to methods of planning for changing and flexible adjustments. [Ref. 3, pp. 17–18; and ref. 14.]

TABLE 1.
Typology of Range of Choice in Adjustments to Floods

1942	1965
Land elevation	Land use A—
Flood abatement	Bearing the loss
Flood protection	Protection
Emergency measures	Emergency measures
Structural adjustments	Structural, including land elevation
Land use	Flood abatement
Crops	Insurance
Urban relocation	Public relief
Public measures	Land use n—
Public relief	Bearing the loss
Insurance	etc.

How Is the Hazard Perceived?

One of the comforting explanations for apparently less than optimal use of flood plains is that there is lack of information as to flood hazard. The obvious corrective—making the information available—was slow in coming in the form of flood hazard maps, and when the first map appeared, it failed to yield the expected results. The U.S. Geological Survey map of Topeka in 1959 did not have a prompt, significant effect upon the thinking of people in Topeka [ref. 15]. Experience there and in the Tennessee Valley pointed out the need for understanding how people habitually perceive hazard and for designing means by which hazard information may become meaningful to flood plain dwellers.

Kates's study of LaFollette and five other communities indicates that perception of flood hazard is a function of direct flood experience and of outlook toward nature, and that the mere supply of information, as to where the water reached and when, does not necessarily lead to more precise recognition of the probability and magnitude of floods [ref. 5]. He shows how the ambiguity of flood risk and the difficulty of facing uncertainty foster a division between flood plain dweller and the scientist in recognizing the hazard for what it is to each of them [ref. 16].

The pioneering flood reports of TVA [ref. 17] and the wide experimentation of the Northeastern Illinois Metropolitan Area Planning Commission with USGS maps have begun to point out specific steps, such as distribution of hazard reports to financial agencies, which will enhance their reception. Regional studies by the USGS of flood frequency are making possible more reliable estimates of hazard. From the burgeoning number of Corps of Engineers flood plain information reports new experience is accumulating but has not been assessed in detail.

We still have only a rudimentary knowledge of how man perceives the risk and uncertainty of a flood or any other natural disaster [ref. 18] and, until this is refined, the judgment of what information in what form will be useful to him will be largely pragmatic.

What Technology Is Available?

It early became apparent that many flood plain managers, while vaguely aware of the possible range of choice and of the flood risk, did not understand the techniques of certain adjustments such as emergency evacuation, structural change, and insurance. From the LaFollette study there is evidence that those who have lived longest on the flood plain are more aware of alternatives, that those most recently flooded perceive emergency action more acutely, and that the times of construction, normal renovation, or disaster repair are more propitious for adoption of alternatives than are other times. Sheaffer's study of flood proofing in Bristol, Tennessee-Virginia showed systematically for the first time the potentialities of combining emergency and structural measures [ref. 19]. This led to TVA and state discussions with local authorities and those, in turn, to a significant deviation from usual federal flood control policy. At Bristol and White Oak, the TVA authorized federal contributions to partial engineering works on condition that local government regulate further encroachments, flood-proof its own buildings, and take responsibility for advising property managers as to flood proofing of the other structures which would enjoy only partial protection under the feasible engineering works [ref. 20].

Emergency evacuation measures have received little detailed study other than at LaFollette and Bristol, and it is only in recent months that the Weather Bureau has begun to go beyond mail questionnaires to ask how its forecasts are used.

Notwithstanding elaborate engineering studies of flood control spillway and channel design, there is no significant research under federal or any other auspices on methods of using plastics, temporary barriers, electronic control, and similar devices to prevent flood losses, and nothing since 1936 on means of rehabilitating damaged property. Expert services are poured into specifications for a dam, but it still is impossible to get from a federal agency the simplest advice as to technology for flood proofing. This lack becomes especially critical when it is recognized that the number of places receiving unfavorable reports from the Corps of Engineers on local protection projects probably equals those receiving favorable reports; that among the authorized projects more than 200 have not been undertaken because of local complications; and that even where comprehensive reservoir programs have been authorized and are under construction, it may be years before the full effect of protection will be felt. Recently, unfavorable reports have tended to include more references to possible alternatives to protection.

Insurance, while a practicable alternative for the few managers who know how to obtain special coverage for flood-proofed property, or who fortuitously are covered by an all-purpose auto policy, is closed to most others. Partly as a result of caution on the part of the insurance companies and partly the consequence of inept beginnings by the administration of the authorized but abortive Federal Flood Insurance Agency, there has been no systematic experimentation with this device. Were the recent explorations by an industry committee to be extended with Housing and Home Finance Agency encouragement and, using the full technical advice of federal agencies, to offer limited coverage in sample areas, it would be practicable to find out precisely how much could be indemnified at costs and in circumstances that would supplement or substitute for protection and other alternative measures. Insurance may well have its most influential uses in being available as a substitute where protection and structural adjustments are not feasible, or in covering the hazard during a period when old uses are phased out.

Is It Economically Efficient?

Although public approaches to flood problems have centered upon benefit-cost analysis of protection projects, little attention has been paid to the economic efficiency of other adjustments and, particularly, to the efficiency of choices by private managers. As a result, we still have only a sketchy knowledge of how far individuals seek to optimize their uses, and what they would choose if they were to do so rationally using their preferred criteria. It is plain that differences in time horizon, discount rate, perceived benefits, and, most of all, direct costs give many individual managers a view of alternatives that would favor federal reservoir projects and would discourage an alternative such as insurance so long as existing federal policy prevails.

By assuming that managers are both rational and subject to the same efficiency criteria as public agencies, the federal programs predict changes which do not materialize—as with the Soil Conservation Service anticipation of intensification of agricultural land use—and fail to predict other changes that do materialize—as with earlier Corps of Engineers disregard for continued encroachment into valleys partially protected by new reservoirs. Economic research has contributed notably to refinement of public analysis without confronting these problems. The recent study of industrial losses in the Lehigh shows that loss and benefit estimates may be sharpened by improved methods, but that a more important step is to recognize differences in the economic stance of an industrial plant versus its region versus the nation [ref. 21].

How Are Other Places Affected?

A principal deficiency of most economic efficiency analysis has been the handling of external economies and diseconomies. In physical terms, little attempt has been made to assess the full physical consequences of changing the regimen of a stream or altering its channel. These go largely unmeasured [ref. 22]. In economic terms, the impacts of a change in land use upon other parts of the same community and region are rarely and imperfectly traced. It is much easier to compare possible adjustments for a store in the Dallas flood plain than to estimate what would be the effects upon Dallas of sharply or progressively shifting that use to recreational or residential. Hopefully, the current Pittsburgh study will throw some light on this. And analysis, such as that attempted at Towson, Maryland [ref. 23, 24], of the social costs of alternative uses will help make choices in the light of impacts upon the whole community.

The early studies of flood plain adjustments tended, as Kates has pointed out, to attribute much of the behavior of flood plain dwelling to ignorance, cupidity, or irrationality [ref. 16]. We took a long time—far too long—to begin to test these riverside opinions as to motives and as to the decision process itself. Perhaps we lacked a handy model of how decisions are made if they are not made by rational, economic men. Perhaps the relative simplicity of manipulating a benefit-cost ratio fascinated us. Perhaps we had too much faith that if a government commission charted a path, both property owners and government officials would follow it sheepishly. At any rate, we went many years aiming at what people should do about floods without trying to deepen our understanding of the different paths which people actually take in living with floods.

To do this requires a much more complex model of human behavior than the optimization model. It must be a model which takes sufficient account of differences in perception, decision criteria, and the effect of social guides to permit a reasonably accurate description of what and how people decide to cope with flood hazard.

How Does Society Guide the Choice?

The role of social guides in constraining or encouraging the flood plain manager has been noted at several points. More is known about how public managers respond to pressures [ref. 25, 26] than about how individual managers respond to public guidance. We have just begun to identify the ways in which federal policies of flood control, flood forecasting and urban renewal, state regulatory action on stream channels and highway location, municipal building codes, urban plans and renewal programs, and financing agency policy can be integrated to promote maximum choice in adjusting to flood hazard and in use of flood plains. We have learned, for example, that while a flood hazard map alone may have little influence upon the decision of a property owner to build in a flood plain, it becomes powerful when placed in the hands of a professional appraiser who has been instructed in its use, and even more powerful when mortgage insurance officers in the Federal Housing Administration and Veterans Administration are instructed to look for it and use it. We have learned that a cost-sharing requirement for a protection project may change a manager's view not only of the project, but of the alternatives open to him. Reactions to enforcement of encroachment lines, zoning ordinances, and subdivision regulations are better known. The legality of setting encroachment lines now appears well established, but no solid test yet has been made of restrictive zoning of the plain above [ref. 27] the channel, or of the liability of a property owner who knowingly exposes others to the damages of flood.

Perhaps the most baffling single problem in achieving any significant advances in public action with respect to flood loss reduction is the set of mind and institutional position of public agency personnel. To ignite the field staff of an agency like the Corps of Engineers or the Bureau of Reclamation with a new approach in contrast to a new technique is like setting fire to a pile of soggy newspapers—time, patience, and systematic ventilation are required. And a new organization can mismanage a promising innovation, as in the case of flood insurance. But there are exciting exceptions, as in the Tennessee Valley Authority where one man gave the leadership for a new federal-state-local co-operative approach to flood loss reduction.[1]

Basic to the action of the administrators and the public pressures they feel are the attitudes toward nature, water, and floods which they and other resource managers share. The sense of man as a conqueror of nature, the view of access to water as a divine right, these and other attitudes combine to condition the position of a city manager who argues that restriction on channel encroachment is a denial of a right to share nature's largess, or of an engineer who after daily travelling a hazardous expressway to his office concludes that the only suitable engineering works are those promising virtually complete safety from loss of life.

Unlike the larger enterprise of river basin development, difficulties in flood loss management cannot be charged primarily to splintering of responsibility among agencies operating under divided congressional authority. True, the number of federal, state, and local agencies having a hand in guiding decisions about floods is large, but they now have little conflict or duplication—except where the Soil Conservation Service bumps into the Corps of Engineers as it moves downstream with larger dams and smaller local requirements—and the greatest opportunity for co-ordination appears to rest in the application of an integrated federal approach within existing legislative policy.

Side Effects of Normative Analysis

Emphasis upon normative economic analysis by federal agencies and their academic reformers may have retarded the attainment of optimal goals. Refinement of the benefit-cost practices has directed attention to

---

[1] The work which has been carried out under the leadership of James E. Goddard is reported briefly in two papers [see ref. 28, 29].

what should be engineering investment in flood plains rather than to explaining their present use. While there is much room for improvement and while benefit-cost analysis would be enhanced by insight into managerial behavior, it detours the realistic prediction of future use. By assuming the managers of flood plain property are either optimizing, rational men, or narrow, inflexible men, it avoids difficulties that would arise were account taken of information lacks; interpretation of information; differing perception of hazard, technology, and efficiency; differing decision rules; and inconsistent social guides. Having prescribed a simple cure, there is little incentive for the government doctor to return to the bedside to find out what happened to the patient. Public doubts about economic justification are soothed by B/C ratios exceeding unity while public side-effects are largely ignored. It should not be abandoned, but the weight of its authority should not be carried unless it is used to help explain the vital question of what will be the future use if a given adjustment or use is adopted.

One day a short, sturdy Maine blacksmith, after long wooing the willowy village belle, won her consent to marriage as they talked in his shop. Enthusiastically, he jumped onto the anvil and kissed her. Then they walked hand in hand out across the meadows. "Shall we kiss again?" he asked. "Not yet," she said. Farther on he again put the question. "But why do you keep asking?" she replied. "Because," he said, "if there isn't going to be any more kissing, I'll stop carrying this anvil." Normative economic analysis is an anvil that can serve several important uses, including intangible aesthetic ones, but there isn't much point in carrying its weight unless it is used properly.

WARRANTED PUBLIC ACTION

Given optimal use as our distant aim, what do we know sufficiently well to warrant immediate prescription of public program? I think we know enough about human use of flood plains to assert that if the burden of annual losses is to be reduced without concomitant expenditures for engineering works, federal policy and program must be revised and supplemented in several ways. These would help to see to it that managers of flood plain land are supplied with full information, in intelligible form and at the right times, as to the range of choice in use and adjustment open to them in using the flood plain. This means piecing together a genuine program from diverse parts.

Solid data on flood losses would help. There are grounds for believing that sufficient research has been done to enable us to design and carry out a new system for collecting flood loss data which would substitute synthetic for reported losses, estimate the degree to which potential losses are averted, and rely upon a stratified, systematic set of samples [ref. 3, pp. 111–14]. We ought to end our unhappy plight of having to say that mean annual flood losses are "in the neighborhood of $300–900 million."

Technical studies on flood proofing and insurance and on relationships between flood characteristics and flood losses should be pushed, and their results disseminated where and when people will use them.

A profound change in approach would result if the Corps of Engineers were to exercise its present authority to require, as a condition of further construction, state agencies to regulate encroachments upon stream channels, and to require local agencies to regulate land uses in reaches of streams where federal protection is to be provided.

Perhaps more important is the opportunity for the Corps of Engineers and the Soil Conservation Service, in collaboration with the appropriate federal agencies dealing with urban problems, to encourage local communities to assure that consideration of flood hazard enters into public and private planning decisions [ref. 3, p. 124]. This would include expansion of reports on flood areas and frequencies, interpretation of the results to interested managers and key people such as architects and mortgage officers, stimulation of flood-forecasting and warning systems, dissemination of information on alternative measures for loss reduction, promotion of improved land use regulations, and support of selective public acquisition of hazard areas. Reconciliation of cost-sharing policy is in order.

In brief, the chief threats from clearly uneconomic encroachment should be curbed. Next to this, the major opportunity now seems to rest in promoting choice by private managers among combinations of protection, emergency, structural, and insurance measures. In the light of our knowledge of decision making and of a few practical experiments, it seems likely that public action with that aim would improve flood plain use and that it would be politically acceptable. Only a few aspects would require new federal legislation.

In contrast to earlier times when proposals for federal policy, whatever their theoretical merit, fell on inhospitable ground, three aspects of the present scene make action seem more hopeful: (1) There is a rather widespread feeling in both federal and state agencies that engineering works are not enough. (2) At the same time practical experience is building respect for new analytical techniques and for such social guides as flood information reports, mortgage insurance policy, and zoning. (3) The public groups concerned with flood damage management have been expanded significantly in recent years. To the flood sufferers have

264

been added citizen and government contingents seeking speedy urban renewal and greater open space, and their support for a broadened approach seems assured.

Now let us list points at which understanding is so lacking that it is necessary to be cautious about recommending public action.

While there are rough methods for weighing alternative adjustments for the same land use, such as protection and flood proofing, there is no satisfactory method of comparing the feasibility of different land uses, having in mind the external economies and diseconomies accruing to other parts of the same urban area. Until this is achieved the public choice of alternative uses in hazardous areas, a choice which at best is subject to highly political pressures, is bound to be vague.

In the case of both urban and rural reaches, much more needs to be known about the precise factors affecting individual choice, particularly the managerial perception of uncertainty and of economic efficiency. Without such refinement of relationships, U.S. Department of Agriculture's predictions of flood plain land use in Watershed Protection projects, and Corps of Engineers' estimates of urban land use changes will remain speculative. We need to find out precisely how many alternatives people can consider and in what conditions.

DENVER AS AN EXAMPLE

With the June 1965 disaster in Denver in mind [ref. 10, pp. 127–33], how would these conclusions apply to that inundated South Platte flood plain as its residents dug out of the mud and repaired their bridges behind them? After Red Cross and federal disaster assistance had been assured and people began to look to the possibility of future floods (including some which, they have been told for many years, will bring a flow twice as large as that of 1965), a program of the type suggested could have affected the city in the following fashion.

The Corps of Engineers, while open to discussion about getting funds for an upstream dam, would announce that no federal funds would be available for protection until the state took steps to curb further encroachment on stream channels. Any further protection for Denver would also be contingent upon the city showing it had extended its present regulation of land use from a few of the tributary dry washes to the full South Platte flood plain. Assistance would be offered to the municipal authorities in getting accurate, intelligible reports on the hazard areas and likely frequency of flooding, and in advising them as to how the results could be put in the hands of property managers. Technical assistance would be available to owners, architects, and city officials, not only on how to speed up appropriations by Congress but on how to save on salvage operations, how to flood-proof existing buildings against future losses, how to improve the flood-warning service, and how to draw up building codes which would prohibit dangerous uses such as flammable gas installations. Highway officials and the Federal Housing Administration and Veterans Administration would be alerted to hazard areas. Appraisers would state flood hazards, like termite infestation, as a routine part of their reports. The new urban affairs agency would offer to collaborate in planning of renewal for part of the area and in preparing schemes for open land reservation and acquisition for other parts of the area. Insurance would be available, perhaps through private companies at rates reflecting the risk, to property owners who already were within the reach of floods and could not be protected or who must wait years for protection.

What would all of this mean in terms of future occupance of the South Platte? As a minimum, the harmful encroachments on natural channels and needlessly hazardous invasion of adjoining flood plains at last would stop. No further increase in damage potential would take place without both property managers and public agencies being aware of the hazard and the possible choices. Emergency damage reduction plans would become a part of industrial and municipal preparations. Structural changes would receive routine consideration in any rehabilitation or construction of buildings in hazard areas. Insofar as renewal or open space schemes were studied, there would be conscious public judgment of the merits of changing existing uses. As a maximum, Denver might find itself after two decades of progressive adjustments with only as much property in the path of floods as city and owners feel warrants the risk. Thus, the optimal adjustments to flood hazard would be approached. The present policy of permitting dangerous invasion of the channel and of restricting many flood plain dwellers to a choice between bearing flood losses or seeking federal aid would be abandoned.

LESSONS FROM THREE DECADES

This rich and partly distilled experience of the United States in coping with the risk and uncertainty of floods is relevant to broader efforts at water management in several ways. Wherever growing cities spread into flood plains and whenever governments feel obliged to curb the losses from inundation there is danger that public investment may take the course which has been etched in buildings, earth, and concrete along American river valleys during the past three decades. This need not be repeated in growing countries with rapid urbanization.

Beyond the flood plain, there are three more general lessons that may apply to other sectors of water management. One is to guard against becoming bemused by commitment to a single engineering solution to the exclusion of other alternatives. Just as devotion to dams, channels, and levees obscures the view of possible gains in flood management from changes in emergency action, structures and insurance, or from other land uses, the preoccupation with stream dilution may divert attention from alternative waste treatment, and the search for new water supplies may prevent the exploration of methods of saving water already available.

Another lesson is to beware of easy, unsupported explanations of why people manage resources as they do. Willingness to believe that flood plain dwellers are rational managers who will seek the optimal economic adjustments to floods, can sidetrack our understanding of the complex factors which in fact affect their decisions. In the same way, simple curbstone explanations of manufacturers' preferences may delay measures to improve the efficiency of their water use, and casual assumptions concerning an irrigator's aims may obstruct the public attempts to help him adopt soil- and water-saving practices.

In both the exploration of alternatives and the understanding of the intricate process of resource decisions it is essential, if the results are to be useful, to be continuously alert to ways of reporting and interpreting findings so that they will be employed at the right time by farmer or manufacturer or government official. It is better to know that flood plain dwellers interpret the same sequence of flood events differently than to believe erroneously that a single government statement of hazard will have similar significance to all. It is even more important to learn by both study and trial what form of information will be meaningful to them and in what circumstances decisions will be made. The manager must not only see the choices, but see precisely how he or others can carry out each alternative.

When we address ourselves to lessons such as these, we are confronting—whether in flood plain or upland or city or farm—the fundamental problem of how man, in the face of diverse cultural tradition, social rigidity, and resource disparity, manages peacefully to gain a more fruitful living from the earth.

REFERENCES

[1] Senate Select Committee on National Water Resources. *Report*. 86th Congress, 1st Session, Report No. 29. Washington: U.S. Government Printing Office, 1961, p. 24.

[2] Burton, Ian. *Types of Agricultural Occupance of Flood Plains in the United States*. Department of Geography Research Paper No. 75. Chicago: University of Chicago, 1962.

[3] White, Gilbert F. *Choice of Adjustment to Floods*. Department of Geography Research Paper No. 93. Chicago: University of Chicago, 1964.

[4] Tennessee Valley Authority, Technical Library. *Flood Damage Prevention: An Indexed Bibliography*. Knoxville: Tennessee Valley Authority, 1964.

[5] Kates, Robert William. *Hazard and Choice Perception in Flood Plain Management*. Department of Geography Research Paper No. 78. Chicago: University of Chicago, 1962.

[6] Hoyt, William G., and Langbein, Walter B. *Floods*. Princeton: Princeton University Press, 1955.

[7] Hufschmidt, Maynard M., Krutilla, John V., and Margolis, Julius. *Report of Panel of Consultants to the Bureau of the Budget on Standards and Criteria for Formulating and Evaluating Federal Water Resources Developments*. Washington: U.S. Bureau of the Budget, 1961.

[8] *Policies, Standards and Procedures in the Formulation, Evaluation, and Review of Plans for Use and Development of Water and Related Land Resources*. Senate Document No. 97, 87th Congress (approved by the President on May 15, 1962).

[9] Cook, Howard L., and White, Gilbert F. "Making Wise Use of Flood Plains," *United States Papers for United Nations Conference on Science and Technology*, Vol. 2. Washington: U.S. Government Printing Office, 1963.

[10] White, Gilbert F., *et al. Changes in Urban Occupance of Flood Plains in the United States*. Department of Geography Research Paper No. 57. Chicago: University of Chicago, 1958.

[11] ——. *Rural Flood Plains in the United States: A Summary Report*. Department of Geography (mimeo.). Chicago: University of Chicago, 1963.

[12] ——. "Limit of Economic Justification for Flood Protection," *Journal of Land and Public Utility Economics*, Vol. 12, 1936.

[13] ——. *Human Adjustment to Floods*. Department of Geography Research Paper No. 29. Chicago: University of Chicago, 1945.

[14] James, Douglas. *A Time Dependent Planning Process for Combining Structural Measures, Land Use and Flood Proofing to Minimize the Economic Loss of Floods*. Report EEP-12. Stanford: Stanford University Institute in Engineering Economic Systems, 1964.

[15] Roder, Wolf. "Attitudes and Knowledge in the Topeka Flood Plain," in *Papers on Flood Problems*. Department of Geography Research Paper No. 70. Chicago: University of Chicago, 1960.

[16] Kates, Robert W. "Variation in Flood Hazard Perception: Implications

for Rational Flood-Plain Use," *Spatial Organization of Land Uses: The Willamette Valley*. Corvallis: Oregon State University, 1964.

[17] Senate Select Committee on National Water Resources. "Flood Problems and Management in the Tennessee River Basin," *Committee Print No. 16*. 86th Congress, 1st Session. Washington: U.S. Government Printing Office, 1960.

[18] Burton, Ian, and Kates, Robert W. "The Perception of Natural Hazards in Resource Management," *Natural Resources Journal*, Vol. 3, 1964.

[19] Sheaffer, John R. *Flood Proofing: An Element in a Flood Damage Reduction Program*. Department of Geography Research Paper No. 65. Chicago: University of Chicago, 1960.

[20] *Plan for Flood Damage Prevention at Bristol, Tennessee-Virginia*. Bristol: Bristol Flood Study Committee, 1962.

[21] Kates, Robert W. *Industrial Flood Losses: Damage Estimation in the Lehigh Valley*. Department of Geography Research Paper No. 98. Chicago: University of Chicago, 1965.

[22] Wolman, M. Gordon. "Downstream Changes in Alluvial Channels Produced by Dams." U.S.G.S. Professional Paper, in preparation.

[23] McHarg, Ian, and Wallace, D. A. *Plan for the Valleys*. Towson: Worthington and Green Valley Planning Commission, 1964.

[24] Sutton, Walter G. *Planning for Optimum Economic Use of Flood Plains*. A.S.C.E. Environmental Engineering Conference, Atlanta, 1963.

[25] Maass, Arthur. *Muddy Waters: The Army Engineers and the Nation's Rivers*. Cambridge: Harvard University Press, 1951.

[26] Murphy, Francis C. *Regulating Flood Plain Development*. Department of Geography Research Paper No. 56. Chicago: University of Chicago, 1958.

[27] Beuchert, Edward W. "Recent Natural Resource Cases: Constitutional Law–Zoning–Flood Plain Regulation," *Natural Resources Journal*, Vol. 4, 1965.

[28] Goddard, James E. "The Cooperative Program in the Tennessee Valley," in *Papers on Flood Problems*. Department of Geography Research Paper No. 70. Chicago: University of Chicago, 1960.

[29] ——. "Flood Damage Prevention and Flood Plain Management Improve Man's Environment," *Proceedings American Society of Civil Engineers*, Vol. 89, 1963.

Policy Problems in the Field of Water Resources

*Irving K. Fox**

W̶ater resources policy issues have been studied intensively and
reported on frequently since the end of World War II. In this paper, it is
proposed to examine several overriding problems which promise to be of
major, if not dominant, significance in the conduct of water resources
activities in the next few decades. The over-all environment within which
policies evolve and programs are undertaken will have much to do with
the future course of events in the water field. In our concentration on the
technical aspects of water uses, we may fail to see the restraints on what
is feasible that are imposed by our cultural and institutional environment.

The three problems to be considered are:

1. How to achieve a rational public understanding of water resource
use problems and opportunities.

2. How to achieve a reasonable approximation of a social optimum
through public decision-making process.

3. How to change policy to accord with the changing environment
within which water resources activities are undertaken.

PUBLIC ATTITUDES ON WATER RESOURCE USE PROBLEMS AND OPPORTUNITIES

In reviewing the history of water resources activities in the United
States, one is struck by the extent to which water development has been
influenced by major political or social goals that have become prominent
during particular periods. Although promoters of canals were compelled

* Vice President, Resources for the Future, Inc., until August 31, 1966; now
Professor of Regional Planning and Associate Director of the Water Resources
Center, University of Wisconsin.

to provide economic justification for each investment proposed, it seems doubtful that the Canal Era was the product of rational consideration of the benefits and costs of canal investments. The surge of canal building activity may have resulted from a combination of economic and political forces that led people to believe much was to be gained through canal construction. Whatever the forces may have been, the conviction grew that it was sound public as well as private policy to invest large sums in canal development. There was widespread belief that canals were needed, and this view determined the course of public and private decisions for several decades.

The story of irrigation in the arid and semi-arid West is a somewhat similar one. It is difficult to say what all the forces were that caused the settlement and investment which resulted in the present level of irrigation in western United States. I question that it was a response to a considered judgment that irrigation of new lands was the best way to increase the agricultural output of the nation or that the economic opportunities offered by irrigation were so much brighter than other available opportunities. I suspect that it was the result of a variety of forces, such as the concept of political leaders that settlement of the West was in the national interest and a general feeling that making the desert bloom is intrinsically good. In part because of these drives, individuals saw opportunities for private gain or political advancement and added to the pressures for action. Another widely held conviction took root: Western lands should be irrigated. This idea has remained with us to this day (although somewhat diminished) and influences public and private investment in water resources development in the West. Many of the decisions made in the past seem irrational to us now. Much that was done was costly if not disastrous. Yet, one wonders whether the general course of history would have been changed significantly even if modern engineering, economic theory, and systems analysis had been used.

The province of British Columbia has recently undertaken an enormous program of hydroelectric power development. Included in this program is the construction of the largest reservoir in North America, on the Peace River, together with a system of dams on the Columbia to be constructed under an international agreement. Many economists advised against this program, holding that incremental additions to supply should be made in response to growth in demand. Yet the program is going forward, because public opinion in the province appears to be that the program will stimulate the social and economic development of the region. Here again, the course of water development is being determined by public viewpoints resulting from a combination of social, political, and economic forces that are difficult to identify.

This brief history suggests that the broad outlines of water resources development in North America may not be determined by what we would consider to be a rational engineering-economic approach to water problems. Possibly more attention should be directed to understanding how the public makes up its mind on the pros and cons of water development issues.

An immediate question is: What public attitudes will influence, if not determine, the course of future water resources development in the United States (and possibly North America)? No doubt there are many; but two might be identified as having a profound potential influence upon the future course of policy and decision making. One of these is the view that an abundance of water, especially in the West, is a dynamic factor in fostering social and economic advancement. The other is the view that disposal of wastes to waterways is intrinsically evil and that some way must be found to abate it if not discontinue it. Let us examine each of these views.

Water Abundance and the Development of the West

Concern about the adequacy of water supplies is nationwide: the recent experiences of New England and New York come freshly to mind. For our present purposes, however, we will consider only the arid and semi-arid West, because it is in that region more than any other that the availability of water is associated with economic advancement. Broadly speaking, there are two generalized views of the western water situation. One of these might be termed the "economic rationality view," the other, the "developmental view." The distinction is not a sharp one, for many people hold views that lie somewhere in between; nevertheless, it is useful to make such a distinction at the outset of our discussion.

Most economists, engineers, and others with predilections similar to mine tend to subscribe to the economic rationality view. Briefly summarized, it is as follows:

> Throughout the West most of the water used is applied to agriculture. In a society that is predominantly urban-industrial this is a relatively low-value use. Even to meet future increased demands for agricultural output at reasonable cost, the amount of water used for western agriculture could be reduced substantially. Western municipal and industrial requirements are increasing rapidly, but modest reductions in agricultural use combined with more efficient use of available supplies through reuse and reclamation practices can readily meet these demands for several decades. According to estimates made by the Resources for the Future staff, for example, a

transfer to municipal and industrial use of 10 per cent of depletions for irrigation projected for the year 2000 could nearly double the projected levels of depletions for municipal and industrial activity [ref. 1].

To launch one of the ambitious diversion schemes now being entertained—such as the North American Water and Power Alliance (NAWAPA) proposal or the suggestion for a major diversion from the Columbia—would be a mistake, for they are costly in comparison with the foregoing alternative and they involve enormous capital investments to serve needs which can be only dimly perceived. Demands cannot be projected with confidence into the twenty-first century because of the rapid pace of economic and social change and scientific and technological advancement. Who is to say today what techniques are best for supplying water in the twenty-first century or how much will be demanded? In view of the enormous capital cost and the uncertainty, is it wise to chew up as much of the landscape as is contemplated by these proposals?

In brief, sound public policy involves the application of improved techniques of engineering, economics, and systems analysis to develop economically efficient systems that take into account marginal costs and returns from alternative system design. Over the next several decades one can envisage a substantial shift in water use from agriculture to municipal, industrial, and recreation uses. Modest increments to total supply may also be necessary. These changes, combined with substantial advances in the technology of water use and possibly significant advances in the technology of supply, will assure adequate water for economic growth in the region.

I do not claim that this is the right viewpoint, but it is one that is supported by much of the research conducted over the last couple of decades.

Let us turn now to the developmental view. Possibly no one will subscribe unreservedly to the following summarization, but in view of some of the proposals made by advocates of major diversions, I believe the interpretation to be not unreasonable.

The country's greatness is founded on grand visions of future growth. If economic rationality had been adhered to by our forebears, westward settlement would hardly have moved beyond the Appalachian Mountains, the Louisiana Purchase would never have been consummated, the transcontinental railroad system would never have been built, and the arid and semi-arid West would have

274

remained a barren desert. The proposed major water diversions are in the tradition of a dynamic America.

In a narrow economic sense it may be demonstrable that the proposed diversions are too costly, but a dynamic future for the West depends upon the availability of a plentiful supply of water at a low price. Shifting water out of agriculture, increasing prices, waiting for technology to improve, and similar measures will induce a psychology that will discourage investment and will in general foster stagnation of the western economy.

The major diversions will have the opposite effect. The West will be assured of plentiful water. Industry and cities will be encouraged to expand. The agricultural sector will grow instead of decline. The large investments in the works of diversion themselves will add further stimulus to the western economy. The total effect will be a dynamic West experiencing tremendous advances and contributing enormously to the national economy.

The application of traditional benefit-cost analysis misses the dynamic character of the situation. Certainly, economics, engineering, and systems analyses are useful tools for arriving at minimum-cost arrangements for the grand design. But these tools fail to measure adequately the benefits, because the impact a large venture of this nature has upon the psychology of the people of the region is not susceptible to engineering-economic analysis.

My purpose in presenting these two contrasting views is to suggest that the broad outlines of western water development may not be determined by a combination of conventional economic criteria, federal reimbursement policy, public power policy, the application of the acreage limitation, and other specific policy guides. They may, instead, be determined by the way the western situation is broadly perceived by political leaders and the public generally. If, in response to broad public support or possibly only with public acquiescence, the political leadership of the West adopts the developmental view, a major developmental effort would conceivably be launched. This effort might not be as grand as NAWAPA but one can envisage political arrangements that would permit the Pacific Northwest to export large quantities of water to the more arid sections of the Southwest. If this idea takes a strong hold, reimbursement policy, benefit-cost analysis, and other criteria will be the handmaidens of the grand design rather than its determinants.

The situation has important implications for research designed to improve the basis for water resources policy, a matter that will be discussed further after consideration of a somewhat parallel situation.

Waste Disposal and the Preservation of Water Quality

The nation's concern about water pollution is evidenced by the attention given it by the press and by the activities of federal, state, and local governments. As in the case of western water supply, two broadly contrasting views of the nature of the waste disposal problem are discernible. One might be termed the "management view," the other, the "complete abatement view."

Most economists, engineers, and other specialists in the water field tend toward the management view. The rationale is as follows:

> Disposal of wastes in waterways is a valuable use of the nation's water resources. It represents a special problem largely because the waste discharger imposes costs upon others that do not enter the calculus of his own decisions concerning the extent to which he should use the waterway for this purpose. By viewing the waterway as an integrated system and applying modern techniques of analysis, it is practicable to develop optimal arrangements that take into account the values of using the waterway for waste disposal in comparison with the social cost thereof, and also to take advantage of potential scale economies such as those realized through low-flow augmentation, large-scale treatment facilities, and so forth.
>
> Consequently, waste disposal is a legitimate use of a waterway which should only be limited by the costs of such use as compared with the returns. The research problem is to provide an improved basis for designing and implementing efficient systems which embrace waste disposal as well as other potential uses of water resources.

This view is well supported by much of the research on water quality management conducted in recent years, including the economic analyses of Allen Kneese [ref. 2, 3]. It also seems to be supported by common sense. Rivers and lakes are valuable for waste disposal purposes. What could be more logical than balancing the returns against the costs of such use and managing the river system and waste disposal in accord with an optimum result? However, the contrasting view of complete abatement, held by a great many people, appears to be embedded in our framework of law. It may be summarized as follows:

> The original riparian doctrine is basically sound in providing that the riparian owner is entitled to have the flow of the waterway pass his property unchanged in quality as a consequence of upstream uses. Waste disposal to waterways results in pollution; pollution is an evil thing and as such it should be eradicated.

It is true that waterways are extensively used for waste disposal purposes and that to require complete discontinuance of these practices at once would seriously disrupt many economic activities. Returning our waterways to conditions existing when wastes were not discharged into them, however, remains the long-range basic objective.

The way to achieve this objective is through the development of new techniques of handling wastes and the persuasion and regulation of those who dispose of wastes. Water pollution control agencies should apply pressure to waste dischargers to treat wastes to the fullest extent practicable under existing technology. Research should be directed to improving technology with the objective of reducing waste contributions to continuingly lower levels.

Public policy appears to be oriented toward this latter approach: "clean streams at almost any price" is the watchword. As I understand the law, a waste discharger cannot obtain a right to use a waterway for waste disposal purposes, although the courts have refused to prevent such use when important economic considerations seemed to justify it. Public agencies have directed their attention toward reducing waste discharges of cities and other public bodies through support of waste treatment, regulation, and research on treatment techniques. It is true that flow augmentation is recognized as a legitimate purpose of a federal reservoir—which suggests that the river should be managed for waste disposal as well as other purposes. However, low-flow augmentation is not viewed as a substitute for treatment of wastes at the source, but only as a supplement to be used after all other practicable means of treatment have been utilized. There is good reason to believe that low-flow augmentation has been supported more as further justification for all-purpose dams than as recognition of its place in a comprehensive approach to managing water quality. Proposals for instituting features of a management approach to water quality have been noticeably absent in congressional legislation dealing with water pollution.

There are indications of a growing understanding of the management approach. The comprehensive surveys being conducted by the U.S. Public Health Service appear to be founded on this concept, and industrial groups, some regional agencies, and certain federal agency personnel have displayed increasing interest. It is quite possible that when the costs of complete abatement are fully appreciated the management approach will be accepted. Yet, today the trend is still toward complete abatement and may continue so for many years. It is possible that those of us who specialize in water problems have failed fully to understand the value

Americans attach to clean water. Perhaps mass media have helped to develop a popular mystique. People may not be properly informed about acceptable degrees of water quality and the costs of pursuing the mirage of totally clean water. The largest question in water quality management centers around the views people will hold of the nature of the water quality problem. Is waste disposal, seen as pollution, an evil to be eradicated or is waste disposal a legitimate use of a river to be managed with due regard for aesthetics but in accordance with the costs and returns?

Public Views and Water Resources Policy

The work of Robert Kates and Gilbert White [ref. 4, 5] and the two situations just examined point up the questions which, while bearing directly upon water resources policy, have not received the emphasis they may merit.

First, are there large and seldom recognized gaps in our techniques for measuring benefits and costs of water programs? Can we in fact appraise the consequences of alternative decisions when we move from the addition of modest increments to large-scale changes? Is the intuition of our political leaders more accurate than our analysis? If large public investments do, in fact, provide an enormous stimulus to economic advancement, what are the relative merits of alternative investment opportunities?

Second, since the views of the general public and political leaders largely determine the course of water development, should we not seek a better understanding of what these views are and how they are formed? With a better understanding of public viewpoints, research could be more explicitly directed to the clarification of issues about which there is confusion or where public views do not appear to accord with the results of scientific inquiry.

PUBLIC DECISION-MAKING PROCESSES

Much of the water resources research undertaken by government, universities, and other institutions is aimed at improving public programs. Heavy emphasis has been placed on engineering and economic aspects, but, as has been indicated, comparatively little attention has been given to the study of decision-making processes as they relate to the use of water. Yet, if water resources programs are, in fact, to be improved, we need to know much more about the decision-making process and how it should function in order to estimate what cost-sharing policies are appropriate, what constitutes a good framework of water law, what are desirable patterns of relationship among the three levels of government, and what is an appropriate organizational structure for the conduct of water resources activities.

It is important at the start to clarify what we mean by "good" decisions or "good" policies relating to water resources; there is much confusion on this point. Furthermore, we need to examine the structure and process of decision making so that we may understand how public and private institutions involved in water management can be organized and related to one another to produce "good" results.

"Good" Public Decisions

There is a great deal of loose talk about whether a given decision or action is in "the public interest." For what, in fact, is the public interest? As a concept, it eludes scientific analysis. Even the techniques of welfare economics, invaluable as they are to those of us who are analyzing water resources activities, suffer in their application, for they are limited in the following ways:

- Many values people associate with water use cannot be measured satisfactorily in quantitative terms for purposes of analysis.
- The value preferences of an analyst influence the alternatives he considers and the way data are utilized. Complete objectivity is an impractical ideal.
- Welfare economic theory cannot objectively take into account values associated with income redistribution. Yet income redistribution has always been associated with public water development programs.

The limitations listed in no way minimize the importance of the analytical tools developed in recent years. But these tools are not infallible, and I feel strongly that in the case of water systems planning we should be careful not to equate the optimum arrived at through their use with the public interest.

Since the public interest cannot be determined through objective analysis of alternative decisions, it is necessary to seek some other approach. Western society has traditionally sought to resolve the problem by means of rules and institutions governing the pattern of relationships among the individuals affected by a decision. Thus, with regard to economic institutions the economic theorists have developed an optimizing model based upon the operation of the competitive market through which goods and services are exchanged in accordance with individual value preferences. A "good" result is not predetermined through scientific analysis. Instead, it is achieved through the process of purchase and sale in which the value placed upon a commodity by an individual is reflected in the price

279

he is willing to pay to obtain it or the price he must be paid to part with it. Equity is achieved because buyers bear the cost of their purchases and sellers are rewarded through payments for the costs they have incurred. Under this model an optimal solution reflects the value standards of the individuals affected by the decision; any appraisal of the result is based upon the opportunity afforded individuals to participate in the decision rather than upon an evaluation of the result itself.

Political theorists have also used an optimizing model, although it is not as precisely defined as the economist's. It is based on the participation of individuals in the selection of governmental officials and on a division of power among branches and jurisdictions of government, including an assignment to the judiciary to enforce certain principles of liberty and justice which have evolved through centuries of human experience. Implicit in the classical political model is the assumption that the individual affected by a decision would be able to express his value preferences through the system of governmental representation.

It has long been recognized that the market does not always work in accordance with classical economic theory, and economists have specified the conditions under which it could not be expected to function. This, in turn, has stimulated a demand for public action to compensate for the limitations of the market. It is because of these limitations that government is so deeply involved in the water resources field. But it is also true that the classical political model is no longer applicable to American government. It seems reasonable to say that no well-defined modern theory of public decision making has evolved which one might consider as offering an optimum result, that is, one best serving the public interest.

It seems evident that any theory of public decision making which best serves the public interest in a modern democratic society must be concerned with the relationships among the individuals and groups that will be affected by a given decision. It must be concerned, that is, with the individual's ability to express his value preferences and with a balancing of his preferences against the preferences of others who are involved in the decision. In brief: Are those who benefit and those who pay satisfactorily represented in the decision-making process? Without trying to define what constitutes a "satisfactory" measure of representation, certain blocks to its achievement can be identified.

Problems in Achieving "Good" Results through Public Decision Making

Any effort to develop a framework of public decision making that best serves the public interest must be concerned with at least five major problems.

First, the large number of complex decisions which must be made through modern governmental institutions inhibits sustained interest in any one facet of governmental activity. Broadly speaking, everyone has a stake in the management of the nation's water resources, although some have a much larger stake than others; but each citizen has a stake in various other governmental activities. How can he be expected to react intelligently about each one of these? He is also concerned with Vietnam and the Dominican Republic. He is concerned with the operation of his local school system and the city plan. He is helping to pay for the space program and the maintenance of the defense establishment. He has interest or concern about the use of pesticides, air pollution, the construction of highways, and so on. How can the individual participate effectively in decisions about water when so many other aspects of public life also demand his attention? If he cannot participate effectively, how can his interests be adequately represented?

Second, the diffusion, and in some instances the concentration, of costs and returns from water programs makes it difficult to achieve a balance in the relationship among those affected by a given decision. Federal water resources repayment policy widely distributes the costs of a water resources project among federal taxpayers. The benefits from a given project may accrue to a limited number of individuals. This sort of relationship provides those who benefit with a major incentive to use their influence to bring about favorable public decisions. On the other hand, the diffusion of costs obscures the consequences of a given decision by those who pay. The net values lost by the many who pay for a project may exceed the benefits of those who receive the returns from it. But those who pay the costs may not be heard because the costs are so widely distributed. The reverse situation may also occur: benefits from a program may be so widely diffused that support is difficult to mobilize. How can one achieve a proper balancing of interests in situations of this kind?

Third, many public decisions about water are based upon a complex scientific and technological foundation. This, however, does not endow the scientist or the technician with special ability to determine what is best. He can evaluate physical consequences of alternative decisions and he can measure certain types of values to the extent permitted by the tools of economic analysis, but he cannot judge the worth of a given service or its cost to the individuals affected. Under these circumstances, can the individual affected by a water resources decision utilize the scientific and technological knowledge required for an intelligent decision, or must he abdicate to the scientist responsibility for making value judgments?

Fourth, how can minority tastes and preferences as well as majority tastes and preferences be satisfied through public decision-making processes? Western philosophy stresses the importance of the individual. The competitive market makes provision for satisfying the demands of those whose tastes or preferences differ from those of the majority. But public decision making tends to be less responsive to minority interests, especially if that minority is relatively small, and especially if those finally responsible for decisions are dependent upon popular elections.

Fifth, there is a tendency for decisions about substantively unrelated programs to become politically intertwined. The President at times may trade his support for a water resources project for the support of senators and congressmen on such other matters as foreign aid or civil rights legislation. Similar agreements are reached among legislators. This is a political fact of life which undoubtedly complicates one's consideration of an appropriate decision-making framework.

The Research Task

Clearly, there are no simple or obvious solutions to the problem of providing decision-making structures which best serve the public interest. Governmental activities promise to remain complex and to impose a heavy burden upon the ordinary citizen. Technical and scientific expertise will be called upon to an ever-increasing extent for the development of information and analyses required for intelligent decision making. The situation in which those who receive the benefits will not bear all the costs, and the situation in which costs are diffused so as to offer little mobilization incentive for those who pay, will no doubt continue.

Some would propose to remove water resources management from the political arena, or at least to insulate it from political pressure. Under these proposals, reliance would be placed upon the judgment of the professionally trained individual. Water resources would be scientifically managed by individuals who are well-trained technically and devoted to the public service. In my judgment, this is no solution. Decisions about water resources are frequently political in the best sense of the word. The issues which must be faced involve value judgments as well as scientific and technical determinations. The answer is not to be found in insulating the management of water resources from politics, but in increasing the effectiveness of the political process. Certainly, the professionally trained individual and advanced techniques of engineering and economic analysis merit an important part in such an improved system.

It has also been suggested that adherence to certain prescribed roles by the legislature, the executive, and planning agencies would assure good results. "Objectives should be set by legislative action; these would be translated into design criteria in a budget or planning agency at the center of government; and the actual design of river systems would be accomplished by planners in the field." [Ref. 6.] Under this arrangement, it is assumed, the value judgments would be made through legislative action at a stage when an interest in specific projects would have a minimum influence on the judgment of legislators. The planners would, in effect, be largely engaged in a technical operation, subject to legislative oversight and administrative accountability to the executive.

This, it seems to me, is an incomplete, if not unrealistic, view of the way American government functions. It is doubtful that legislative bodies would specify objectives of water programs in terms sufficiently precise to embrace the major value judgments that must be made. One has only to observe how many policies imposed by legislative bodies are built incrementally in response to quite specific problems. But even if this were not the case, important value judgments are made in the interpretation of engineering and economic data. Value judgments are also made in selecting the alternatives considered in the planning process. No matter how well trained individuals are, they have motivations stemming from their background, their aspirations, and the aspirations of the agency with which they are identified. These result in value preferences that may or may not reflect accurately a balancing of the interests of those affected by a particular decision.

To provide an over-all context for specific research on decision-making processes, advances in political and administrative theory seem to be needed to bring theory abreast of the conditions of modern governmental problems. Through many centuries our culture has evolved concepts of the individual, his rights and obligations, and his relationship to the community and to government. These concepts, rather than science or art, are the hallmark of western civilization. Yet, the uneasy feeling remains that we have failed to relate these concepts in a systematic manner to the realities of governmental administration in the modern world. Would it not be desirable to define these concepts in the light of the last few decades of human experience and then interpret their significance for the objectives or goals of governmental decision making in fields such as water resources? Is not this an appropriate task for a student of political theory and political philosophy? Such an approach may be considered old-fashioned, but I should like to see it seriously explored.

Let me explain more fully my own view of this problem. It would appear that we are seeking a pattern of relationships among individuals, groups, and agencies to accomplish two objectives, namely:

1. to illuminate the issues about which value judgments must be made; and
2. to provide representation in the decision-making process for all parties having an interest, including those individuals who in total have a substantial interest, but who individually have so small an interest as to be inarticulate.

This means that there should be built into the governmental decision-making framework units which can be expected to reflect differing values and as a consequence opposing points of view. It also means that these units must be armed with the scientific and technical expertise to penetrate fully the ramifications of proposed programs. The most difficult aspect of this task is that of providing adequate representation within the governmental structure of those interests that bear a large share of the costs, or potentially would realize a large share of the returns when such costs and returns are spread over a large number of individuals. These interests generally are not articulate, and thus they offer little in the way of political support to any unit of government that might be assigned this role. In the absence of political support, a unit serving this purpose may find it difficult to survive. Yet this problem is so widespread in modern government that it merits special study and attention.

Pending further theoretical advances, study and experimentation might well be directed to the following areas:

The system of prices and charges. Certainly there is nothing wrong with the use of subsidies provided they serve a legitimate policy objective. There is considerable doubt that existing subsidies in the water resources field do in fact serve an accepted policy objective. Furthermore, there is good reason to feel that the pattern of prices and charges impairs the decision-making process. Although much study has been given to this subject, would it not be desirable to gain a deeper understanding of the consequences of alternative cost-sharing policies?

The relationship among differing interests in the governmental structure. Within government, individual agencies have differing objectives and as a result tend to reflect and promote different values. It seems to me that there are possibilities here of taking much greater advantage of these differences than heretofore to illuminate the issues in program situations. How would a program for a river basin devised by a park and recreation agency compare with a plan devised by either the Bureau of Reclamation or the Corps of Engineers? Possibly instead of trying to integrate these planning operations, we should be fostering to a degree the development of competitive proposals. Possibly agencies such as the

National Park Service and the Bureau of Sport Fisheries and Wildlife should be staffed with some engineers and hydrologists, as well as with park and recreation specialists, to prepare carefully analyzed alternative possibilities, especially where sharp differences of opinion exist over what constitutes a best solution. This might offer one way of providing technical expertise on water resources planning in support of views and values which differ from those of a water resources agency.

The hierarchy of relationships in the federal system. The geographical division of power under our federal structure has always been considered an important factor in achieving "good" results through our system of political and administrative processes. (See, for example, [ref. 7].) I wonder whether in the water resources field we have taken adequate advantage of dividing power geographically to achieve the most effective decisions. For much of our investment in water resources facilities, critical decisions are made by federal agencies. This has often meant that the local office of the federal agency has identified itself with the interests of the local area and promoted programs of questionable desirability from a national point of view. Although headquarters offices counteract this tendency to some extent, there is good evidence that the broad national interest has been underrepresented in the political process. Could this situation be improved by modifying the system of relationships among levels of government in the water resources field? If, for example, a local or regional agency had responsibility for planning, building, and managing water resources facilities, but secured a portion of its funds from a federal agency that had no direct responsibility for the program, might not a system of relationships develop under which the national viewpoint would tend to be better represented in the investment of federal funds?

Specific possibilities for representing the widely diffused interests in water resources problems. As pointed out earlier, under existing arrangements the federal taxpayer may bear a major share of the cost of a project which results in such a diffusion of the costs that there is no effectively organized clientele concerned with whether federal funds for water development are invested in accordance with the interests of those who pay. Similarly, certain benefits may be widely diffused and not command organized support. Where conflicts arise, such as between the park and recreation interests on the one hand and the developmental interests on the other, the issues may be illuminated and a decision which more accurately reflects a consensus will result. However, many investments are made without any such conflict. In those instances, how is the interest of those who pay to be represented and reflected? The First Hoover Commission suggested a board of review which was designed to serve this purpose. This and other possibilities appear to merit more careful study and critical evaluation than they have received.

PUBLIC POLICY CHANGE

Politics has been described as the art of the possible. It may be that students of government could devise decision-making structures which would achieve "good" results—if adopted—but the hope for adoption is remote if not non-existent. This prompts the suggestion that the process of policy change itself merits research attention so that the desirable can be related in a useful way to the practical.

Implicit in much of the research and study undertaken in the water resources field is the confidence that new knowledge will eventually be reflected in public policy. There is considerable evidence to support this view but, on the other hand, some policies appear to change at a glacial rate when more rapid advances would appear called for. It is true that over the last fifteen years water resources policy has changed a great deal. The changes that have occurred, however, are largely additions to policy to provide for such activities as federal participation in the development of municipal and industrial water supplies and in the control of pollution —activities not previously covered by federal policy. On the other hand, the policy framework for such fields as flood control, irrigation, hydro-electric power, and navigation have remained relatively unchanged in spite of new conditions and the advancement of knowledge which most of us would agree call for important adjustments. Why does this situation exist? What does it take to achieve substantial innovations in policy? If, as many feel, a continuous change in water resources policy should occur in the years ahead, what conditions must exist to make changes possible?

In raising these issues another question may arise about the appropriateness of undertaking studies that bear directly upon the process of policy change. Yet, it appears reasonable for a society in which public policies are so important to seek a systematic understanding of the processes of policy change and to make that knowledge widely available. It is essential that policy be flexible and be adjusted to the new requirements of a rapidly changing society. We should seek to avoid those situations, which are frequent, in which policies become frozen and totally unsuited to the changing environment in which they must function. Understanding the processes of policy change better than we now do does not assure that policies will be adjusted to meet new needs. Yet knowledge about the processes of policy change could contribute to that end, especially as this knowledge reaches the hands of the practitioners of the art of politics.

It is abundantly evident to those working in the water resources field that the configuration of forces tending to maintain the status quo in water resources policy are enormous. Federal cost-sharing or reimbursement policy offers an excellent example. Cost-sharing policies that would impose a larger share of the cost of water resource development activities on the beneficiaries would result in a pattern that would serve better the over-all public interest. Modifications in federal policy to achieve this result have been recommended from time to time for at least two decades by high-level study commissions and prominent individuals. Nevertheless, most changes in federal cost-sharing policies have been in the opposite direction. For example, Public Law 566 was eventually amended to extend certain features of flood control reimbursement policy to the small watershed programs of the Department of Agriculture. One might almost conclude that a kind of Gresham's Law is at work here: bad policies drive out good ones. The rationale for this particular change was that, in fairness, flood control beneficiaries of small watershed programs should not be faced with higher charges than the beneficiaries of the larger projects of the Corps of Engineers. However, no one gave serious consideration to making the adjustment in the other direction.

The forces in favor of preserving existing cost-sharing policies for federal water resources development activities are powerful indeed. The present beneficiaries certainly do not want to change. Possibly of even greater significance are the potential beneficiaries. At any suggestion of change they remind us that many others have already benefited from existing policies and ask why they should be discriminated against. The agencies which administer federal water programs are not in a position to advocate major changes in cost-sharing policies even though some individuals in those agencies favor such changes. The basic interest of these agencies demands that they maintain a position consistent with that of the clientele that supports their programs. A contrary position would be very difficult to sustain. Finally, there is the force of inertia. All of us hesitate to move from a situation in which the consequences are known to a situation in which the consequences are less clear unless the benefits promise to be large.

The forces which favor a revision of federal cost-sharing processes are for the most part diffused and not very articulate. The costs are borne mostly by the general taxpayer and since no single taxpayer is affected very much by existing policies (federal water programs are a little over 2 per cent of the federal budget), it is difficult to arouse much popular interest in changing the situation. A few interest groups that are well organized would support such changes but generally they have other matters of higher priority on their agendas.

A somewhat similar situation exists in other water policy areas. The forces for maintaining the status quo are powerful and by comparison the forces for change are relatively weak. Yet changes appear desirable.

Were one to devise a program of research in the area of policy change, it would seem to be desirable also to look beyond water resources to other fields with similar problems to see what can be learned about policy change generally. Three specific lines of study come to mind:

Historical studies of the origins and the changes which have led to the existing water resources policies. It is doubtful that sufficient attention has been given to the history of policy in the United States in seeking to understand how we have gotten where we are.

Detailed studies of specific policy changes with a view to understanding as well as possible the forces that brought the changes about. Such studies might include changes in water resources policy as well as policy changes in transportation, power, and other similar fields.

Comparative studies of different policy areas in an effort to determine why some are dynamic and others are rigid.

If these lines of research are undertaken we might eventually have a clearer view of the kind of activity that will contribute to policy change in a manner consistent with our democratic traditions. The lessons learned should be particularly useful to educators and those directly involved in policy formulation and implementation.

REFERENCES

[1] Landsberg, Hans H., Fischman, Leonard L., and Fisher, Joseph L. *Resources in America's Future.* Baltimore: Johns Hopkins Press, 1963, p. 385.
[2] Kneese, Allen V. *Water Pollution: Economic Aspects and Research Needs.* Washington: Resources for the Future, Inc., 1962.
[3] ——. *The Economics of Regional Water Quality Management.* Baltimore: Johns Hopkins Press, 1964.

[4] Kates, Robert William. *Hazard and Choice Perception in Flood Plain Management.* Department of Geography Research Paper No. 78. Chicago: University of Chicago, 1962.

[5] White, Gilbert F. *Choice of Adjustment to Floods.* Department of Geography Research Paper No. 93. Chicago: University of Chicago, 1964.

[6] Maass, A., Hufschmidt, M. M., Dorfman, R., Thomas, H. A., Jr., Marglin, S. A., and Fair, G. M. *Design of Water-Resource Systems.* Cambridge: Harvard University Press, 1962.

[7] Maass, A. (ed.). *Area and Power: A Theory of Local Government.* Glencoe, Ill.: The Free Press, 1959.

Politics and Efficiency in Water Development

Hubert Marshall*

While a very large number of federal government agencies are in one way or another involved in development of the nation's water resources, only three—the Corps of Engineers, the Bureau of Reclamation, and the Soil Conservation Service—are engaged directly in the *construction* of water facilities.[1] The three agencies vary substantially in the functions they perform, but between them they are variously engaged in flood control, navigation improvement, the irrigation of arid lands, the conservation of municipal and industrial water, recreation development, and the enhancement of fish and wildlife values. Despite differences in size, age, function, and doctrine, these agencies live in the common environment of the federal government and are shaped by it in ways that leave them much alike in outlook, in the need to mobilize political support, and in the procedures they use to justify projects and secure appropriations. In particular, all three agencies have their projects authorized and funded by Congress principally on a project-by-project basis (with the consequence of heavy congressional involvement in the details of the water program),[2] and all three agencies make generally similar efforts to

---

* Professor of Political Science, Stanford University.

[1] The Soil Conservation Service does not contract directly for construction. Local units of government do this, but SCS (which bears a major share of the costs) has substantial control over both design and construction.

[2] This is a generalization which needs some modification. All three agencies may authorize and fund certain small projects without prior congressional approval of the specific project. The Soil Conservation Service is somewhat freer in this respect because its projects are relatively smaller than those of the other two agencies. As a general proposition, however, the fact of congressional involvement in the details of project development remains one of the principal characteristics of our national water program.

measure the economic efficiency of their projects through the use of benefit-cost analysis.

ECONOMIC EFFICIENCY

The notion that public works projects should be subject to economic analysis goes back for a considerable period in history. Until the last twenty years, however, the matter received relatively little attention and only recently has it been the subject of intensive study by government agencies, engineers, and economists. Despite neglect over so long a period, the question of economic efficiency is of the utmost importance to the public which both finances and is served by government. Large sums are everywhere spent on public works; today the federal government's expenditures on water development alone are well in excess of a billion dollars a year. If these projects have reliably calculated benefit-cost ratios in excess of unity, they are likely to make a net contribution to real national income. Given the magnitude of the annual federal investment in these projects, they are capable of making an important contribution to rising levels of living if their economic benefits genuinely exceed their economic costs. On the other hand, if their benefit-cost ratios, reliably calculated, are less than unity these projects are likely to result in a deduction from real national income, and in some measure reduce the national standard of living.

The concept of economic efficiency in water development is thus an important one, involving, as it does, the allocation of substantial resources and the confidence that citizens can place in the decision-making processes of their government. It is thus a matter of concern that as I read the literature (principally by economists) I can find no truly independent review, appraisal, or check of the economic evaluation of a federal water project which confirms the benefit-cost ratio calculated by the construction agency. Some studies, of course, record the obvious benefits of water projects but do not deal with the relationship of benefits to costs. Other studies, many of them critical of agency procedure, are confined to a review of published agency reports. But those that go deeper into a check of the field estimates of the benefits claimed by the agencies are universally critical in their findings.

How can we categorize the criticisms of the benefit-cost ratios calculated by the agencies?[3] Perhaps the most frequent criticism found in the

---

[3] I have documented a number of these criticisms in my "Rational Choice in Water Resources Planning." (See [ref. 1], pp. 403–24.) For another recent discussion of agency practices in the economic evaluation of water projects, see [ref. 2].

literature involves the overestimation of direct benefits. On flood control projects these criticisms involve variously the overestimation of the value of property in the flood plain, the inflation of estimates of the actual damages caused by floods, and overestimation of the frequency and severity of floods.[4] On irrigation projects they involve inflation of the estimated value of crops to be grown on the projects. And on navigation projects the literature contains frequent reference to the double counting of benefits, particularly of the traffic benefiting from such projects.

Today there is also a substantial body of literature on the problem of secondary benefits. The question here is not principally one of overestimation but of the appropriateness, under conditions of full employment, of counting them at all. The issue is an important one because the justification of nearly all irrigation projects depends upon them, and in some instances the secondary benefits claimed for projects are in excess of the primary benefits. Yet the literature reveals nearly universal professional disapproval of the degree to which the Bureau of Reclamation depends upon them to achieve favorable ratios.[5]

On the cost side of the ratio, much the same story is repeated, although the literature here is less voluminous. One study holds that the costs of irrigation projects are underestimated by approximately one-third, and other studies have alleged the underestimation of costs on flood control projects. Perhaps more serious is the question of the appropriate discount rate to be used in project evaluation. A small change in the discount rate can have a large impact on the calculated ratio. Although the appropriate

---

[4] Estimates of the value of property in the flood plain and of actual flood damages are usually made by economists and engineers. Hydrologists supply the data on flood frequencies. The periods of record are often short, but with a considerable degree of confidence could sometimes be extended on the basis of newspaper accounts and interviews with long-time residents of the flood plain. Linsley, for example, describes a project with an eighteen-year period of record composed of two segments of eleven and seven years, separated by nine years of missing record. The project had a benefit-cost ratio of 1.04. No flood during the period of missing record, however, equalled the maximum recorded flood. If the record had been extended to twenty-seven years, as would have been dictated by imaginative hydrology, the benefit-cost ratio would have fallen to 0.74 and the project would not have met the test of economic feasibility. (See Ray K. Linsley's "Engineering and Economics in Project Planning," in [ref. 1, pp. 99–100]).

[5] Very little empirical work on secondary benefits has been done. As a consequence of this, little is known about the level of unemployment that must exist nationally, or the level of underutilization of resources that must exist in a locality before secondary benefits become national in character and are appropriately counted in the benefit-cost ratio. [Ref. 3.] Additional research on secondary benefits might justify the Corps of Engineers in changing its present practice of not counting them; but that the Bureau of Reclamation depends too heavily upon them is widely recognized.

interest rates suggested in the professional literature vary over a wide range, the writers on the subject are unanimous in holding that the rate used by the federal agencies is much too low.

Finally we must note frequent references in the literature to the failure of these agencies to explore relevant alternative means of achieving project alternatives. The agencies have preferred solutions that are not necessarily the most efficient ways of achieving project goals or of using project resources. Thus, there are cheaper ways of bringing additional lands into agricultural production than irrigating the arid West, and, as Gilbert White and his associates have shown [see White's paper in this volume], there are numerous alternatives to the Corps' preferred solutions to the flood problem.

Reluctantly, one is forced to conclude that the literature is unanimous in alleging that agency practices have the effect of inflating benefits or deflating costs, or both. Moreover, the differences between agency claims and the findings of independent reviewers are not small. The Missouri Basin Survey Commission, for example, in reviewing the Corps' navigation program on the Missouri River could find only one-twelfth the benefits from erosion control and one-third the savings to shippers claimed by the Corps. The Commission's benefit-cost ratio was half that calculated by the Corps [ref. 4]. Differences of this magnitude are typical of the literature in question. Economic evaluation, of course, is regularly used as a means of killing the more hopelessly uneconomic projects. On this score the Corps of Engineers' record, at least, is clear, and it is likely that the other two agencies use economic evaluation for this purpose as well. But having admitted this, one is still forced to conclude that one of the principal uses of benefit-cost analysis is to clothe politically desirable projects with the fig leaf of economic respectability.

Although much of the critical literature to which I have referred is well known to the construction agencies, they have elected to respond with silence rather than with a defense of their practices. They could readily use the forum provided by a congressional committee hearing or the medium of a congressional document to rebut their critics. With perhaps only a single exception this has not happened. Admittedly, the agency economists who are most qualified to undertake this task are overworked; but all three agencies devote considerable attention to public relations, and to ignore their critics in the area of economic analysis is either a deliberate tactic or an admission of the inadequacy of their staffing. In the agencies' failure to establish a dialogue with their critics, public confidence in the decision-making process is the loser. Had a dialogue been established the critics might by now have been silenced, or agency practices improved.

HUBERT MARSHALL

CONGRESSMAN-CONSTITUENCY RELATIONS

The construction of uneconomic projects is clearly an aspect of the pork-barrel phenomenon which has so long been part of the American political landscape. Since this phenomenon has persisted for so long, we may hypothesize that it performs a function of value to one or more groups, even though it may be dysfunctional for the political system as a whole. While many interests may be served by the construction of these projects, in my view the principal function they perform is to provide a means by which congressmen can curry favor with their constituents.

American political arrangements make it essential that congressmen pay close attention to the demands of their constituents. This fact, which is not nearly so true in Great Britain and a number of other countries, arises simply and almost inevitably out of the way in which congressmen are nominated and elected. An American is nominated for legislative office by securing a modest number of signatures on a petition, filing a small fee, and winning a primary election in which he raises his own campaign funds. Having won the primary, he enters the general election under the banner of his party no matter how widely his views diverge from those of the party leadership or how much independence he will show in Congress if elected. In the general election, he must again raise campaign funds, ordinarily with only nominal assistance from the party's national committee or congressional campaign committee. He may, however, receive substantial aid from the local party organization. The general election won, he enters Congress beholden to no one but the electorate of his constituency and the local interests that financed his campaign and helped deliver the vote. No national party organ or leadership group in the Congress commands his allegiance or has the power to control his vote. More important, no mechanism exists to compel or even to direct his attention to the national interest. The result is a Congress from which the emerging legislation represents not a coherent party view of the national interest but a summation of the parochial views of a large number of separate constituency interests.

For these reasons American political parties are variously characterized as weak, decentralized, and irresponsible. They are said to be irresponsible in the sense that the voter cannot hold his party as a whole accountable. Rather he holds his own congressman accountable; and the congressman, as indicated above, responds by directing his loyalty to his constituents rather than to his party. While it overstates the case, to be sure, the relationship of constituent to congressman may be characterized as that of master to slave.

To state the case this baldly is not to say that the congressman lacks considerable freedom of choice in voting. After all, the master may not exercise his authority on every occasion. On most matters, for example, a congressman's constituents will have no views, either because these matters are unimportant or because they are too complex for ready comprehension. On other matters, constituents will be evenly divided and the congressman, unable to please everyone, will perforce be free to vote on other grounds. Statistically it is a fact that party affiliation is the most important determinant of congressional voting behavior [ref. 5]. But public works are seldom the subject of party differences, and on a matter of this kind the congressman can ordinarily expect the political elites in his constituency to be both nearly unanimous and well informed. They recognize the economic benefits that will accrue to the locality and they appreciate clearly that the costs will be paid by the taxpayers nationally. Under the circumstances, the congressman ordinarily has no option but to accede to his constituents' demands. To co-operate is simply to play the political game.

The pressure on the American congressman, unlike that on his British counterpart, is increased by virtue of the fact that he can act significantly on behalf of his constituents. He can secure appointment to the standing committees that will consider project authorizations, or he may become a member of an appropriations subcommittee that will have jurisdiction over the funding of water projects. Whether or not he is a member of a key committee, he may introduce authorization bills. Moreover, although the budget originates in the executive branch, the congressman may work toward its amendment in Congress to further his constituents' interests. And finally, he may join with other members of Congress to override presidential vetoes either of authorization measures or of appropriations bills. It is this capacity to act, widely appreciated by constituents, which ensnares the congressman and makes it difficult for him to resist constituency pressures.

It might be hypothesized, of course, that while congressmen respond to constituency demands for public works, they do so in the conviction that the economic returns will be in excess of the costs. My interviews during 1964 with congressmen and their legislative assistants reveal, however, that this is not the case. There is widespread appreciation in Congress that benefit-cost ratios are inflated and that they are not a reliable index of economic efficiency. Perhaps most members of Congress do not realize the magnitude of the distortions that are present in benefit-cost ratios, but that distortion exists is seldom denied in off-the-record conversations. Yet the unreliability of benefit-cost ratios is never openly discussed, except by one or two mavericks in the Senate. There is an unwritten agreement not to discuss it. A form of "senatorial courtesy" exists in both chambers in which it is regarded as being in bad taste for a member to question publicly the economic desirability of a project in another member's constituency. When open criticism does occur, the offending congressman may be told to mind his own business.[6] Moreover, such defense of a questioned project as is made is usually irrelevant to the question of economic efficiency. Thus the congressional critics of benefit-cost analysis as it is employed by the agencies have been no more successful than have the academic economists in establishing a meaningful dialogue with the defenders of the system.

The sacrosanct nature of the unreliable benefit-cost ratio is appreciated in the General Accounting Office as well as in Congress. This agency, which reports to Congress, is perhaps best known for its audit of executive branch expenditures. Less well known is the fact that it conducts intensive investigations of executive agency programs and activities in a search for waste and extravagance. Its reports are sent to Congress and often provide the basis for congressional hearings and for corrective legislation. The relevant officials in the GAO are fully aware that many water projects constitute a waste of resources. They are surprisingly well informed on all aspects of economic evaluation, cost allocation and related matters, and are wholly familiar with the literature by Eckstein, Krutilla, McKean, Hirshleifer, Milliman and others. They keep abreast of academic thinking and agency practice in the field of economic evaluation in the event that Congress should request a report on the matter. But, of course, Congress never has requested such a report and no one really expects it to. The GAO, on its own initiative, might report its conviction that the benefit-cost ratios calculated by the agencies are a poor index of economic efficiency, but its officials suspect that Congress would resent such a report and, in any event, would pay no attention to it. Since the GAO's resources are limited and it has no desire to engage in an exercise in futility, it naturally—and perhaps quite appropriately—devotes its energies to those areas in which Congress seems likely to take constructive action.

THE PRESIDENT

The United States Constitution divides governmental power not only between the national government and the states, but also between the

---

[6] When Senator Proxmire questioned a project to be built in Indiana, Senator Hartke of that state retorted, "The bill contains more than $38 million worth of commitments for the state of the distinguished Senator from Wisconsin. I feel that in good conscience he should be making a start to reduce those projects before he attacks ours. . . . We will stay in Indiana. We will not interfere with the business of Wisconsin. If the Senator from Wisconsin will let us alone, we shall be happy." [Ref. 6.]

executive, legislative, and judicial branches. With uncanny genius the founding fathers devised this atomization of power to ensure weak government. As a consequence, successive Presidents have had to grasp for power wherever they could find it as a means of meeting the responsibilities placed upon them by the American people.[7] This being the case, we might hypothesize that Presidents have used public works as an instrument of presidential leadership; or, more specifically, that they have used water projects as part of a system of rewards and deprivations in order to secure congressional support for their policies and programs.

The notion that projects are sometimes used in this fashion was seemingly given support when, in the first weeks of the Kennedy Administration, it was alleged that Secretary Udall had threatened to withhold a seawater conversion plant which had been promised a North Carolina congressman who, at the moment, was reluctant to support the packing of the House Rules Committee. Nevertheless, presidential memoirs never refer to the use of projects for this purpose, nor do the memoirs of cabinet officers or presidential aides. Moreover, presidential enemies in Congress seem to do as well in securing projects as do their friends. It would thus seem a better interpretation of the facts to hypothesize that Presidents recognize the proprietary nature of Congress' interest in water projects and, recognizing this, have not sought to reduce the support of their friends or exacerbate the opposition of their opponents by opposing too directly or too often those projects which enjoy the requisite political support. Presidents appear to be unable to use these projects positively as an instrument of their own leadership and they seem to be too weak to attack successfully the network of political forces which results in the allocation of such substantial resources to projects which fail to meet the test of economic efficiency.

The role of the Bureau of the Budget is curiously similar to that of the General Accounting Office. Personnel in the Bureau are aware of the unreliability of benefit-cost ratios and, like their counterparts in the GAO, are familiar with the relevant literature on economic evaluation. Yet the Bureau has never sent a team of engineers and economists into the field to review at first hand the reliability of the estimates of benefits claimed by the construction agencies. Like the GAO, it has sensed the futility of expending its own limited resources on investigations which could well bring into question the economic desirability of nearly all water projects and hence would be appreciated neither in the White House nor in the Congress.

Despite its reluctance to conduct investigations which might have the

[7] For an incisive discussion of presidential weakness, see Neustadt [ref. 7].

effect of striking at the heart of the system, the Bureau must, of course, review all project proposals before they are submitted to Congress. The office review which takes place is conducted with an eye to determining the individual project's conformance with the criteria found in Senate Document 97 and with commonsense notions of reasonableness regarding the project's purposes and its integration with the programs of other agencies.[8] The Bureau's objections, when they occur, are thus likely to be directed to specific projects or specific aspects of projects rather than to the reliability of agency estimates of benefits and costs as a general matter.

Prior to 1957, a Corps of Engineers project report which was disapproved by the Bureau was nevertheless transmitted to Congress, accompanied by a statement from the Bureau indicating that the project was not in accord with the program of the President. The Bureau frequently recorded its opposition to projects in this fashion without consulting the President personally; and as is well known, Congress commonly authorized such projects and appropriated funds for their construction despite the Bureau's opposition. In the middle years of the Eisenhower Administration, the Bureau recorded its opposition to the proposed deep water channel up the Delaware River to the projected Fairless plant of the U. S. Steel Corporation without consulting the President. When the Bureau's action became personally known to the President, there was considerable reverberation in the White House, and the Bureau subsequently abandoned that means of opposing objectionable projects.

Today the Bureau returns objectionable project reports to the Corps, making its views known to the Office of the Secretary of the Army and the Office of the Chief of Engineers. In recent years these offices have been more responsive to the Bureau than was once the case, and it can now fairly be said that they are more concerned than formerly with the quality of the Corps' economic justifications. Not only does the Bureau's current procedure capitalize on changing attitudes in the Department of the Army and in the higher echelons of the Corps, but it has the advantage of bringing the Bureau's influence to bear before the reports are published and hence before political support has had an opportunity to crystallize. It is now not unusual for project proposals to be modified at the Bureau's request. But, as indicated above, the Bureau's review does

---

[8] Senate Document 97 [ref. 8] is the current official statement of the standards and criteria to be employed in the economic evaluation of federal water projects. It supersedes the earlier Budget Circular A–47 [ref. 9], used during the Eisenhower Administration, and the still earlier "Green Book" [ref. 10]. The standards set forth in Senate Document 97—including particularly the discount rate, the period of analysis, and the treatment of secondary benefits—are regarded as too liberal by many economists.

not extend to field checks on the reliability of the estimates of benefits and costs, and the Bureau accepts the criteria of Senate Document 97 which have been so widely criticized outside the government service [ref. 11].

It is not beyond the realm of possibility that future Presidents will act to ensure the reliability of the benefit-cost ratios presented by the agencies. Secretary MacNamara's insistence upon the closing of inefficient defense installations holds out the hope that some day a strong Director of the Budget or one or more Cabinet secretaries may secure the support of a sympathetic President in making certain that the calculated ratios reflect the true economic merits of our water projects. That the President has such authority is hardly open to question. Senate Document 97, which presently embodies the criteria used in economic evaluation, is an executive document and could be changed by presidential order. A President could order the construction agencies to refuse to send to Congress project reports containing economic evaluations made with any criteria other than those meeting his approval. In an extremity, he could refuse to spend money appropriated by Congress. Presidents in the past have refused to spend appropriations for manned bombers desired by Congress and, more relevantly, they have impounded money appropriated for water projects. Whether any President *will* take action to improve the reliability of economic evaluations is another matter. The political costs to the President of such an action would be very great indeed. On the other hand, pressure from the Executive Office for improvement in present practices might well be a factor, if not the principal one, in any correctives that the future may bring.

THE CONSTRUCTION AGENCIES

If Congress seems actively to foster the unreliable economic evaluation and if Presidents seem to acquiesce in the practice, what can be said about the role of the construction agencies themselves? Generally speaking, it is a universal characteristic of organizations that they wish to survive and grow. Gordon noted this some years ago when he observed that business organizations tend to expand their operations even when it is not profitable to do so [ref. 12]. Growth adds to the power and prestige of the organization's officials and to the income and status of its members. And survival of the organization contributes to the economic and psychological security of all those associated with it.

The behavior of organizations, of course, is rooted in the perceptions, the aspirations, and the identifications of those who make them up, and it is at these factors that one must look for the explanation of organizational behavior. In this regard, nearly all those who have studied voluntary organizations are impressed with the extent to which their members tend to identify with the group. This is due in part to the process of self-selection by which those who have an attachment to the service goals of the organization join it, and those who are indifferent or opposed do not. Thus, without conscious effort on its own part an organization ordinarily commands a considerable degree of loyalty from its members. Organizations that employ their members and pay them remuneration, however, recruit selectively, and one of the criteria employed will ordinarily be enthusiasm for organizational goals. Thus, selectivity in recruitment by the organization combines with self-selection to ensure a very considerable loyalty to the group and its goals. To extend the argument to professions as well as organizations, and to overstate the case for purposes of emphasis, it is for these reasons that doctors tend to view the ideal world as one in which everyone is in good health. And it is for these reasons that highway engineers perceive the ideal world as one which is largely paved, while water engineers perceive it as one in which slack water extends from the mouths of our rivers to the farthest reaches of their headwaters. This tendency, of course, is a useful one, for it imbues agency personnel with enthusiasm and commitment, and contributes to the efficiency of the organization.

Another force which ensures the loyalty of employees to organizational goals is the socialization process which is applied to new recruits. Whether it is more important than self-selection and selective recruitment is difficult to say, but it cannot be less important in shaping the specific aspects of employee behavior. In a multitude of ways the new recruit is taught that the organization can prosper only as organizational goals are served. He is praised when he meets organizational needs and reprimanded when he does not. Social pressures of greater or less subtlety are constantly brought to bear: the deviant employee can be excluded from important meetings, given less desirable work assignments, or omitted from the guest list on social occasions. Promotions and pay raises, and advancement in status, prestige, and power come only if the recruit conforms to organizational expectations.

The new recruit may not conform, of course, and in that case he may find it expedient to resign. The organization in this case will probably get along quite well without him. If others of a similar bent leave, the organization will have purged itself of internal dissent and those who remain can push forward toward the achievement of organizational goals without the foot-dragging of those who are plagued with doubts and reservations. Over a period of time the employee who stays will have acquired a loyalty that guarantees his decisions will be consistent with the values and goals of the group. Through the internalization of organizational values, the participant in time acquires an organizational personality distinct from his personality as an individual. Ultimately, he may so completely accept the organization's goals that he senses no cross-pressuring and no conflict with competing values.

The implications of these processes of selection and socialization are, of course, clear. The water development agencies cannot survive without projects; and to have projects they must have favorable benefit-cost ratios for the simple reason that neither the Congress nor the public would tolerate projects that were openly admitted to be economically inefficient. In producing favorable ratios for the politically desired projects, the employee knows that he is loyally serving not only his agency but the Congress and perhaps the President as well.

Admitting the existence of these forces that tend to corrupt economic evaluation, why cannot we count on the integrity of the employee to resist them? Undoubtedly there is resistance to a degree, but apparently not enough. Why? The answer would seem to lie in part in the fact that benefit-cost ratios are the product of group effort, the work jointly of economists, hydrologists, geologists, agronomists, and several kinds of engineers. Where an individual is solely responsible for a decision, there is likely to be a strong ethical link between the man and the decision. But where a decision is the responsibility of a sizeable staff and is subject to review by other technicians and by a hierarchy of superiors, subtle changes take place in individual attitudes, including a dilution of the sense of individual responsibility for the final product. Ethical questions do arise within large hierarchical organizations, but there is greater opportunity for reaching decisions on general policy grounds instead of solely on the basis of one individual's ethical convictions.

Large-scale organizations, with their complex division of labor, seem to dilute the sense of immediacy and the directness of responsibility involved in the decision-making process. The ethical difficulty is shared and the individual's responsibility is fulfilled by group sanction of the final product. In the case of economic evaluation, each member of the group may sense that a particular benefit-cost ratio is not an accurate reflection of the project's economic efficiency, yet feel little personal responsibility for that fact. As one looks broadly at human behavior it seems to be true that guilt which is shared is not strongly felt. This thesis was elaborated years ago by Niebuhr in his *Moral Man and Immoral Society* [ref. 13].

These moral dilemmas which members of organizations face in such acute form were discussed, eloquently I think, by C. P. Snow in his address a few years ago to the American Association for the Advancement of Science. Drawing on his long experience as a scientist and civil servant he said:

> Scientists have to question and if necessary to rebel. I don't want to be misunderstood. I am no anarchist. I am not suggesting that loyalty is not a prime virtue. I am not saying that all rebellion is good. But I am saying that loyalty can easily turn into conformity. . . . So can obedience, carried to the limit. When you think of the long and gloomy history of man, you will find that far more, and far more hideous, crimes have been committed in the name of obedience than have ever been committed in the name of rebellion. . . .

Then, speaking of his own twenty years' experience in the British Civil Service, he said:

> Yet the duty to question is not much of a support when you are living in the middle of an organized society. . . . I was coming to hide behind the institution; I was losing the power to say no. Only a very bold man, when he is a member of an organized society, can keep the power to say no. We can't expect many scientists to do it. [Ref. 14, p. 258.]

If Sir Charles is correct, we may conclude that ordinary men will not often be heroes. Our civil servants may not be ordinary men, but they are not supermen either, and in the nature of things we cannot depend upon heroes for good government. Good government must have a stronger institutional base than that. Moreover, if we are to understand the nature of our problem we must recognize that conflict between ethical obligation and hierarchical loyalty is a universal phenomenon of administrative life. All professional groups in government suffer from such conflict at times, and the difficulties are most likely to arise precisely when the technical task is performed in an atmosphere suffused with political tension. There is no ready solution for such difficulties, but it is more likely that adequate solutions can be found if it is realized that the difficulties arise from the character of organizations and are not caused solely by the weakness of man.

PROFESSIONALIZATION

If the pressures on employees to conform to agency goals are as strong as I have indicated, and if these pressures are abetted by Congress to the degree I think they are, what counterpressures might be developed or enhanced to bend employee behavior in the direction of more reliable economic evaluations? There is, of course, no simple or single answer to this question. But I am convinced that a greater sense of professionalization on the part of agency employees and greater professional support for them in the situation in which they find themselves would measurably improve the quality of the economic analysis that today underlies the decision to authorize and construct our major water projects. The discussion of professionalization that follows deals with economic analysis and not with the more traditional aspects of engineering science. On matters of engineering analysis, design, and construction, the three construction agencies are perhaps among the most professionalized to be found anywhere. These aspects of their work are seldom the subject of criticism. But the decisions involved in whether to build, on what scale and when, are decisions of a different order and are those, I shall show, which engineers are poorly equipped to make. It is in this aspect of their work that professionalization is so conspicuously lacking.

What are the characteristics of a profession? What attributes must one look for in judging the degree of professionalization in any group of men? The professions have been defined in various ways, and not all students of the professions are in agreement on matters of definition. For our purposes, however, there are four characteristics of the professions that have behavioral consequences of relevance to the present discussion. It can be said of the professions, first, that their members are ordinarily university trained and possess a body of esoteric knowledge. Possessing this body of knowledge that is denied to others, they are more likely than other workers to claim the prerogative of defining the nature of the problems they deal with and of prescribing methods and solutions. In all aspects of their work they are less likely than others to brook interference from laymen; and in particular they are likely to hold that neither client nor lay employer can be a true judge of the quality of the services he receives. As a consequence of this, the true professional is more willing to submit himself to what the sociologist calls colleague authority than hierarchical authority. In this sense, the professional accepts the judgment and the criticism of his colleagues more readily than he will accept them from a lay superior. The bonds of professional knowledge have psychological dimensions, too, for they create a sense of solidarity among members of a profession and cause them to relate more strongly to each other than to the organizations that employ them.

A second characteristic of the professions is that their members are detached in the sense of having schooled themselves to have no personal interest that would influence their actions or advice. Thus, the truly professional physician is as ready to find the patient healthy and not in need of treatment as he is to find him ill. The truly professional lawyer is as ready to advise against expensive litigation as he is to recommend it. To put the matter more abstractly, the true professional tries to find an intellectual base for the problems he handles by taking those problems out of their particular setting and making them part of some more universal order.

Third, it is true of the professions that they are oriented toward the community interest. The professional will not do anything his client or employer asks of him, but only those things which the profession has defined as being consistent with the general interest.

Finally, it can be said of the professions that they seek and in large degree succeed in instilling in their members a high degree of self-control of behavior through codes of ethics which are so internalized that they become part of the personality. The professional socialization which leads to the internalization of codes of conduct begins in the universities and is continued by intermittent association with academic members of the profession in later years. This association takes the form of refresher courses, of participation in conferences, and of a continuing dialogue between practicing and academic members of the profession in professional journals. Professional associations play a major role in the process.

The relevant behavioral consequence of professionalization is that loyalty to the organization is balanced by loyalty to professional standards. When the professional feels that adherence to bureaucratic norms will lead to a violation of the norms of his professional group, he is more likely than the non-professional to rebel or resist. Recent studies by sociologists provide a wealth of empirical evidence to support this proposition.

Scott, in a study of social workers in a public social work agency, found that professionally oriented workers were more critical of their supervisors and of agency policy on certain matters than were non-professionally oriented workers.[9] In another study of social workers it was found that the more professionally oriented workers were more likely than their bureaucratically oriented counterparts to deviate from agency rules that were perceived to interfere with professional performance. [Ref. 16, pp. 73–74.] In a quite different study of technical experts —including economists—employed by labor unions, Wilensky found that those who were professionally oriented reported that their major problems stemmed from a conflict between the requirements of their jobs and

---

[9] He also found exactly what one would expect when organizational goals and professional norms coincide and hence reinforce each other: 84 per cent of the social workers he interviewed felt that "residence requirements governing client eligibility for assistance should be removed or reduced, and 99 per cent of the workers felt that budgetary ceiling set by the state to govern the amount of assistance should be either removed entirely or raised." [Ref. 15, p. 69.]

the standards of their professional groups. [Ref. 17, pp. 129–44.] Finally, to cite only one further study, Corwin found in questioning a sample of nurses who held either strong bureaucratic or strong professional role conceptions, that the two-role orientations prescribed opposing programs of action. In addition, his data indicate that nurses trained in degree programs in universities were likely to be professionally oriented while nurses trained in diploma programs conducted in hospitals were likely to hold bureaucratic role conceptions [ref. 18].

Since the engineers employed by the federal agencies under consideration here are by any test professionals, why is it that there is so little apparent resistance to the distortion of benefit-cost ratios? One reason, of course, is the rather extraordinary combination of pressures favoring distortion. But aside from this there are, I think, three factors which conspire to weaken resistance to these pressures. The first has to do with professional knowledge. When it is said that a profession possesses a body of esoteric knowledge, it is implied that there is a relatively high degree of certainty about that knowledge and that it is widely accepted in the profession. But this is not yet entirely the case with the notions of engineering economy applied to water development. It has been, after all, only sixteen years since publication of the "Green Book," and only in the last ten years have we had what might be described as a substantial output of professional literature on the subject. Moreover, no real consensus has yet been reached on some aspects of the standards and criteria that are appropriate for the economic evaluation of water projects. This being the case it is not surprising that bureaucratic norms take precedence over professional norms in the calculation of benefit-cost ratios.

In some degree, time should change this. Most of the engineers who hold key positions in these agencies were trained before there was any substantial body of professional literature applying specifically to the economics of public works investment. As men better acquainted with the new literature move into the agencies, change is almost certain to take place. Already this seems to be so in the Corps of Engineers, where substantial interest in the improvement of the standards of economic evaluation has been present for perhaps the past five years. Nor is it surprising or in any way inconsistent with my thesis that this change began to take place first in Washington and is not yet substantially apparent in the field. The personnel of agency headquarters are more mobile, and they come into contact with more groups and a wider variety of ideas than do personnel in the field.

The second reason for the failure of professional engineers to resist the distorted benefit-cost ratio is their inadequate academic training in engineering economy. In this respect the universities have clearly failed in their task. This failure cannot be explained away on grounds that economic considerations lie outside the province of the engineer. Just the contrary is true, for the engineers themselves are the first to claim that economic notions lie at the heart of their discipline. Thus the Recognition Committee of the Engineers' Council for Professional Development (closely associated with the American Society for Engineering Education) defines engineering as "the Profession in which a knowledge of the mathematical and physical sciences gained by study, experience and practice is applied with judgment to develop ways to utilize, economically, the materials and forces of nature for the progressive well-being of mankind." [Ref. 19, p. 484.] Used as it is here, "economically" modifies the entire definition. The Committee recognizes this, for in an explanatory note it adds that "economics is a primary consideration in all engineering."

Despite the centrality of economics to engineering, the engineering schools devote little time to it in their curricula. Nearly a quarter of the schools require no economics whatsoever of their students, ignoring even the introductory course which is widely assumed, at least, to have important citizenship values [ref. 20]. The introductory course, however, is not likely to have much *professional* value to the prospective civil engineer because it commonly ignores the notion of discounting which lies at the heart of benefit-cost analysis. Looking at course offerings in engineering economy, the picture is equally dismal. In one study of 200 institutions offering engineering curricula, it was found that slightly more than a third did not offer engineering economy in any of their programs. Focusing on civil engineering curricula in these 200 schools, it was found that only 54 or about a quarter, *required* a course in engineering economy of their students [ref. 21]. A more recent study of the 82 principal civil engineering departments in the nation reveals much the same pattern. Of these 82 departments, only 19 *required* a course in engineering economy and an additional 21 schools offered but did not require one [ref. 22]. Thus in only half of these 82 schools were civil engineering students given so much as an opportunity to be exposed in a concentrated way to a set of notions which the profession claims to be central to the engineering discipline. It is not surprising, then, that young engineers enter professional practice with a bias toward construction hardly offset by notions of economic efficiency in the use of resources.[10]

---

[10] The disinterest of the universities is further illustrated by Winfrey's survey of engineering economy research in 155 institutions. Only 70 responded to his inquiry. Of these, 22 reported some research in engineering economy and 48 reported no research. He found only six projects currently active in civil engineering departments. Most projects were in *industrial* engineering with emphasis on problems of private investment. [Ref. 23.]

307

Finally, it is unfortunately true that agency personnel find little explicit moral guidance in the Code of Ethics of the American Society of Civil Engineers [ref. 24]. Most of the ten provisions of the Code concern the financial and commercial dealings of consulting engineers and engineers employed by firms engaged in design and construction. Eight of the ten fall in this category. One provision is summary in nature and is wholly lacking in specificity. The remaining provision holds that it is unprofessional for the engineer "to act for his client or for his employer otherwise than as a faithful agent or trustee." Explanatory material makes it clear that loyalty to the employer should not extend to the engineer's giving "professional advice which does not fully reflect his best professional judgment." Nevertheless, the over-all tenor of the Code is such that it is not particularly helpful to the engineer who would at once be loyal to the large-scale organization which employs him and at the same time be faithful to the highest standards of his profession.

These three factors may account in substantial part for the failure of engineers to resist more than they do the political demands placed upon them by the environment in which they work. Recent federal legislation providing support for water resources research in universities throughout the country may in time have some impact on the economics content of engineering curricula. The lack of agreement on standards and criteria for economic evaluation seems more readily remediable. Indeed, the current outpouring of literature on economic evaluation leads one to hope that in the not too distant future there may be reasonably widespread agreement on minimum standards.

The process of professionalization will, in any event, be slow. But it offers as much promise in correcting the present abuse of benefit-cost analysis as does any other change that can be reasonably foreseen. If the economists, *as an organized profession,* can be induced to show an interest in the quality of the economic analysis that finds its way into the benefit-cost ratios published by the agencies, progress will be even more rapid. Ideally, one can hope that the day will come when a joint committee representing the American Economics Association, the Engineers' Joint Council, and perhaps the Universities Council on Water Resources will publish a statement of minimum standards for the economic evaluation of public water projects. Such a statement of standards might never be issued between green covers; and it might never be made a Budget Circular or be printed as a Senate Document. But it would be widely appreciated by agency personnel who badly need the support they now lack from their colleagues in the universities and the professional societies.

REFERENCES

[1] Smith, Stephen C., and Castle, Emery N. (eds.). *Economics and Public Policy in Water Resource Development*. Ames: Iowa State University Press, 1964.

[2] Fox, Irving K., and Herfindahl, Orris C. "Attainment of Efficiency in Satisfying Demands for Water Resources," *American Economic Review,* Vol. 54 (May 1964).

[3] Kimball, Norman D., and Castle, Emery N. *Secondary Benefits and Irrigation Project Planning*. Technical Bulletin 69. Corvallis: Agricultural Experiment Station, Oregon State University, 1963.

[4] U.S. Missouri Basin Survey Commission. *Missouri: Land and Water*. Washington: Government Printing Office, 1953, p. 122.

[5] Stone, Clarence. "Inter-Party Constituency Differences and Congressional Voting Behavior: A Partial Dissent," *American Political Science Review,* Vol. 57 (September 1963), pp. 665–66.

[6] *Congressional Record,* 88th Congress, 2nd Session (August 7, 1964), p. 18492.

[7] Neustadt, Richard. *Presidential Leadership*. New York: John Wiley, 1960.

[8] S. Doc. 97, 87th Cong. 2nd Sess., May 29, 1962.

[9] U.S. Bureau of the Budget. *Circular A-47*. Mimeo. Washington, December 31, 1952.

[10] U.S. Federal Inter-Agency River Basin Committee, Subcommittee on Benefits and Costs. *Proposed Practices for Economic Analysis of River Basin Projects*. Washington, May 1950.

[11] Castle, Emery, Kelso, Maurice, and Gardner, Delworth. "Water Resources Development: A Review of the New Federal Evaluation Procedure," *Journal of Farm Economics,* Vol. 45 (November 1963).

[12] Gordon, Robert A. *Business Leadership in the Large Corporation*. Washington: The Brookings Institution, 1945, p. 306.

[13] Niebuhr, Reinhold. *Moral Man and Immoral Society*. New York: Charles Scribner's Sons, 1936.

[14] Snow, Charles P. "The Moral Un-Neutrality of Science," *Science,* Vol. 133 (January 27, 1961).

[15] Scott, W. Richard. "Reactions to Supervision in a Heteronomous Professional Organization," *Administrative Science Quarterly,* Vol. 10 (June 1965).

[16] Blau, Peter M., and Scott, W. Richard. *Formal Organizations: A Comparative Approach*. San Francisco: Chandler Publishing Co., 1962.

[17] Wilensky, Harold L. *Intellectuals in Labor Unions*. Glencoe, Ill.: The Free Press, 1956.

[18] Corwin, R. G. "The Professional Employee: A Study of Conflict in Nursing Roles," *American Journal of Sociology,* Vol. 66 (May 1961).

[19] *Journal of Engineering Education,* Vol. 48 (February 15, 1958).

[20] Holstein, Edwin J. "Economics in American Engineering Schools," *The Engineering Economist,* Vol. 5 (Winter 1960).

[21] Matchett, Gerald J. "Engineering Economy Courses in Educational Institutions," *Journal of Engineering Education,* Vol. 50 (February 1960).

[22] "A Survey of Engineering Economy Instruction Available to Civil Engineering Students in United States Universities." Typescript (August 1965), prepared for the writer by David Evans.
[23] Winfrey, Robley. "Survey of Engineering Economy Research in Educational Institutions," *Journal of Engineering Education,* Vol. 51 (April 1961).
[24] American Society of Civil Engineers, *Code of Ethics.* New York, adopted July 1961.

Benefit-Cost Analysis: Its Relevance to Public Investment Decisions

Arthur Maass*

$\mathbf{T}$he U.S. government has for some time used benefit-cost analysis in the design and justification of dams and other water resources improvements. Currently the government is trying to adapt the technique to other public investment programs. At the request of the Bureau of the Budget, The Brookings Institution held a major conference on the topic in November 1963, with papers on applying benefit-cost analysis to urban highways, urban renewal, outdoor recreation, civil aviation, government research and development, and public health [ref. 1]. In 1965 the Bureau of the Budget established a special unit to adapt and apply benefit-cost and cost-effectiveness studies to a broad range of government programs. It is appropriate, therefore, to examine and evaluate this important branch of welfare economics.

WHAT IS THE PROBLEM?

The major limitation of benefit-cost analysis, as it has been applied to public investments in the United States, is that it ranks projects and programs in terms only of economic efficiency. (At the national level this

* Professor of Government, Harvard University. This paper, which appeared in substantially the same form in the May 1966 issue of the *Quarterly Journal of Economics,* results from several studies of the public investment decision process by members of the Harvard Water Program. The program has been supported by the U.S. Army Corps of Engineers, Resources for the Future, Inc., and the U.S. Public Health Service.

means that projects and programs are judged by the amount that they increase the national product.) But the objective of most public programs is not simply, not even principally, economic efficiency. The redistribution of income to classes or to regions is an important objective in government plans—witness the Appalachia program. And there are other objectives, too—the promotion of national self-sufficiency, for example.

In other words, the objective functions of most government programs are complex; yet benefit-cost analysis has been adapted to only a single objective—economic efficiency. Thus, benefit-cost analysis may be largely irrelevant, or relevant to only a small part of the problem of evaluating public projects and programs. We should not settle for the current state of benefit-cost analysis, but rather find ways to make it applicable to the real issues of public investment.

Now, in all complex objective functions for government programs, economic efficiency will be one term. A second will frequently be income redistribution, as has been noted—to classes (the poor) or to regions (depressed areas). These two objectives may be complementary in some ways: a program designed to transfer income from the rest of the nation to Appalachia, or from the wealthy to the poor, may also increase national product.[1] But a government program that maximizes efficiency will not necessarily, indeed is not likely to, achieve a specified high level of income redistribution. Thus, a planner who is responsible for developing a program or project for both purposes will need to know the relative weights to assign to efficiency and income redistribution.

Assume that the problem is to design an irrigation project on an Indian reservation so as to increase the income of the Indians as a group and to increase food production for the nation as a whole. The relation between income for the Indians (income redistribution) and food production (national economic efficiency) in this case can be stated in any one of three ways as follows. The example is based on Marglin [ref. 3]:

1) Maximize net income to the Indians, subject to a constraint that the ratio of efficiency benefits to efficiency costs is at least 1.0 to 1.0, or 0.9 to 1.0, or some other.

2) Maximize net benefits from food production in national terms—i.e., economic efficiency—subject to a constraint that the Indians net $X thousand/yr.

3) Maximize a weighted sum of net benefits from economic efficiency

---

[1] For conditions under which regional redistribution in the United States can be achieved without significant loss in economic efficiency, see Mera [ref. 2]. For a more general statement of the relationship between economic efficiency and income distribution, see Marglin's discussion on "Objectives of Water Resource Development: A General Statement" [ref. 3, ch. 2, pp. 63–67].

and income redistribution in which $1 of income to the Indians is valued at $(1+X) of efficiency. (In this case the X can be called a shadow premium on redistribution benefits.)

With proper values these three statements will be equivalent. Any constraint can be converted into a shadow price and any shadow price into a constraint.

The efficiency benefits and costs of this two-term objective function can be measured fairly well by the art of benefit-cost analysis in its present state. There are problems, to be sure, resulting from such factors as the collective character of the benefits of many public programs, the need to measure costs in terms of resource displacements rather than market prices where these two measures diverge, the selection of an appropriate discount rate, and various so-called external effects—but great progress has been made on these in recent years.[2] Thus, all that is needed to solve the maximization equation is to specify the tradeoff ratio between efficiency and income redistribution. If there is a way of finding this ratio, the maximization problem can be solved in any of its three forms, and we can design projects and programs that are responsive to a realistic two-factor objective function.

There is a way to determine the tradeoff—through the political process. For the federal government my studies indicate that there is a capacity in the legislative process to make the tradeoff decisions that can then govern the design of projects and programs. The President initiates the legislative process; the Congress examines the President's proposals in the light of alternatives and accepts, modifies, or rejects them. Thus, the experts in the executive departments need to develop data that show the effects on the design of programs and projects of different tradeoff ratios. This the executive can do. The President needs to select one or a range of these ratios and thereby initiate formally the legislative process. This the President can do. And finally, the Congress, when presented with such data and such a presidential initiative, needs to and can respond in order, as we shall see.

Ironically but understandably, the field of public investment for which the present benefit-cost technique is most advanced, water resources, is the field for which the political technique for determining tradeoffs among efficiency and other objectives is most primitive. The legislative process for water resources consists principally of omnibus bills that authorize individual projects, rather than of legislation that sets standards and criteria. In the housing and urban renewal area, by contrast, stan-

---

[2] For discussions of these problems as of 1961, see Marglin and Dorfman ([ref. 3] ch. 2, 3, and 4); also see [ref. 4]. For examples of more recent developments, see papers by Peter O. Steiner and Kenneth J. Arrow, in this volume.

dards and criteria, based on both income redistribution and economic efficiency, are determined in the legislative process, and benefit-cost analysis is primitive.

The problem is to combine the advanced state of the art of efficiency benefit-cost analysis, as found in water resources planning, with an equally sophisticated technique for relating efficiency benefits and costs to those stemming from other objectives.

HAVE BENEFITS BEEN OVERESTIMATED?

In this context it is interesting to examine the arguments over so-called secondary benefits and how they should be included, if at all, in project analyses. There is no such thing as a secondary benefit. A secondary benefit, as the phrase has been used in the benefit-cost literature, is in fact a benefit in support of an objective other than efficiency.[3] The word "benefit" (and the word "cost," too) has no meaning by itself, but only in association with an objective; there are efficiency benefits, income redistribution benefits, and others. Thus, if the objective function for a public program involves more than economic efficiency—and it will in most cases—there is no legitimate reason for holding that the efficiency benefits are primary and should be included in the benefit-cost analysis, whereas benefits in support of other objectives are secondary and should be mentioned, if at all, in separate subsidiary paragraphs of the survey report. Using the current language and current standards, most of the benefits to the Indians in the Indian irrigation project are secondary benefits. How silly!

In this context it is interesting also to examine the conclusion of many non-governmental studies of government planning for water resources projects, namely, that benefits have been overestimated. Hubert Marshall has recited the evidences of chronic overestimation in his paper, "Politics and Efficiency in Water Development," elsewhere in this book. The principal cause of such benefit "overestimation" is, I believe, the unreal restrictions placed on the analysis of projects by the unreal but virtual standard that the relation of efficiency benefits to efficiency costs is the indicator of a project's worth, when in fact the project is conceived and planned for objectives in addition to efficiency. In such an incongruous circumstance one might expect project planners to use a broad definition of efficiency benefits. The critics, either not understanding or unsympa-

---

[3] The term has been used also to describe a small class of efficiency benefits that are *in*duced, rather than *pro*duced directly, by public investment, but the usefulness of this distinction is questionable.

thetic to the planners' plight, have judged them by a more rigorous definition of efficiency.[4]

HOW DID WE GET TO WHERE WE ARE?

Why has benefit-cost analysis developed in this way? Certainly not because of any myopia on the part of the Congress, though executive officers are frequently quick to blame Congress for their ills. To be sure, we do not have adequate legislative objectives, standards, or tradeoff ratios for the design and evaluation of water resources projects, but this is because the President has failed to initiate the legislative process, not because of a lack of receptivity to such initiatives by Congress. In fact, certain committees of Congress, impatient with the President for not proposing legislation to set standards, have tried to initiate the legislative process themselves; but without co-operation from the executive they have failed, understandably [ref. 3, p. 588]. The task of assembling and analyzing data, the necessary first step in the legislative process, is beyond the capacity of Congress and its staffs in complex areas like this one. Insofar as there is a general standard for the design of water projects that has been approved by Congress in legislation, it is a thirty-year-old statement that "the benefits to whomsoever they may accrue should exceed the costs."[5] This standard, you will note, does not specify efficiency benefits, but "benefits to whomsoever they may accrue."

The executive agencies have painted themselves into the efficiency box. In 1950 the Subcommittee on Benefits and Costs of the Federal Inter-Agency River Basin Committee gave overwhelming emphasis to the efficiency ranking function in its now well-known "Green Book" report [ref. 5]. In 1952 the Bureau of the Budget, in a Budget Circular that neither required nor invited formal review and approval by the Congress, nailed this emphasis into national policy, adopting it as the standard by which the Bureau would review agency projects to determine their standing in the President's program [ref. 6]. And soon thereafter agency planning manuals were revised, where necessary, to reflect this Budget Circular. In this way benefits to all became virtually restricted to benefits that increase national product.

The federal bureaucrats, it should be noted, were not acting in a vacuum; they were reflecting the doctrines of the new welfare economics

---

[4] Causes for so-called benefit overestimation, with the exception of the cause I consider to be the principal one, are given in Hubert Marshall's paper, in this volume.

[5] Incidentally, this provision of the Flood Control Act of 1936 (49 Stat. 1570) did not originate in a presidential initiative.

which has focused entirely on economic efficiency. Non-efficiency considerations have been held to be outside of the domain of the welfare economist. They have been called by such loaded names as "inefficient," "value-laden," "altruistic," "merit-wants," "uneconomical."[6]

WHAT CHANGES IN WELFARE ECONOMICS THEORY ARE NEEDED?

From a practical point of view, the new welfare economics has dealt exclusively with efficiency because for it, and not for other objectives, benefit and cost data are provided automatically by the market, though market prices sometimes have to be doctored. Theoretically, however, the preoccupation of present-day welfare economics (and its branch of benefit-cost analysis) with economic efficiency results from its very basic assumptions, and two of these in my view can and should be abandoned.

First is indifference to the distribution of income generated by a government program or project—the assumption that each dollar of income from the program is of equal social value regardless of who receives it. In benefit-cost analysis that maximizes efficiency, an extra dollar to a Texas oil man is as desirable socially as one to an Arkansas tenant farmer, and an additional dollar of benefits for Appalachia, West Virginia, is no more worthwhile than one for Grosse Pointe, Michigan.

Few welfare economists support the social implications of this basic assumption, and they would compensate for them in one of two ways. Some hold that the professional planners should design projects and programs for economic efficiency, for which benefit-cost analysis can provide the necessary ranking function; and that thereafter these project designs can be doctored and modified by a political process to account for any "uneconomic" objectives.[7] But this response is unsatisfactory for reasons already given. Where government programs are intended for complex objectives they should be designed, where this is possible, for such objectives, not designed for one objective, which may not be the most important, and subsequently modified in an effort to account for others. Almost inevitably economic efficiency will be overweighted in such a scheme. How relevant is this type of planning for our Indian irrigation project? Furthermore, such a planning process calls on political institutions to perform a task for which they are not well equipped.

---

[6] For example, see Musgrave [ref. 7]. The first of these nomers is perhaps correct technically, but even this cannot be said of the others, for efficiency is not necessarily less or more value-laden, altruistic, or meritorious than other objectives.

[7] In essence, this is what Dorfman proposes for West Pakistan [ref. 8].

Where the approval and modification of individual projects, rather than a debate on objectives and standards for designing projects in the first place, is the *principal* activity of the legislative process, decision making for the nation can disintegrate into project trading. In the legislature, for example, the voices of the whole house and of committees are muted at the expense of those of individual members, each making decisions for projects in his district and accepting reciprocally the decisions of his colleagues. Nor does the executive under these circumstances play a more general or high-minded role. The public investment decision process can be organized, hopefully, to play to the strengths rather than to the weaknesses of political institutions.

An alternative response of some welfare economists to the inequitable social consequences of the basic assumption of indifference to income distribution is as follows: It is more efficient to redistribute income directly from one group of individuals to another through government programs of taxation and subsidies, than to do so indirectly through government investment programs that are designed also to increase national product. If the government's objectives are, for example, to increase both national food production and income of the Indians, it should plan to accomplish these by two programs rather than a single one. Government planners should design the most efficient program for increasing food production, which may mean additional irrigation facilities in the Imperial Valley of California, where there are no Indians. Then, with taxes collected from the irrigators and representing their willingness to pay for their new benefits, the government should make subsidy payments to the Indians. In this way, so goes the argument, the government can achieve the best of both worlds. "Best" in this context means "efficient," however, and there is no reason why a community need prefer the most efficient method for redistributing income, especially if it requires transferring cash from one group to another. As Marglin points out in his treatment of this subject [ref. 3, pp. 17–18, 63–67], the means by which a desired distribution of income is achieved may be of great importance to the community.[8] In our example, the

---

[8] Tinbergen [ref. 9] observes that in the normal case, *n* programs (or instruments) are required to maximize a welfare function that includes *n* objectives (or targets). But for his normal case Tinbergen assumes that only the results of the programs, not their qualitative characteristics, affect welfare and that planners are free to select that level of achievement of each objective that maximizes the over-all welfare function. This freedom is theirs only if *n* programs are available to the planners. Our discussion, on the other hand, proceeds from the assumptions that the qualitative characteristics of the programs affect welfare, and that the number of acceptable programs may be fewer than the number of objectives, which necessitates the tradeoff among objectives. This would be an abnormal case in Tinbergen's formulation.

community would probably be willing to give up some efficiency to see the living standard of the Indians improved by their own labors rather than by the dole. In short, the community may quite properly want to realize multiple purposes through public investment projects and programs, and if benefit-cost analysis is to be of great use in planning these activities, then the basic assumption of indifference to their distributive consequences must be abandoned.

It should be noted, however, that where, as in the case of the Indian irrigation project, a government program produces benefits that can be sold or otherwise charged for, a desired redistribution of income can be achieved by both the quantity of benefits produced and the prices charged for them. For any given quantity of irrigation water, the smaller the repayment required from the Indians, the greater the income they will receive. Thus, when the agency men prepare data showing the effects on public programs of alternative tradeoffs between economic efficiency and income redistribution, these alternatives should include different repayment possibilities.

The second basic assumption of the new welfare economics and of benefit-cost analysis that needs to be challenged is consumers' sovereignty —reliance solely on market-exhibited preferences of individuals. This assumption, to be sure, provides normative significance for the familiar prescriptions of welfare economics on which the efficiency calculus is based—for example, that price ought to equal marginal costs. Nonetheless, it is not relevant to all public investment decisions, for an individual's market preference is a response in terms of what he believes to be good for his own economic interest, not for the community.

Each individual plays a number of roles in his life—social science literature is filled with studies of role differentiation—and each role can lead him to a unique response to a given choice situation. Thus an individual has the capacity to respond in a given case, to formulate his preferences, in several ways, including these two: (1) what he believes to be good for himself—largely his economic self-interest, and (2) what he believes to be good for the political community. The difference between these two can be defined in terms of breadth of view. To the extent that an individual's response is community, rather than privately, oriented, it places greater emphasis on the individual's estimate of the consequences of his choice for the larger community.

Now, the response that an individual gives in any choice situation will depend in significant part on how the question is asked of him, and this means not simply the way a question is worded, but the total environment in which it is put and discussed. This can be illustrated with a small group experiment. Questions with relevance for the church (for example, should birth control information be provided to married individuals who desire it?) were asked of Catholic students randomly divided into two groups. One group met in a small room where they were made aware of their common religious membership. The other group met in a large auditorium, along with hundreds of other students of many religions, where no effort was made to establish awareness of common religious beliefs. Although all of the students were instructed to respond with their "own personal opinion," there was a significant difference between the replies of the group that were aware of their common religious membership and the unaware group, the former approximating more closely the orthodox Catholic position against birth control [ref. 10].

An individual's response depends, then, on the institutional environment in which the question is asked. Since the relevant response for public investment analysis is community, not privately, oriented, the great challenge for welfare economics is to frame questions in such a way as to elicit from individuals community-oriented answers. The market is an institution designed to elicit privately oriented responses from individuals and to relate these responses to each other. For the federal government, the electoral, legislative, and administrative processes together constitute the institution designed to elicit community-oriented responses. The Maass-Cooper model describes these processes within such a context [ref. 3, p. 588].

Although several welfare economists have recognized explicitly that individuals play several roles and that these roles influence preferences, they go on to say that in making decisions relating to social welfare each individual uses a composite utility function, a total net position representing a balance of all of his roles [ref. 11, 12, 13]. This last hypothesis, which is not supported by experimental evidence, is unfortunate. It misses the point that an individual will respond differently depending on how the question is asked of him, and it fails to give proper emphasis to the differentiation of institutions for putting the question—for example, the market institution to elicit privately oriented responses, and political institutions for those that are community oriented.

Ideally, we want community, not market, responses of individuals with respect to both factors in our complex objective function—economic efficiency and income redistribution. Fortunately, however, market-determined prices are a fairly good surrogate for the economic efficiency factor, providing adjustments are made for so-called externalities and the like.[9] This is opportune. Were it not for the propriety of using market-related prices for efficiency benefits and costs, benefit-cost analysis for

[9] Marglin's 1962 analysis [ref. 3] is one demonstration of this.

public projects and programs would be beyond the capacity of available economic techniques and of political institutions as they operate today.

Some day, I am confident, we shall be able to use institutions that elicit community-oriented responses to measure all factors in a complex objective function—efficiency, income redistribution, and others. The very recent search by a few economists, inspired largely by the work of Kenneth Arrow, for a new criterion of social welfare may contribute to this end.[10] The more modest proposal of this paper is that we use political institutions to measure the tradeoff ratio between a basically market-determined efficiency and the single most important non-efficiency objective of a government program—which is likely to be income redistribution but may be some other.

WHAT IS THE EVIDENCE THAT TRADEOFFS
CAN BE DETERMINED?

It remains to be demonstrated that there is a capacity in the legislative process to select tradeoff ratios in a way that will be useful for the design of government programs and projects. As stated earlier, the legislative process involves three steps. First, the officials in the executive departments prepare data showing what would be the effects on programs and projects of alternative tradeoffs between economic efficiency and another objective; second, the President, with these data in hand, selects a trade-off ratio and proposes it to Congress as the legislative standard; and third, Congress examines the President's proposal, in the light of the alternatives developed in the departments and of others that may come from outside sources, and accepts, rejects, or modifies it.

The first step should not involve great difficulties, especially in water resources where analysis of the efficiency factor is well advanced, although there will be obvious problems in areas where economic efficiency analysis is primitive. For continuing programs, the data necessary to initiate the legislative process need not relate to projects and programs being designed or to be designed; they can be drawn from projects already in operation and in some cases from hypothetical or prototype projects. Agency men can re-examine completed projects and programs and estimate how differently they would have been built and would have operated with different tradeoffs among objectives. At the same time they can reflect in the data that they prepare for new investment programs information generated during previous planning periods, thereby using a sequential planning process. (See Marglin [ref. 14, p. 22].)

---

[10] For an excellent summary of this research, see Rothenberg [ref. 13].

It is at the final, or congressional, stage that doubters will raise most questions, and it is, of course, this stage that is most difficult to prove, because in the water resources area, for which the legislative initiative could be taken most clearly, the President has failed to act. To demonstrate Congress' capacity we must, therefore, turn to public investment programs for which standards have been set in legislation, and these are ones for which benefit-cost analysis is so rudimentary that it is necessary to examine the record very carefully for implicit evidence of a concern for tradeoffs between efficiency and other objectives.

Legislation authorizing the National System of Interstate Highways, principally the Act of 1956, furnishes one example.[11] The legislation provides that the system should consist of 41,000 miles of roads which are identified generally as to location, and it sets design criteria for these roads. The criteria depart from those of earlier highway legislation in three important respects, apart from the taxing methods for financing the federal government's share of the costs. First, roads are to be designed for predicted traffic volumes of 1975, and the monetary authorizations are calculated from this standard.[12] Second, the federal-state matching ratio is changed from 50:50 to 90:10. Third, the formula for apportioning funds among the states is changed. The earlier formula for the primary system of roads was one-third on the basis of each of the following ratios: a state's population to the total U.S. population, a state's area to the total U.S. land area, a state's rural delivery and star routes to the total U.S. mileage of such roads. The new formula provides a single ratio: the estimated cost of completing the interstate system within the borders of a state to the total estimated cost of completing the entire system by a fixed date, 1972.[13] This last criterion was agreed to after considerable discussion involving numerous alternatives, but principally two: the one adopted and one that would continue to give considerable weight to a state's area and its population.

As Major has shown, these alternatives represent respectively economic efficiency, or more properly a surrogate for efficiency, and income redistribution. Given the requirement of completing a given mileage, by a given date, to a given capacity (1975 traffic volume), an apportionment based on cost of completion would be efficient; and one based on such factors as a state's area would introduce other objectives into the pro-

[11] My data are taken from Major [ref. 15]. See this thesis for citations of statutes and reports referred to here.

[12] This design standard was amended in 1963 to provide for predicted traffic volumes twenty years from date of approval of project plans.

[13] The Act of 1956 contemplated completion by fiscal year 1969, but both estimated costs and year of completion were later amended.

gram, namely, redistribution of income (largely federal construction funds) to rural states where traffic volumes and highway construction costs per mile are typically lower. This is especially true because the alternative provided that if a state received more funds than necessary to complete its portion of the interstate system, it could divert a percentage of the excess for use on its other federally aided roads.

A study of the legislative process in which these new program criteria, especially the third one, were adopted has some useful lessons for our inquiry. There was a vigorous and effective executive initiative of the process. The concept of uniform completion of an interstate system in all states at approximately the same time appears to have been recommended first by a non-federal entity, the American Association of State Highway Officials. Thereafter, the Bureau of Public Roads made a detailed factual study of the costs of building an interstate system. The President, in an address before the 1954 Governors' Conference, proposed that the nation develop a new master plan for highways, and he appointed an Advisory Committee on a National Highway Program, chaired by General Lucius Clay, to prepare one. The Clay Committee used the Bureau of Public Roads report as its empirical base. It recommended the three design standards that were finally adopted, presenting them in the context of alternatives about which debate in the legislative process could and did revolve.[14] Both the BPR and the Clay reports were sent to the Congress, along with a presidential recommendation. The discussion in Congress, in committee and on the floor, was informed and extensive. Information was available on the expected consequences in terms of investment of choosing alternative standards, the participants were aware of the nature of the choices they had to make, and their debate was rich in relevant arguments pro and con on the alternatives, especially on apportionment formulae.

What we have called economic efficiency in this case—i.e., the most efficient way of satisfying a fixed requirement—is of course quite different from economic efficiency as an objective in benefit-cost analysis for water resources, where it means to maximize the contribution of a project to national product. The latter concept played no part in setting the standards for the highway program. The art of efficiency benefit-cost analysis is much less well developed for public investments in highways than in water resources developments, and this was even more true ten years ago than it is today. It is not unreasonable to suggest, from the record of the legislative process for the interstate highway system, that

[14] The Clay report's proposals on tax policy and accounting procedures for financing the road system, which we do not discuss here, were altered significantly in the legislative process.

had data been available on real economic efficiency and on alternative tradeoffs between it and income redistribution, these would have been used intelligently in setting standards.

Comparing the legislative processes for the interstate highway system and water resources, the former is less concerned with authorizing individual projects that have been designed and more concerned with setting standards for project design. To be sure, the Highway Act authorized 41,000 miles of roads and fixed their general locations. Design of the roads, including definite locations for them, was left, however, for administrative action insofar as the federal government was concerned.

In federal programs for housing and urban renewal, standards and design criteria have been set in the legislative process, and the recent legislative history of the rent supplement program is an instructive example.[15] In his Housing Message of 1965, President Johnson described a proposed program for rent supplement payments as "the most crucial new instrument in our effort to improve the American city." The federal government was to guarantee to certain private builders the payment of a significant part of the rent for housing units built for occupancy by moderate-income families. These are families with incomes below the level necessary to obtain standard housing at area market prices, but above the level required for admission to publicly owned low-rent housing units. The rent payments were to be the difference between 20 per cent of a family's income (the proportion of income that a moderate-income family is expected to allocate to housing) and the fair market rental of the standard housing to be built. The President proposed an authorization of $200 million over four years which was designed to encourage the construction of 500,000 new housing units in this period. The housing supported in this way would constitute some but not all of the rental units in new housing projects.

The Housing Act of 1961 had also included a program designed specifically for moderate-income families, but this program had encountered certain problems that slowed its expected impact. Section 221d(3) of the 1961 Act provided for 100 per cent loans to qualified private builders at below-market interest rates. The low interest rates were to keep rents within the reach of moderate-income families. The law provided, however, that the interest rate was to be the average rate on all outstanding marketable federal obligations. This was $3\frac{1}{8}$ per cent when the program began, but it had risen to approximately $4\frac{1}{8}$ per cent by

---

[15] Except where otherwise noted, the facts of this case are derived from legislative documents relating to the Housing and Urban Development Act of 1965 [ref. 16]. David C. Major has assisted in developing the facts and interpretation of this case.

mid-1965. This meant that rents would be significantly higher and beyond the capacity of most moderate-income families. Another problem with the 1961 program was that the low interest mortgages constituted a heavy drain on the special assistance funds of the Federal National Mortgage Association, the federal housing credit agency that purchased them. Because these mortgages were below market rates, FNMA could not issue against them debentures for sale in private capital markets, and they remained a 100 per cent charge on federal funds. Nonetheless, the Administration recommended in 1965 that the 221d(3) program be continued for four years with a mortgage authorization of $1.5 billion, for about 125,000 new housing units. But this program was to be phased out if the rent supplement proposal worked as its backers hoped that it would.

The Administration had three principal objectives in proposing rent supplements. The first was to increase the number of housing starts. This derived from a desire to expand the national housing stock and a concern about the possibly failing health of the housing industry and the industry's impact on the national economy. We can equate this objective roughly with increasing national product, or economic efficiency. The government's housing experts found that there was a large untapped market for new housing among moderate-income families, and that rent supplements for them would stimulate the rapid construction of substantial amounts of new housing.

The second principal objective of the Administration in recommending a rent supplement program was to give direct assistance to a large group of families with incomes above the public housing level but below the level needed to obtain standard housing at market prices. This objective we can equate with income redistribution—to moderate-income families.

As for direct assistance to low-income families, the Administration bill would authorize additional public housing units. Over a four-year period 140,000 new units were to be built and 100,000 units purchased or leased from private owners and rehabilitated. Using the trickle-down theory, the Administration could claim that all other housing programs that increased the national stock of standard housing would ultimately improve the housing of the poor, but certainly the primary and direct impact of the rent supplement program, insofar as its objective was income redistribution, favored moderate-income families.

The Administration's rent supplement program contained, then, as one design criterion of a tradeoff ratio, relating the objectives of efficiency and income redistribution, and as a second, a specification of the group to be favored by the redistribution. The second criterion was explicit in the Administration's legislative initiative, though the first was largely implicit.

The Administration's third principal objective for the rent supplement program was "economic integration." Families being aided by the government would live in projects with families who would pay normal market rentals for their housing. In this respect the new program differed from most other federal housing programs for disadvantaged groups, for the latter promoted economic segregation. Only the poor live in public housing; all units in 221d(3) projects are for occupancy by designated groups. To encourage economic integration even where local authorities may oppose it, the Administration proposed that in certain cases projects supported by rent supplements need not conform to locally approved "workable programs" for housing development.

After hearings, and debates, and conferences, Congress modified drastically the Administration's design criteria for a rent supplement program. Briefly, the supplements are to be given for new standard housing units that are to be occupied by low-income families. As a result, both the tradeoff ratio between efficiency and income redistribution and the impact of the redistribution itself have been changed.

The relative contributions of the program to increasing national product and to redistributing income have been altered because, with a given authorization or appropriation, there will be fewer housing starts if rents of low, rather than moderate, income families are supplemented. The unit costs of standard housing are the same in either case, but the supplement required to make up the difference between what the family can pay and what is needed to support the new housing varies greatly. The new law authorizes $150 million for rent supplements (rather than the $200 million proposed by the President). According to December 1965 estimates of housing experts, this $150 million would result in 350,000–375,000 housing starts over four years if it were available for the Administration's program of aiding moderate-income families. As rent supplements for low-income families, the same money will induce only 250,000–300,000 starts.[16]

As for the criterion that governs the group to be benefited, the relative impacts on low- and moderate-income families of the original and revised programs for rent supplements and closely related activities are shown in Table 1.

[16] Under the Administration bill the rent supplement would be the difference between rent for standard housing and 20 per cent of a moderate-income family's income; under the Act as approved, the difference between the same rent and 25 per cent of a *low*-income family's income. The two changes made by Congress work in opposite directions, but they do not offset each other.

TABLE 1.

Impact on Low- and Moderate-Income Families of Certain Provisions of
1965 Housing Act

Program	Administration proposal	Congressional action
(All figures are thousands of housing units over four years)		
Low income		
Public housing	240	240
Trickle down from all programs that increase national stock of standard housing	ok	ok
Rent supplement program	zero	250–300
Moderate income		
Rent supplements	467–500	zero
221d(3)	125 (*but* problems in achieving this because of high interest rate and drain on FNMA funds)	125 (*and* this likely to be achieved because interest rate fixed at 3% and provision made for tapping private capital)

The impact of Congress' revisions on the Administration's third objective of economic integration is not so clear. Insofar as it is poor rather than moderate-income families who are enabled to live in housing developments along with families that are able to pay normal rents, a more dramatic integration can be achieved. On the other hand, it is clear from the legislative history that Congress does not intend that the housing agency exempt any rent supplement projects from the "workable plan" requirement, which means that local controls will continue.

The housing case study, like that of the highway program, shows that there is a capacity in the legislative process to discuss and adopt standards and criteria to control the design of public projects and programs; that the Congress is prepared to focus its efforts on such standards and forego authorization of the projects themselves—public works for housing, urban renewal, and community facilities are not individually authorized by law; and that the legislative process for setting standards can be used to select tradeoff ratios where a program has two objectives. On this latter point, the rent supplement case is a bit weak, to be sure. The Administration in its legislative initiative did not make sufficiently explicit the tradeoff between economic efficiency and income redistribution that was involved in its proposal for approximately 500,000 new housing starts for the benefit of moderate-income families. Administration witnesses failed to give a clear statement of how the two objectives were related and how the program would differ if alternative tradeoff ratios were assumed. One reason for this failure is that efficiency benefit-cost analysis has not been perfected for housing programs as it has for water resources. Nonetheless, the Congress, in reviewing the President's program, managed to focus on the relevant design criteria and, after extensive consideration, including some confused debate, revised them in a way that apparently was consistent with its policy preferences. Also, the executive now has a legislated standard that it can use in redesigning the relevant housing programs. How much better the process would have been if the initiative had been better prepared!

THE LESSON

To those in the executive departments of the U.S. government, the lessons of this article should be clear. If the subject is water resources, initiate a legislative proposal for setting a tradeoff value between economic efficiency and the most important non-efficiency objective that is relevant to your agency's program. Once this is approved, you can forget about secondary benefits, probably be relieved from the drum-drum and profession-wise insulting charges that you persistently overestimate benefits, and you can design projects that are more in accord with the nation's objectives. If the subject is highways, or housing, or most other public investment programs, perfect the efficiency benefit-cost technique for your agency's program. Once this is done, there should be no difficulty in deriving through the legislative process a tradeoff between efficiency and another objective. As a result, the design and selection of projects will be more intelligent and the program should be more convincing to those who judge it.

After the agencies have learned how to work with two-term objective functions, they can try to solve far more complex ones. For the time being, however, purposes other than efficiency and the most important non-efficiency objective will need to be treated descriptively in the familiar "additional paragraphs" of program and project reports.

REFERENCES

[1] Dorfman, Robert (ed.). *Measuring Benefits of Government Investments*. Washington: Brookings Institution, 1965.
[2] Mera, Koichi. "Efficiency and Equalization in Interregional Economic Development." Ph.D. thesis, Harvard University, 1965.
[3] Maass, Arthur, Hufschmidt, Maynard M., Dorfman, Robert, Thomas, Harold A., Jr., Marglin, Stephen A., and Fair, Gordon Maskew. *Design of Water-Resource Systems*. Cambridge: Harvard University Press, 1962.

[4] Hufschmidt, Maynard M., Krutilla, John, and Margolis, Julius, with assistance of Marglin, Stephen A. *Standards and Criteria for Formulating and Evaluating Federal Water Resources Development: A Report of Panel of Consultants to the Bureau of the Budget.* Washington: U.S. Government Printing Office, 1961.

[5] U.S. Federal Inter-Agency River Basin Committee, Subcommittee on Benefits and Costs. *Proposed Practices for Economic Analysis of River Basin Projects.* Washington, May 1950.

[6] U.S. Bureau of the Budget. *Circular A-47* (Mimeo.). Washington, December 31, 1952.

[7] Musgrave, Richard A. *The Theory of Public Finance.* New York: McGraw-Hill, 1959.

[8] Dorfman, Robert. "An Economic Strategy for West Pakistan," *Asian Survey,* Vol. 3 (1963).

[9] Tinbergen, Jan. *On the Theory of Economic Policy.* Amsterdam: North-Holland Publishing Co., 1952.

[10] Charters, W. W., Jr., and Newcomb, Theodore M. "Some Attitudinal Effects of Experimentally Increased Salience of a Membership Group," in Maccoby, Eleanor E., Newcomb, Theodore M., and Hartley, Eugene L. *Readings in Social Psychology.* New York: Henry Holt, 1958.

[11] Downs, Anthony. "The Public Interest: Its Meaning in a Democracy," *Social Research,* Vol. 29 (1962).

[12] Colm, Gerhard. "The Public Interest: Essential Key to Public Policy," in Friedrich, C. J. (ed.), *The Public Interest.* New York: Atherton Press, 1962, p. 121.

[13] Rothenberg, Jerome. *The Measurement of Social Welfare.* Englewood Cliffs, N.J.: Prentice-Hall, 1961, pp. 296–97.

[14] Marglin, Stephen A. *Public Investment Criteria.* London: Allen and Unwin, 1966.

[15] Major, David C. "Decision Making for Public Investment in Water Resource Development in the United States." Ph.D. thesis Harvard University, chap. 5.

[16] President's Message (H. Doc. 89–99); Hearings before Subcommittees on Housing of the House and Senate Committees on Banking and Currency (March–April 1965); Reports of House and Senate Committees on Banking and Currency (H. Rept. 89–365, S. Rept. 89–378); Debate in House and Senate (*Congressional Record* for June 28–30 and July 14–15, 1965); Conference Report (H. Rept. 89–679); Debate in House and Senate on adoption of Conference Report (*Congressional Record* for July 26–27, 1965).

RESEARCH ON HYDROLOGY AND ENGINEERING

Synthetic Hydrology: An Assessment

Myron B. Fiering*

"*Now, in the waning days of the second World War, this ship lies at anchor in the glassy bay of one of the back islands of the Pacific. It is a Navy cargo ship. You know it is a cargo ship by the five yawning hatches, by the house amidships, by the booms that bristle from the masts like mechanical arms. You know it is a Navy ship by the color (dark, dull, blue), by the white numbers painted on the bow, and unfailingly by the thin ribbon of the commission pennant flying from the mainmast.*"

Thus Thomas Heggen begins *Mister Roberts* [ref. 1], a little book which became a classic story of embattled life at sea during World War II—a story which rings especially true to former Naval Reservists. It describes the combat record of this ship:

"*It has shot down no enemy planes, nor has it fired upon any, nor has it seen any. It has sunk with its guns no enemy subs, but there was this once that it fired. This periscope, the lookout sighted it way off on the port beam, and the Captain, who was scared almost out of his mind, gave the order: 'Commence firing!' The five-inch and the two port three-inch guns fired for perhaps ten minutes, and the showing was really rather embarrassing. The closest shell was three hundred yards off . . .*"

So it is with the application of synthetic hydrology to the design and management of water resource systems. No enemy planes have been downed, or fired upon, nor is there absolute certainty that any have been

* Assistant Professor of Engineering and Applied Mathematics, Harvard University.

seen. No enemy subs have been sunk, although a few salvos have been fired. And while confirmation of a direct hit must await the judgment of history, at least a few substantial oil slicks have risen to the surface and hopes run high.

Nor does the analogy end here, because just as a naval salvo is preferred to individual, sporadic firing, so our research program is a team effort. Maynard Hufschmidt has more to say about this elsewhere in this volume.

Synthetic hydrology, or what is now called "operational" hydrology,[1] was developed to correct a fallacy. Adoption of the word "operational" in place of the ill-chosen, but now accepted, adjective "synthetic" is an effort to remind the user that hydrologic sequences generated by recursive models, of whatever sort, are meaningless unless transformed into some metric and then ranked to aid and abet in the exercise of a decision. There is an element of P. W. Bridgman's operationalism subsumed in the new title "operational" hydrology; after all, what could be duller than long sequences of hydrologic inflows which did not really occur anywhere but in the central processing unit of a digital computer?

Problems in water resource design are solved by one or a combination of ways. Rigid codes, political expedience, rules of thumb, engineering judgment, and standard office practice are among those most frequently used. The lowly, busy beaver designs and builds dams in accordance with some blend of these inputs and a large dose of genetic sophistication and natural selection. Operational hydrology cannot help in these methods, useful as they may be in some cases. The remaining design regime is that of the model, encompassing analog techniques and mathematical or symbolic representations. The latter are further subdivided into analytic models and simulation models. In this paper attention is focused on the use of simulation models.

THE TECHNOLOGICAL FUNCTION

The technological function, frequently called the production function by economists, represents the physical limits of the process or system under study. Thus, if the inputs to some economic enterprise or production process are limited by a budgetary constraint or by resource availability, the technological function specifies the capability of the system to produce output by defining the maximal levels of the outputs which can be attained from a given level of inputs. Conversely, for every set of system outputs, the production or technological function indicates the

---

[1] I am indebted to Professor Gordon M. Fair for suggesting the term.

least-cost combination of inputs required to produce the specified outputs.

While most real systems are so complicated that a simple analytical relation between inputs and outputs cannot be formulated, the concept of a technological function as the locus of economically efficient points along which the production process should be undertaken is a useful guide to planning.

The technological function for very simple resource systems, such as those characterized by one of a handful of well-behaved inflow distributions, might be derived by analytical techniques. For example, consider the storage-yield problem investigated in 1883 by Rippl [ref. 2], who routed the hydrologic record through a semi-infinite storage and calculated the range of the cumulative departure of the inflow from the outflow. If the outflow or release equals the mean inflow, the requisite storage would fill once and go dry once, but would never spill and would never fail to meet the demand or target release. Rippl could thereby derive a mapping between storage size and firm yield.

Feller [ref. 3] and others (e.g., Alexander, Annis, Lloyd) saw the fallacy in Rippl's argument—the probability that the historical flow pattern will recur within a few years is infinitesimally small, so any design conclusions based solely on one pattern or hydrologic trace are subject to vigorous attack. If the inflows are normally and independently distributed, and if the outflow in each period is the population mean inflow, Feller's results give the expected value and the variance of the required storage as functions of the length of the period of analysis and the standard deviation of the inflows; the coefficient of variation of required storage is 29 per cent.

But for non-normal or serially correlated inflows, for release patterns which do not utilize the mean flow, or for short periods of analysis, the analytical solution fails. Alternatively, long traces of inflows x_i might be synthesized by the familiar recursion relation

$$x_i = \mu(1 - \rho) + \rho x_{i-1} + t_i \sigma (1 - \rho^2)^{1/2} \tag{1}$$

where μ and σ are the mean and standard deviation, respectively, of the inflows, ρ is the lag one serial correlation coefficient among the inflows, and t_i is a standardized random-sampling variate with zero mean and unit variance.

Suppose the index i runs from 1 to n, where n is large, and that m flow samples of N periods (say years) are extracted so that $n \geq m \cdot N$. If the m traces are routed through a Rippl or mass curve analysis, m required storages are educed. Let these storages be written $S_1, S_2, \ldots, S_m$, whereupon the distribution and the moments of the S_i may be estimated empirically. Clearly the moments of the S_i depend on hydrologic factors and operating parameters. Among the hydrologic factors are the moments of the inflows and the serial correlation coefficient, while operating parameters include the length of economic analysis N, the degree of regulation (which in turn determines the release pattern), and the reservoir operating policy.

For normal inflows, the t_i in equation (1) are normally and independently distributed with zero mean and unit variance. For gamma inflows, the t_i have zero mean, unit variance, and skewness γ_t functionally related to the skewness of the observed values [ref. 4, 5]. Similarly, for distributions whose specifications require higher moments, the t_i are further transformed so as to preserve all their lower moments and to satisfy each newly imposed requirement, whereby the x_i can be molded to any distribution and the generated sequences are statistically indistinguishable from the observed events.

It is clear that the generating mechanism, equation (1), can be generalized to a model of lag r and that it would then include the additional independent variables x_{i-2}, x_{i-3}, ..., x_{i-r}. Current studies are directed at identifying the best distribution and lag for any record. Spectral analysis of records, the standard technique for discriminating among alternative generating models of various lags, is not immediately applicable in hydrologic problems because the record lengths are typically so short that discrimination between models at the ordinary levels of significance is often inadequate.

Even in the simple storage-yield example, involving only one reservoir, one stream, and a trivial rule curve or operating policy, operational hydrology must generally be used in tandem with simulation to produce a statistical description of system response because the conditions of the analytical solution are violated. The next question, inevitably, concerns how operational hydrology facilitates the formulation and evaluation of a meaningful objective function for a water resource system.

THE OBJECTIVE FUNCTION

Returning to our storage-yield example, suppose we generate n years of operational hydrology and route the flows through a storage facility of given capacity, each year trying to meet a given target release. The proportion of years in which the release can be met is p^*, the ratio of the cumulative shortage to the cumulative target is q, and the complement $p = 1 - q$ is one alternative to p^* for defining the probability of meeting the target.

The set of alternative storages can be mapped into a set of costs, while the set of target releases can be mapped into a set of benefits. The result of simulating many combinations of storage and yield can be expressed on a contour map for which the axes are storage and yield, or cost and benefit, and on which the contours represent various levels of fulfillment of the target draft, or the statistic p defined above. A typical map is shown in Figure 1. Now the designer must specify two parameters—any two—of the three represented on the map, and the third is uniquely defined. That is, storage and yield uniquely define the confidence level p, storage and p jointly define the maximum yield attainable (at p), and yield and p together define the minimum storage required. Of course, cost can be substituted for storage and benefit can be substituted for yield in the foregoing.

Operational hydrology has bought us a handle, then, for a statistical description of the system. It no longer suffices to say that some level of yield can be achieved from some investment in storage, or conversely. A statistical measure of fulfillment, p, must accompany all such statements.

For more sophisticated systems, involving the interplay between many reservoirs and components, a three-dimensional surface (represented by a contour map) is inadequate to express the optimization problem. Thomas [ref. 6] has prepared a scheme for evaluating the magnitude of an insurance or sinking fund which is augmented when the system

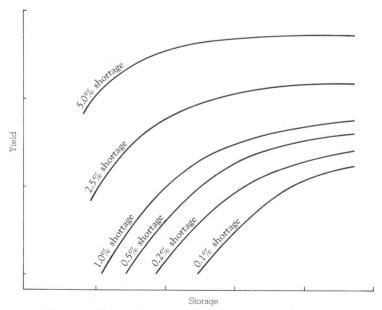

Figure 1. Storage-yield contours at several levels of reliability.

335

operates at a profit and depleted when the system sustains a loss. The value of the fund at any time depends on its initial value, the discount rate, and the statistical characteristics of the system's response. If the benefits are independent and normally distributed, Thomas shows that a consistent (i.e., rational) objective function to be maximized by varying the several decision variables is

$$\text{Objective function} = \mu_B\,(r\,,N) + a\,\sigma \qquad (2)$$

where $\mu_B\,(r\,,N)$ is the present value of expected net benefits, discounted at rate r over N years, where σ is the standard deviation of annual benefits, and where a is a parameter related to the decision-maker's propensity to risk.

The parameter a is functionally dependent on the discount rate r, the time horizon N, and a probability α that the sinking fund will be non-negative after N years. The dependence is such that for risk-averse decision-makers, $a < 0$; for gamblers, $a > 0$. If $a = 0$, the decision-maker is indifferent to risk or, equivalently, makes decisions based on expectation only. The product $(-a\sigma)$ is the initial value of the sinking fund.

There are gaps in this analysis. For example, the technique does not penalize the system for having a negative fund at any time before year N. If benefits are not independent and normally distributed, their standard deviation is not readily attainable by analytic techniques. But simulation and operational hydrology together provide a basis for evaluating the initial size of the insurance fund when analytical techniques fail; while much remains to be done in this type of analysis, we are encouraged.

FURTHER GENERALIZATIONS

The application of operational hydrology to a multiple-reservoir system is a more substantive problem, because not only must the several temporal or auto-correlation coefficients at each site be maintained by the model, but the moments and covariances (i.e., spatial correlations) between sites must be preserved if the synthetic flows are to be indistinguishable from their historical counterparts. Subjecting the observations to a principal component analysis transforms them into a set of orthogonal variables which serve as the bases for independent synthetic records at each pseudosite, each generated independently by recursive use of equation (1). The inverse transform, applied to the generated components, reconstitutes an array of flow data which, like frozen orange juice, retains all the relevant features (moments) of the original observations and which could be another sample drawn from the same multi-variate population as the historical observations.

There are many other ways to generate flows which preserve the serial and cross-correlations of the historical observations. However, all these alternatives appear to require a prior specification of the order in which the several sites are treated; thus, they lack one of the main advantages of principal component analysis, namely, freedom from prior arbitrary ordering of the sites.

THE DYNAMICS OF SIMULATION

Commonly used time horizons are 50, 75, and 100 years. It is trite, but true, that during these substantial intervals much water can flow over the dam, resulting in a changing pattern of supply and demand levels which dictates the desirability of augmenting the system in due course. Operational hydrology can be used to design a dynamic system; the analysis distinguishes between the length of demand periods and the length of each associated simulation period. Suppose the time horizon is 50 years, that it is segmented into three demand periods of 10, 20, and 20 years, and that the objective function is the maximization of the present value of expected net benefits less the contribution to an insurance fund. The design proposed for the first demand period, covering the time from year 0 to year 10, is simulated using as a long sequence of operational hydrology, say 100 or 500 years, as required for stable results. From this simulation period we impute the distribution of the benefits, and can discount the relevant moments to time zero, the present. Design and demand changes are then instituted, generally by reading a few new input cards, and the program simulates the second demand period, year 11 to year 30, again discounting the relevant moments to their present values. Finally, after the last of the design and economic changes are invoked and read into the computer, the terminal 20-year demand period is simulated and discounted. The discounted values are summed, or otherwise combined as dictated by the objective function, and the value of the alternative is calculated and saved for ultimate ranking. The use of dynamic programming as an aid to scheduling system modification is currently being examined.

A BIT ABOUT COMPUTERS

Rippl published his technique for mass-curve analysis in 1883, and the art of designing reservoirs was stagnant, except for a few innovations introduced by Allen Hazen and Charles Sudler, until a few years ago.

Why, suddenly, has the problem become so attractive? Part of the answer lies in the random nature of things—in coincidence—but part is closely interwoven with the advent of, and faith in, the electronic digital computer. One man, or an office full of men, could not undertake either segment of the proposed analysis—synthesis or simulation—without the support of a substantial computing facility. Thus, when we speak of instituting design changes by inserting a few new cards into a deck, it is understood that the detailed simulation analysis has been coded for a computer and that the program either accepts or generates the operational hydrology required by the simulation.

THE SALVOS

The first application to a real situation was undertaken in connection with a study by the Meramec River Basin Commission [ref. 7]. It was a modest simulation program, at least by present standards, and was integrated into the planning of a few small reservoirs in the St. Louis area.

The next effort was made at flank speed and under forced draft. In response to a request from Pakistan's President Ayub Khan, President Kennedy directed his Scientific Advisory Council to undertake a technical assistance program for relief of waterlogging and salinity of agricultural lands in the Punjab region of West Pakistan. To evaluate the technological response of the proposed remedies, a group at Harvard with which I am associated simulated a well field of truly heroic proportions, and generated synthetic traces of river flow, irrigation diversions, and rainfall. The output comprises a trace of ground-water depth versus time and an evaluation of the economic benefits of increased agricultural productivity. A near-optimal design was recommended [ref. 8] and is soon to be implemented.

The group studied the disposal of radioactive wastes in streams by simulating hydrologic events and the introduction of radioactive pollutants. The technologic function is such that during periods of low flow the pollutant is deposited in the stream bank while during periods of high flow the radioactive material is removed by scouring action and is carried downstream toward the zone of water use. All the while, both in transit and in bank storage, the material is subject to exponential decay governed by the half-life of the pollutant. Any attempt to deduce the concentration of radioactive flux at downstream use points by analytical techniques would be intractable, but stable estimates of the parameters of the concentration distribution can be obtained by simulation with long synthetic traces [ref. 9].

The Harvard group's current research efforts are focused in the Delaware River basin and one of its sub-basins, the Lehigh River. Using economic data developed by the U.S. Army Corps of Engineers in its Summary Report [ref. 10], our analysis of the Lehigh encompasses six reservoirs, nine turbines, water supply diversion works, and storage facilities for flood control and recreation. The capacity of core storage in our IBM 7094 is utilized, save for three registers, and preliminary results indicate that we can improve on the best of the Corps' designs by approximately 50 per cent. The study has been generalized to include the forty-two reservoirs and turbines of the entire Delaware basin, and results have recently been published [ref. 11].

PROSPECTS

Operational hydrology has permitted some striking advances in the rational design of water resource systems. It cannot improve faulty or biased records; there is no mathematical rubric that can serve in place of an abundant and reliable record. But it is a significant advance in the direction of statistically efficient use of the data, however good or bad they may be. Thus one might be justified in using several estimates of the population moments required in equation (1) or its more complicated descendants. For example, if $\bar{x}$ is the sample (observed) mean and s the sample standard deviation drawn from a record of length n, then the standard error of the sample mean is $\sigma/\sqrt{n}$ which is estimated, in turn, by $s/\sqrt{n-1}$. If u is a standard normal random sampling deviate such that $u \sim N(0, 1^2)$, then trial values of the population mean might be constructed by the linear combination $\bar{x} + u\,s/\sqrt{n-1}$; similar demonstrations could be made for the estimates of σ and ρ.

Experience with this modification is inadequate to draw any general conclusions, but it offers one suggestion for answering a common criticism of operational hydrology, namely: that population estimates that are very wide of their marks yield biased results. Of course, such criticism hardly deserves an answer, because there is no technique which can undo the harm introduced by erroneous or biased records.

A major decision to be made at the start of any analysis is the form of the generating model. The distribution, or distributions, and lag of the population must be estimated so that the appropriate transforms and parameters can be incorporated in the model. Multivariate and spectral techniques are being applied to real and generated records to ascertain which tests of actual observations adequately discriminate between several alternative models. In cases where two distributions appear equally plausible, simulation runs can be made using both candidates to generate inputs, thereby imputing a dollar value to the process of obtaining those extra data which might distinguish between distributions.

But even more exacting and exciting than awakening the statistical conscience of the civil engineering profession are the current and proposed developments in operational hydrology.

Operational hydrology is being applied to preliminary screening in a river basin. From among all the potential sites and development alternatives in a basin, a small number must be isolated for intensive study; this is so because intensive study is expensive, and to examine every alternative in microscopic detail would be prohibitively costly. Thus, while current use of synthesis and simulation is directed mainly toward final or detailed design, we envision schemes for scanning the inventory of possible designs, in a macroscopic fashion, and identifying likely candidates for further study.

All these examples and ruminations are based on the synthesis of annual, monthly, or seasonal data. But our experience shows that short-term records, say for an hour or a day, can be synthesized equally well. Such traces are useful in studies of flood routing, peak-power generation, pollution control, drought management, and other short-term phenomena; the generation of short-term records will surely become increasingly important.

Operational hydrology plays a role in the specification of a system operating policy. It appears likely that conjunctive use of operational models and forecasting techniques can be used to devise optimal hedging rules, whereby several small losses are accepted to ward off the possibility of one or a few major catastrophes.

Our goals are formidable, but not unrealistic. We envision the collection of flow and meteorological records, their transmittal to a computer, the passage of a few minutes, and the production, without manual intervention, of an optimal design.

CONCLUSIONS

Use of synthetic hydrologic traces does not provide a mechanism for overcoming biased or faulty data; it merely provides a convenient numerical device for dealing with the paucity of hydrologic records typically available to the planner. It is not a substitute for analytical solution, and indeed those who have matched wits with computing devices are inevitably those most anxious to introduce analytical solutions. But when system simulation appears necessary, it is statistically unjustifiable to rely solely on the observed sequence of hydrologic events; in these circumstances the concomitant use of synthetic traces allows the planner to sample the distribution and to approximate the moments of economic benefits. It is with these moments that meaningful objective functions are written, so that simulation with synthetic inflows allows a complete ordering to be made on system performance.

REFERENCES

[1] Heggen, Thomas. *Mister Roberts*. New York: Houghton Mifflin, 1946.
[2] Rippl, W. "The Capacity of Storage Reservoirs for Water Supply," *Proceedings Institute of Civil Engineering*, Vol. 71, 1883, p. 270.
[3] Feller, William. "The Asymptotic Distribution of the Range of a Series of Independent Random Variables," *Annals of Mathematical Statistics*, Vol. 22, 1951, p. 427.
[4] Fiering, M. B. "The Nature of the Storage-Yield Relationship," *Proceedings Symposium on Streamflow Regulation*, U.S. Public Health Service. Cincinnati, April 1963.
[5] Thomas, H. A., Jr., and Fiering, M. B. "The Storage-Yield Relationship," *Water Resources Conference, American Society of Civil Engineers*, Vicksburg, 1964.
[6] ———. "A Method of Accounting for Benefit and Cost Uncertainties in Water Resource Project Design." Unpublished memorandum to the Harvard Water Program.
[7] Meramec Basin Research Project. *The Meramec Basin—Water and Economic Development* (3 vols.). St. Louis: Washington University, February 1962.
[8] Fiering, M. B. "Revitalizing a Fertile Plain," *Journal of Water Resources Research*, Vol. 1, No. 1, 1965.
[9] Thomas, H. A., Jr., and Fiering, M. B. *Fate of Radioactive Wastes in Streams*. Report for the U.S. Atomic Energy Commission. Cambridge: Harvard University, Division of Engineering and Applied Physics, 1964.
[10] U.S. Army Corps of Engineers. *Report of the Chief of Engineers on the Delaware River Basin*. House Doc. No. 522, 87th Congress, Washington, D. C.
[11] Hufschmidt, M. M., and Fiering, M. B. *Simulation Techniques for Water Resource Systems*. Cambridge: Harvard University Press, 1966.

Some Observations on Rainfall and Runoff

Norman H. Crawford*

The processes that cause one storm to produce damaging flood flows while another with apparently similar characteristics does not, are easily misinterpreted. For the hydrologic cycle has a superficial simplicity that can trap the unwary public, and occasionally also the hydrologist. In studying the relationships between rainfall and runoff, basic to hydrologic behavior, two major questions have to be answered: First, "What is the volume of runoff?" and second, "What is the time distribution of this runoff?" Finding answers to each of these questions involves several complex and detailed processes which it is my purpose to explain in this paper without, I hope, erring on the side either of misleading oversimplification or confusing elaborations.

Some illustrations from synthesis models (Stanford Watershed Model IV) of the role of the various basic processes will be used but, except where necessary, the way in which the synthesis models are constructed will not be developed here, these details being readily available in other publications [ref. 1, 2, 3].

A schematic description of a watershed, presented in the first section of this paper, provides background for the concepts and terms which will follow. The second section discusses the volume of runoff, and the third gives some illustrations of timing and runoff distribution. In the conclusion some comments are made about education in the response of watersheds to rainfall, and about the application of synthesis methods of investigation to water resource studies in general.

* Assistant Professor of Civil Engineering, Stanford University.

A SCHEMATIC WATERSHED

Why does a given discharge occur in a river?

What are the factors that determine the variation of observed discharge in a stream with time?

Before attempting to identify these factors it may be useful to look at the components of a watershed. Consider first a strip of land from the drainage divide to a stream channel. Figure 1(a) shows a plane impervious surface subject to rainfall that varies with time. In this simple case the volume of rainfall will equal the volume of runoff, but their time distributions will differ due to transient storage during overland flow. The characteristics of the land surface are already influencing watershed response. In Figure 1(b) infiltration and evapotranspiration that vary with time have been added. Both processes are dependent on partially saturated flow in porous media and vary with the moisture content, porosity, and permeability of the soil profiles. In the case of transpiration, vegetal cover is an additional variable. Where the local rate of infiltration exceeds the rainfall rate, overland flow will not occur. In Figure 1(c) ground water and interflow are included, and the land surface is irregular and diverts some rainfall to depression storage before overland flow can reach the stream channel.

In this form the watershed element contains most of the components needed to simulate a natural watershed, with the additional caution that infiltration rates, depression storages, the length and slope of overland

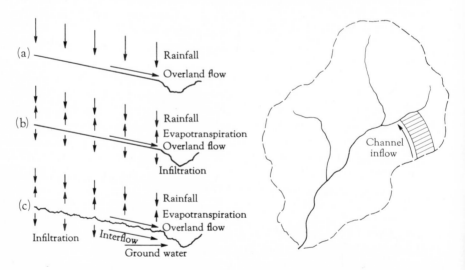

Figure 1. Components of a watershed.   *Figure 2.* Channel system of a watershed.

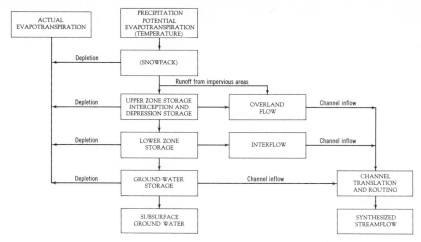

Figure 3. Watershed model flowchart.

flows, the volumes of discharge from ground water and interflow, and the volumes of storage in the soil profile will vary throughout the watershed. Also, in many watersheds snowfall occurs, creating temporary storage that dissipates through a heat exchange process with the atmosphere and the land surface [ref. 3].

To complete the schematic description of a watershed, Figure 2 shows the channel system. Inflows from the land surface that are dependent on time and location occur throughout the channel system. These inflows are the combined overland, interflow, and ground-water discharges, and after modification in the channel system they are responsible for the observed flow at the outlet of a watershed.

In a digital computer model the processes above appear in outline as shown in Figure 3. The chart is self-explanatory except for the fact that the soil moisture storages are divided into three parts: The upper zone and lower zone storages model the effects of the vertical distribution of moisture in the soil profile, while the ground-water storage is responsible for the movement of water as ground-water discharge into the stream channels.

INFILTRATION AND RUNOFF VOLUMES

Significant amounts of overland flow can result from a broad spectrum of circumstances. On one side, the limits of this spectrum are storms that cause overland flows into stream channels despite the capacity of watershed soil profiles to store more of the rainfall. Runoff can occur because of an infiltration rate limitation; the soil profiles are unable to absorb the rainfall before it reaches the stream channels. Typically this may result from storms of high rainfall intensity or in areas where surface soils are of low permeability.

At the other side of the spectrum are storms that are able to cause overland flows because infiltration rates in the watershed have been greatly reduced by high soil moisture levels that reduce capillary heads in watershed soil profiles. Capacity limitations under natural conditions are normally responsible for high percentages of rainfall becoming runoff. Rate limitations can also cause high percentages of runoff but appear to be more typical of moderate to low percentages of runoff. A sketch of this behavior is shown in Figure 4.

All watersheds experience storms in which rate limitations are dominant. These are smaller storms and storms that occur after several days of dry weather. However, watersheds differ greatly in the degree to which storage capacities may become limiting, and some watersheds may never advance very far toward this condition.

In Figure 5, the maximum clock-hour rainfalls observed over a period of years are plotted against the maximum combined overland and interflow runoffs calculated during the same period. A stream that characteristically tends toward a capacity limitation will maintain 70 to 80 per cent runoff for most of these maximum events relatively independent of rainfall intensities. In a stream that tends to remain in the rate limitation range, the percentage of runoff is much more closely associated with rainfall rates and will decrease as rainfall intensities decrease.

These interpretations of watershed behavior may be checked by the use of synthesis runs. Figure 6 compares the recorded and synthesized streamflow for 1955–56 on the Russian River near Hopland. This stream, one of those shown in Figure 5, appears to reach capacity limitation conditions and should do so in 1955–56, a wet year. Two modifications in the model structure that simulates this river were tried. First, as is indicated in Figure 7, watershed infiltration rates were doubled and the modified synthesis output for the year was plotted against the control synthesis output shown in Figure 6. The small storms and the early season low soil-moisture storms were modified much more than storms during high soil-moisture conditions. Note also the increase in ground water that results from the increase in infiltration rates. Second, storage

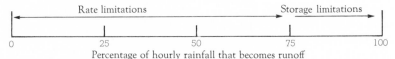

Figure 4. Rainfall compared with runoff.

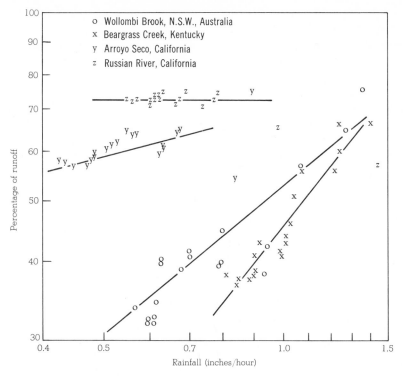

Figure 5. Rainfall rates and percentage of runoff plotted for four watersheds.

calculations were changed to reduce the tendency toward capacity limitation, and infiltration rates were returned to their original values. Figure 8 shows this modified output plotted against the control synthesis output. In this figure, storms that were modified most by the infiltration rate increase of Figure 7 have recovered and are close to their original response. Ground-water outflow has been reduced sharply as the soil profiles are able to retain more water which eventually leaves the watershed through evapotranspiration.

To this point the role of interception, depression storage, and the soil profile at the land surface has not been discussed. These are temporary storages that typically have high or infinite inflow rates but low storage capacities. They are grouped in Figure 3 in the upper zone storage. The role of these factors in watershed response is to retain or delay water for later infiltration that might otherwise reach a stream channel. These elements will completely dominate showers and small storms and are important in the early stages of larger storms. These smaller storms would generally tend toward the rate limitation side of the spectrum, and

347

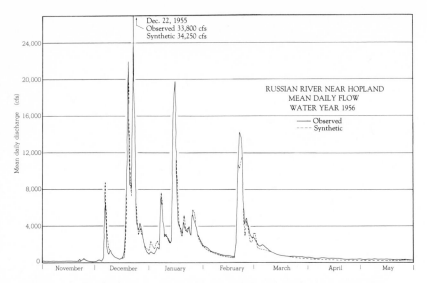

Figure 6. Synthesis runs: comparing recorded and synthesized streamflow.

retaining and delaying water in these temporary storages is just what is needed to allow infiltration rates to absorb more of the storm rainfall. The temporary storages still operate but tend to become less important under capacity limitation conditions, since their effectiveness is dependent

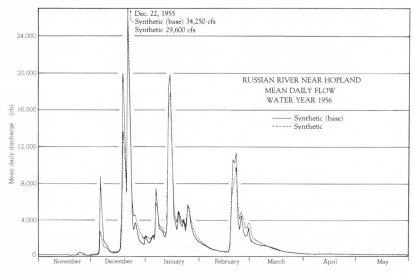

Figure 7. Synthesis runs: comparing modified synthesis output with control synthesis output.

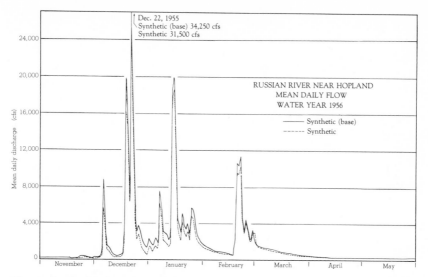

Figure 8. Synthesis runs: comparing a further modified synthesis output with control synthesis output.

on the existence of moderately high infiltration rates. This would also suggest that the ability of surface conditions, such as vegetation, to modify over-all hydrologic response would vary in different watersheds, depending on their tendency toward capacity limitation. These responses can be investigated in synthesis runs by modifying the appropriate model components.

TIMING AND RUNOFF DISTRIBUTION

Watershed behavior is closely connected with timing considerations. Everyone knows that one twenty-minute thunderstorm will not cause a flood on a large river. It is equally clear that low intensity rainfall over several days is unlikely to cause flooding in a small stream. Synthesis models can be used to provide interesting illustrations of timing relationships that support these intuitive conclusions.

How will the appearance of a storm change at various points in a watershed? In Figure 9, a storm in Beargrass Creek, Kentucky (18.5 sq. mi.), is shown with the rainfall rates, the average channel inflow hydrograph, and the synthesized and recorded hydrographs at the stream gauge all plotted in inches per hour for the drainage area. Note the time delay and attenuation that takes place in the channel system. The channel system, except in very small watersheds, will modify the time distribution of the channel inflows greatly, delaying and reducing maximum discharges. Except in arid areas, the volume of runoff is usually not greatly changed.

In a very small watershed where the outflow hydrograph is very nearly equivalent to the channel inflow hydrograph, the reaction of the watershed to rainfall in the preceding ten to thirty minutes determines the outflow at any time. In a larger watershed the cumulative reactions to rainfall in the preceding two or three days, or even two or three weeks, may be determining outflow. This variation in response is quite evident in Figure 9.

The distribution of channel inflow begins to affect hydrograph shape and peak discharge as the areas of the watershed increases. Again, synthesis models can provide illustrations. Two hypothetical storms were constructed that each caused 7.25 inches of runoff during a 48-hour period from the watershed of the Russian River above Guerneville, California (1,340 sq. mi.). One of the storms was devised to give a maxi-

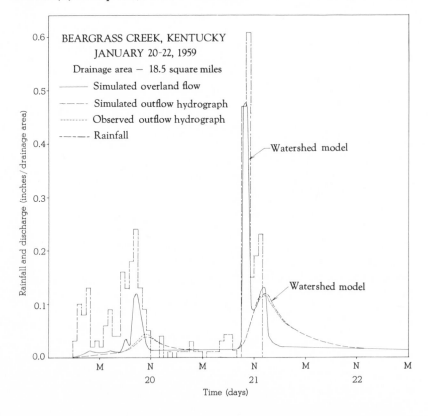

Figure 9. Hydrographs of rainfall, channel inflow, and watershed outflow.

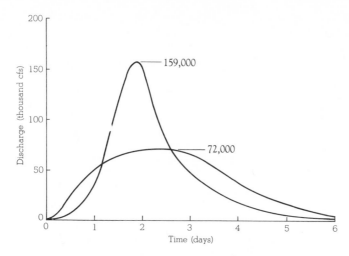

Figure 10. Hydrographs of two hypothetical storms.

mum peak flow; the other to give a minimum peak flow. Rainfall was prepared and entered for nine recording stations in the watershed.

The hydrographs that resulted are shown in Figure 10. The variation in this figure is primarily due to time and areal distribution of channel inflow during the storms, since both storms contained the same volume of rainfall and runoff and were of approximately the same duration. It is, of course, very unlikely that two natural storms would even approach the variation that resulted in the hydrographs shown in Figure 10, but the figure does indicate that the influence of runoff distribution can be large.

CONCLUSIONS

A brief review of hydrologic behavior has been given together with examples of hydrologic response from digital synthesis models. These examples serve a dual purpose: they provide illustrations for the text, and they also provide examples of the potential application of digital models in the investigation of the characteristics of other hydrologic regimes.

This second application is of particular interest for education in the response of watersheds to rainfall. It is difficult for students to gain a quantitative appreciation, or in some cases even a qualitative appreciation, of the factors responsible for the broad range of hydrologic regimes. To derive the volume of continuous watershed rainfall and runoff is time-consuming. When answers are found, the student is often unable to relate the academic explanation of rainfall time distributions, interception, interflow, infiltration, channel flow, and all of the other factors to his rainfall hyetograph and outflow hydrograph. It would be helpful if a student could interrogate a computer model, watch an oscilloscope screen, and observe the change in a hydrograph or series of hydrographs if, for example, watershed potential evapotranspiration rates were changed. Such an approach, of course, requires stored programs and quantities of stored data, a collection of closely simulated watersheds, and carefully developed simulation models that will not mislead the student. Stanford has experimented with this type of instruction and hopes to expand its use in the future.

What are the current and future applications of basic hydrologic studies, such as the study of rainfall and runoff, in the general field of water resources? Research in water resource problems is growing rapidly, spurred by awareness that the current practice of building another reservoir or aqueduct to meet increasing demands for water supplies will eventually reach a physical limit. Political, economic, and legal problems have all quite correctly become major concerns in water resources research.

In the light of all of this activity it may be well to reflect that the natural processes that govern water supplies are not as well understood as one might wish. For example, Plass [ref. 4] relates the increase in atmospheric carbon dioxide caused by man's activities in the last hundred years to a rise in world atmospheric temperatures, and anticipates a further temperature increase and a decrease in precipitation. How would higher temperatures and increased potential evapotranspiration, combined with decreased precipitation, affect rivers and streams? Synthesis models indicate that streamflow can be quite sensitive to each of these factors [ref. 5], and in some hydrologic regimes streamflow could be highly sensitive if both factors were changed adversely.

The common problems of design and operation of reservoir and aqueduct systems are becoming more complex as systems expand and interconnect. It will be increasingly necessary to use all of the available hydrometrological data as effectively as possible in order to plan and operate these systems. Thus, the detailed synthesis of hydrologic behavior and other approaches to basic technical problems of hydrology seem destined to remain essential to the evaluation of water resources.

REFERENCES

[1] Crawford, N. H., and Linsley, R. K. *The Synthesis of Continuous Streamflow Hydrographs on a Digital Computer.* Technical Report No. 12. Stanford: Stanford University, Department of Civil Engineering, 1962.

[2] ———. *A Conceptual Model of the Hydrologic Cycle.* International Association of Scientific Hydrology, No. 63, 1963.

[3] Anderson, E. A., and Crawford, N. H. *The Synthesis of Continuous Snowmelt Runoff Hydrographs on a Digital Computer.* Technical Report No. 36. Stanford: Stanford University, Department of Civil Engineering, 1964.

[4] Plass, G. N. "Carbon Dioxide and Climate," *Scientific American,* Vol. 201, No. 1 (1959).

[5] Crawford, N. H. *Some Illustrations of the Hydrologic Consequences of Weather Modification from Synthesis Models.* Paper given at the Symposium on Economic and Social Aspects of Weather Modification. Boulder, July 1965.

Integrating Snow Zone Management with Basin Management

*Henry W. Anderson**

T he snow zone is a principal source of the West's water supply, important both for the amounts supplied and for a favorable time of delivery of the water. Perhaps half of the water of the major river systems of the West comes from melting snowpacks. These snowpacks act as huge reservoirs, "spilling" their water over long periods in the spring and in the early summer. Research has indicated that we can manage the snowpack reservoirs, both to yield more water and to improve the time of delivery to meet our water needs.

Management includes control of the snow itself and also of the water from melted snow. Snowpacks are managed by controlling snow accumulation, snowmelt, and evaporation; the snowmelt water is further managed by controlling vegetation-induced losses—interception and transpiration—by controlling evaporation from soil and water surfaces, by modifying the retention characteristics of the soil "reservoir," and by modifying the surface and subsurface paths that the water takes in its runoff.

For some of these management possibilities, little or no knowledge or technique has been developed; for others, a considerable amount exists, but for the most part it has not been integrated into comprehensive programs of basin management. This paper summarizes some of the present techniques and what they can accomplish, and points out how water

* In charge of Water Source Hydrology Studies, Pacific Southwest Forest and Range Experiment Station, Forest Service, U.S. Department of Agriculture, Berkeley, California.

management can take its place in basin management. In the following pages, the role of cutting of forests, brushland conversion, and artificial snow barriers in management for water supply and control is illustrated with results from Colorado and California. Tentative criteria are suggested for design of forest cuttings for particular objectives of water yield improvement, flood prevention, and sediment control. Finally, further studies are suggested, both of physical applications to forest sites and of appraisal methods which will allow the integration of physical knowledge in the design of systems of basin management.

WATER PRODUCTS

Before considering management of the water from the snow zone, let us first consider some of the water products that must be delivered and how they are delivered. These products involve the quantity and quality of water, which affect its usefulness, and the timing of the delivery of the water, which affects its value: enhanced value, if the water is delivered at a time when the demand to refill reservoirs or supply water is at a maximum; reduced value, if the water comes off as flood waters which are wasted or carry damaging amounts of sediment or debris. Four aspects of water supply are discussed briefly: the total annual yield, including its variability from year to year; the seasonal distribution of streamflow; floods; and sediment damage.

Annual Water Yield

Water yield is usually greater from the high-elevation snowpack zones than from the lower-elevation forest, brush, and grassland zones. Although these separations are bound to be somewhat crude, information from runoff maps [ref. 1] can be combined with vegetation-type maps to give estimates of the water contributed by various vegetation zones [ref. 2]. In California, for example, the snowpack zone (the zone where more than one-half of the water comes from a melting snowpack in the average year) yields about 51 per cent of the total streamflow in the state. In contrast, the lower forest zone yields 32 per cent and the foothill woodland zone about 12 per cent of the state's water. Similar figures would undoubtedly pertain to much of the West where large contrasts in elevation and vegetation zones occur.

Variability of annual streamflow presents a major problem in water management. If the average runoff from our watersheds were received each year, there would be relatively few management problems. But this is not so. Some years are dry, and the cry is for water; other years are wet, and water is lost in flood runoff. In those areas with wide variation in annual streamflow, the snow zone area becomes especially important. The snow zone not only yields the greatest amount of water on the average, but in the most critical dry years it shows much less variability than the other zones [ref. 3].

If we define "dry years" as those years in which streamflow is less than one-half of the average annual flow, how often do dry years occur in the snow zone in contrast with the lower-elevation zones? An area with high year-to-year variation in precipitation is the southern Sierra Nevada which supplies water to the southern San Joaquin Valley of California. In the snow zone there, less than one year in ten is a dry year. Conifer forest below the snow zone has two or three dry years in ten. In the foothill woodland zone lower in the Sierra Nevada, not only is there less water, but it is more variable: three to five years in ten are dry years. The lesser variability of the snowpack zone has been attributed to fundamental differences in the precipitation and distribution of evaporation opportunities in these zones [ref. 3].

In forest and brush zones below the snow zone, precipitation is mostly in the form of rain or light snowfall that melts after a few hours or days. Part of the rain of every storm is caught by the forest trees or brush, evaporates rapidly during breaks in the storms and between storms, and is thus lost. In this zone, whenever water is stored in the soil transpiration by the vegetation is likely to be active. Between storms, vegetation, litter, and the soil surface dry by evaporation. Small storms contribute little except to replenish and keep active these evaporative losses. Only in large storms does significant water penetrate the soil mantle and add to the streamflow. Large storms in these lower zones are almost always rainstorms which in some places often produce floods and erosion problems rather than usable water.

In contrast, the water stored in the snowpack is relatively immune from evaporative losses, flash flood runoff, and rapid melt. Water loss by evaporation from snowpack is small. In California it is about 4.5 inches per year on exposed ridges, 2 inches in large open areas, and less than 1 inch in forest stands [ref. 4]. Snow held until late spring gains water by condensation rather than losing it by evaporation. The surface of the snow during winter reflects most of the heat from the sun: 90 per cent is reflected from new snow, and 60 per cent from older snow surfaces [ref. 5]. Small snow storms, thus, become hydrologically important, in contrast to small storms in the lower-elevation zones; even the small snow storms restore the high reflectivity of the snow surfaces, thereby minimizing snowmelt. Further, snow zone soils at some places and in some years may not lose all their water during the summer; some unused water remains in the soil to contribute to the next year's streamflow [ref. 6]. The net result is that although different years bring wide differences in the number, size, and distribution of storms, the hydrology of the snow zone tends to minimize year-to-year differences in streamflow. By management, such variability can be further minimized to produce increased water values from snow zone management.

Seasonal Distribution of Streamflow

Seasonal variability in streamflow may influence the objectives of management for water. Consider the variability of monthly streamflow in one snow zone watershed, the Kings River of the southern Sierra Nevada in California. The seasonal distribution of runoff differs widely between dry and wet years (Table 1). In the average year, the critical period from June to September yields 24 per cent of the water; but in the driest of ten years, not only is the flow low for the year, but the same critical period yields only 7 per cent of the water. Analysis of other snow zone watersheds in this area shows similar results—flows come earlier in the dry years [ref. 7]. Management that would prolong water yield in these dry years would be most beneficial.

Floods

Flood frequencies from snow zone watersheds may change as management makes changes in the basic hydrologic processes: precipitation

TABLE 1.

Streamflow Distribution, in Inches, in a Watershed Whose Yield Is Chiefly from Snowmelt, North Fork of Kings River, California, at Cliff Camp
(elevation 6,144 to 12,955 feet)

| Month | Streamflow | | |
	Medium	10-year minimum[1]	10-year maximum[1]
Oct.	0.05	0.04	0.33
Nov.	0.12	0.05	1.00
Dec.	0.30	0.06	0.98
Jan.	0.39	0.08	0.82
Feb.	0.53	0.14	1.06
Mar.	1.33	0.36	1.97
Apr.	4.72	2.24	7.29
May	10.52	3.20	17.20
June	6.00 ⎫	0.73 ⎫	17.37 ⎫
July	0.81 ⎬ 24%	0.12 ⎬ 7%	4.55 ⎬ 42%
Aug.	0.11 ⎪	0.04 ⎪	0.46 ⎪
Sept.	0.04 ⎭	0.02 ⎭	0.14 ⎭
Year	29.00	12.00	53.00

[1] 10-year minimums and maximums are flows expected to be not exceeded and exceeded, respectively, in 10 per cent of all years.

TABLE 2.

Rain and Snowmelt Frequency, Relative Precipitation, and Flood Potential,
by Elevation Zones, Willamette River Basin above Salem, Oregon

Elevation (feet)	Relative rain area frequency	Relative snowmelt frequency	Relative precipitation	Relative flood potential
0–1,000	1.00	1.00	1.0	1.0
1–2,000	.96	.99	1.5	1.5
2–3,000	.87	.92	2.1	1.9
3–4,000	.74	.82	2.4	1.9
4–5,000	.60	.74	2.4	1.7
5–6,000	.39	.48	2.4	1.0
6–7,000	.17	.38	3.1	0.6

supply; storage and detention on the watershed surface, in the soil, and in channels; the loss processes of interception and evapotranspiration; and the flow process, including surface and subsurface waterflow [ref. 8]. These processes operate differently into two fundamentally different types of floods—the snowmelt floods and the rain or rain-on-snow floods.

Snowmelt floods periodically produce inundation in small mountain valleys and along upstream channels, but particularly in the great valleys below the mountains. The amount of snowpack and the rate of melt are the primary "cause" variables, together with the available soil-moisture storage space. Since land management can influence each of these, one may expect management to influence large snowmelt floods significantly. Some quantitative expressions of management effects will be outlined later.

Rain and rain-on-snow floods have historically produced many of the larger floods of the West. In contrast to snowmelt floods, these floods are complex events of a dozen or more hydrologic processes combined to determine flood size [ref. 8]. The effects of management on floods depend on the effects of management on each of these processes. The effect of the snowpack itself on the rain-on-snow floods depends mostly on the depth of the snowpack and its condition.

Deep snowpacks may modify such floods in two primary ways: by storage of the rainwater and by increasing the surface detention of flood runoff, sometimes delaying the delivery of the water until rainwaters from lower elevations have safely passed. Shallow snowpacks, in contrast, may augment the precipitation by adding snowmelt water, increasing flood peaks correspondingly. Table 2 shows the frequency with which snowmelt water contributes to floods in different elevation zones. Snowmelt, combined with the frequency and amount of rainfall, make up the flood potential for western Oregon. We see that the combination of events makes for the greatest flood potential at elevations from 2,000 to

4,000 feet. That is where the greatest care in management for flood prevention will be needed.

One of the primary functions of the snowpack is in preventing or minimizing the freezing of the soil, which in this case acts as a reservoir, thereby keeping the soil open for floodwater retention or detention. It becomes obvious that the effects of management practices on floods involve effects on snow and snowmelt water; so floods are not simply related to a single-cause variable such as soil-moisture deficit or total storm size, as some hydrologists have implied.

Sedimentation

Sedimentation from snow zone watersheds is usually less than from similar watersheds at lower elevations. Precipitation falls mostly as snow or rain-on-snow, and rain penetrating a deep snowpack causes little soil erosion. Transport of stream sedimentation is generally low because peak flows, which carry most of the sediment, are dampened by the snowpack. However, other conditions of high-elevation sites may offset the subduing effects of snow on erosion in the snow zone. Slopes are more frequently steep, and more areas are naturally bare. In some places soil erodibility is high because of low cohesiveness of many soils at a high elevation [ref. 9]. Once sediment from mountain slopes reaches the channel, it can cause damage in several ways: It can restrict channel capacities, reduce water quality, and fill or clog downstream improvements, like reservoirs and percolating basins. Principal sources of sediment that management can influence include roads, landslips, logging-skid trails, and land-clearing and vegetative-type conversions.

MANAGEMENT EFFECTS ON SNOW AND SNOW WATER YIELD

Research throughout the West has shown that snow accumulation and melt and loss of snow water can be modified. This modification comes about when forest trees are cut, when brushy vegetation is removed, and when we install mechanical barriers, such as snow fences or trenches.

Logging Effects

Logging effects on snow and on snow water depend not only on how the cutting is done, but on the characteristics of the timber stand before and after the logging, the type of logging-associated treatments such as skid trails, landings, and roads, and how these change with time after logging.

Early studies of forest effects on snow and snowmelt gave clues to the important differences in snow brought about by forest conditions, and furnished some information about specific management designs. Church [ref. 10], after observing snow in forests and openings, advocated the use of forest screens instead of solid forest to create snow drifting and to delay snowmelt. From observations and measurements of snow on many sites, he concluded:

> ... the ideal forest is one honey-combed with glades whose extent is so related to the height of the trees that the sun cannot reach the surface of the snow. Such a forest will permit far more snow to reach the ground than will a forest of great and uniform density, and yet will amply protect the snow from the effects of sun and wind. [Ref. 11, p. 538.]

Connaughton [ref. 12] measured snow in ponderosa pine stands, sagebrush, and denuded areas in central Idaho. He concluded that management of ponderosa pine on a shorter rotation, avoiding the high, spreading crown canopies, would accumulate almost as much snow as accumulated in completely denuded areas, and yet would retard melt for a number of days. He found that sagebrush was quite effective in accumulating snow but was not as effective as trees in retarding snowmelt.

Wilm [ref. 13] reported studies conducted in north central Colorado from 1938 to 1943. Comparison of commercial selection cutting of mature lodgepole pine stands, with different amounts of residual commercial trees left, showed that removal of all commercial-sized trees increased the "water available for streamflow" by 31 per cent.

Kittredge [ref. 14] made studies in the central Sierra Nevada mixed-conifer belt at elevations between 5,200 and 6,200 feet, where snow accumulation ranged from 3 to 30 inches. He sought to find out what kinds of forests and what densities and sizes of openings in forests were effective in promoting snow accumulation and melt. He concluded that openings with a width of about one to two times the tree height had the most snow. The species and densities of trees were so tied in with topographical variation as to make impossible direct comparison of their effect on snow accumulation. Kittredge further concluded that ". . . clear-cutting in small groups should yield both the most water and prolong the summer flow. Strip-cutting might also give results if the clearcut strips are narrow, if they follow, as far as possible, the contours, and are oriented east and west rather than north and south" [ref. 14, p. 92].

More recent studies in Colorado and California have elaborated on the suggestions of Church and Kittredge, have tested some of the interrelationships between forest management and terrain, and have tested the effects of different methods of management not only on snow, but also on soil moisture and streamflow. These studies add to our knowledge of how forests influence snow accumulation and melt, and how forests may be cut so as to maximize water yields, delay snowmelt runoff, or minimize local floods and sedimentation.

Cutting Effects on Streamflow

Experiments at Fraser, Colorado, started in 1943, have contributed substantially to our knowledge of the effects of logging on water yield. The predicted effect on streamflow of forest cutting (Wilm and Dunford [ref. 15]) was tested on a whole watershed, Fool Creek, and the data were analyzed by Goodell [ref. 16]. Cutting of 39 per cent of a lodgepole-spruce-fir forest in strips 1, 2, 3, and 6 chains wide (1 chain = 66 feet) was begun in 1954 and completed in 1956 (Figure 1). Associated with the logging was an average of 4.0 inches of streamflow increase from the watershed for 1956 and 1957. After logging, the peak discharges from the logged watershed were 50 per cent and 45 per cent greater in two years, 1956 and 1958, and 23 per cent less in one year, 1957. No significant increases in sedimentation were reported. Year-by-year increases for the years 1957 through 1961, as reported by Martinelli [ref. 17], are shown in Table 3.

TABLE 3.
Streamflow Yield, in Area Inches

Year	Predicted	Actual	Increase
1957	19.6	23.0	3.4
1958	11.4	13.5	2.1
1959	10.5	13.6	3.1
1960	11.1	14.9	3.8
1961	8.8	10.9	2.1

Notice that if all of the increase in the flow is said to be associated with the 39 per cent of the watershed which was cut, the increase ranged from 5 to 10 inches for the cut area in the different years.

Similar results were found from a commercial selective logging in central California. One square mile of the 4-square-mile Castle Creek watershed near Donner Summit was logged in 1957, with 2.8 million board-feet being removed—30 per cent of the volume of the logged area, and 12 per cent of the total volume of the 4-square-mile watershed. Most of the trees, predominently red fir and lodgepole pine larger than 20 inches in diameter, were cut, leaving a good stand of pole-sized trees. Water yield as streamflow increased by the equivalent of 7 inches (in the logged area) for at least two years after logging [ref. 3, 18]. These increases were brought about in the two subnormal runoff years of 1959

Figure 1. Fool Creek experimental timber harvest for snow and water yield, 1956.

and 1960. About one-half of the increase came in June each year. How much longer the effect might have persisted is not known, because a freeway was built across the watershed.

Logging Effects on Snow Accumulation and Melt and Soil Moisture Losses

Several studies have compared the effects of different types of logging, such as selective cutting, strip cutting, block cutting, and sequential cutting, on snow accumulation and melt and on soil moisture losses. These studies furnish clues to relative effectiveness of management techniques in improving water yield from snow.

Selective cutting of forests in the Rocky Mountains of Colorado and in the Sierra Nevada of California has increased snow accumulation. Goodell [ref. 19] compared two types of selective cutting, both of which reduced the original stand by 50 per cent: single tree selection, which reserved from cutting the better trees spaced 8.5 feet apart, 649 trees per acre being left; crop tree selection, which produced openings 8 feet in radius around 100 selected crop trees per acre, 2,072 trees per acre being left. Increases in snow of 2.3 and 1.7 inches (24 per cent and 17 per cent) were associated with the single tree and the crop tree selection, respectively. This study demonstrated that thinning of the forest permitted more winter precipitation to reach the forest floor.

For red fir forest in the central Sierra Nevada in California, selective cutting of forest may increase the maximum snow accumulation by 5 inches of water if the average crown cover is reduced from 90 per cent to 50 per cent; if the cover is further reduced to 35 per cent, the snowpack would be another 4 inches greater [ref. 20]. In another study, 7 inches more water were measured in a commercial selective cut than in the uncut forest in 1958, and 6 inches more in 1959 [ref. 6, 21]. For late spring yield of water, these California studies showed 35 per cent density had no advantage over the 50 per cent density; stands with both these lower densities had about 4 inches more water on June 1, 1958, than stands of 90 per cent density [ref. 20]. Savings in soil moisture losses amounted to only 2 inches the first year after logging and had been reduced to about 0.8 inch the fifth year. However, selective cutting was differentially effective in drought years versus wet years. A reduction in forest density by selective cutting from 90 per cent to 35 per cent increased snow storage in the drought year of 1959 by 34 per cent, but the increase in the wet year of 1958 was only 17 per cent.

In contrast to the small amount of sediment produced in Fool Creek, sedimentation in Castle Creek was greatly increased after logging. Long-term average sediment discharge from the 4-square-mile watershed before logging was 900 tons per year. The first year after logging, sediment discharge soared to 4,600 tons. The second year after logging, it dropped to 1,800 tons per year. If the increases are considered to have come from only the logged area, sediment production was increased by seventeen times the first year, and by five times the second year after logging [ref. 3]. Erosion from roads and landings, which were constructed as part of the logging operation, provided most of the sediment. Minor rivulets diverted down logging roads caused erosion of all fine material. Landings made by building deep fills across ephemeral stream channels now have deep V-notched gullies across them [ref. 18]. These landings have been an obvious source of increased sedimentation. Rice and Wallis concluded that ". . . even though the total disturbance of the Castle Creek watershed was not great, the location of the roads and landings created a large sediment source. More attention to water values could have eliminated much of this source." [Ref. 18, p. 40.]

Strip cutting has some advantages over block cutting. Maximum snowpack in cut strips occurs when strip widths are approximately equal to the height of the surrounding trees [ref. 22, 20, 10, 14]. Melt of the pack is more rapid in wide strips than in narrow; as the spring season progresses, the maximum unmelted snow is found in narrower and narrower strips. In the California study, for example, on the average the maximum snow water equivalent on June 9 was in strips only one-half as wide as the trees were tall [ref. 22].

Figure 2 shows differences in snow accumulation and timing of snow

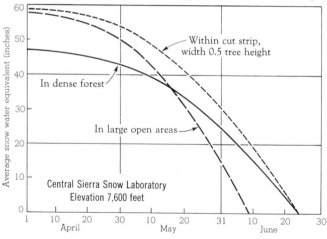

Figure 2. Snowpack water equivalent at various dates in an average year for two forest conditions and in large open areas.

water delivery in a dense forest, in a large open area which simulates a clearcut block, and a narrow clearcut strip. Both the open area and the strip had about 12 inches more water in the snowpack at time of maximum accumulation, April 1. However, the advantage of cutting in strips shows up in the amount of water delivered later in the spring. On June 9, for example, when all snow was gone from the large open block, 16 inches of water remained in the dense forest and 20 inches in the cut strip. The last snow disappeared from the dense forest and the cut strip at about the same time—sixteen days later.

Studies have shown that the full effectiveness of strip cutting cannot be evaluated by simple comparison of the amount of snow in the strip and in the adjacent forest [ref. 3]. From analyses of fifty-eight to sixty-six snow courses in the central Sierra of California, the conclusion was drawn that only about one-half of the difference in snow between a cut opening and the adjacent forest was found in the opening itself, the rest being found in the adjacent forest. An experimental cutting in the Tahoe National Forest, near Yuba Pass, California, gave similar results.

The Yuba Pass cutting consisted of five east-west strips, 0.6 mile long, 135 feet wide, 400 feet apart. The cutting permitted comparison of the total snow accumulation and rate of snow melt under five different treatments of the strips. Cutting was in an old-growth red fir stand on a 15 per cent north slope at an elevation of 6,700 feet. First results were for measurements of the snowpack at some 400 points on April 24, 1963 —about the time of the maximum pack—and again on May 21, when about 60 per cent of the pack had melted [ref. 3]. The snow in the center of uncut forest averaged 19 inches on April 24, and 7.7 inches on May 21. Increases in the snow associated with the cut strip for the five treatments ranged from 4.4 inches to 18.9 inches of water (Table 4). These increases amounted to 1.1 to 4.7 inches of water for the whole forest. The greatest increase was for a simulated wall-and-step forest, shown in Figure 3 [ref. 22]. Even though the simulation was incomplete, it increased total snow accumulation by 25 per cent for the forest as a whole. Such an increase is important enough to encourage management for water yield of these high elevation forests. Table 4 shows that 70 per cent of the increase (3.3 inches) persisted as delayed melt until May 21. The concomitant reports by forest officers of "little or no blowdown in the severe October storm" and "an economical logging show" gives at least preliminary conclusions that such treatments may be feasible.

Comparisons of selective, strip, and block cutting of mature spruce-fir forest in Colorado showed only small differences in these three treatments when equal numbers of trees were removed; however, all treatments increased water available for streamflow by 20 to 24 per cent [ref.

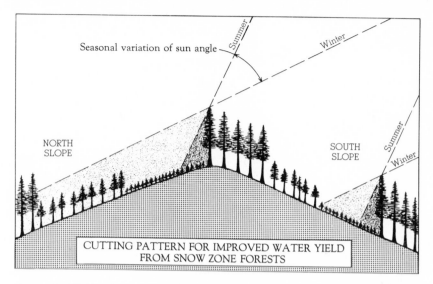

Figure 3. Wall-and-step forest for maximum snow accumulation and delaying melt.

23]. We conclude that differential treatment effects may be associated with different amounts of snow and different vegetation sites, and that further research will provide better answers of how forest stands may be cut for improved yield of snowmelt water.

TABLE 4.

Excesses of Snow Water Equivalent, in Inches, Associated with Cutting Compared with Uncut Forests, Yuba Pass, California

Date and area considered	Excess of snow associated with treatment				
	Slash piled	Slash lopped	Small trees left	Slash dozed downhill	Wall-and-step[1]
April 24, 1963:					
Cut strip only	4.4	6.4	8.0	14.4	18.9
Whole forest	1.1	1.6	2.0	3.6	4.7
May 21, 1963:					
Cut strip only	7.2	7.2	−5.2	−1.2	13.2
Whole forest	1.8	1.8	−1.3	−0.3	3.3

[1] In wall-and-step cutting, one-fourth of stand was clearcut with slash bulldozed down to the lower edge; in an equal width to the north, the taller trees were removed. In the other cuttings, only the strip was cut.

Duration of Logging Effects

How many years does the excess of snow in cut strips persist? Snow accumulation was measured in a strip made by a power-line clearing ten years ago and also in an area of that clearing widened five years ago. The excess of snow in the five-year-old cut area was the same as that expected the first year after the cut—13 inches; the excess in the ten-year-old cut area—where the red fir reproduction was 7 feet tall—was 10 inches.

In the Fraser study in Colorado, remeasurement of the cuttings thirteen years after the logging showed no apparent decline in the excess of snow in the cuttings [ref. 23].

Duration of summer soil moisture savings resulting from cutting of strips is important to any evaluation. Savings were greatest the first years after the cutting and in the deepest soils. For 4-foot soil, the saving was 4.9 inches the first two years, but decreased to 3.4 inches the fourth year after the logging [ref. 3].

In another study, Ziemer [ref. 24] traced the long-term effects of logging by measuring soil moisture losses in forests logged at times ranging through the previous twelve years. He found that the logging effect averaged 6.9-inch increase the first year after logging, and this effect diminished to zero by the sixteenth year. Total savings in the cut strip for the sixteen-year period were estimated as 34 inches.

Other data are consistent with the above indicated duration of soil moisture savings after strip cutting. For example, the power line cleared ten years ago, then widened five years ago, showed savings of soil moisture of 1 inch and 3 inches, respectively. It must be pointed out that savings other than summer soil moisture diminish much more slowly with time, interception taking perhaps thirty-five years to "recover" and evapotranspiration during the spring, fall, and winter somewhat less. These slower diminutions are suggested by the slow decrease in snowpack differences—only 23 per cent in ten years.

Mechanical Treatments

Possibilities of increasing late season snowmelt runoff through the use of fences near windswept ridges have been demonstrated in the Rocky Mountain area. Lull and Orr [ref. 25] found that fences as well as natural tree screens were effective in piling snow in melt-delaying drifts. Martinelli [ref. 17] reported that it took 100 to 125 feet of fence, 8 feet high, to give 1 acre-foot of extra water delivered after July 1. These studies have indicated the physical practicality of mechanical treatments in snow zone management of windswept sites.

Brushfield Management

Studies have also indicated that high-elevation brushfields may be converted to forests with benefits to water supply. During the conversion period, interception and transpiration losses will be reduced. After the forests are established, snowmelt may be delayed with resultant benefits from water yielded later in spring and summer [ref. 3]. In the central Sierra, melt in brushfields was 3 inches greater than in comparable large areas bare of brush, and nearly 8 inches greater than in nearby forests of 50 per cent density. Conversion of such high-elevation brushfields to forest may be expected to give 7 inches more snowmelt water at that time of year when all of the snow would have been gone from the brushfield.

Savings in water by reduction of losses from the soil ranged from 4 inches the first two years after a brushfield was cleared by bulldozing to only 0.3 of an inch the fourth year, after sprouting brush had returned [ref. 3]. Thus, temporary benefits in total water yield and long-term benefits in delayed yield, as well as timber values, may be expected from conversion of brushland to forest. Such combined water and timber benefits may justify the conversion of brushfields when this is not justified by either single benefit.

. . .

To sum up: Research results have suggested that high-elevation snow-pack forests and brushfields can be managed for water production—that is, for such objectives as increasing water yield, delaying yield, and maintaining water quality. Further study is needed not only in techniques of snow management, but in the broad fields of resource management, to allow integration of snow zone management with other uses of the mountain lands.

PRESENT POSSIBILITIES IN SNOW BASIN MANAGEMENT

Management for increasing water yield may be undertaken where downstream reservoir storage and water needs are not fully met. Production curves such as in Figure 2 may be drawn, and snowmelt water yield routed into reservoir storage. Changes in snowmelt water production for different elevations and slopes may be calculated [ref. 3]. Just as reservoir-stored water is routed to power production and downstream users [ref. 26], in the same way snow storage and snowmelt water may be simulated. Then decisions can be made on management for water yield, for minimizing floods, and for controlling sedimentation.

We would expect these techniques to be effective for particular outputs:

• Maximum increase in yield will result from cutting of trees or removal of brush from areas of deep soils, from areas with direct drainage to channels (slopes adjacent to channels or strips perpendicular to contours), from areas of least runoff per unit precipitation (densest forests, sites with most heat, and/or frequent drying).

• Maximum delay in yield will result from piling of snow, as in cut strips or by snow fences, by maximizing the length of water flow paths (as by clearcut strips from ridge to channel), and by removing riparian vegetation along and adjacent to streams.

• Maximum flood prevention will result from (a) maintaining maximum use of water by vegetation (in order: no cutting, selective cutting, strip cutting on contour, other types of cutting, and maintaining deep-rooted vegetation on deep soils and adjacent to channels); (b) maximizing lengths of water flow paths (maintenance of surface infiltration and deep percolation, prevention of soil freezing, and draining roads away from channels); (c) maximizing diversity of snowmelt (selective cutting on south slopes with no cutting or strip cutting on north slopes, also drifting of snow with natural or artificial barriers).

• Sediment damages may be minimized by (a) preventing erosion (patch or contour strip cutting on steep slopes, leaving strips of trees adjacent to channels of headwater streams, keeping road fills away from streams, revegetating road cuts and fills, spilling road-drainage water away from channels); (b) maintaining channel bottoms and bank stability with vegetation, with rip-rap, or with check dams at critically unstable spots; (c) using care in logging (location of landings out of drainages, diversion of skid trails after use, removal of temporary stream crossings, after logging covering soil with pulverized slash on critical sites); and (d) using care in type conversions (contour piling of brush in brush removal, seeding of grass on critical sites).

These are only a few possibilities. What is needed for control at a particular site will depend on the impact of meteorological events as well as the terrain and forest condition. Simulation of alternatives with computers before application of management seems a promising technique.

FUTURE POSSIBILITIES IN SNOW BASIN MANAGEMENT

Our ability to combine snow management with other basin management is dependent on several improvements: better inventories, more knowledge of the physics of snow and snow water, better management techniques, and better means of synthesizing these factors in planning to meet water demands.

Inventory techniques around the corner include machine interpretation of aerial photos, including such simple inventory characteristics as forest species, densities, and tree heights, but also including special characteristics such as radiation, extent of snow cover, and snow volumes (as in cornices). Instruments for aerial appraisal of the depth and densities of the soil and fractured rock mantle in mountain watersheds hold promise of becoming available. Current ground-operated seismic techniques are slow, but they have indicated our ignorance of the hydrologic characteristics of watershed surface soil and rock.

Snow physics research will give a basis for prediction of snow and snow water behavior. The alternative is "cut and try tests" on the some 6,000 different "forest sites" of the West. Further understanding of heat and water budgets, together with knowledge of surface winds and turbulence, may serve to explain the extreme variation in snow accumulation, snowmelt, and evapotranspiration loss. Such explanations will inevitably lead to better designed management techniques and reduction in the number of experimental tests that need to be made of alternative techniques.

Some testing of management techniques by controlled experiments may quite possibly be accomplished largely by finding and evaluating analogous situations in nature. Interactions of forests and terrain seem to be suited to such testing by selection. Other experimental testing obviously involves laboratory and field tests. Methods of control of the melting of snow, such as by albedo control, need further development. Control of evaporation and condensation of snow by chemicals, such as the long-chain alcohols [ref. 27], should be pursued. Further tests of control of snow drifting, of piling snow by avalanche initiation, and of creation of artificial glaciers might be considered. The soil-water "reservoir" is practically uninvestigated from the viewpoint of management of its characteristics, except by simple recourse to vegetation removal and type conversion. Sterilization of the deeper soil layer to prevent root penetration and transpiration losses seems possible.

The use of electronic computers in studying basin management is changing so rapidly that significance of "the literature" is largely historical rather than reflecting current possibilities. Today it is not *what* you know, but who do you know that knows how. Mention of such techniques as linear programing, simulation, and systems engineering can help introduce the manager to current tables of computer software techniques. Applications in water resource and forest management include those of Maass [ref. 26], and Gould and O'Regan [ref. 28]. These techniques permit testing of different management combinations for expected outcomes before they are applied.

The computer can give the manager another planning tool—a map to meet specific management needs [ref. 29]. Now the manager may ask for a map of a combination of hydrologic and other management criteria and get it in minutes. Programs that will produce maps of 2,000 different classifications have been written.[1] Soon we shall be able to apply functions to these classes, integrating snow storage and melt, soil water, and path lengths, to obtain hydrologic outputs—maximum water yield versus flood control, pure water versus maximum yield, winter flow versus delayed yield.

REFERENCES

[1] Langbein, Walter B., *et al. Annual Runoff in the United States.* U.S. Geological Survey, Circ. 52. Washington, 1949.

[2] Colman, Edward A. *Proposed Research in Snowpack Management in California.* Berkeley: U.S. Forest Service California Forest and Range Experiment Station, 1955.

[3] Anderson, Henry W. *Managing California's Snow Zone Lands for Water.* U.S. Forest Service Research Paper PSW-6. Berkeley: Pacific Southwest Forest and Range Experiment Station, 1963.

[4] West, Allan J. "Snow Evaporation and Condensation," *27th Annual Western Snow Conference Proceedings.* Fort Collins: Colorado State University, 1959.

[5] Miller, David H. *Snow Cover and Climate in the Sierra Nevada, California.* University of California Geography Publication 11. Berkeley, 1955.

[6] Anderson, Henry W., and Gleason, Clark H. "Logging Effects on Snow, Soil Moisture, and Water Losses," *27th Annual Western Snow Conference Proceedings.* Fort Collins: Colorado State University, 1959.

[7] Court, Arnold. *Larger Meltwater Flows Come Later.* U.S. Forest Service Pacific Southwest Forest and Range Experiment Station Research Note 189. Berkeley: 1961.

[8] Anderson, Henry W. *A Model for Evaluating Wildland Management for Flood Prevention.* U.S. Forest Service Pacific Southwest Forest and Range Experiment Station Technical Paper 69. Berkeley, 1962.

[9] Willen, Donald W. "Surface Soil Textural and Potential Erodibility Characteristics of Some Southern Sierra Nevada Forest Sites," *Soil Science Society of America Proceedings,* Vol. 29, No. 2 (1965).

[10] Church, J. E. "Snow Surveying: Its Principles and Possibilities," *Quarterly Journal of the Royal Meteorological Society,* Vol. 40, No. 169 (1914).

[11] Church, J. E. "Snow Surveying: Its Principles and Possibilities," *Geographic Review,* Vol. 23, No. 4 (1933).

[1] Personal communication from Elliot Amidon.

[12] Connaughton, Charles A. "The Accumulation and Rate of Melting of Snow as Influenced by Vegetation," *Journal of Forestry,* Vol. 33, No. 6 (1935).

[13] Wilm, Harold G. "The Influence of Forest Cover on Snowmelt," *American Geophysical Union Transactions,* Vol. 29 (1948).

[14] Kittredge, Joseph. "Influence of Forests on Snow in the Ponderosa-Sugar Pine-Fir Zone of the Central Sierra Nevada," *Hilgardia* (Berkeley), Vol. 22 (1953).

[15] Wilm, Harold G., and Dunford, E. G. *Effect of Timber Cutting on Water Available from a Lodgepole Pine Forest.* U.S. Department of Agriculture Bulletin 968. Washington, 1948.

[16] Goodell, Bertram C. "Watershed Studies at Fraser, Colorado," *Society of American Foresters Proceedings.* Washington, 1958.

[17] Martinelli, M., Jr. *Watershed Management in the Rocky Mountain Alpine and Subalpine Zones.* U.S. Forest Service Research Note RM-36. Fort Collins: Rocky Mountain Forest and Range Experiment Station, 1965.

[18] Rice, R. M., and Wallis, J. R. "How a Logging Operation Can Affect Streamflow," *Forest Industry,* Vol. 89, No. 11 (1962).

[19] Goodell, Bertram C. "Watershed Management Aspects of Thinned Young Lodgepole Pine Stands," *Journal of Forestry,* Vol. 50, No. 5 (1952).

[20] Anderson, Henry W., Rice, Raymond M., and West, Allan J. "Snow in Forest Openings and Forest Stands," *Society of American Foresters Proceedings,* 1958.

[21] Anderson, Henry W., and Gleason, Clark H. "Logging and Brush Removal Effects on Runoff from Snow Cover," *International Association of Scientific Hydrology Pub. No. 51.* Merelbeke, Belgium, 1960.

[22] Anderson, Henry W. "Forest-cover Effects on Snowpack Accumulation and Melt, Central Sierra Snow Laboratory," *American Geophysical Union Transactions,* Vol. 37, No. 3 (1956).

[23] Rocky Mountain Forest and Range Experiment Station. *Annual Report.* Fort Collins: U.S. Forest Service, 1956.

[24] Ziemer, Robert R. "Summer Evapotranspiration Trends as Related to Time After Logging at High Elevation Forest Stands in Sierra Nevada," *Journal of Geophysical Research,* Vol. 69, No. 4 (1964).

[25] Lull, H. W., and Orr, H. K. "Induced Snow Drifting for Water," *Journal of Forestry,* Vol. 48 (1950).

[26] Maass, A., et al. *Design of Water Resource Systems.* Cambridge: Harvard University Press, 1962.

[27] Anderson, Henry W., West, A. J., and Ziemer, R. R. "Evaporative Loss from Soil, Native Vegetation and Snow as Affected by Hexadecanol," *International Association of Scientific Hydrology Pub. No. 62,* 1962.

[28] Gould, Ernest M., Jr., and O'Regan, William G. *Simulation, a Step toward Better Forest Planning.* Harvard Forest Papers No. 13, Petersham, Mass., 1965.

[29] Amidon, Elliot. *A Computer-oriented System for Assembling and Displaying Land·Management Information.* U.S. Forest Service Research Paper PSW-17. Berkeley: Pacific Southwest Forest and Range Experiment Station, 1964.

Stochastic Problems in Design of Reservoirs

Vujica M. Yevdjevich*

DESIGN OF STORAGE RESERVOIRS

Independent and Dependent Reservoirs

For the purposes of this paper, an independent reservoir is defined as a storage reservoir that is operated independently of any other reservoir. A dependent reservoir is defined as a storage reservoir whose design and operation are dependent upon other reservoirs. Dependent reservoirs are of three general types:

a) reservoir inflow depends partly or fully on the regulated outflow of upstream reservoirs;

b) reservoir outflow is imposed by joint operation with downstream reservoirs; and

c) reservoir water outflow is affected by water released from reservoirs in adjacent river basins.

This study deals with the stochastic problems encountered when designing independent reservoirs. Investigations also probe design problems connected with dependent reservoirs whose characteristics of eventual inflows dependent on upstream reservoirs and/or imposed outflows are known or prescribed in advance. The study does not deal with complex stochastic problems encountered when designing a system of several dependent reservoirs, since the solution of these problems involves

* Professor of Civil Engineering, Colorado State University. The research leading to this paper is sponsored by the National Science Foundation.

further reservoir design generalizations, whereas the solutions of stochastic problems connected with individual independent reservoirs become the basic design elements in a reservoir system.

Basic Storage Equation

The classical basic continuity equation used in the design of reservoirs is

$$I - O = S \tag{1}$$

with I = inflow, O = outflow, and S = change in reservoir storage, in a
given time interval T. If one neglects the ground-water portion and the
seepage of a predominately surface storage reservoir, but includes the
evaporation and sedimentation of the reservoir, expressing equation (1)
in the form of rates of inflow, outflow, evaporation and storage change,
then

$$P_t - Q_t - E_t = \frac{dS}{dt} \tag{2}$$

with P_t = inflow rate (a stochastic variable or a combination of cyclic
and stochastic processes); Q_t = outflow rate (a stochastic variable or a
combination of cyclic and stochastic processes); E_t = evaporation rate
from the reservoir which depends on the climatic stochastic and cyclic
movements as well as on the reservoir surface. The last term in equation
(2) is the rate of change in stored water.

Storage volume of a reservoir is a function of both the reservoir elevation and the time. It can often be approximated by the storage volume
function

$$S = aH^m \tag{3}$$

with $a = \psi(t)$, and $m = f(t)$ which are functions of time. This time
function is the result of the sedimentation process which is a function of
time. The inflow of sediments into a reservoir has a stochastic component. The result of this variable is that storage function parameters a and
m are stochastic variables. The basic input-storage-output relationship,
equation (2), is an ordinary differential equation of stochastic variables.
By determining dS/dt in equation (2) from equation (3), with a and m
functions of time, equation (2) becomes a partial differential equation.

The storage capacity, S_f, of a reservoir is always a finite value. It is a
stochastic variable because $S_f = a(H_{max}{}^m - H_{min}{}^m)$, with H_{max} and
H_{min} the maximum and the minimum reservoir heights, where a and m
are stochastic variables. These variables and evaporation are neglected
in practical applications when the average annual evaporation, E_t, from

a reservoir is small in comparison with the average annual inflow and outflow, and when the sediment inflow is small in comparison with the finite storage capacity. In this case, the basic stochastic variables in equations (1) and (2) are the inflow and the outflow. Therefore, the water storage in a reservoir at a given time must also be a stochastic variable.

Change of Inflow and Outflow with Time

Natural fluctuations cause the inflow to change with time. However, various changes and developments in a river basin may cause the inflow's mean, variance, skewness coefficient and time dependence to change with time. These changes can be assessed with only a small degree of accuracy, thus limiting precision when determining inflow parameters. Various river basin developments and unavoidable changes in storage objectives cause the outflow to change with time.

A reservoir designer is faced with the problem of solving an ordinary or partial differential equation with stochastic variables, which are made nonstationary by environmental conditions and changes. These facts are responsible for the complexity of problems and for the many approaches used in solving stochastic problems in reservoir design.

Method of Solving Stochastic Problems in Reservoir Design

Approaches currently used in solving stochastic problems in reservoir design and operation may be classified into three groups:

1) *The empirical method* consists of deriving properties of various storage variables by using mass curves of available historical flow time series.

2) *The data generation method* solves stochastic storage problems by generating large samples of data. Statisticians call it the Monte Carlo method; hydrologists use various terms, such as synthetic hydrology, simulation, data generation, and operational hydrology. In this study, the term "data generation method" will be used. This method uses random numbers of one or several variables which are distributed as independent normal, log-normal, gamma, or according to other theoretical distributions, or as an empirical distribution. The stochastic dependence process or cyclic movement are processes superimposed on the sequence of these independent variables. Data accumulated by the generation method is analyzed by a procedure that is similar to the empirical method.

3) *The analytical method* consists of mathematical derivations of exact properties of variables involved in the analysis of storage problems.

Because of difficulties in integrating exact distribution equations, it usually employs a numerical finite differences approach in solving problems.

A brief analysis of the potentials and limitations of these three methods of solving reservoir design and operation problems is the main objective of this paper.

PROPERTIES OF INFLOWS INTO RESERVOIRS

Variables which Describe Inflows

The instantaneous discharge is the basic variable for a description of inflows. However, practical problems are concerned with such variables as the daily, monthly, and annual flows. The latter two variables are discussed here to illustrate the mathematical description of properties of inflows into reservoirs. Since properties of instantaneous inflows are often roughly approximated by the properties of monthly flows, the following information on monthly flows, when it is refined, may be applied to daily or instantaneous inflows.

Properties of Annual Flows

By using data from a number of river-gauging stations, the writer concluded in a recent study that there are no cycles greater than a year in the sequence of annual river flows [ref. 1]. However, the change in water carry-over in river basins from year to year creates a dependence in time series of annual flow. This dependence can be best described mathematically by the first or second order Markov models (autoregressive schemes), or in general by moving average schemes.

Figure 1 represents the annual flow series of the Rhine River at Basel,

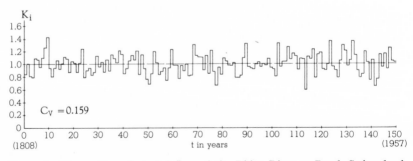

Figure 1. Time series of annual flow of the Rhine River at Basel, Switzerland, 1808–1957, in modular coefficients, $K_i = X_i/X$, with $\bar{X}_i$ = annual flow and $\bar{X}$ = average annual flow.

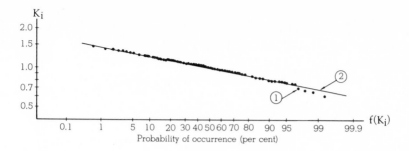

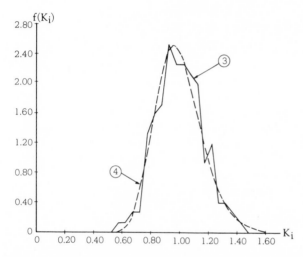

Figure 2. Frequency distribution (upper graph) and frequency density curve (lower graph) of annual flows of the Rhine River at Basel: (1) Observed; (2) Fitted log-normal function; (3) Observed densities; (4) Fitted log-normal function.

Switzerland, for 150 years, from 1808 to 1957. The purpose of this figure is to emphasize the fact that one of the longest annual flow series available in hydrology looks like many series of generated random numbers. Figure 2 gives the distribution of the river's annual flow as expressed in modular coefficients, $K_i = X_i / \overline{X}$, with X_i the annual flow, $\overline{X}$ the mean annual flow, and K_i the modular coefficient. Figure 3 represents the correlogram of this series. For all practical purposes, Figure 3 illustrates, by confidence intervals, that the annual flow of this river is an independent variable. Figure 2 shows that it approximately follows a log-normal distribution.

Figure 4 shows the correlogram of annual flow series of the St. Lawrence River at Ogdensburg, New York, for ninety-seven years, from 1861 to 1957. This river has a large time dependence. Assuming that a stochastic independent variable represents the inflow into all storage

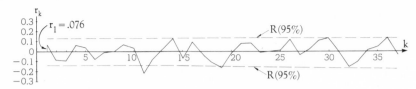

Figure 3. Correlogram of annual flows for the Rhine River at Basel: $r_1 = 0.076$, the first serial correlation coefficient; R (95%), confidence limits at 95% level; r_k, k-th serial correlation coefficient; and k, the lag.

capacities of the river basin, particularly of the Great Lakes, the following mathematical model may be applied to the outflow:

$$K_i = K_{i-1}^\rho \epsilon_i. \tag{4}$$

It may be written as

$$\ln K_i = \rho \ln K_{i-1} + \ln \epsilon_i \tag{5}$$

or the first order linear Markov model is applied to logarithms of this variable. The correlogram for the variable K_i is

$$\rho_k = \frac{e^{\rho k} - 1}{e - 1} \tag{6}$$

with the variable K_i being log-normally distributed when ϵ_i is log-normally distributed, with the dependence model given by equation (5). Figure 4 shows the fitting of equation (6) to the correlogram of this river, with $\rho = 0.77$. The model of equation (6) fits the correlogram better than the general model $\rho_k = \rho^k$ of the first order Markov linear model generated by the scheme $K_i = \rho K_{i-1} + \epsilon_i$.

The two examples given above are the extremes encountered by the writer while investigating the annual flow series of several hundred rivers. It was found that two types of variables—independent and dependent—which are well fitted by the first order linear Markov model, are two extreme cases. In some cases, the second order linear Markov model fits the correlograms of annual flows.

Whenever a large storage capacity for over-year flow regulations is being designed or operated, the inflows on an annual basis may be described by the corresponding stochastic mathematical models. If flows are not affected by accidents in nature such as fires and land slides, and if the inconsistency (man-made systematic errors in data) and non-homogeneity in data (man-made changes in river basin) are negligible, the series of annual flow are usually second order stationary and ergodic, i.e., the expected mean, the variance, and the autocovariance are independent of the position in the series, and the ergodicity requirement is satisfied. If the above conditions do not exist, the non-stationarity (linear

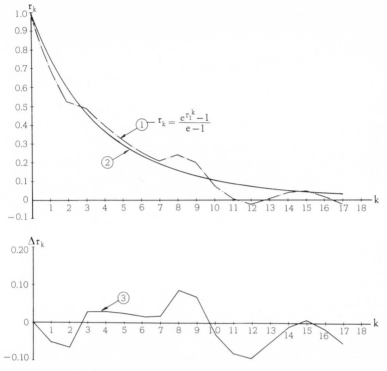

Figure 4. Correlogram (upper graph) and difference between observed and fitted correlogram (lower graph) for annual flows of St. Lawrence River, Ogdensburg, New York, 1861–1957: (1) correlogram of observed annual flows; (2) fitted correlogram of the model $r_k = (e^{r_1^k} - 1)/(e - 1)$; (3) Difference between the curves (1) and (2).

or non-linear trends) must be replaced with the new stationary series (that which is expected to be experienced in the future).

Properties of Monthly Flows[1]

The time sequence of monthly flows, x_t , usually shows a cyclic movement of twelve months and its harmonics (six, four, three months) plus a stochastic movement. The time series mathematical description of x_t is made feasible by taking into account the sampling errors inherent in any limited period of monthly flow observation.

Figure 5 gives the sequence of monthly flows of the Gasconade River, near Waynesville, Missouri, for forty years, from 1921 to 1960. This hydrograph of monthly flows is shown here to underline the cyclic move-

[1] This example and mathematical description of monthly flows are taken from Roesner's recent Master's thesis at Colorado State University. See [ref. 2].

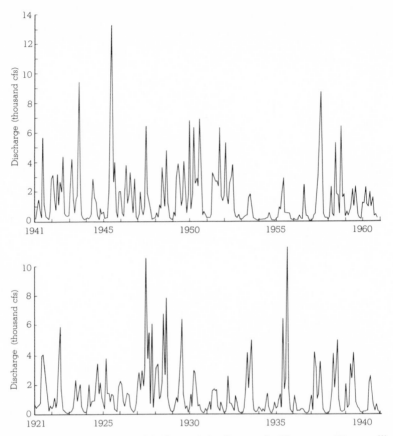

Figure 5. Times series of monthly flows of the Gasconade River, near Waynesville, Missouri, 1921–1960 (forty years). Discrete values of monthly flows are shown as a hydrograph with twelve ordinates per year.

ment as well as stochastic superimposed process. Figure 6 shows the correlogram and power spectrum of x_t. Figure 7 gives the sequence of the average monthly flows for each of the twelve months, m_τ; the standard deviations, s_τ; and the coefficients of variation for each month, C_τ, where τ represents the calendar months 1, 2, ... , 12. The monthly flow time series is not stationary even of the first order. The expected mean, variance, and covariance of monthly flows depend on the calendar month. A rigorous mathematical statistical analysis of monthly flows requires a series to be stationary. A second order stationarity is obtained by transforming monthly flows x_t to

$$y_t = \frac{x_t - m_\tau}{s_\tau} \tag{7}$$

382

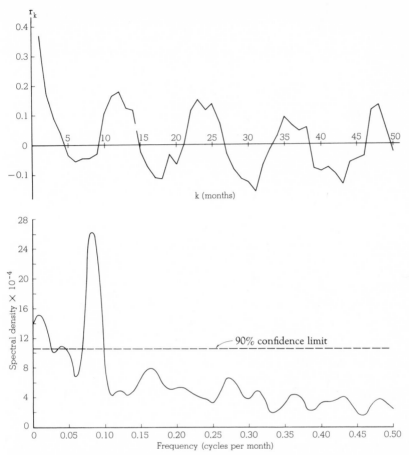

Figure 6. Correlogram (upper graph) and power spectrum (lower graph) of monthly flows (x_t) of the Gasconade River for the period of observation 1921–60 (forty years, 480 monthly values).

with m_τ and s_τ of Figure 7, and with y_t a new second order stationary time series. Figure 8 shows the correlogram and power spectrum of y_t. When using equation (7) twenty-four m_τ and s_τ empirical constants must be extracted from data and considered as parameters. The coefficient of variation C_τ may replace s_τ in equation (7) as

$$y_t = \frac{1}{C_\tau} \left(\frac{x_t}{m_\tau} - 1 \right). \tag{8}$$

C_τ usually shows a much smaller variation than s_τ. The standard deviation s_τ is used in this study.

The sequences of m_τ and s_τ are composed of harmonics. Figure 6

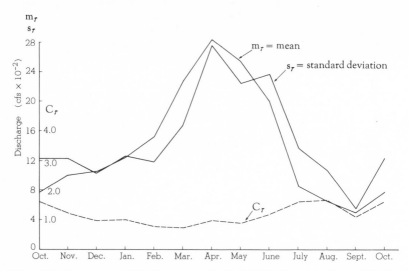

Figure 7. Average monthly flow, m_τ; standard deviation, s_τ, of monthly flows about m_τ; coefficient of variation, $C_\tau = s_\tau / m_\tau$, for each of the twelve months, for the Gasconade River for the period of observation 1921–1960 (forty years, 840 monthly values).

shows that the only pronounced cycle in x_t is a twelve-month period with some low frequency noise. When equations for the twelve-month cycle are fitted to m_τ and s_τ, these symbols are designated as m_t and s_t. In the case of the Gasconade River these two equations are:

$$m_t = 1433 - 878.8 \cos \frac{2\pi}{12}t - 419.2 \sin \frac{2\pi}{12}t \qquad (9)$$

and

$$s_t = 1480 - 494.4 \cos \frac{2\pi}{12}t - 493.0 \sin \frac{2\pi}{12}t. \qquad (10)$$

To approximate the third order stationary—i.e., the skewness coefficient, C_s, should be approximately equal for all months—the logarithmic transformation of x_t may be used for data analysis. The use of an estimating cycle to find m_t and s_t—the values $\bar{x}_t$ and $\bar{s}_t$ are the averages of m_t and s_t—then six parameters in the cycle allows the replacement of the twenty-four constants in equation (7). By using equation (7) for y_t, with m_t and s_t given by equations (9) and (10), the new variable y_t has the mean $\bar{y} = 0.02$, and the standard deviation 1.18. The new standardized variable is now:

$$z_t = \frac{y_t - \bar{y}}{s_y}. \qquad (11)$$

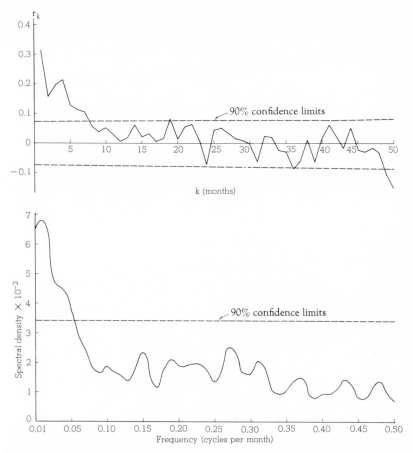

Figure 8. Correlogram (upper graph) and power spectrum (lower graph) of stationary standardized time series $y_t = (x_t - m_\tau)/s_\tau$ of monthly flows for the Gasconade River, with 90% confidence limits for both graphs.

The correlogram and power spectrum of z_t are given in Figure 9. The stochastic variable z_t follows a moving average scheme. It is roughly approximated in this example by the first order linear Markov model, with $\rho = 0.316$. Then:

$$z_t = \rho z_{t-1} + \sqrt{1 - \rho^2}\ \epsilon_t \tag{12}$$

with ϵ_t an independent variable with the distribution given in Figure 10 and with $E(\epsilon_t) = -0.001$ and variance of $\epsilon_t = 0.902$. The skewness coefficient of ϵ_t is $C_s = 2.64$. The skewness coefficients of ϵ_t for each month $C_s(\tau)$ are given in Figure 11. It shows that the ϵ_t series has not

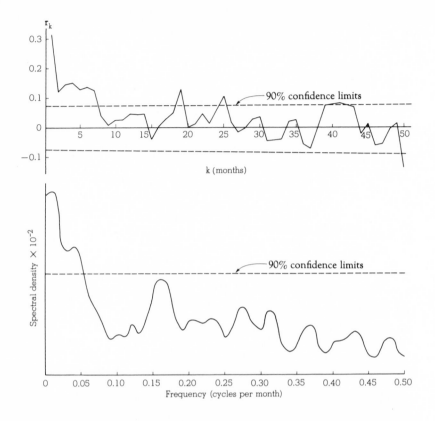

Figure 9. Correlogram (upper graph) and power spectrum (lower graph) of stationary standardized time series $z_t = (y_t - y)/s_y$, with $\bar{y} = 0.02$ and $s_y = 1.18$, and $y_t = (x_t - m_t)/s_t$, with m_t and s_t given by equations (9) and (10), for the monthly flows of the Gasconade River.

a third order stationarity. The non-uniformity of C_s (τ) is a measure of this third order non-stationarity.

The mathematical model of x_t is obtained from equations (7) through (12) as:

$$x_t = \rho(x_{t-1} - m_{t-1})s_t/s_{t-1} + m_t + \bar{y}\, s_t(1 - \rho) + s_t\, y_t \sqrt{1 - \rho^2}\, \epsilon_t \quad (13)$$

with ρ, $\bar{y}$, s_y given as above, and m_t, m_{t-1}, s_t and s_{t-1} given by equations (9) and (10). Equation (13) is the mathematical description of this river's monthly variable. The third order stationarity may be approached much closer if $\ln x_t$ is investigated and described by an equation similar to equation (13) instead of x_t being investigated.

386

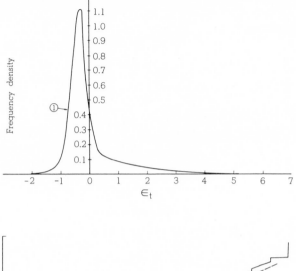

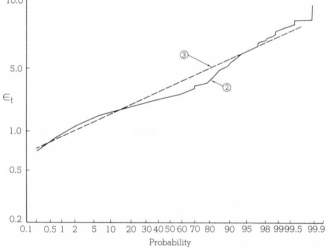

Figure 10. Frequency density curve (upper graph) and frequency distribution (lower graph) of the independent stochastic component, ε_t, of monthly flows of the Gasconade River: (1) frequency density curve; (2) frequency distribution; and (3) log-normal fit for frequency distribution, with the lower boundary $\varepsilon_0 = -2.20$.

The advantage of separating the cyclic from the monthly flow stochastic component lies in the fact that a constant storage capacity is necessary to regulate the flow in order to eradicate the cyclic movement. The stochastic movement gives a distribution of storage variables, which has to be superimposed on the constant storage of cyclic movement.

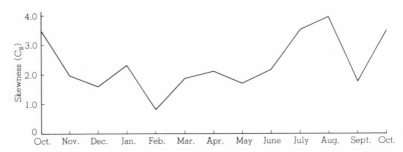

Figure 11. Skewness coefficients for each of the twelve months of the independent stochastic component, ε_t, of monthly flows of the Gasconade River. The non-uniformity of C_s (τ) is a measure of the third-order non-stationarity of ε_t.

Properties of Daily or Instantaneous Flows

A mathematical model for daily or instantaneous river flows may be obtained similarly as equation (13) for monthly flows. Within the limits of sampling errors, any variable which describes the river flows may be represented by the corresponding stochastic process. The basis of this process is the transformation of independent variables, ϵ_t.

PROPERTIES OF OUTFLOWS

Variables which Describe Reservoir Outflows

The reservoir outflows are usually expressed as the same variable (instantaneous, daily, monthly, or annual flow) as the inflow, and the same mathematical approach may be used in describing reservoir outflows. In the case of lakes with no artificial flow regulation, the outflows are usually subject to a larger time dependence and smaller variations than the inflows, but their description is similar. The rigorous mathematical description of outflows as stochastic processes is less suitable in the case of outflows regulated by reservoirs.

General Types of Reservoir Outflows

A systematization of the types of regulated outflows, from a mathematical point of view, gives the following cases:

1. Outflow is constant and equal to the estimate of the mean $(Q = \overline{Q} = \overline{P})$, assuming that $\overline{Q} = \overline{P}$, so that:

$$P - \overline{P} = \frac{dS}{dt}. \tag{14}$$

2. Outflow is constant for a given period of n-time units and is equal

388

to the average inflow of that period, so that $Q = \bar{P}_n$, with $\bar{P}_n$ a stochastic variable. The value $\bar{P}_n$ changes from one n-time unit period to another. Its variation decreases with an increase of n. Then:

$$P - \bar{P}_n = \frac{dS}{dt}. \qquad (15)$$

This means that after each n-time unit the reservoir storage is always at its initial stage.

3. Outflow is prescribed only by the water demand function as $Q = \bar{Q}$ $[1 + \psi(\tau)]$, with $\psi(\tau)$ a fluctuation function in a given time (say τ are 12 months of the year), and $E[\psi(\tau)] = 0$. Its variation about zero usually depends on the seasonal patterns of water demand. Then:

$$P - \bar{P}[1 + \psi(\tau)] = \frac{dS}{dt}. \qquad (16)$$

The integration of equation (16) depends upon how well $\psi(\tau)$, as a mathematical function with stochastic components, describes the actual water release.

4. Outflow depends on the storage in the reservoir as $Q = \bar{Q}$ $[1 + f(S)]$, so that:

$$P - \bar{P}[1 + f(S)] = \frac{dS}{dt} \qquad (17)$$

with $E[f(S)] = 0$. The variation of outflow depends on storage variation, which in turn depends on inflow variation and reservoir characteristics.

5. Outflow depends on the inflow into the reservoir, or $Q = \bar{P}$ $[1 + \psi(P)]$, so that

$$P - \bar{P}[1 + \psi(P)] = \frac{dS}{dt} \qquad \text{with } E[\psi(P)] = 0. \qquad (18)$$

6. Outflow depends on both storage in the reservoir and inflow, or $Q = \bar{P}[1 + \phi(S, P)]$, so that

$$P - \bar{P}[1 + \phi(S, P)] = \frac{dS}{dt} \qquad (19)$$

with $E[\phi(S, P)] = 0$. The variation of $\phi(S, P)$ depends on the type of function, and the weight by which each S and P affects the outflow.

7. Outflow is generally prescribed by the water demand, but is also dependent on reservoir storage and inflow, or $Q = \bar{P}[1 + \psi(\tau) \phi(S, P)]$ so that

$$P - \bar{P}[1 + \psi(\tau)\phi(S, P)] = \frac{dS}{dt} \qquad (20)$$

with $E [\psi (\tau) \phi (S, P)] = 0$. The variation of $[\psi (\tau) \phi (S, P)]$ depends on the weight of each of three variables: τ, S, P. This last case is the general type of regulated outflows. In practice, the demand is prescribed, but it is usually modified by the water available in the reservoir and by the anticipated inflows.

There may be various shapes of functions $\psi (\tau)$, $f (S)$, $\psi (P)$ and $\phi (S, P)$, and their combinations. When expanded into power series forms, the linear terms yield first order approximations which are the simplest to investigate. When these functions become complex, the mathematical analysis is difficult to apply. Usually the investigation must apply the finite difference method of integration of equations (16) through (20). Outflow regimes in cases 1 and 2, equations (14) and (15), are theoretical regimes. They have limited practical applications. However, these regimes supply storage capacity information which is required to develop theoretical regulation patterns.

TYPES OF STORAGE

Concept of Infinite Storage

Even though reservoir storage capacities are always finite, the theoretical concept of infinite storage is useful as a limit when investigating stochastic problems in design of reservoirs. Authors may refer to this concept as: infinite reservoir, infinite dam, infinite storage, infinite sum of deviations, and similar terms. A reservoir fitting the infinite storage concept is assumed to be capable of storing any water surplus as incurred by the difference of inflow and outflow, and to supply any deficit for the difference between outflow and inflow.

This concept introduces three basic and important variables into the stochastic analysis of storage problems: the range, the surplus, and the deficit. In general, the concept of infinite storage is not necessary for the definition of these three variables, but it is useful as soon as these variables are associated with or applied to storage problems. It is assumed that infinite storage does not mean that at the initial stage the storage is empty. It is assumed that on both ends of actual storage there is infinite storage for accepting the surplus or supplying the deficit.

Definition of Range, Surplus, and Deficit

Figure 12 shows a graph of accumulated deviations from the mean, $\sum \Delta P = \sum (P - \bar{P})$. For a given period of n-time units, the difference between the maximum and the minimum of $\sum (P - \bar{P})$ is the range, R_n ;

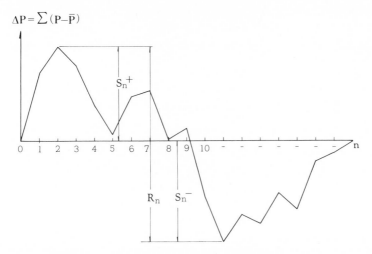

Figure 12. Definition graph for the surplus (S_n^+), deficit $(S_{\bar{n}})$, and range (R_n) on the curve of accumulated deviations of flows P_i from the mean flow $\bar{P}$.

the maximum positive sum is the surplus, S_n^+ ; and the absolute value of the maximum negative sum is the deficit $|\,S_{\bar{n}}\,|$. Characteristics of these three variables measure stochastic variations in reservoir design. The sum of departures, $\sum (P - Q)$, may be determined not only by using a constant value of $\bar{P}$ as the outflow, but by applying an outflow function. Properties of these three variables depend on the character of outflows for given inflows. By this definition $R_n = S_n^+ - S_{\bar{n}}$, or the range is the surplus plus the deficit. When $\bar{P}$ is replaced by $\bar{P}_n$ as the mean for each n-time unit, the range, surplus, and deficit are referred to as the adjusted range, adjusted surplus and adjusted deficit [ref. 3]. Further discussion of stochastic problems in this paper is restricted to the range, R_n . The distributions of R_n , S_n^+ and $S_{\bar{n}}$, and their patterns in sequence under various conditions of inflow, storage, and outflow, are the fundamental stochastic properties when investigating flow regulation problems.

Finite Storage

All reservoirs have limited storage capacities, resulting in the practical problems of finite storage. Finite storage is conceived as a stochastic process with two barriers: the upper with the full storage capacity, S_f , and the lower with the empty reservoir. The initial storage content may be anywhere between 0 and S_f . This initial condition parameter plays an important role in the operation of reservoirs until this operation becomes independent of the initial conditions. The existence of two storage boundaries, 0 and S_f, and the impact of initial storage make the analytical integration of storage differential equations (1) and (2), or of any other equation (14) through (20) very complex.

EMPIRICAL METHOD FOR INVESTIGATION OF STORAGE PROBLEMS

Mass Curve Approach

The empirical method of analyzing stochastic problems has dominated engineering practice ever since Rippl applied this approach in 1883. This approach is used to such an extent that any new variable may be considered as being empirically obtained. If the sample size is N, and a variable is related to n units of the time series, then the sample size of a derived variable is $m = N/n$. For example, if the maximum annual flow in ten-year subsamples ($n = 10$) in a sample of 150 years represents a new variable, its derived sample is $m = N/n = 15$. The main characteristic of the empirical method is a decrease of the derived variables sample size with an increase of subsample size to which the new variables are related.

The accuracy of mass-curve approach depends on: original accuracy of data; the size of the sample; and the accuracy of mass-curves. The sampling errors resulting from the available sample size dominate the accuracy of results.

The main disadvantage in using mass-curves is the assumption that river flows are known in advance. This assumption is based on the classical approach of "matching the best outflow regime for the known inflow mass-curves." In other words, a sample among an infinite number of possible samples of the same size is "idealized" and the outflow is "fitted" to this unique sample. The characteristics of the empirical method are relatively irregular frequency density curves for derived variables.

Example of the Empirical Method

Figure 13 gives the empirical distribution of range R_3 (for $n = 3$). The mass-curve of departures $\Delta K_i = K_i - 1$, with $K_i = Q_i/\overline{Q}$ the modular coefficients of annual flows of the Rhine River for 150 years, is used to determine each subsample of $n = 3$ and the corresponding frequency density of R_3 from $m = 150/3 = 50$ values. This distribution is compared with the same distributions obtained by the data generation method and the analytical method.

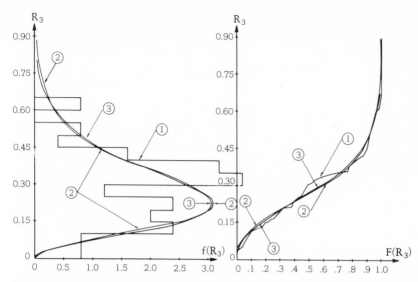

Figure 13. Probability density (left graph) and probability distribution (right graph) of the range R_3 ($n = 3$) for annual flows of the Rhine River (1908–57) determined by three methods: (1) empirical method; (2) data generation method; and (3) from exact distribution of R_3 and finite differences procedure of integration.

DATA GENERATION METHOD FOR INVESTIGATION OF STORAGE PROBLEMS

Data Generation

The data generation method is defined as the simulation of large samples of data from observed data, or of data from inferred properties of a variable population. The latter are usually defined by distribution functions and by mathematical models of the stationary time series dependence. At present, the generation of independent random numbers and their transformation to obtain the selected population sample are carried out on digital computers.

The main property of this method is the absence of any limitation in the generated sample size. The size is limited by either of two criteria: sampling error of final results, and economics of generating and processing a large sample.

Example of Method's Application

Annual flow logarithms of the Rhine River are considered as being normally distributed. Using the sample of modular coefficients the mean

393

is $\overline{K} = 1$ and the standard deviation $S_n = 0.159$. The variance of logarithms $\sigma_n^2 = \ln(1 + s_n^2) = 0.02517$ with $\sigma_n = 0.1582$, and the mean of logarithms $\mu_n = -0.0126$ with $\ln K = 0.1582t - 0.0126$, where $t =$ standard normal independent variable. The transformation

$$K = e^{0.1582t-0.0126} \tag{21}$$

is used for data generation. The use of random normal independent numbers, t, will generate a very large annual flow sample of the Rhine River.

A large sample of 30,000 annual flows is generated to determine the distribution of maximum range R_3 for $n = 3$, so that the range sample is of the magnitude of 10,000. This distribution is determined by digital computers, and is represented in Figure 13 for comparison with the same distribution obtained by the empirical method. This distribution is much smoother than that obtained by the empirical method.

Generation of Large Samples from Theoretical Distribution Functions and Dependence Models

The data generation method is useful when studying the properties of variables with given theoretical distributions and dependence models, when these properties cannot be obtained by analytical derivations. In the writer's opinion, this characteristic of the data generation method is most valuable in research activities and applications of stochastic problems in reservoir design.

Assume that programs are available for generating the random normal independent variable, t, with a mean of zero, variance unity, and the first autocorrelation coefficient of zero, $(0, 1, 0)$. The generation of samples for the following functions is then as follows:

1. *Normal independent variables:* Mean is μ and standard deviation, σ. Then any normal independent variable is generated by

$$X_i = \sigma t_i + \mu. \tag{22}$$

2. *Normal dependent variables.* Several dependence models can be used for river flows according to the properties of variables. The first order linear Markov model generally represents one of the hydrology's dependences on a change in water carryover. Then,

$$X_i = \rho X_{i-1} + t_i \tag{23}$$

with t_i the normal standard independent variable, ρ the first autocorrelation coefficient estimated by the first serial correlation coefficient, r_1, and X_i the generated normal dependent variable, usually with $X_1 = t_1$, $\overline{X} = 0$, var $X_i = 1/(1 - \rho^2)$. To generate a variable with a standard deviation of $s_r = 1$, the generating model is

$$X_i = \rho \, X_{i-1} + \sqrt{1 - \rho^2} \, t_i. \tag{24}$$

The generated samples have correlograms

$$r_k = r_1{}^k \text{ with}$$

$$E(r_k) = \rho_k = \rho^k, \text{ and } E(r_1) = \rho. \tag{25}$$

3. *Log-normal independent variables.* For an independent variable X_i log-normally distributed, with mean μ and standard deviation σ, the mean μ_n and standard deviation σ_n of $\ln X_i$ are

$$\mu_n = \ln \frac{\mu^2}{\sqrt{\mu^2 + \sigma^2}} \tag{26}$$

$$\sigma_n = \left[\ln\left(1 + \frac{\sigma^2}{\mu^2}\right)\right]^{1/2}. \tag{27}$$

The generating model is

$$X_i = e^{\sigma_n t_i + \mu_n} \tag{28}$$

with μ_n and σ_n given by equations (26) and (27), respectively.

4. *Log-normal dependent variables.* When obtaining a log-normal dependent variable from a standard normal variable, only the product of log-normal variables becomes a log-normal variable, so the transformation

$$X_i = e^{\rho \ln X_{i-1}} e^{\sqrt{1-\rho^2} \, t_i} \tag{29}$$

gives a dependent log-normal variable. However, the correlogram of the X_i series is

$$r_k = \frac{e^{r_1 k} - 1}{e - 1} \tag{30}$$

with $E(r_1) = \rho$ and $E(r_k) = \rho_k$. Investigations show that for annual flows of many rivers the model of equation (30) fits better the observed series of correlograms rather than the model of equation (25).

5. *Gamma independent variables.* Only gamma distributions with one parameter are discussed. Gamma distributions with two or three parameters (Pearson Type III function) can be reduced by appropriate transformations to one parameter gamma distributions.

The transformation, using the principle that the sum of gamma distributions is a gamma distribution, gives

$$X_i = \tfrac{1}{2} \sum_{j=1}^{m} t_j^2 \tag{31}$$

with X_i the gamma density distribution function and t_j^2 a gamma distribution, so that

$$f(x) = \frac{1}{\Gamma(\alpha)} x^{\alpha-1} e^{-x} \tag{32}$$

395

with $\alpha = m/2$, mean α, variance α, and skewness coefficient $(4/\alpha)^{1/2}$; and t_j represents m independent normal standard variables uncorrelated among themselves. Equation (31) enables the generation of skewed distribution with any value of $C_s = 2/\sqrt{\alpha}$, for $\alpha = m/2$ and m any integer number.

6. *Gamma dependent variables.* Using the transformation of equation (31) with any obtained variable

$$U = \tfrac{1}{2} \sum_{j=1}^{m} x_j^2 \tag{33}$$

and each variable of x_j obtained by the transformation

$$x_i = \sqrt{\rho}\, x_{i-1} + \sqrt{1 - \rho}\, t_i \tag{34}$$

where t_i is the standard normal independent variable $(0, 1, 0)$, and the variable x_i is the dependent normal variable with mean zero, variance unity, and expectation $E\,(r_k) = \rho^k$. It can be shown that the variable U, obtained from m x_j-variables, which are independent among themselves, by equation (33), is a gamma distribution with mean α, variance α, $C_s = 2/\sqrt{\alpha}$, and an expected correlogram of $\rho_k = \rho^k$, which is the Markov first order linear model.

Some properties of the above six cases may be derived analytically. However, the data generation method is the fastest way to obtain properties of range, surplus, and deficit; and other characteristics of storage problems for most of the above cases.

Example with Gamma Dependent Variables

This study cites only two of the many examples of the use of the data generation method.

Figure 14 gives the range mean values for $n = 2 - 50$, for $\alpha = m/2 = 1$, or $E\,(C_s) = 2.0$, and six values of $\rho = 0.0, 0.1, 0.2, 0.4, 0.6$, and 0.8. This is an example of the gamma dependent variable obtained by generating normal independent random numbers t_i, with two transformations. First by equation (34), then by equation (33) for $m = 2$. The generating of 100,000 numbers for t_1 and t_2, or x_1 and x_2, yields a gamma U-variable with a mean of 1.001, a variance of 0.98 and a skewness coefficient of 1.92. These values are close to expected theoretical values. The departure of these parameters from the expected theoretical values $(1, 1, 2)$ is explained by the fact that the t-values are squared. The extreme t-values of very small probability have the largest sampling variation, and squares of these values emphasize this fact even more.

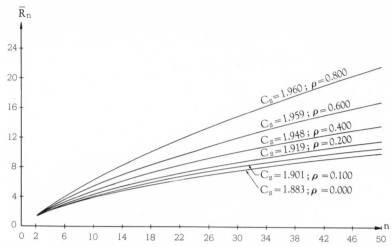

Figure 14. Mean values of range for $n = 2 - 50$ for gamma variable with $C_s = 1.9$ $[E(C_s) = 2.00]$, and six values of ρ (0, 0.1, 0.2, 0.4, 0.6, 0.8).

Figures 15 and 16 give the variances and skewness coefficients of range for the same example as used in Figure 14, respectively. Figure 16 shows that skewness coefficients of range, R_n, as plotted versus n, are not smooth curves like the curves for the mean range and the variance of range. This is a result of sampling errors. The 100,000 random numbers are not sufficient to produce smooth curves of $C_s (R_n)$.

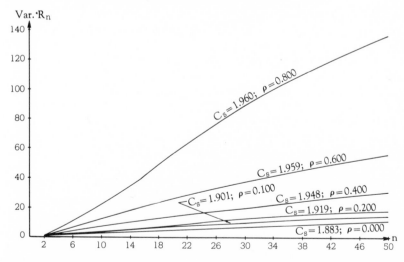

Figure 15. Variances of range for $n = 2 - 50$ for gamma variable with $C_s = 1.9$ $[E(C_s) = 2.00]$, and six values of ρ (0, 0.1, 0.2, 0.4, 0.6, 0.8).

397

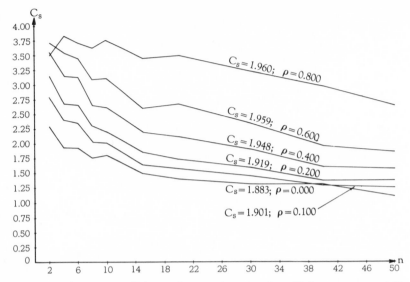

Figure 16. Skewness coefficients of range for $n = 2 - 50$ for gamma variable with $C_s = 1.9$ [$E (C_s) = 2.00$], and six values of ρ (0, 0.1, 0.2, 0.4, 0.6, 0.8).

With $\overline{X}$, s^2 and C_s of range distributions from Figures 14 through 16 for any value of $n = 2 - 50$, and gamma distribution with $\alpha = 1$ for $\rho = 0.0 - 1.0$ (with interpolations), any distribution of the range can be approximated by methods available in the literature for fitting distributions for the first three moments given. Figures 17 and 18 represent examples of some of these probability distributions obtained by the data generation method on a digital computer: Figure 17 for $\rho = 0$, $C_s = 1.883$ and for $n = 1, 2, 4, 8, 10, 15, 20, 30, 40$ and 50; and Figure 18 for $\rho = 0.2$, $C_s = 1.919$ and the same values of n. Distributions are relatively smooth. This proves that the data generation

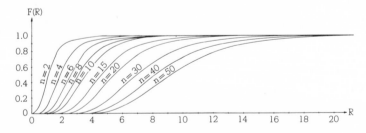

Figure 17. Distributions of range of gamma independent variable, $\rho = 0$, with mean and variance unities for $C_s = 1.883$ and for $n = 2, 4, 6, 8, 10, 15, 20, 30, 40$, and 50, obtained by data generation method.

398

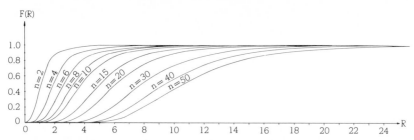

Figure 18. Distribution of gamma dependent variable, $\rho = 0.2$, with mean and variance unities, for $C = 1.919$, and for $n = 2, 4, 6, 8, 10, 15, 20, 30, 40,$ and 50, obtained by data generation method.

method gives smooth solutions of mathematical problems if enough random numbers are used.

Properties of the Data Generation Method

It has been contended that small sample properties can be used to generate large samples of data which in turn can increase information about the sequences. The reasoning behind this contention is this: The mean, variance, skewness coefficient, serial correlation coefficients, probability distribution itself as well as the mathematical model of dependence of a stationary time series, are to be inferred from the sample. Their reliability cannot be improved by generating large samples of data. However, the flow regulation properties resulting from a given cluster of sequence (small sample time series) may be improved by generating more such sequences. In other words, the value of a reservoir's water yield for a small given inflow sample may be improved by generating a large number of similar sequences with the corresponding number of water yields. It is not claimed that the mean outflow of a reservoir may be improved by the data generation method. It is claimed, however, that the range reliability is improved (or the information is increased) by this method. It should be noted that this claim is a point of controversy.

The data generation method may be viewed from the following three points:

as producing storage variable distributions that are smoother than these produced by the small sample;

as a technique to increase information concerning sequential properties; and

as a method of solving intractable analytically mathematical problems of stochastic variables.

There is often confusion between smoothness and information. In Figure 13, lines (1) and (2) show the same distribution as obtained by the empirical method and by the data generation method. The latter is very smooth, while the former has an opposite look. It is questionable whether the second smooth distribution curve has more information when compared with the first. Smoothness and information, as related to the distribution of stochastic variables, should be considered as two different properties.

The usual statistical approach to sample analysis assumes that maximum information may be extracted from a sample by using statistical inferential techniques. This approach also assumes that once these techniques are applied, no more information can be obtained from the sample. But this second assumption raises the question of whether the proper techniques are used or not. Assume that the best estimation techniques were used for the parameters of probability distribution, and the model of corresponding stationary time series dependence for a hydrologic sample. They should contain all the information that the sample can produce. Is it feasible to expect that techniques like large sample generations can extract more information?

There is also confusion in the use of terms. The data generation method is an excellent technique for solving many mathematical problems concerned with stochastic variables, but it is questionable whether it will increase information. Here is the essence of the controversy: Can a problem-solving technique yield an increase in information? The data generation method as a technique for solving mathematical problems with stochastic variables may be compared with the numerical finite differences method for solving differential equations when both cannot be solved analytically. As the numerical finite differences method does not improve the "information" contained in ordinary or partial differential equations, except to produce their solutions, it may be expected that the same conclusions would be valid for the data generation method as currently used in solving stochastic problems. Less confusion will be introduced in the data generation method by separating these two aspects of the method. In the writer's opinion, the data generation method is an excellent technique in solving stochastic mathematical problems when they are analytically intractable. The need for smoothness of distributions as a property of the data generation method is a question of interpretation. Smoothness should not be misinterpreted as the information. Any claim that the data generation method increases information should be subjected to a rigorous mathematical statistical analysis.

ANALYTICAL METHOD FOR INVESTIGATION OF STORAGE PROBLEMS

Analytical Method

This method consists of analytical procedures for deriving new variable properties by using the probability distribution and dependence model of the basic variable (usually inflow in the case of storage problems). It should be noted that at the present time very few cases have been solved analytically. Problem solving is usually restricted to asymptotic conditions and some other cases of distributions and means and variances of range, surplus and deficit for large or small values of n for normal independent variables, or simple dependent normal variables. There is, however, a need for research efforts to find analytical solutions for various cases of theoretical distributions and dependence models.

Properties of Means of Range of Normal Independent Variables

Hurst [ref. 4] developed the asymptotic expression for the mean of an adjusted range. Feller [ref. 3] obtained, theoretically, the mean of asymptotic distribution of range as

$$E(R_n) = 2\left(\frac{2n}{\pi}\right)^{1/2} = 1.6\sqrt{n}. \qquad (35)$$

Anis and Lloyd [ref. 5] developed exact value of the mean of range as

$$E(R_n) = \sqrt{\frac{2}{\pi}} \sum_{t=1}^{n} t^{-1/2} \qquad (36)$$

for a standard normal independent variable $(0, 1, 0)$. For any normal independent variable with the standard deviation σ, the mean of range is the right-hand expression of equations (35) and (36) multiplied by σ, respectively, for asymptotic and exact mean.

Figure 19 is a comparison of equations (35) and (36), and values from a data generated sample of 100,000 of the variable x, and an approximation to equation (35) in the form

$$E(R_n) = 2\left(\frac{2n}{\pi}\right)^{1/2} - 1. \qquad (37)$$

Figure 20 gives the absolute differences between the three range means curves and the exact mean determined by equation (36), and the difference between mean ranges of data generation method and equation (37).

The conclusions from Figures 19 and 20 are:

    a. Feller's formula, equation (35), yields too large a value of $\overline{R}_n$ for any values of $n = 1 - 50$;

401

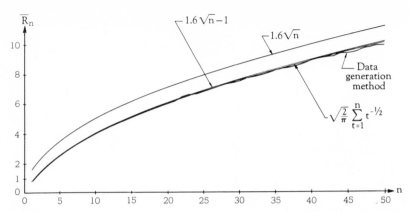

Figure 19. Comparison of asymptotic mean of range $1.6 \sqrt{n}$ with exact mean $\sqrt{\frac{2}{\pi}} \sum_{t=1}^{n} t^{-\frac{1}{2}}$, the approximation of asymptotic mean $(1.6 \sqrt{n} - 1)$, and the mean determined by the data generation method, for standard normal independent variable.

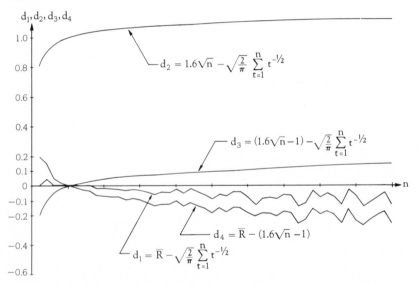

Figure 20. Absolute differences between (1) means of range computed by data generation method and exact means, d_1 ; (2) asymptotic means of range and exact means, d_2 ; (3) asymptotic means of range minus unity and exact means, d_3 ; (4) means of range computed by data generation method and asymptotic means of range minus unity, d_4 .

    b. Anis-Lloyd formula, equation (36), is well confirmed by the data generation method with a large generated sample; and

    c. An approximation for $n = 1 - 50$ is given by equation (37).

Properties of Variance of Range for Normal Independent Variables

Feller [ref. 3] gives the following expression for the variance of asymptotic range distributions for various n values:

$$\text{Var } R_n = 4n\left(\ln 2 - \frac{2}{\pi}\right) \approx 0.218n \tag{38}$$

Figures 21 and 22 compare the variances for asymptotic distributions with the variances determined by the data generation method with 100,000 random numbers. This comparison shows that the asymptotic values are smaller for a small n and greater for a large n than the range variances of generated data. However, the relative differences, as shown

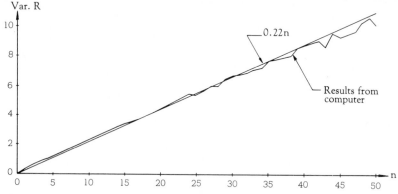

Figure 21. Comparison of asymptotic variances of range with the variance determined by data generation method for $n = 2 - 50$, and for standard normal independent variable.

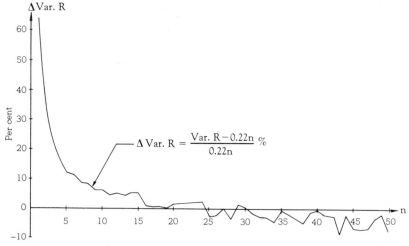

Figure 22. Relative differences of asymptotic variances of range and the variances computed by data generation method for standard normal independent variable.

in Figure 22, are equal to or less than 5 per cent for $n = 10 - 50$, but these differences increase for a decrease of n. It may be assumed that equation (38) can be used for the variance of range, even though it has been derived for asymptotic distributions.

Skewness Coefficient of Range

At present no literature offers an analytical expression of a skewness coefficient for the range for normal independent variables. Figure 23 gives the computed values obtained by the data generation method using 100,000 random numbers.

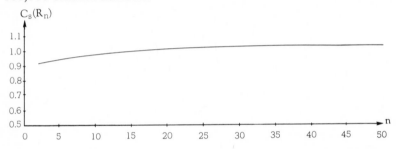

Figure 23. Skewness coefficient of range for various values of n for normal independent variable.

Equations (36) and (38) and Figure 23 give the three parameters (and from them the first three statistical moments) necessary for fitting mathematical functions to range distributions by procedures available in the literature when these statistical moments are known.

Exact Distributions of Range for n = 3

The exact distribution of range can be practically developed only up to $n = 3$ or 4, because beyond $n = 4$, or $n = 5$, the treatment of various cases involved becomes intractable.

Figure 24 shows eighteen cases of sums of $S_3 = x_1 + x_2 + x_3$ with their range values. The combined cases give the final expression for any symmetrical distribution, as developed by the writer,

$$f_3(R_3 = R) = 2 \int_0^R f(R - y) \left[\int_0^R f(y - x)f(x)dx \right] dy +$$

$$+ 2f(R) \int_0^R \left[f(y) \int_{-y}^{R-y} f(y - x)f(x)dx + \int_0^{R+y} f(y - x)f(x)dx \right] dy +$$

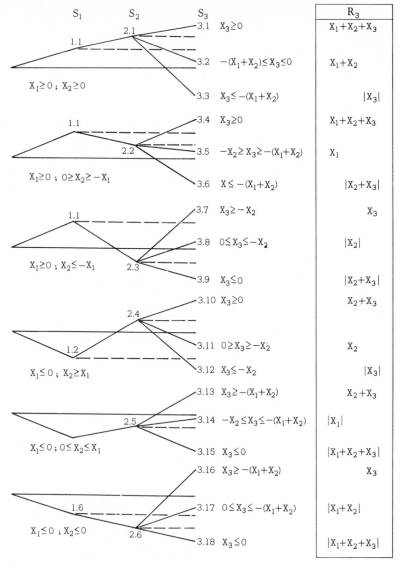

Figure 24. Eighteen cases for derivation of exact distribution of range, R_3, for any basic function, $f(x)$.

$$+ 4 \int_0^R f(x)dx \int_0^R f(R-x)f(x)dx + 2f(R)\left[\int_0^R f(x)dx\right]^2 \quad (39)$$

with $f(x)$ the probability density function of the basic variable x. The purpose of giving this expression in this study is to show how complex the exact probability density functions of range become even for a small n such as $n = 3$ and a symmetrical density function of x.

Another more complex asymmetric distribution $f(x)$ equation was used to find the exact distribution of R_3 of the Rhine River for a log-normal variable, where $\overline{K} = 1$ and $C_v = 0.159$. Figure 13 gives the probability density and distribution curves of R_3 as obtained by the numerical difference integration of the exact distribution.

There is no appreciable difference between the distribution functions of R_3 obtained from the empirical, data generation and analytical methods for the Rhine River's annual flows.

Future Development of the Analytical Method

It is expected that in time many properties of range and other variables associated with stochastic problems in design and operation of reservoirs will be solved by the analytical approach. This new approach is expected to solve problems for some basic distributions and dependence models of storage inflows. At present, the data generation method is filling this gap in knowledge and will be useful in checking the results of the analytical method. It can also be expected that the future trend will be to replace the empirical method in solving storage problems with the data generation method, and that further in the future the analytical method will replace them both in many instances.

Comparison of the Three Methods

The empirical method is acceptable as long as the data are sufficiently consistent, homogeneous and the sample is not too small. The data generation method is appropriate when the mathematical problems, with stochastic variables, are such that either the empirical method or the analytical method cannot produce the required answers. Assume the following problem: What should be the storage capacity of a reservoir in order to produce a safe water yield of a given probability for a period of fifty years, while there is only twenty years of observation data available? The problem may be solved by either the analytical or the data generation method. The latter method should be used whenever the problem is too complex to be successfully approached by an analytical treatment. The analytical method, with its developed formulas, is useful as reference in the analysis of many storage problems. The good approach may be to use all three methods alternately or in combination. This approach should be used when it is found that each of them can shed some light on a stochastic storage problem.

CHARACTERISTICS OF RANGE FOR OUTFLOW LINEARLY DEPENDENT ON STORAGE AND INFLOW

Storage Equations for Outflow Dependent on Reservoir Storage or Inflow

Putting $P - \bar{P} = p_t$, deviations of inflow from the mean inflow, and using the linear case of equation (17)

$$f(S) = \frac{\alpha S}{\bar{P}} \tag{40}$$

then equation (17) may be written as

$$\frac{dS}{dt} = p_t - \alpha S. \tag{41}$$

Putting in equation (18)

$$\varphi(P) = \beta \frac{p_t}{\bar{P}} \tag{42}$$

then equation (18) becomes

$$\frac{dS}{dt} = (1 - \beta)p_t \tag{43}$$

with α and β the proportionality coefficients.
Assuming in equation (19)

$$\phi(S, P) = \frac{\alpha S + \beta p_t}{\bar{P}} \tag{44}$$

then equation (19) becomes

$$\frac{dS}{dt} = (1 - \beta)p_t - \alpha S. \tag{45}$$

As $(1 - \beta)$ is a constant in each particular case, equation (45) can be written as

$$\frac{dS}{dt} = w_t - \alpha S \tag{46}$$

with equation (46) being a general linear case and w_t proportional to p_t.

Distribution of Range for the Outflow Linearly Dependent on Storage[2]

For a standard normal independent variable the expected value of range R_n is

$$E(R_n) = C_1 \sum_{t=1}^{n} \frac{\sqrt{\text{var } S_t}}{t} \tag{47}$$

with

$$C_1 = \sqrt{\frac{2}{\pi}}(1 + 3\alpha^2 e^{-2\alpha}) \tag{48}$$

and

$$\text{var } S_t = \frac{1 - e^{-2\alpha t}}{2\alpha} \tag{49}$$

where the main form is determined analytically, the constant C_1 by fitting the mathematical expression of equation (48) to the values obtained by the data generation method, and α is the proportionality parameter of equation (40).

The variance of range R_n is

$$\text{var } R_n = C_2 \sum_{t=1}^{n} \frac{\text{var } S_t}{t} \tag{50}$$

with

$$C_2 = 4\left(\ln 2 - \frac{2}{\pi}\right)(1 - 8e^{-20\alpha})\left(\frac{1 - e^{-2\alpha}}{2\alpha}\right). \tag{51}$$

For n between 2 and 50, and α between -0.04 and 2.00, the values of $\bar{R}_n$ of equation (47) are given in Figure 25, the values of variance R_n of equation (50) are given in Figure 26, and the values of the skewness coefficient of $\bar{R}_n$-distributions are given in Figure 27, as obtained by the data generation method.

These three figures and the expressions of equations (47) and (50) point out that the mean range, and by it the necessary storage for regulations, decreases with an increase of α, and increases at a faster rate for negative values of α. The same is valid for the variance of R_n.

Therefore, a compromise between large storage, as expressed by its range and good regulation, versus smaller storage, with less effective regulation, may be measured by the corresponding parameters α, $\bar{R}_n$, variance R_n, or similar factors.

In practice, the actual dependence of the outflows on inflows and/or storage is not linear. The second order approximations are a subject for

---

[2] This case was investigated by Melentijevich in a recent Ph.D. dissertation at Colorado State University [ref. 6].

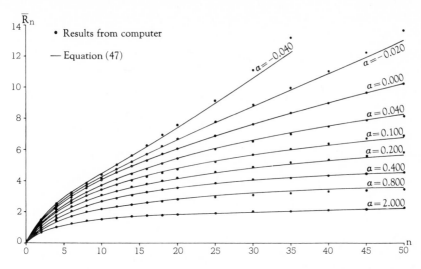

Figure 25. Mean of range for the case outflow is proportional to the storage volume, for various constraints of proportionality, α.

further investigations. The service function, or the relationship of outflow to any parameter or variable, can vary in large limits from simple to complex functions. The more complex the function, the more an investigation must depend on the data generation method to derive the stochastic properties of storage variables.

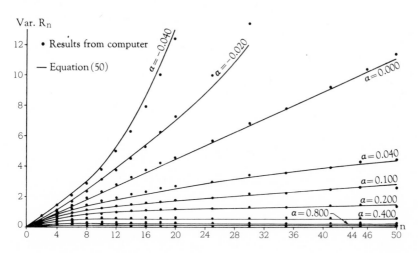

Figure 26. Variance of range for the case outflow is proportional to the storage volume, for various constants of proportionality, α.

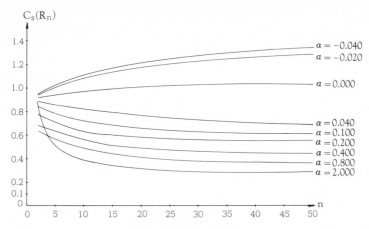

Figure 27. Skewness coefficient of range for the case outflow is proportional to the storage volume, for various constants of proportionality, α.

FINITE STORAGE

The Stochastic Variables of Interest in Design and Operation of Finite Storage Capacities

The general stochastic variable distributions of interest in practical storage problems are:

Probability distribution of water volumes stored in a reservoir at a given time, for given conditions;

Probabilities that a given storage volume is not exceeded in a given time;

Probability that the storage volume reaches either barrier (full or empty reservoir) in a given period;

Probability that the reservoir is full or empty at a given moment, under given conditions;

Probability of time-on that a reservoir stays full or of time-off that a reservoir stays empty for a given period, once either of the two barriers are reached;

Probability of water excess beyond demand, once the reservoir is full and stays full, for a time period, or probability of water excess for each case of full storage; the same probabilities for the water deficiency for empty reservoirs;

Probabilities of range, surplus, and deficit for the case of finite storage capacities; and similar problems;

Probabilities of water yields in a given time period, and so on.

Solution of Above Problems

At present, the most efficient way of solving the problems listed above is by the data generation method for given properties of inflows. The basic assumption is that the population characteristics of reservoir inflows are estimated from the best available information and estimating techniques. Attempts to solve the above problems by analytical means yielded very little success. There is a great need for solving some of them, at least for simple cases, by the analytical method.

REFERENCES

[1] Yevdjevich, V. M. *Fluctuations of Wet and Dry Years, Part II, Analysis by Serial Correlation.* Colorado State University Hydrology Paper No. 4. Fort Collins, Colo., June 1964.

[2] Roesner, Larry. "Analysis of Time Series of Monthly Precipitation and Monthly River Flows." Master's thesis, Colorado State University, July 1965.

[3] Feller, W. "The Asymptotic Distribution of the Range of Series of Independent Random Variables," *Annals of Mathematical Statistics,* Vol. 22 (September 1951), p. 427.

[4] Hurst, H. E. "Long-term Storage Capacity of Reservoirs," *American Society of Civil Engineers Transactions,* Vol. 116, No. 2447 (1951), p. 776.

[5] Anis, A. A., and Lloyd, E. H. "On the Range of Partial Sums of a Finite Number of Independent Normal Variates," *Biometrica,* No. 40 (1953).

[6] Melentijevich, M. J. "Characteristics of Storage when Outflow is Dependent upon Reservoir Volume." Ph.D. dissertation, Colorado State University, June 1965.

Analog Models for Stream Hydrology

*J. A. Harder**

The original analog model for river systems was the hydraulic model familiar to hydraulic engineers; it simulated, at a reduced and more manageable scale, the behavior of its prototype. More recently, models have appeared that depend for their operation on certain analogous relationships between the flow of water and the flow of electricity. Digital computers can be programmed to simulate or model river basins, too, and can in addition perform other accounting functions important to economic evaluations. In this paper I wish to discuss how analog models, or simulators, can be used in the study of the decision problems encountered in managing a large flood control system during times of emergency. My approach will be problem oriented; only after the problem has been defined is it useful to describe the methods available for its solution.

Flood control system management is only one aspect of the problem of lowering flood damages. Gilbert F. White discusses the role of flood plain regulation in his paper, which appears elsewhere in this book; and of course the Corps of Engineers has its ongoing program of constructing physical works for flood protection. Many billions of dollars have been spent in the United States for the construction of such physical works; in a moderate-size basin such as that of the Kansas River, costs running to several hundred million dollars are justified on the basis of flood control benefits. These engineering works might be called the hardware of flood

* Associate Professor of Hydraulic Engineering, University of California, Berkeley.

413

protection, and, using a term popular in the computer field, the plans for making the best use of these works might be called the software. Good software can be counted on to add value to the hardware, but in the case of flood control operation the funds available for this aspect of the job have been relatively small compared to the physical plant investment. In addition, until recently only the most general sort of planning has been considered feasible; we simply have not had the means to process the enormous amounts of information inherent in the response of a large river basin to a complex storm pattern in time to do very much good during an actual emergency.

THE RIVER BASIN AS AN INFORMATION PROCESSOR

Relative to its response to a storm pattern, the river basin may be considered a system: local watersheds respond to local rainfall patterns according to soil moisture, ground cover, average slope, etc., and contribute runoff to tributary streams. Here the drainage channels combine the flows, and waves of discharge are propagated to downstream areas on the main stem. Often the response has been modified by man: forests have been cleared, dams have been constructed across streams, levees alter the flood wave propagation velocity. But whatever its current configuration, if left alone or subjected only to rigid operating rules for reservoir releases, it is in theory a deterministic system. With enough information and computing power the response in terms of flood heights and consequent damages can be predicted for any of an infinite number of storm patterns. This sounds like a large order, but it is just what engineers have been doing to the best of their ability for a long time. An important part of the design of a dam is the determination of the inflow expected from a "design storm" based on the best available statistics of rainfall and runoff. The downstream channel is then designed on the basis of the expected release rates from the dam.

However, in the design process only a few storm patterns can be used out of the infinity of possibilities. After the design process is complete and the physical works are constructed, the response to each storm pattern as it occurs is then subject to further calculations so that within the physical limitations the best operation is carried out. This is not a simple problem, even for a single reservoir. Consider the position of a decision maker in the midst of a moderate storm as he plans the release rates from a reservoir: his first responsibility is the safety of the dam, but within that restriction he must make releases so that long-term damage to the downstream area is minimized. What information does he have on which to base his decisions? He knows the current inflow rate to his reservoir, and can project this for a day ahead with fair confidence; he knows how much of the reservoir volume remains vacant and available to take up the difference between inflows and releases; and if there are uncontrolled areas downstream between the dam and a potential damage area, he may know how much of a flood may be coming from such areas and regulate his own releases accordingly. The number of combinations and permutations of these few factors can be accommodated by a set of rules, charts, and nomograms in many cases. That is, there need be no ad hoc human judgment applied for this single reservoir problem. Indeed it has been argued convincingly that we should make such an operation completely routine in emergencies, for to introduce spur-of-the-moment decisions may be detrimental in the long run. Let me illustrate with an example: suppose that the amount of reservoir capacity is strictly limited, which is usually the case, and that we can make releases of whatever magnitude we wish independent of the reservoir level. This is not usually the case, but can be assumed here. Further assume that a moderate flood, having a 10 per cent probability of occurring in a given year, can be handled by making releases that will hold the flood levels downstream to a point where even minor damage will not occur. If this is true there is likely to be public demand for it.

However, no one can be sure at the midpoint of a flood whether it is going to be moderate, or whether another day's heavy rain will make it severe. If, indeed, the flood turns out to be severe, we may find that by holding back water in the early stages of the flood, we have run out of storage capacity just when it is needed, and that by the time the worst of the flood has arrived we have spent our capacity and must release the whole of the inflow to the downstream channel.

An operator who tries to do the most short-term good in this case is not only destroying his capacity to act effectively in the rarer but more damaging instances, but may contribute to encroachments on the flood plain. For people who see low-lying lands protected for relatively long periods of time may incline toward forgetfulness when real estate transactions are pending.

What is really needed at the wheel of the release gate is an operator instructed by a committee of expert gamblers who follow a plan—men who know how to trade short-term losses for long-term gains, and who are not afraid of incurring damaging flows in a given instance, if this is required by the plan, when 20-20 hindsight might indicate that they could have been avoided. And after such a plan has been devised, there would be no harm in turning over the detailed calculations to a computer.

For a computer can contribute a bit of magic to the decision-making process and further insulate the committee from the misplaced wrath of damaged citizens, and will as well give the operator greater peace of mind.

Two features of this simplified decision model stand out: First, the amount of information that must be handled is small, so that standard engineering calculations, perhaps carried out by a small computer, suffice to give an optimum. Second, since there are fixed rules, only one calculation need be carried out each time the hydrologic input data are updated. This will be a flood forecast for downstream areas.

MULTIRESERVOIR SYSTEMS

Were the effect of operating all reservoirs in a river basin strictly additive, the above ideas could be extended easily, perhaps with the help of linear programming. Unfortunately, the interactions among elements of the system cannot be neglected, and so no such simple methods are feasible. We could, of course, still consider operating with a fixed set of rules, thus simplifying the calculations so that even a small computer could keep up with the work of producing forecasts during the intervals between the times the hydrologic information is updated. By fixed rules, however, I mean that upstream reservoirs would be operated without regard to downstream and subsequent events, for to take these into account would involve a very complicated iteration procedure.

If we were to adopt a management method that does not take into account interactions, we would sacrifice many opportunities for achieving damage reduction through a joint operation of facilities.

Let a simple example illustrate the way interaction and joint operation can work. Assume that we can see, coming down the main stem of the river, a large flood wave that will arrive at our damage center in about two days. Meanwhile, a local tributary, equipped with a regulating reservoir, is threatening to produce damaging flows in about twelve hours' unless we use up storage volume to prevent its doing so. By taking all the upstream information into account, we can arrive at a reasonable estimate of and probable lower limit to the damage from the main stem flood acting alone.

By appropriately manipulating the tributary releases, we can allow an initial heavy flow from a local area in order to save storage space, even though this will produce damages that would not otherwise have occurred so soon. Later this storage space will be used to allow the tributary to be completely shut down as the main flood goes by. Thus, by taking our damages ahead of time, we may be able to reduce the over-all damages during the worst period.

In a large system there are likely to be many such opportunities during a flood emergency; however, each of them will be unique, and there is likely to be an astronomical number of possible situations. On an ad hoc basis, we may be able to take advantage of each as it comes along if we have a quick and sure way of predicting the result of several alternative courses of action and can try out one after another until we are satisfied that we have the best local operational plan. Because of the interaction of each part of the system with other parts, each change we make will require a completely new computation for the basin response. And on the basis of the over-all response, we will often find that a local optimum, or a number of local optima, do not add up to an over-all optimum.

Thus, if we wish to inject flexibility into the operational decisions, the computational problem is compounded three ways: (1) Because of the astronomical number of situations that can arise in a large basin subject to an almost infinite number of storm patterns, we must wait until the actual flood emergency to make our calculation. (2) Because of interactions, each decision in a part of the basin must be followed by a computation to acertain the resulting effects in other parts. (3) Because each decision must to some extent be an educated guess of what is best, many trials must be made in arriving at each decision.

So far we have been considering the flood management problem; now it is time to consider the appropriate methodologies for finding solutions. Since we are in effect asking that an optimum plan be discovered, it is natural to turn first to those methods that have been well developed for maximizing or minimizing a function (in the present case, flood damages) in the presence of restraints. Linear and dynamic programming are capable of analyzing problems of astonishing complexity—so long as the independent variables enter in a linear way. Non-linearity of a limited sort can also be handled through the device of piecewise linearization; however, when interactions and other non-linearities do enter, they compound the problem not in an additive way, as would the introduction of yet another linear variable, but in an exponential way. This is a morass into which we can only dimly see, but it appears that we could step up computer speed and memory capacity by a factor of a hundred and still not feel any more hopeful about the usefulness of these programming methods for the problem we are discussing.

An important factor in extending the number of variables is that each physical variable changes with time, and in the ordinary optimization schemes its value during each interval of time becomes a new mathematical variable. However, this new sequence is ordered, for later values cannot affect earlier ones; dynamic programming takes advantage of this fact. Simulation takes advantage of it too, in an implicit way, for it is a method of calculating at each instant the progress of phenomena that would take place in the prototype according to the parameters and inputs assumed.

Whatever the physical means of carrying out the simulation, there will be a branch point each time a decision must be made; and as in a chess game, the number of individual paths through all the branches quickly becomes astronomical. Thus it appears that introducing human judgment at critical points, interior to the simulation, will be very helpful; some would say essential.

This leads us towards the concept of man-machine interaction in which the machine provides the high-speed computing or simulation under the currently prescribed conditions and decisions, and the human operator provides the decisions that steer successive simulations towards an optimum.

Although no substitute for the intelligence part of this partnership is likely to be found, two ways can provide the simulation: (1) through a digital computer program, and (2) through an analog simulator. Before describing the analog simulators we have been developing at the Hydraulics Laboratory at the University of California, Berkeley, let me say a few words about using computers for the simulation. The advantage of a computer simulation is that incidental calculations of flood damage figures can be carried out alongside the flood routing and other simulation calculations. The disadvantage is that the communication between computer and man tends to be either slow and clumsy or else very expensive. It is not possible to conjecture which of the two methods is likely to be better for a given system in the future, for this would depend on many factors, such as the kind of computer and the input-output equipment that is available. Normally one expects that a rather large memory and fast arithmetic unit are needed, and these do not come cheaply.

The analog simulators the laboratory at Berkeley has been building are designed for very fast operation and for easy communication to and from the human operator. The Kansas River analog model, for example, completes sixty simulations per second; consequently, the output display on a cathode ray oscilloscope is presented without a flicker that is apparent to the eye.

The basic idea of such simulators, or analog models, is that they obey the same equations, relative to the electrical currents and voltages involved, as govern the actual prototype variables. In this case, electrical current corresponds to discharge, and voltage corresponds to water levels above a local datum. The analog, which is a large network of special

418

circuits, simulates all the pertinent properties of the flood control system: the ability to transmit waves having the correct celerity from one point to another, to attenuate these waves or to allow them to build up according to the channel properties, to store electrical charge in the way reservoirs store water, and to be subject to all the manipulations that the flood control system is subject to. This is quite an order, and has been achieved through a large number of ingenious circuit designs. The details of these circuits cannot be given in the space here available, but I will describe in a general way some of the components.

The flood control channels are divided into reaches that are about eight miles long; within this distance the channel properties are averaged, and these average values are used to set the river reach units of the analog. The channel conveyance, its ability to transmit a flow, and the channel storage are each introduced as functions of the local stage. This means that the non-linear properties are built in, so that the propagation speed and attenuation of flood waves are properly conditioned by the instantaneous water level in the reach.

When the flow encounters a reservoir simulation circuit, the discharge is retained and raises the simulated water level at that point. Again the stored volume is an adjustable non-linear function of the reservoir stage. Discharge from the reservoir is according to an operator-determined release schedule and is independent of the reservoir stage unless it is empty or completely full.

These channel units and reservoir units simulate the physical features of the flood control system. There is yet to be simulated the hydrologic inputs. At the beginning of each flood period, initializing circuits reset the reservoir levels and establish initial flow profiles in all the river reaches. This requires about eleven milliseconds. The ten-day flood period then commences, requiring five milliseconds of time in the simulator. During this ten-day period the rainfall excess reaching each of twenty-six subwatersheds is simulated by current generators that inject current according to schedule. Each of these current pulses simulates six hours' rainfall excess and is adjustable in magnitude from zero to an equivalent of four inches; there are thus forty pulses during the flood period. Each of these trains of pulses makes its way through a linear shaping network that has a transfer characteristic corresponding to the unit hydrograph for that subwatershed, and thence to the river reach units that comprise the main channels.

Flood routing then proceeds, modified where appropriate by reservoirs. The time history of water surface elevation or river discharge is then sampled and displayed on the oscilloscope tube face. Provision is made for displaying any two waveworms, which may be of either discharge or stage, from any two points in the system. The operator then can see displayed before him in almost instantaneous fashion the results of whatever reservoir release schedule he has established. He can increase by an arbitrary amount the release from an upstream reservoir during a particular six-hour period, note that the resulting flood wave will overtop a levee fifty miles downstream, and reduce the release back to its original amount, all in less time than it takes to describe his actions. Because the machine is so responsive, he can try out all kinds of schemes, and can just as quickly reject the unworkable ones.

INFORMATION NEEDED IN CONSTRUCTING
A SIMULATOR

From the above brief description it can be seen that there are two general kinds of input information: (1) the relatively permanent description of the channels and reservoir characteristics, and (2) the hydrologic inputs that change from storm to storm. Of the channel characteristics, the flooded area as a function of stage is relatively easily obtained from surface surveys; most of the time the areas involved are dry. This information must be updated whenever new levees constrict the floodplane. (A special circuit accommodates the situation where flood waters inundate a low-lying area protected by levees that may fail, by diverting current when the voltage exceeds a fixed amount and not allowing it to return to the river sections.)

Information about the discharge as a function of stage is easily obtained for low and moderate flows through standard river gauging techniques; however, the all-important extreme flows are both rare and hard to measure. Between such rare events, changes in the vegetation, that will be reflected in changes in the hydraulic friction, must be continuously monitored, and careful hydraulic calculations must be made of the resulting effect on the stage-discharge relationship. Those occasions when the floods are so extreme that measurements are both difficult and hazardous are golden opportunities for checking the results of such calculations. In this connection, we should consider the availability of helicopters equipped with dye bombs and cameras that can make spot measurements of surface water velocities.

Of the hydrologic inputs needed, the initial water surface levels and stream flows give little difficulty. The "rainfall excess" provided for each subwatershed is the difference between actual rain, determined from gauging records, and infiltration losses. Each of these is subject to the usual uncertainties. However, very often there is a river gauging station

420

at the downstream end of a subwatershed; this provides a check, albeit a day late, of the rainfall excesses; on the basis of the gauging station records the rainfall input is then readjusted on the rainfall pinboards. Thus the hydrologic inputs have three degrees of accuracy: the best is attained by the river gauging records; next are the records from actual measurements of rainfall; and least accurate are inputs of predicted rainfall.

APPLICATION TO THE KANSAS RIVER BASIN

The first application of the analog simulation technique described above has been in the Kansas River basin. The Kansas City District of the Army Corps of Engineers began supporting the development of analog work at the University of California, Berkeley, in 1959, where the work was under the direction of H. A. Einstein and myself. As completed in 1964, the analog simulates 7,000 square miles of the lower Kansas River basin plus all the reservoirs and other inflow points to the lower basin. Four reservoirs are included; each of these has its own inflow generator calibrated in cubic feet per second rather than in inches per six hours, but is otherwise programmed the same as a subwatershed. The effective flood period is ten days, which is appropriate to the flood travel times experienced in the basin.

A set of selector buttons enables the operator to quickly change his observations from one point on the river to another, and to monitor either discharge or stage. Because of the high repetition rate of sixty floods per second, there is no apparent lag between the time that a new release schedule or an updated hydrologic input is introduced and the time at which the operator perceives the result in terms of stage or discharge. Thus, the whole of whatever time delays occur between trials is used by the human operator as he ponders what new decision needs to be made in a search for an optimum operation.

The completed analog consists of a desk console that contains the output display, reservoir release controls, and other controls; an electronics cabinet with about twelve feet of rack space, and two rainfall tables, about five feet long, for the input. The machine contains some 3,000 transistors and diodes, 25,000 precision resistors, and 350 printed circuit cards. It cost the government under $200,000, a figure that is but a small fraction of the annual flood control benefits expected from its use. Thus, with mean annual damages in the basin on the order of $20 million, were the analog able to increase the flood fighting efficiency there by as little as 1 per cent, it would pay for its original cost each year.

CAN ANALOG SIMULATORS BE USED FOR BASIN PLANNING?

The obvious advantages of analog simulation for optimizing flood control operations have suggested that the idea might be extended to the problem of planning river basin management systems. Here the answer is not so clear, for one of the advantages of the analog—high-speed operation with continuously changing hydrologic inputs during emergencies —is not so applicable to the less hurried atmosphere of planning. On the other hand, it is true that the digital computer has the decided advantage of being able to do cost accounting on the side with no additional hardware or trouble. From the planning engineer's standpoint, the directness of the man-machine interaction using the analog is a great attraction, and more attention should be paid to incorporating this sort of feature into computers—down to the point where computer input is accomplished by easily visualized pinboard settings, and output is in the form of maps and graphs. To be sure, this kind of communication equipment is becoming available in connection with digital computers, but only at substantial costs.

CONCLUSIONS

In looking back over our experience with analog simulators at Berkeley, it seems to me that the most important conclusion has been that the human mind, with its capacity to integrate and hold together a vast amount of information and to formulate decisions on this basis, must be brought into interaction with computing machinery, of whatever sort, if we are to successfully optimize the operation of large systems. At one time we were dazzled by the seemingly inexhaustible capacity of the computer for enormously extended analysis. Now we realize that as the degree of system complexity goes up, the permutations rise exponentially, and some commonsense limitations must be made on the alternative possible paths to optimizing a solution. So far as I can see, there will never be a substitute for this function of the human mind; therefore we must search for ways that can accommodate this important part of the man-machine team as a real equal, and not as a second-class partner off at a desk somewhere. In this search the analog simulators have made a significant contribution.

Sea Water Conversion: Its Potential and Problems

J. W. McCutchan and *Walter M. Pollit**

Sea water conversion has always been one of the great "engineering dreams." In the search for large supplies of high-quality water, a great deal of research and development effort has focused on the large underground sources of brackish water that exist throughout the world. Most of the U.S. effort is being conducted under the aegis of what is loosely termed the Saline Water Conversion program. Brackish waters are considered to be those natural sources whose total dissolved solids content ranges from 1,500 ppm to 25,000 ppm. Most brackish waters being processed have less than 5,000 ppm salts, but at Roswell, New Mexico, the well water being used in the demonstration plant shows an analysis of 15,860 ppm.

In view of the many conversion plants now in operation throughout the world, one might say that, technologically, saline water conversion is here today. However, from an economic point of view, desalted water must still find its place in the total water complex of a particular locality.

The costs of water from a conversion plant are generally considered in four categories: capital (including the original cost of equipment), amortization, labor, and energy or fuel. Each process under study must first satisfy the criterion of "Will it work?"; then, if further development is to be justified, it must show a cost advantage in one or more of the above categories. The cost estimates derived in this way have been

* Respectively, Associate Professor of Engineering, and Senior Engineer, Department of Engineering, Saline Water Conversion Research Program, University of California, Los Angeles.

criticized because they do not include the cost of water distribution, but so long as one is fully aware of this limitation the value of the economic studies that are made is not impaired.

Progress in developing the various conversion processes is discussed in the annual reports of the Office of Saline Water [ref. 1]. These are essentially summary reports of the work being done by the OSW contractors, but they also contain references to work by industry and universities, such as the University of California, who independently issue their own reports [ref. 2, 3]. In addition, a number of articles appearing in professional journals have reviewed technological progress. The most recent, by Bell [ref. 4], highlights the progress made in the reverse osmosis process. Its basic conclusion is that "flash evaporation is the most economic process to date."

That there is no essential disagreement on the promise implied in Bell's conclusion is indicated by the following, quoted from the letter of transmittal from Assistant Secretary Kenneth Holum to the Secretary of the Interior, in the Secretary's 1964 report to the President on "A Program for Advancing Desalting Technology." [Ref. 5, p. 2.]

On the basis of today's technology, the cheapest water for large coastal communities will be produced by dual-purpose plants, coupling desalters with electric generators. The desalter will utilize a distillation process which must be improved and perfected. The cost of energy will continue to be one of the most important cost factors in a plant of this size. . . . Membrane processes hold great promise, particularly for brackish and minerally charged waters. Although the reverse-osmosis process is in the early stages of development, it is so promising that it merits accelerated efforts aimed at its improvement and perfection.

This report makes twelve specific recommendations, those most pertinent to this discussion having to do with the building of at least one dual-purpose, power-distilled water plant of approximately 50 million gallons per day. The plant is to be based on design studies to be undertaken in the next two years and is to be backed by the testing of full-size modules and components at a proposed West Coast test center. A comprehensive study of all phases of comparative water costs and needs is also proposed as a parallel study.

The classification of processes used for desalting water has gone through several phases. If one is interested in the broad approach, the first report, written in 1952 [ref. 6], contains many ideas based on physical phenomena. In the ensuing years these ideas have been shaken down to a point where they may be classified into three groups: distillation— liquid to a pure gas phase—then condense; freezing—liquid to a pure solid phase—then melt; processes where separation takes place from the liquid phase.

The household tea kettle with condensation of steam coming out the spout is probably the best example of simple distillation. Such a process takes approximately one thousand times the theoretical minimum energy requirement, since the bulk of the heat needed for evaporation is carried away by the condensing water and the balance is in the water left behind which contains the salts. The tea kettle also serves to illustrate the number one problem holding back low-cost converted water, namely, mineral deposit which forms on the walls of the tea kettle. These deposits known as "scale" will form in any type of evaporating equipment if the solubility limits are exceeded.

Sea water contains approximately 3.5 per cent inorganic solid material in solution. If, in the process of distillation, the water were evaporated to dryness, all dissolved material would deposit as solids. In distillation practice, however, sea water is rarely concentrated in the evaporator by a factor of more than three or four times. Of the total dissolved solids in sea water, less than 0.3 per cent is potentially capable of forming scale. Nevertheless, these minute quantities of insoluble material are capable of producing great engineering difficulties.

The principal components of scale from sea water distillation are calcium sulfate, calcium carbonate, and magnesium hydroxide. Small quantities of silica and alumina are sometimes found in scale deposits due to the turbidity of certain coastal waters, for instance, bays and river outlets. A summary of the solubility of scale-forming compounds in pure water has been compiled by Partridge [ref. 7], and is shown graphically in Figure 1. Recent research is directed toward establishing the reliability of using solubility data in the prediction of the scaling threshold of any feed water of known chemical composition when this water is to be desalted by an evaporation process.

DISTILLATION PROCESSES

Since single-effect distillation would be ruled out on the basis of energy costs alone, methods of achieving greater thermal efficiency must be devised. Multiple-effect distillation has long been utilized. First, evaporators were built of the submerged tube type; that is, the tubes were submerged in sea water and the steam was condensed on the inside of the tubes. The steam produced in the first effect heats the second which produces steam to heat the third, and so on, so that a 10-effect evaporator would ideally use only one-tenth the energy of a single-effect evaporator.

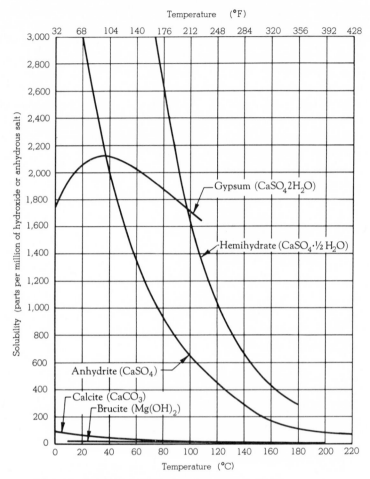

Figure 1. Solubility of scale-forming compounds in pure water.

A 12-effect distillation cycle was chosen as the first demonstration plant of the federal program, at Freeport, Texas. This design is known as the long-tube vertical system and utilizes the falling film principle for the evaporating surface. Figure 2 is a cross-section of one of the effects. The contract for plant design was awarded to W. L. Badger and Associates, and that for plant construction to the Chicago Bridge and Iron Company. One of the primary objectives of the demonstration plant program was to obtain performance data on actual plants and their operating costs. Annual reports are available for the Freeport plant, prepared by the Stearns-Roger Manufacturing Company, the operating contractors for the

426

plant [ref. 8]. The plant experienced some difficulties with corrosion and scale control. McIlhenny described a study of the operating cycle in relation to scale formation in a paper presented at a 1965 meeting of the American Chemical Society [ref. 9]. From this, it appears that the plant stayed out of calcium sulfate hemihydrate trouble by holding the temperature down to 230° F., and out of gypsum trouble by maintaining a concentration factor below 3. It has recently been reported that this plant is now operating at a top temperature of 270° F. with an output of

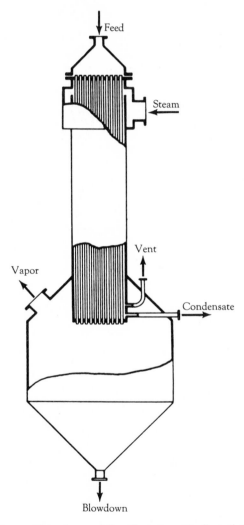

Figure 2. Cross-section of one of the effects in a 12-effect distillation cycle.

1,140,000 gallons per day. If reliable, scale-free operation can be maintained, this process will improve its competitive position.

The multi-stage flash process was chosen for demonstration at Point Loma, California. This plant was jointly sponsored by the U.S. Department of the Interior and the California Department of Water Resources. The Fluor Corporation served as the architect-engineering firm and Westinghouse Electric Company constructed the plant. Burns and Roe, Inc. were awarded the contract for management, operation, and maintenance. In flash distillation the term "multi-stage" is used rather than "multi-effect." The use of the word "stage" in place of "effect" is to differentiate between the case where the sea water is heated under pressure prior to entering a series of flash chambers or stages, and the case where the vapor of one effect is used to boil water in the next effect. The Point Loma flash plant had thirty-six stages and was operated successfully in California from March 1962 until March 1965, when it was dismantled and shipped to Guantanamo Bay, Cuba. The theory and practice of multi-stage flash evaporators has been discussed by Frankel [ref. 10], and Brice and Townsend [ref. 11]. A simplified diagram is shown in Figure 3. Ambient sea water is heated to about 200° F. in the brine heater under non-boiling conditions and then transferred to a series of flashing chambers. In each chamber a portion of steam is "flashed off" and condensed, thereby reducing the pressure in the system and the temperature of the brine. The plant was designed to operate normally at 212° F. and experimentally at 250° F. with a brine discharge temperature of 90° F. The plant was normally operated in a range of con-

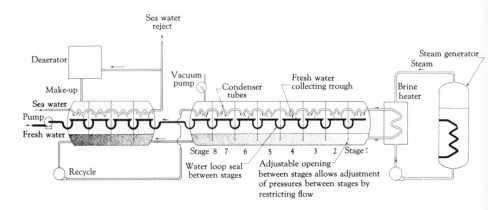

Figure 3. Diagram of a multi-stage flash evaporator.

centration factors between 1.5 and 2.0, but in some tests of short duration concentration factors as high as 2.9 were achieved.

Other flash plants in the news are the Harvey Aluminum Company's 750,000-gpd flash plant at St. Croix, Virgin Islands, built by Westinghouse. This plant has a unique feature—the tubing and some of the plates will be made of titanium, which should prove highly successful from the corrosion and erosion point of view and provide meaningful cost data on the use of titanium in flash evaporators.

Baldwin-Lima-Hamilton Corporation is building a 16-stage, 25,000-gpd flash distillation plant to operate at the Wrightsville Beach Test Station to study scale control. BLH has already made valuable contributions to scale control in tests on their 10,000-gpd unit, and additional information is anticipated from this new unit which is designed to operate up to 350° F. Data should also be available shortly on the 1,000,000-gpd flash plant built by BLH for Israel. This water plant is coupled with power generation and is termed a Dual-Purpose Plant. The plant was commissioned in April 1965 and is now undergoing the acceptance tests [ref. 12]. The 100,000-gpd Cleaver-Brooks unit, operated by the Edison Company of Southern California at Mandalay Beach, California, has been moved to Catalina Island where it is helping to supply the water needs of the resort community of Avalon.

The vapor compression process illustrated in Figure 4 was chosen as the third distillation process, for demonstration at Roswell, New Mexico, in the hope of realizing the advantage of the relatively low energy requirement of that process. This plant, dedicated in July 1963, has been plagued with maintenance problems, and until a reasonable degree of reliable operation is achieved it will not be possible to make accurate cost estimates. Ion-exchange equipment was installed to remove 75 per cent of the Ca^{++} and Mg^{++} ions with the intention of regenerating the ion exchange bed with the concentrated brine. This ion exchange process was reviewed in a recent paper by Crits, McIntire, and Raffel [ref. 13]. It now appears that a higher percentage reduction in Ca^{++} and Mg^{++} is desirable as well as a thorough study of other scaling components, namely, silica. Greater reliability of the mechanical components, such as the compressor, would help to make this process more competitive.

The best performance record of a vapor compression still known to the authors was achieved by a 15,000-gpd unit built by the Mechanical Equipment Company in New Orleans. This design has gone in the opposite direction from most thinking on thermodynamic cycles. The unit boils the water at 109° F., a relatively low temperature, utilizing a specially designed forced circulator and operating at a relatively high brine blowdown rate. It is reported to operate free of scale. We have no

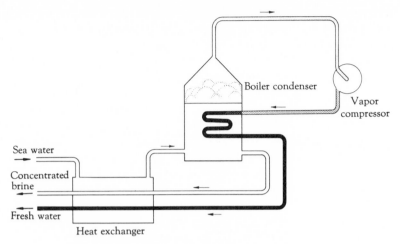

Figure 4. Schematic of the vapor compression process.

report on mechanical maintenance, but if operation is scale-free and the mechanical components show reasonable maintenance, the type of design should be thoroughly studied.

Since Roswell is an inland city, it serves to highlight the third problem following scale control and mechanical reliability. That is the disposal of the waste brine. Few ideas have been proposed to solve this problem. At present, probably the most acceptable method is that chosen for Roswell, namely, an evaporation pond which has an impermeable liner so that the salts will not re-enter the soil and further increase the problems in the natural underground water storage. The University of New Mexico is currently studying the performance of the 90-acre pond at Roswell so that this evaporation process can be operated in an optimum manner.

A word of caution is in order, even though it is based on experience with a water-softening operation rather than with demineralization. An interesting article by Lawrance [ref. 14] on the new water system at Lompoc, California, includes a photograph illustrating what happens when the evaporating ponds do not operate optimally. The photograph shows a severe problem of disposal of the calcium carbonate precipitate in an evaporation pond. Problems such as these give added arguments for seaside plants.

A number of other designs for distillation equipment have been proposed, such as wiped-film evaporating surfaces, secondary heat-transfer media, vapor reheat, diffusion stills, and rotating stills. A promising approach, which is receiving considerable attention at present, is to devise designs that will include the advantages of a multi-stage process and

multiple-effect designs in a single plant. The proposed replacement demonstration plant for San Diego, when built, will be one physical realization of this approach.

FREEZING PROCESSES

Theoretically, a single freezing should produce potable water from salt
water. However, ice frozen from saline solution occludes or entraps brine
between the interstices of the ice crystallites and some brine is also
adsorbed on their surfaces. Thus, one of the major problems to be solved
before this process can be considered competitive is how to develop
satisfactory methods of separating the ice crystals from mother liquor.
Research sponsored by the Office of Saline Water and the work of others
has shown that several separation procedures are technically feasible.

Figure 5 is an early schematic of the freezing process. It is shown here
in place of more recent cycles because of the clear way in which it illustrates the freeze separation principle. In addition, it illustrates the separa-

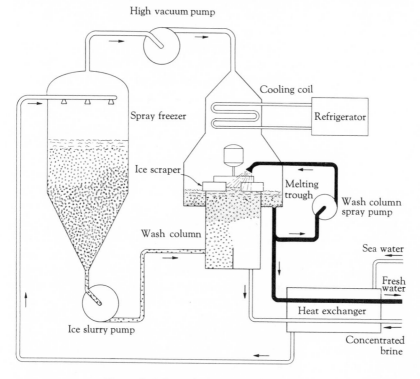

Figure 5. Schematic of the freezing process.

tion of the brine from the ice crystals by use of a wash column. Hydraulic forces are used to move a porous bed of ice upward while wash water moves downward and carries away the salt. At present this system of cleaning the ice still appears to be most promising. A 200,000-gpd freezing pilot plant, built at Wrightsville Beach, North Carolina, by Struthers Scientific and International Corporation, was completed in June 1964. This plant employs the Struthers-Umano controlled-crystallization freezing process, which uses direct contact heat exchange with a secondary refrigerant. The ice and brine are separated in a centrifugal separation process.

The advantages of freezing processes are, first, that low energy requirements hold promise of lower cost and, second, that low-temperature operation minimizes the maintenance problems associated with scale and corrosion.

Other developments using the freezing process have been reported by the Carrier Corporation, Blaw-Knox Company, and the new plant now in operation in Elath, Israel, which was built by Colt Industries, Inc. through its subsidiary company, Fairbanks Morse, Inc.

The hydrate process is similar to freezing, but is listed by the Office of Saline Water as a chemical process since it involves a hydrating agent such as propane or one of the chlorofluromethanes to form an insoluble hydrate. The hydrate crystals must then be separated and washed and the hydrate decomposed so that the hydrating agent can be recovered.

ELECTRODIALYSIS

The electrodialysis process is probably our best example of the results of research and development effort in the desalting field. It has come from bench scale models in 1952 to many installations of significant size, such as those at Webster, South Dakota, and Buckeye, Arizona. The latter, built by Ionics, Inc., has a capacity of 650,000 gpd, reporting water costs as low as 50¢/1,000 gallons when operating on a feed water of 1,800 ppm [ref. 15].

Electrodialysis is still the leader in the brackish water field. It is the process of ion transport through alternately spaced cation and anion membranes in which the driving force is an electrical field. Figure 6 is a schematic of the system. Recent advances are the availability of less expensive membranes with greater stability and polarization control by a current pulsing technique. One of the greatest problems is keeping the membrane surface clean. Prefiltering and the addition of chemicals to the feed brine have kept plants operating, but a thor-

432

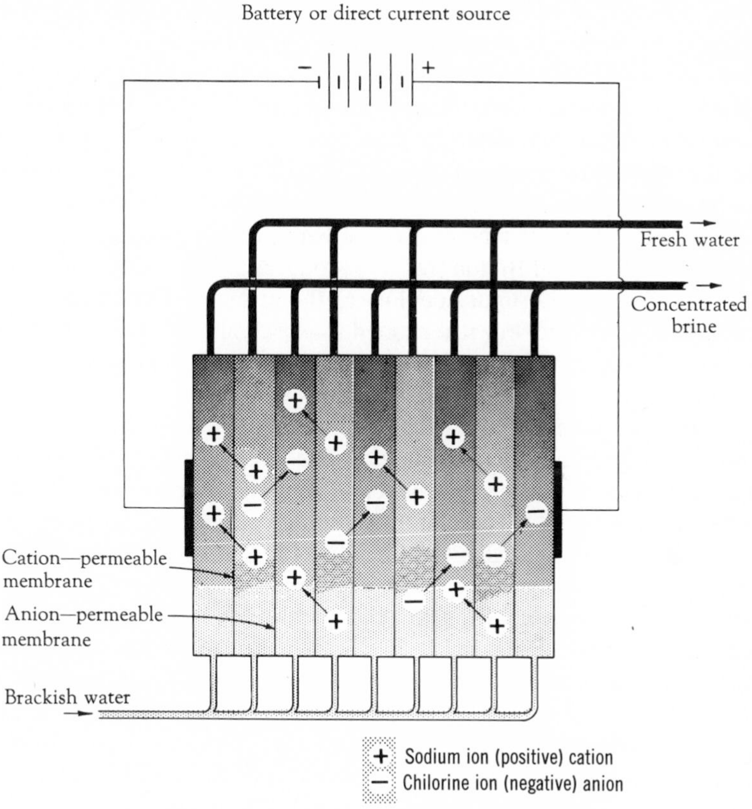

Figure 6. Schematic of the electrodialysis process.

ough study of feed water conditions is a most important step in planning the installations. A major advantage of the electrodialysis process for treating brackish water lies in the fact that the energy consumed is proportional to the salt removed. Also, the process is controlled to produce a water that meets drinking-water standards of less than 500 ppm, yet does not present the problems associated with handling distilled water of less than 50–25 ppm.

The Bureau of Reclamation's Division of Research at Denver, Colorado, prepared the specifications for the Webster, South Dakota, plant. They have continued under an OSW-sponsored program to study, evaluate, and develop electrodialysis equipment and membranes. Seven pilot plants with different membranes and cell designs have been tested and evaluated.

REVERSE OSMOSIS

The term "osmosis" is used to describe spontaneous flow of water into a solution, or from a dilute to a more concentrated solution when separated from each other by a semipermeable membrane. In order to obtain fresh water from saline water, the flow must be reversed from the solution into the fresh water stream. Hence, the term "reverse osmosis." Figure 7 illustrates the principle.

The most successful membranes are being made of cellulose acetate. The work of Reid and Breton [ref. 16] produced the first published report aimed at fundamental understanding of the cellulose acetate type semipermeable membrane, but it remained for Loeb and Sourirajan [ref. 17] in 1960 to formulate the casting solution, containing magnesium perchlorate, which led to desalination membranes with high enough flow to be commercially interesting. In a recent report Manjikian [ref. 18] explains how this casting solution formulation has been simplified to a three-component system: cellulose acetate, acetone, and formamide. The new casting solution can be cast at room temperature and the membrane properties are more reproducible. Because of recent advances, enthusiasm is high—as high, in fact, as it was for electrodialysis ten years ago. However, one must be careful not to expect too much too soon. Membrane surface fouling problems are already being encountered, so that questions of maintenance records and the membrane life will have to be answered for reverse osmosis membranes just as they have for electrodialysis membranes. Nevertheless, designers are ingenious and a number of units are now being tested. The University of California, Los Angeles, first reported tests of a 500-gpd flat plate unit in 1962 [ref. 19], and more recently Aerojet-General [ref. 20] has reported on the design and

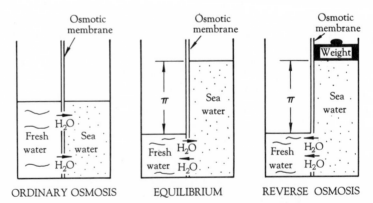

Figure 7. Illustrating the principle of reverse osmosis.

construction of a desalination pilot plant. The General Atomic Division of General Dynamics is working on a spiral wound unit [ref. 1, pp. 42–43].

On June 10, 1965, Sidney Loeb, of the University of California, Los Angeles, announced a new tubular unit which is now operating at Coalinga, California. The news release stated, ". . . the membrane, four-thousandths of an inch thick is cast in the form of a tube, wrapped in two layers of filter paper and nylon net material and inserted into a copper tube 10 feet long and one inch in diameter. Along each tube are small holes, three inches apart, from which the purified water flows." The unit currently has fifty-six tubes in series and is producing 3,000–4,000 gpd. The conversion process lowers the salt content of the town's brackish water from 2,500 to under 500 ppm, the recommended standard for drinking water.

Since the city of Coalinga is actually using this water to augment that produced by the 28,000-gpd electrodialysis unit built by Ionics, Inc., this is an important development and its performance will be watched with great interest.

USE OF NUCLEAR ENERGY

This report would not be complete if it did not comment on the use of nuclear energy. The Oak Ridge National Laboratory is taking an active part in this program. Dr. K. Kraus and his group are doing basic re-search, but by far the most discussed proposal has been the plan of coupling a nuclear reactor with a power and water plant, described by Hammond in 1962 [ref. 21], but support for this idea has been cautious. Two articles from engineers outside the Atomic Energy Commission have recently been published. Lewis [ref. 22] in December 1964 reported costs of 0.283¢ to 0.358¢ per 1,000 gallons based on a capacity of 50 million gpd. Skinner [ref. 23], discussing this question in June 1965, concluded that a large-size desalting unit and reactor should be built so that actual costs can be obtained. He states: "It is the author's belief that Southern California's future water supply—that is after 1990, the pre-dicted end of the period of sufficiency of the current State water project —will come from a combination of desalting plants and additional importations."

Finally, mention should be made of a study undertaken by the Bechtel Corporation of San Francisco under the joint sponsorship of the Depart-ment of the Interior, the Atomic Energy Commission, and the Metro-politan Water District of Southern California. The resulting report [ref. 24], issued in 1965, indicates that fresh water can be produced from the sea at a cost of 22¢–30¢ a thousand gallons. This is based on the use of nuclear fuel to produce 1,800 megawatts of electricity and 150 million gallons of fresh water daily. Cost of such a combination plant is estimated at $300 million.

REFERENCES

[1] U.S. Department of the Interior, Office of Saline Water. *Saline Water Conversion Report for 1964*. Washington, 1965.

[2] University of California, Berkeley and San Diego campuses. *Saline Water Conversion Research—1964 Progress Report*. Sea Water Conversion Laboratory Report No. 65–1, 1965.

[3] *Saline Water Conversion Progress Summary*. Department of Engineering Report No. 65–1, WRC No. 95. University of California, Los Angeles, September 1961.

[4] Bell, D. A. "Review of Desalination Processes," *Chemical and Process Engineering*. London, March 1965.

[5] U.S. Department of the Interior. *Program for Advancing Desalting Technology*. Stewart L. Udall, Secretary, Report to the President, September 22, 1964.

[6] U.S. Department of the Interior. *Demineralization of Saline Waters: A Compendium of Existing and Potential Separation Processes, Phenomena, and Energy Sources with Discussion and Literature References*. Report PB 161373, October 1952.

[7] Partridge, E. P. *Engineering Research Bulletin No. 15*. University of Michigan, Department of Engineering Research, 1930.

[8] U.S. Department of the Interior. *Second Annual Report, Saline Water Conversion Demonstration Plant, Freeport, Texas*. Report PB 181681, R&D 100, March 1964.

[9] McIlhenny, W. F. "Calcium Sulfate Scale in Sea Water Evaporators." American Chemical Society Division of Water, Air and Waste Chemistry, Symposium on Saline Water Conversion. Detroit, Mich., April 4–9, 1965, p. 42.

[10] Frankel, A. "Flash Evaporation for the Distillation of Sea Water," *Proceedings, Institute of Mechanical Engineers*, Vol. 174, No. 7 (1960).

[11] Brice, D. B., and Townsend, C. R. "Sea Water Conversion by the Multistage Flash Evaporation Method," in *Advances in Chemistry Series No. 27*. Washington: American Chemical Society, 1960, p. 147.

[12] Vilentchuk, I. "Survey of Water Desalination in Israel," *First International Symposium on Water Desalination Proceedings*. Washington, October 3–9, 1965.

[13] Crits, G. J., McIntire, W. Y., and Raffel, D. L. "Ion Exchange Softening of Brackish Feedwater for Saline Water Conversion Plant at Roswell, New Mexico." American Chemical Society Division of Water, Air and Waste Chemistry, Symposium on Saline Water Conversion, Detroit, Mich., April 4–9, 1965, p. 160.

[14] Lawrance, Charles H. "Quality Improvement for Lompoc, California," *Journal of American Water Works Association,* May 1965.

[15] Hammer, W. George, and Katz, William E. "Electrodialysis in Buckeye," *Journal of American Water Works Association,* Vol. 56, pt. 2, December 1964.

[16] Reid, C. E., and Breton, E. J. "Water and Ion Flow Across Cellulosic Membranes," *Journal of Applied Polymer Science,* Vol. 1, No. 2 (1959).

[17] Loeb, S., and Sourirajan, S. "Sea Water Demineralization by Means of an Osmotic Membrane," Sea Water Conversion II, *Advances in Chemistry Series 38.* Washington: American Chemical Society, 1963.

[18] Manjikian, S. "Semipermeable Desalination Membranes from Organic Casting Solutions." UCLA Department of Engineering Report No. 65–13, March 1965.

[19] Loeb, S., and Milstein, F. "Design, Development, and Testing of a 500 Gallon Per Day Osmotic Sea Water Desalination Cell," *UCLA Department of Engineering Report No. 62–52,* November 1962.

[20] U.S. Department of the Interior. *Design and Construction of a Desalination Pilot Plant* (A Reverse Osmosis Process), by Aerojet-General Corp. Office of Saline Water Report PB 181574, R&D 86, January 1964.

[21] Hammond, R. P. "Large Reactors May Distill Water Economically," *Nucleonics,* Vol. 20 (December 1962).

[22] Lewis, George T. "Nuclear Energy for Water Desalination," *Power,* December 1964.

[23] Skinner, Robert A. "Sea Water Conversion Study in Southern California," *Journal of American Water Works Association,* June 1965.

[24] Bechtel Corporation. *Engineering and Economic Feasibility Study for a Combination Nuclear Power and Desalting Plant* (3 vol., also summary report). Sponsored by Metropolitan Water District of Southern California; U.S. Department of the Interior, Office of Saline Water; U.S. Atomic Energy Commission. December 1965. (Available from Clearinghouse for Federal Scientific and Technical Information, National Bureau of Standards, U.S. Department of Commerce, Springfield, Va.)

MAJOR RESEARCH PROGRAMS AND NEEDS

The Harvard Program: A Summing Up

Maynard M. Hufschmidt*

In 1959, Arthur Maass and I presented the first public report of the Harvard Water Program to a national audience at the first Western Resources Conference at Boulder (3).[1] It is particularly appropriate, therefore, that the seventh Western Resources Conference should have been the forum for a summing up of ten years of work at Harvard on water resource planning and development. The Harvard Water Program has completed the second phase of its work and is now embarking on the third phase. This paper reports on the first two phases and refers briefly to plans for phase three.

Genesis of the Program. The Program owes its existence to a fortunate combination of circumstances at Harvard in 1955. Several faculty members in political science, economics, and engineering had special research interests in water resource planning and were disposed to work together in pursuit of their interests; the Graduate School of Public Administration (Littauer) offered a means of combining advanced training of public servants with research on problems of public policy and administration; a research associate with long experience in the public service was available to work with the faculty group; and, of major importance, federal water resource agencies were willing to support a combined re-

* Professor of City and Regional Planning and of Environmental Sciences and Engineering, University of North Carolina.
[1] References in parentheses are to publications included in the Bibliography of Selected Publications of Members of the Harvard Water Program, at the end of this paper.

search and training program by releasing experienced staff members to spend an academic year at the Littauer School for advanced training and participation in a research seminar on water resource planning. Finally, the Rockefeller Foundation was favorably disposed to support the Program.

The broad multidisciplinary approach taken by the faculty group in 1955 is revealed in the following quotation from the application to the Rockefeller Foundation for a grant of funds:

> This is . . . . a program of research and advanced training for public servants in the field of water resources planning and development. It is proposed to conduct concentrated research in a water resources Seminar on problems of the design and operation of multiple purpose systems of water resources developments. The basic objective will be to test the validity and utility of certain new methods and techniques of economic, engineering, and governmental analysis. The problems of system design and operation will be related to broader economic data, overall engineering design and economic analysis, public policies, and legal and institutional factors affecting water resources development.

This proposal initiated the first sustained program of multidisciplinary research on water resource planning in this country. Significantly, the research undertaken over the entire ten-year period has conformed remarkably well to the initial statement of objective and content.

The first phase—1955–61. After one year of preparatory work, the research seminar began operation in September 1956, and continued for three academic years. Another two years were used to complete the research and report the results. Publication of the report in February 1962 (7) brought this first phase to a close.

The research and training seminar in water resource system design was the central focus of the work during this period. Public servants with many years of experience in water resource planning in federal and state water resource agencies participated with faculty, graduate students, and special consultants. Emphasis was on basic research.

The second phase—1961–65. Following completion of the basic research under the Rockefeller grant, the faculty group turned to the testing of methodology and techniques on realistic planning cases, as well as continuing work on basic research. Support was provided by the U.S. Army Corps of Engineers, U.S. Public Health Service, and Resources for the Future, Inc.

Unlike the first phase, there was no regularly scheduled research seminar with full-time participants from the water resource agencies. Instead, the faculty group and graduate students met from time to time, sometimes with key staff members from the federal agencies. However, a new teaching seminar on public investment planning was started in September 1962; this course has now become a regular fixture at Littauer, and a comparable course is being taught also at the University of North Carolina.

Also, with support of training grants from the Public Health Service, the Ph.D. program in environmental sciences and engineering in the Graduate School of Arts and Sciences was expanded and reformulated to include work in systems analysis and in the social sciences.

The third phase—1965– . With the completion on June 30, 1965 of the research contract with the Corps of Engineers, the Harvard Water Program is entering its third phase. A major new program of research will begin on the economics of water supply and water quality for a regional system. It will address the problems associated with using a combination of economic projection models, river system simulation models, and hydraulic models (involving both water quantity and quality) in the optimal solution of water resource investment and management problems, especially as they relate to municipal and industrial water supply and water quality management. The Delaware River system will be used as the test region; full advantage will be taken of the research results, experience, and data on the Delaware River system, which were obtained from earlier research at Harvard. In addition, research and training will continue in operations research and systems analysis for water quality management, and the course in public investment planning will continue to be taught.

From the very start of the research seminar in 1956, four faculty participants (Arthur Maass, the chairman, a political scientist; Robert Dorfman, an economist; Harold A. Thomas, Jr., a civil and sanitary engineer; and myself, public administration) have worked together. Others have been associated for extended periods: Gordon M. Fair, a sanitary engineer, 1956–61; Otto Eckstein, an economist, 1956–58; Stephen A. Marglin, an economist, since 1958; Myron B. Fiering, an engineering scientist, since 1959. This continuity has been a major source of strength to the Program.

THE RESEARCH: RESULTS AND APPLICATION

First Phase

Because research results of the first phase were reported rather fully in *Design of Water-Resource Systems* (7), only a summary is presented here. The scope of the work was broad, covering the complete planning process from establishing basic objectives to the detailed technical studies leading to final selection of a system design. Among the major research topics covered in the book are the following:

1. Multiple-objective functions. The multiple-dimension nature of the social welfare function was emphasized, and the several means of dealing with multiple-objective functions were presented; for example, national income and income redistribution objectives could be handled in a composite objective function. This concern with multiple objectives turned out to have practical consequences for U.S. water resource planning, as is shown later in this paper.

2. Discount rate and opportunity cost. A consistent position was developed on use of concepts of social rate of time discount and opportunity costs in public investment planning. This, too, continues to be an important issue in public investment planning, as is demonstrated in Kenneth J. Arrow's paper, elsewhere in this volume.

3. Public investment decision-model. The complete structure of a public investment decision-model for water resources was developed, which incorporated the notions of objective function, design criteria, cost-input functions, benefit-output functions, technological or production functions, and dynamic analysis, and which merged political, economic, and engineering aspects. This model provided the framework for research on specific aspects of water resource planning.

4. System planning techniques. Major work was on simulation and mathematical (analytical) models. As many readers will recall, a simplified river basin system—with realistic cost, benefit, and production function data and the hydrologic record of the Clearwater basin, Idaho—was used to test both conventional planning methods (those then in use by the water resource agencies) and new techniques that were suggested or devised. One such technique was simulation on the high-speed digital computer, combined with procedures for systematically searching the domain of alternative system designs to map the "net benefit response surface," and so, hopefully, to identify the "optimal" design. Perhaps of greatest significance was the development of a workable model and technique for generating synthetic streamflow sequences from the historic record of flows. This involved statistical analysis followed by use in the model of important statistical characteristics, such as mean, standard deviation, skewness, and correlation coefficients.

Two points are of significance here: (a) the synthetic streamflow technique was not practicable until computers of high speed and capacity were available; and (b) the need for long traces of hydrology was not fully appreciated until complex simulation models were constructed. After all, it is not a very exciting prospect to build an elaborate simulation model and computer program, and then to run the simulation with only a short trace of hydrologic events—an actual record of twenty-five to thirty years, for example. With simulation, one wants to examine the outcomes of trials using many different patterns of hydrologic occurrence, operating rules and the like.

The second class of technique examined was mathematical or analytical models. Linear and non-linear programming had been developed and refined by applied mathematicians and experts in operations research, and it was a great temptation and challenge to apply these methods to water resource design problems. Here, computer capacity soon became a severe limitation. Even with drastic simplifications in setting up the design problem, only small systems involving one or two reservoirs and purposes could be handled by the 1959 vintage of standard computer— the IBM 704 class. Nonetheless, much was learned about application of optimizing models to design of water resource systems.

5. Governmental decision-model. Finally, there was presented a normative model of political decision making on public investment in a constitutional-democratic state such as the United States, including applicability of the model to problems of water resource planning and investment.

The first phase produced a substantial volume of research which was not reported in the book. A major theoretical paper was produced by Peter Steiner, involving a conceptual scheme for selecting alternative investments in the water resources field (2). Steiner formulated the first version of this model while participating in the Program's water resources seminar in 1957–58. His model had great influence on subsequent research in the seminar. Otto Eckstein's 1961 survey article on public expenditure criteria (6) was based in part on his participation in the seminar. Also, the first draft of Donald Farrar's monograph on the investment decision under uncertainty (8) was written during his association with the Program.

An opportunity arose in 1961 for application of research results to actual decision making. Early in the Kennedy Administration, the writer was asked to serve as chairman of a panel of consultants to the U.S. Bureau of the Budget to advise on changes in federal standards and criteria for formulating and evaluating water resource investment projects. Other members of the panel were Julius Margolis, economist, then at the University of California at Berkeley, and John V. Krutilla, economist with Resources for the Future, Inc. Both had solid reputations in water resource economics. The staff assistant was Stephen Marglin, whose economic research to that date had been done with the Harvard Water Program. The panel produced a report to the Director of the Budget (5) which was referred to a special interagency group established to formulate new standards and criteria. While it is difficult to trace the precise impact of the panel's report on the final recommendations of the interagency group [ref. 1], the decision process was influenced significantly by the work of the panel.

Finally, three items of research which were first-phase products were published in 1963. All by Stephen Marglin, these were his Harvard Senior Honor's Thesis on dynamic investment planning (18) and two major papers on the social rate of time discount (19) and the opportunity costs of public investment (20). These reports present in detail research results that had been given only in summary form in the early chapters of *Design of Water-Resource Systems* (3).

Second Phase

Unlike the research results of the first phase, most results of the second phase have not yet been published. Some of the results are discussed in papers included in this volume; others will soon be published as journal articles and monographs, as described below; still others exist only in the form of a report to the U.S. Army Corps of Engineers which may choose to reproduce all or parts of it for general distribution.

Consistent with the concern for application, second-phase research was focused on a specific test area—the Delaware River basin. Detailed data were obtained from the Corps of Engineers, including the files and work sheets of the comprehensive survey of the basin which had just recently been completed. (See [ref. 2] for report of survey.) This information on the Delaware was supplemented by materials on the Passaic River basin, New Jersey; Potomac River basin; Texas River basins; Southeast River basins centering on Georgia; and the Snake River basin.

The research accomplished in the second phase is in three broad areas:

a) Setting objectives and deriving design or planning criteria for use in field-level planning;

b) Applying design criteria in field-level planning, including problems of concept and measurement in deriving costs and benefits for the systems under study; and

c) The process of field-level planning, including the techniques of analysis applicable to complex systems.

Objectives and Design Criteria.   Under leadership of Arthur Maass, three major studies were undertaken:

"Decision-making for Public Investment in Water Resources Development in the United States," by David C. Major;

"Passaic Valley Flood Control," by Steven A. Dola; and

"Benefit-Cost Analysis: Its Relevance to Public Investment Decisions," by Arthur Maass (39).

The Major study (Part 4 of the Harvard Water Program's 1965 Report to the U.S. Army Corps of Engineers) investigated the ability of the U.S. governmental process to generate useful statements of objectives and to derive workable detailed criteria from these statements of objectives. Major also investigated the objectives and criteria actually used by Corps planners in the recent surveys of the Delaware and Potomac basins.

The Dola study (Part 5 of the report referred to above) is an analysis in depth of a specific planning problem—Passaic River water resources development—to investigate the crucial role that statements of objectives play in the process of detailed system design.

The general context into which the Major and Dola papers fit is presented in the study by Maass (elsewhere in this book) of public policy issues associated with the use of multiple objectives in system design.

Application: Benefits and Costs.   The conceptual and measurement aspects of benefit-cost analysis were investigated in a series of studies dealing with (a) the use of alternative costs as a measure of benefits, (b) the use of synthetic techniques for estimating industrial flood damages, (c) hydroelectric power evaluation, (d) benefits from water-based recreation, and (e) evaluation of direct irrigation benefits.

The paper on alternative costs by Peter Steiner, elsewhere in this book (37), is a systematic examination of when and to what extent the cost of an external alternative can serve as a substitute for, or provide limits to, benefit measurement. A simple model of two public and two private projects was established. By varying the assumptions of (a) what is alternative to what, (b) what combinations of projects are compatible, (c) what institutional rules govern selection of projects, and (d) what quantities and qualities of services are provided by the projects, the many variations of the general problem can be identified and the extent to which alternative costs can be substituted validly for benefit measurement can be defined.

The study of industrial flood losses by Robert Kates (36) uses the Lehigh basin as its data for analysis. Kates applied the notion of synthetic stage-damage functions to the flood problems of this heavily industrialized valley. This notion had previously been developed by Gilbert White,

Kates, and others [ref. 3, 4] as an improvement to existing techniques for estimating flood losses for commercial and residential land uses. He developed such functions for the Lehigh under several different assumptions of adjustment to the flood hazard and economic evaluation.

"Evaluation of Hydroelectric Power Benefits," by John Wilkinson (Part 8 of the Program's report referred to above), examines (a) the problem of estimating hydroelectric power benefits in cases where the alternative cost test is inapplicable, and (b) the question of defining an upper limit on benefits through use of the alternative cost approach.

"Recreational Benefits of Water-Resource Development," prepared by Leonard Merewitz in 1965 for the Program, is in two parts: (a) a thorough review of previous methods of measuring such benefits using the willingness-to-pay concepts and (b) an application to specific data of a method of measuring recreational benefits, including the consumers' surplus component, by relating reservoir recreation attendance to distance traveled and, hence, to travel costs.

The paper by Henry Jacoby, "Current Practice in the Evaluation of Direct Irrigation Benefits," prepared in 1965 for the Program, contains a brief review of existing methods of benefit measurement and deals with the important problem of determining the "production function" for irrigation water which is basic to benefit estimates.

Field-level Planning: Process and Techniques. The major share of research accomplished during the second phase is in these areas. Research on the planning process includes (a) a series of case studies of current water resource planning practice, and (b) a general discussion of the process in which the underlying economic theory, framework of study, and techniques of analysis are treated together. Work on techniques of analysis resulted principally in the elaborate computer-simulation programs for the Lehigh and Delaware River systems. In addition, there are studies on improved models for synthesis of streamflows for use in simulation and work on formal mathematical models.

John Wilkinson's study of current water resource planning practice in the Delaware, Potomac, Snake, Texas, and Southeast river basins (Part 3 of the Program's 1965 report to the Corps) presents a cross-section of current practice in a variety of institutional, physical, and economic situations. Together with the Major and Dola papers, this paper matches existing practice against the planning model assumed in the research. From these it is possible to draw some generalizations on how existing practice might be changed to accommodate changes in theory, process and technique.

A paper by the author, "The Water Resource Planning Process—Relation to Corps of Engineers Planning" (Part 2 of the Program's 1965 report to the Corps) sets forth the theory, process, and technique of field-level planning and, through use of the findings of the other studies, suggests feasible improvements in existing practice, including ways and means of attaining them.

The major paper on simulation of the Lehigh and Delaware systems, by the author and Myron Fiering (38), reports on the largest single item of research undertaken in the second phase. Involved was a detailed analysis of the voluminous data on the Delaware supplied by the Corps of Engineers. This analysis is reflected in part in a paper by Wilkinson on basic design data for the Delaware River System (Part 10 of the Program's 1965 report to the Corps). Behind the report on simulation are two major simulation programs coded for operation on the IBM 7094 computer at Harvard: the Lehigh basin simulation program, and the Delaware basin simulation program. Copies of the program decks and input data tape, and print-outs of programs and data are on file at Harvard.

Closely related to the research on simulation is the report by Fiering on a multivariate model for synthesis of streamflows (23). This paper presents the statistical theory of an improved method of generating synthetic streamflows for large river systems. Based on this theory, a computer program (model MUSH program) had been coded for the IBM 7094, and 10,000 years of synthetic streamflow data have been generated for twenty-five gauging stations in the Delaware system. The program and data tape are available at Harvard.

Unlike research on simulation, research on application of mathematical models to the Lehigh and Delaware systems was not carried to the point of producing a major report. The paper by Robert Dorfman (27) reports the current state of applicability of formal (mathematical) models to problems of this magnitude, and suggests possible directions for further research.

Related Work during the Second Phase

In the late summer of 1961, two members of the Harvard group (Thomas and Dorfman) were appointed to a special Panel of the President's Science Advisory Committee to study the serious problem of increasing waterlogging and salinization of the huge agricultural area in the Indus River basin of West Pakistan. Their association with the Panel led to a major research assignment at Harvard involving both engineering and economic analysis. The engineering analysis included the development and testing of three large-scale mathematical models, with associated computer programs, to simulate relevant aspects of the hydrological regime of the Indus River basin, and to test performance of various kinds of hydraulic works that may be used to combat waterlogging and salinity and to provide supplemental water for crops. Economic analysis consisted of detailed studies of the problem of raising agricultural productivity in the Indus Plain.

The results of this research are contained, in part, in the report of the Panel which was transmitted in March 1964 by President Johnson to Mohammed Ayub Khan, President of Pakistan [ref. 5], and, in part, in the supporting report of the Harvard group to the President's Science Adviser [ref. 6]. The Harvard group provided four members to the five-man subcommittee of the Panel (chaired by Roger Revelle, then Science Adviser to the Secretary of the Interior) which produced the final version of the Panel's report.

THE TRAINING ASPECT

First Phase

During the three years of operation of the research and training seminar (September 1956 to June 1959), twenty-seven employees of government agencies participated. Upon completion of their year, these men returned to their government positions; many have since attained positions of high responsibility in the field of water resource planning. Two members of the group made important contributions to the research reported in *Design of Water-Resource Systems,* and a third member was a major contributor to the second phase of research. In addition, of the eight graduate students and undergraduates who were regular seminar participants, six have since received Ph.D. degrees in economics or engineering and currently have research and teaching interest in water resource planning or in public investment decision making.

Second Phase

No advance training of public servants was undertaken during the second phase; instead, some fourteen graduate students in economics and environmental engineering have been associated to some degree with the research undertaken during the second phase. Of these, nine are either Ph.D. candidates or have received the doctoral degree. In addition, approximately sixty students from the graduate programs in public administration, city and regional planning, engineering sciences, business and law, and from Harvard College and the Massachusetts Institute of

Technology have taken the course in public investment decision making taught by the faculty group of the Program, which is based on the results of the research.

Summary

About 120 individuals have either received some training or contributed to the research since the start of the Program in 1956. Public service participants have returned to their government agencies, which include the U.S. Army Corps of Engineers, Bureau of Reclamation, Geological Survey, Soil Conservation Service, Forest Service, and California Department of Water Resources. Other alumni are now in the Bureau of the Budget, Department of the Interior, Federal Reserve Bank of Boston, and Resources for the Future; and are in teaching and research at Cornell University and the University of North Carolina, as well as at Harvard. Faculty and students have consulted on or taught public investment and water resource planning in Pakistan, India, United Arab Republic, Argentina, Venezuela, Union of South Africa, and Australia. The impact of the training and the research is being felt in this country and abroad in government as well as in universities and water resource research centers.

CONCLUDING COMMENTS

Any objective evaluation of the Harvard Water Program—its successes and failures—must come from others. Here I offer only a few, admittedly subjective, observations on the work, as follows:

1) The program gained strength through continuity—the same core faculty group worked together for ten years—and through the narrow focus of the research on planning and investment decision making in water resources.

2) Progress in research on techniques of analysis was aided greatly by the rapid advances in computer technology during this period. Problems of simulation as well as hydrologic synthesis now being dealt with on computers could not have been handled with the 1956 vintage computer.

3) A university research group can perform more efficiently on basic research problems than on problems of application. As the work of the Harvard group moved toward problems of application, it became more and more difficult to offer specific and unambiguous guidelines for planning. In general, it appears that university research groups should concentrate on the theoretical and conceptual aspects of planning, and leave the details of application to the practitioners. But the theoretical work is

enriched by access to data from actual planning cases and by contact with practitioners.

4) We made less progress than we had hoped on applying mathematical models to practical use in planning. Simulation still seems to be the most useful computer-oriented technique for water resources systems analysis; further research on simplifying and streamlining this method appears to be worth while.

5) Only a start was made on research on the planning process as a whole; further work on this and on fitting together econometric, simulation, and hydraulic models (now under way in phase three at Harvard) should be productive.

6) Other important subjects of research on water resource planning include (a) political and economic aspects of setting government objectives in our federal system, and deriving the relevant design criteria from these objectives; (b) defining the relevant geographic and functional scope of planning; (c) deriving water resource benefit functions, especially for hard-to-quantify purposes such as recreation; and (d) conducting case studies and evaluations of actual water resource planning operations.[2]

In summary, I believe that the time, effort, and money expended on the Program turned out to be a good investment, which has established a sound basis for future productive work in research, training, and practice on water resource investment in particular, and on public investment in general.

BIBLIOGRAPHY OF SELECTED PUBLICATIONS OF MEMBERS OF THE HARVARD WATER PROGRAM

1959

1. Maass, Arthur, and Hufschmidt, Maynard M. "In Search of New Methods of River System Planning," *Journal, Boston Society of Civil Engineers,* Vol. 46 (April 1959).
2. Steiner, Peter O. "Choosing among Alternative Investments in the Water Resource Field," *American Economic Review,* Vol. 49 (1959).

1960

3. Maass, Arthur, and Hufschmidt, Maynard M. "Toward Better River System Planning," in *Resources Development, Frontiers for Research, Western Resources Conference, 1959.* Boulder: University of Colorado Press, 1960.
4. Maass, Arthur, and Zobel, Hiller. "Anglo-American Water Law," *Public Policy,* Vol. 10 (1960).

---

[2] Further details on needed research are to be found in the author's paper, "Research on Comprehensive Planning of Water-Resource Systems" (35).

1961

5. Hufschmidt, Maynard M., Krutilla, John V., Margolis, Julius, with Marglin, Stephen A. "Standards and Criteria for Formulating and Evaluating Federal Water Resources Developments," Report of Panel of Consultants to the Bureau of the Budget, Washington, D.C., June 30, 1961.

6. Eckstein, Otto. "A Survey of the Theory of Public Expenditure Criteria," in National Bureau of Economic Research, *Public Finances, Needs, Sources and Utilization.* Princeton: Princeton University Press, 1961.

1962

7. Maass, Arthur, Hufschmidt, Maynard M., Dorfman, Robert, Thomas, Harold A., Jr., Marglin, Stephen A., and Fair, Gordon Maskew. *Design of Water-Resource Systems.* Cambridge: Harvard University Press, 1962.

8. Farrar, Donald E. *The Investment Decision Under Uncertainty.* Englewood Cliffs, N.J.: Prentice-Hall, Inc., 1962.

9. Hufschmidt, Maynard M., with Weber, Eugene W. "River Basin Planning in the United States," *Natural Resources—Energy, Water and River Basin Development,* Vol. 1, United States Papers Prepared for the United Nations Conference on the Application of Science and Technology for the Benefit of the Less Developed Areas. Washington, D.C.: U.S. Government Printing Office, 1962.

10. Fiering, Myron B. "On the Use of Correlation to Augment Data," *Journal of the American Statistical Association,* Vol. 57 (March 1962), p. 20.

11. ———. "Queueing Theory and Simulation in Reservoir Design," *American Society of Civil Engineers, Paper No. 3367,* Vol. 127, Part 1, 1962.

12. Watermeyer, Peter, and Thomas, Harold A., Jr. "Queueing Theory and Reservoir Design," in *Proceedings of a Harvard Symposium on Digital Computers and Their Application.* Cambridge: Harvard University Press, 1962.

1963

13. Dorfman, Robert. "Steepest Ascent Under Constraint," in *Symposium on Simulation Models: Methodology and Applications to the Behavioral Sciences.* Cincinnati: South-Western Publishing Co., 1963.

14. Fiering, Myron B. "The Use of a Subsample in Parameter Estimation," *Journal, Boston Society of Civil Engineers,* Vol. 50 (January 1963).

15. ———. "Use of Correlation to Improve Estimates of Mean and Variance," U.S. Geological Survey Professional Paper 434-C (1963).

16. Hufschmidt, Maynard M. "Water Resources System Design," in *Water and Sewage Works,* May 1963.

17. ———. "Simulating the Behavior of a Multi-Unit, Multi-Purpose Water-Resource System," in *Symposium on Simulation Models: Methodology and Applications to the Behavioral Sciences.* Cincinnati: South-Western Publishing Co., 1963.

18. Marglin, Stephen A. *Approaches to Dynamic Investment Planning.* Amsterdam: North-Holland Publishing Co., 1963.

19. ———. "The Social Rate of Discount and the Optimal Rate of Investment," in *Quarterly Journal of Economics,* Vol. 77 (February 1963).
20. ———. "The Opportunity Costs of Public Investment," *Quarterly Journal of Economics,* Vol. 77 (May 1963).
21. Thomas, Harold A., Jr. "The Animal Farm: A Mathematical Model for the Discussion of Social Standards for Control of the Environment," *Quarterly Journal of Economics,* Vol. 77 (February 1963).

1964

22. Fiering, Myron B. "A Markov Model for Low-Flow Analysis," *Bulletin of the International Association of Scientific Hydrology,* Vol. 11, No. 2 (June 1964).
23. ———. "Multivariate Technique for Synthetic Hydrology," *Proceedings of the American Society of Civil Engineers,* Vol. 90, No. HY5 (September 1964).
24. ———. "A Digital Computer Simulation for Well-Field Draw-Down," *Bulletin, Association of Scientific Hydrology,* Vol. 9, No. 4 (1964).
25. ———, with Yotsukura, Nobuhiro. "Numerical Solution to a Dispersion Equation," *Proceedings of the American Society of Civil Engineers,* Vol. 90, No. HY5 (September 1964).
26. ———, with Hufschmidt, Maynard M. "Design of Water Resource Systems," *Proceedings of the Conference on EDP Systems for State and Local Government, Sept. 30–Oct. 2, 1964.* New York University and System Development Corporation.

1965

27. Dorfman, Robert. "Formal (Mathematical) Models in the Design of Water-Resource Systems," *Water Resources Research,* Vol. 1 (3rd quarter, 1965).
28. Fiering, Myron B. "Revitalizing a Fertile Plain," *Water Resources Research,* Vol. 1 (1st quarter, 1965).
29. ———. "An Optimization Scheme for Gaging," *Water Resources Research,* Vol. 1 (4th quarter, 1965).
30. Hufschmidt, Maynard M. "Field-Level Planning of Water-Resource Systems," *Water Resources Research,* Vol. 1 (2nd quarter, 1965).
31. ———. "The Methodology of Water-Resource System Design," in Burton, Ian, and Kates, Robert, *Readings in Resource Management and Conservation.* Chicago: University of Chicago Press, 1965.
32. ———. "Critique of Organization and Management of the U.S. Study Commission, Southeast River Basins," in Kindsvater, C. E. (ed.), *Organization and Methodology for River Basin Planning.* Atlanta: Water Resources Center, Georgia Institute of Technology, 1965.
33. ———. "Systems Analysis," *Water Resources and Economic Development of the South.* Raleigh: North Carolina State University, Agricultural Policy Institute, 1965.
34. ———. "Water Resources Administration," *Proceedings of Fourteenth Southern Water Resources and Pollution Control Conference.* Chapel Hill: University of North Carolina, Department of Environmental Sciences and Engineering, 1965.
35. ———. "Research on Comprehensive Planning of Water-Resource Systems," *Natural Resources Journal,* Vol. 5 (October 1965).

36. Kates, Robert. *Industrial Flood Losses: Damage Estimation in the Lehigh Valley*. University of Chicago Department of Geography Research Paper No. 98, 1965.
37. Steiner, Peter O. "The Role of Alternative Cost in Project Design and Selection," *Quarterly Journal of Economics,* Vol. 79 (August 1965). Also see paper in the present book.

1966

38. Hufschmidt, Maynard M., with Fiering, Myron B. *Simulation Techniques for Design of Water-Resource Systems*. Cambridge: Harvard University Press, 1966.
39. Maass, Arthur. "Benefit-Cost Analysis: Its Relevance to Public Investment Decisions," *Quarterly Journal of Economics,* May 1966. Also, see paper in the present book.
40. Thomas, Harold A., Jr. "On the Efficient Use of High Aswan Dam for Hydropower and Irrigation," *Management Science* (forthcoming issue).
41. Wang, Flora Chu. "Approximate Theory for Skimming Well Formulation in the Indus Plain of West Pakistan," *Journal of Geophysical Research,* Vol. 70, No. 20 (1965).

REFERENCES

[1] S. Doc. No. 97, 87th Congress, 2nd Session, May 29, 1962.
[2] H. Doc. No. 522, 87th Congress, 2nd Session, Jan. 10–Oct. 13, 1962.
[3] White, Gilbert F. *Choice of Adjustments to Floods*. University of Chicago Department of Geography Research Paper 93, 1964.
[4] Kates, Robert W. *Hazard and Choice Perception in Flood Plain Management*. Research Paper 78. Chicago: University of Chicago, Department of Geography, 1962.
[5] The White House—Department of the Interior Panel on Waterlogging and Salinity in West Pakistan. *Report on Land and Water Development in the Indus Plain*. Washington: The White House, January 1964.
[6] Thomas, Harold A., Jr., and Burden, Robert. *Indus River Basin Studies*. Final Report to the Science Adviser. Washington, 1965.

The Impacts of Water Investments in Depressed Areas

G. S. Tolley*

Passage of the Appalachian Act and other recent legislation concerned with low-income regions has brought sharply into focus the need to review some of the basic concepts of traditional benefit-cost analysis and to refine the methods that can be helpful in studying projects involving public investment in depressed areas. The existence of structural unemployment and underemployment highlights a long-recognized need to relax the assumption that market costs of resources employed by a project measure the value they produce in non-project uses—i.e., that the earnings of a worker on a project equal the value of the product he would otherwise produce elsewhere. This is the so-called full employment assumption.

In low-income regions several other project effects, usually treated cursorily or not at all, are important. The effects projects may have on social investments, particularly education, are a case in point. Technique refinement has not kept up with changing emphasis in type of primary benefits for which projects are constructed in low-income regions. For example, in analyzing water projects techniques for measuring recreation and flow augmentation benefits are cruder than for flood control benefits.

That projects can influence the location of economic activity is apparent to decision makers and is reflected in the calculation of local secondary benefits to be gained from the projects. Increasing emphasis at

* Serving as Director of the Economic Development Division, Economic Research Service, U.S. Department of Agriculture; Professor of Economics on leave from North Carolina State University.

the federal government level on regional development makes these locational effects of more explicit national concern. But methods for evaluating secondary benefits need to be refined if they are to provide reasonably accurate estimates of the activities attracted to an area as a result of a government project. There are several shortcomings to using secondary benefits as the sole measure of a project's locational effects. One important defect is that the local area to which secondary benefits apply is not customarily specified. Another defect is the failure to consider where in the rest of the economy activities are displaced.

The present paper will report on progress of a research team at North Carolina State University which has been investigating these and other problems connected with estimating benefits and costs for projects in depressed areas. The research is being undertaken under a contract with the U.S. Army Corps of Engineers. The contract is one of a series by the Corps aimed at refining benefit-cost analysis.

RELATION BETWEEN AREA AND NATIONAL BENEFITS: EMPLOYMENT EFFECTS

This section attempts to lay out an analytical framework for estimating benefits and costs of projects when the assumption of a full employment economy is relaxed.

An Economy where Excess Labor Supplies Would Not All Simultaneously Be Zero

By "excess labor supply" is meant the difference between the amount of labor of a particular kind that could be hired at existing wage rates and the amount of this labor employers wish to hire. Figure 1 depicts two

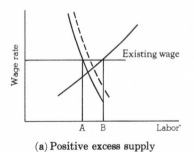

(a) Positive excess supply

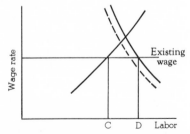

(b) Negative excess supply, equals labor shortage, equals positive excess demand

Figure 1. Labor supply and demand schedules.

different conditions: (a) positive excess supply AB and (b) shortage of labor or negative excess supply $CD;$ these two terms are taken to be identical with positive excess demand. Wages may adjust downward to some extent in response to positive excess supply, or upward in response to labor shortage. In this discussion it will be assumed that wages adjust downward slowly, if at all, in response to the existence of positive excess supply.

Excess labor supply consists of two groups in the labor force and one group not in the labor force. First, there are the measurably unemployed. Second, there are the underemployed, consisting of persons who are in some kind of employment but who would take jobs in an alternative employment if demand for it increased. Low-income farmers who would take factory jobs nearby are an example of persons in this group. Third, there are persons who are not classified as employed or looking for work, but who would take jobs if they were available. Housewives and other potential secondary workers in a family are examples.

One can speak of the absence of a structural unemployment problem if, in response to increases in aggregate demand in the economy which raises the demands for all types of labor and thus reduces excess labor supplies, a point is reached where excess labor supply is zero everywhere in the economy. Whatever the precise definition of structural unemployment, its amount and the seriousness of problems associated with it are reflected in measures of the dispersion of excess supplies (both positive and negative) about their mean.

Nature of the Estimation Problem

As a result of a water resource project, some economic activities will be located in places different from where they would be in the absence of the project. As noted at the outset, in traditional benefit-cost analysis, it is assumed that prices of factors of production are equal to the amount they would be earning if not employed in the project activity. Resources are assumed to be mobile enough to adjust to the locational reshuffling of activities without affecting amounts of excess labor supplies.

Suppose for a moment, at the other extreme, that labor were completely immobile and that a project results in economic activities being located in an area of positive excess labor supply which otherwise would have been an area of labor shortage. Then, as suggested by the dashed lines in Figure 1(a), total employment in the economy would increase. An assumption is that monetary-fiscal policy would allow the increases in aggregate demand necessary for the purchase of increased output. This seems realistic since the increases could come about with little or no effect on price level or interest rates because of the simultaneous increase in output and demand.[1]

In line with traditional benefit-cost analysis, particularly because of small increments to total output usually involved in a project, it is appropriate at least initially to ignore product price effects of locational shifts in output. If such effects are deemed important, they can be introduced at a later stage. Let us take as an example a rubber plant which, in order to aid a depressed area, is located in Appalachia, when it otherwise would have been located in Akron. There is an increment to real national output equal to the difference between the two locations in cost of production of relocated activity—i.e., rubber production and associated economic activity, such as trade and services. Under a full employment assumption, the composition of change in real national output will depend on income elasticities of demand and will be spread among all products with only minuscule further effects on rubber production. A key difference between an analysis based on full employment and the analysis argued in this paper is that dropping the full employment assumption implies that factor prices may not reflect opportunity returns of resources. If as a result of a project labor is employed at going wage rates which would otherwise have zero or at least lower product, then there is a gain in real national output that is not indicated by the procedures of traditional benefit-cost analysis.

Relation between Migration and Employment

The two situations discussed thus far are those of full employment and complete lack of labor mobility. But many difficulties of estimation are associated with a situation where neither of these two extremes is fulfilled—where, that is, projects affect migration in a context of positive excess supplies of some types of labor.

If employment in Akron is growing faster than can be supplied through natural increase of population in the Akron vicinity, Akron will be found to be experiencing in-migration which is most likely to be heavily concentrated among young persons just entering the labor force. If the rubber plant is located in Appalachia, employment in Akron will not grow as fast as it would had the plant been located there; instead, young persons who

---

[1] In the full employment case, it is probably also realistic to suppose that monetary-fiscal policy allows aggregate demand to increase at given prices in response to output effects of projects (primary benefits); but strictly the assumption is not needed for the full employment case, since then there could be a downward adjustment of wages and prices allowing any real output increases to materialize regardless of monetary-fiscal policies pursued.

would have migrated to Akron will either stay where they are or migrate to those points where growth of production other than rubber is occurring. The mobility of young persons throughout the country, who can choose flexibly between migrating to one growth point or another, affords one of the best hopes that a project in Appalachia will result in a net increase in total national employment.

However, if the labor displaced in Akron is of a type that tends to be in excess supply all over the nation—drop-out teenagers, for example —youths who would have been employed in Akron will find no employment at all even though Akron appears to be a place of excess labor demand.

Back-migration to a depressed area can also offset employment-increasing effects. People who grew up in a depressed area and have moved elsewhere to work may return from growing centers and take jobs, leaving those originally unemployed in depressed areas still unemployed. Formally expressed, the downward shift in demand for labor in the rest of the economy tends to be accompanied by downward shifts in supplies in the rest of the economy, concommitant with about equal upward shifts in labor supply and demand in the depressed area.

Net effects on secondary family workers also need to be estimated. If Akron has many and growing employment opportunities for women (excess demand in women's occupations) any loss in openings for women will tend to have no effect on women's employment participation in Akron. On the other hand, if few employment opportunities exist where the rubber plant will be located (excess labor supplies in women's occupations), employment participation there will increase.

One should distinguish the behavior relations for four types of people. National census statistics show that among men, high-income professionals are so highly mobile that net employment effects for them can be ignored, since their employment participation is little affected by the location of jobs. Unattached single women are also quite mobile, as is shown by their high concentrations in areas where there is much white-collar work. Married women and many young women who have not yet left the family home may be considered for all practical purposes to be completely immobile, since migration decisions of the family depend most importantly on job opportunities for the family head. Employment participation for these young women depends on the composition of employment opportunities in the areas where they reside. If these are weighted toward occupations with many opportunities for women, their participation will tend to be high. Finally, there are male workers in lower paying professional occupations. Behavior relations need to be estimated indicating the extent to which these men will migrate or become unem-

461

ployed if there is excess supply for their skills in an area. The relation needs to be estimated separately for different age groups.

In order to understand where economic activity will be displaced, these behavior relations should be used in conjunction with information on the growth of particular industries in various parts of the economy and with information on skill requirements of different types of industries. Attempts can then be made to bring together the various data to predict effects of industry relocation on excess labor demands (both positive and negative) in various areas, on migration, and the resulting changes in over-all employment.

Hypotheses for Choosing Projects to Maximize Net Increases in Employment

The foregoing considerations already suggest that a net increase in employment is most likely to occur if industry is relocated to an area of excess labor supply from growth centers where there is excess demand for labor, and if the industry being relocated demands a skill type which is not in excess supply nationally. Furthermore, the reasoning suggests that larger employment effects are likely to be obtained by concentrating on a few large projects rather than on a number of small projects. Small projects may simply attract back-migration with little net effect, as is illustrated by the dashed lines in Figure 1(b). Back-migration is a slippage that may require a relatively large project before the trend is exhausted and locally unemployed workers are hired.

These hypotheses provide guides for empirical research undertaken with a view to recommending which areas and industries are likely to make the greatest contribution to national income in view of employment effects.

The Valuation Problem

For workers who in the absence of a project would have been unemployed, their opportunity return can be assumed to be zero. That is, from a national point of view their wage cost need not be considered at all. For workers who would have been underemployed, their opportunity cost is their earnings in their underemployed situation, which should be subtracted as a cost. For workers who are attracted into the labor force, there is a problem of valuing their time. For some it is a valuation of leisure. For others it is a valuation of their productivity in activities within the household sector. In either case, since they are not actively seeking work, there is a presumption that the value of their time is greater than zero.

462

Progress has been made on empirical application of some of the ideas that have been presented in this section. G. K. Kripalani is continuing this work.

EFFECTS ON SOCIAL OVERHEAD

It is clear from the foregoing that industrialization has selective effects on migration, often tending to retain in an area workers of higher average product than otherwise would have been there and drawing in from other areas highly skilled persons and management personnel. These effects directly raise per capita income. Higher per capita incomes, together with the greater economic activity generated by a larger population, increase local tax bases and lead to effects on local government expenditures. That local expenditures on education and other social services depend on tax bases is indisputable, but the escalating effects have not been included as benefit estimates, even though greater investment in the human agent via education contributes directly to national income.

To include such effects in estimating benefits from water projects, three steps are required. The first estimates the effect of a project on the tax base; the second, the effect of the tax base on social overhead expenditure; and the third, the effect of social overhead expenditure on real national income. The area of education needs major attention; roads and social services, scarcely less. The statistical inference effort includes estimating the response of education and other social overhead expenditures to local increases in income as a result of projects. For education, and possibly for other social overhead, rates of return—which are measures of contribution to real national income—can be used that have been estimated from other studies.

Eric Olsen is taking responsibility for carrying out the three research steps to estimate project effects on social overhead. Thus far, he has concentrated on explaining local educational expenditures.

REFINEMENT OF REGIONAL MULTIPLIER ESTIMATES

We will now consider techniques for improving estimates of the magnitude and area distribution of secondary benefits. While secondary benefits might be estimated by an extended input-output analysis for each project, such a procedure would be expensive and would, moreover, require the training of planning personnel in extremely advanced economic research techniques. The sensitivity of multiplier estimates to errors due to data inaccuracy and to aggregation has received some attention at the conceptual level for a few special cases, but there has been almost no empirical investigation of these errors.

One part of a strategy for improving estimates of regional multipliers is to push forward the analysis of sensitivity of multipliers to coefficient errors and aggregation. This will enable assigning confidence ranges, and indicates the value of detail in industry-by-industry investigation of input-output coefficients. The analysis should indicate which types of coefficients deserve exacting attention and which types can be estimated only roughly with little effect on multiplier estimates. Hopefully, the analysis will lead to guides for an optimum degree of aggregation. At some point in disaggregation to a more minute industry breakdown, the gain in accuracy of multiplier estimate may not be worth the cost of the additional effort necessary to obtain the additional input-output coefficients. Practically, there could be absolute loss of accuracy if effort in estimating input-output coefficients is spread too thinly. It might be best to concentrate on obtaining accurate input-output coefficients for fewer aggregate industries than inaccurate coefficients for a large number of industries.

Another part of the strategy for improving multiplier estimates has fewer antecedents; it consists in finding out how multipliers vary depending on the component economic structure of an area. Few areas are exactly the same in their economic structure, but many areas have similar sets of component activities in common. Even for areas with completely different industrial structures, the general similarity of household consumption habits throughout the country makes one component column of the coefficient matrix similar. One undertaking that would save duplicated effort and improve estimates of coefficients for areas is to catalogue systematically coefficient estimates from area empirical studies. These would be available for use in further studies, thus eliminating the need for undertaking estimates anew. The study at North Carolina State University will not attempt this large undertaking, but will provide conceptual guides for collecting available coefficient estimates by increasing understanding of their importance and use.

The two principal factors contributing to differences in an area's component economic structure are its industrial composition and its size. Clearly, input-output matrixes differ if they consist of different industrial activities. Size is important because it affects the amount of imports and exports even for areas of similar industrial composition. Visualize estimating at various distances the regional multiplier effects due to new activities located in a place close, say, to the construction of a reservoir. If the site of the activity alone is considered, the value of the regional multiplier is one. For instance, if the new activity is increased agricultural production as a result of flood control, the increased production is all exported directly from the farm site and the increased personal income is all spent off the farm. Now suppose the size of the area considered is expanded to include a nearby town. The processing of the new agricultural products, the increased purchases of farm inputs such as fertilizer, and the local expenditures of farm residents from their increased personal income will lead to a multiplier effect greater than one. As the size of area considered is expanded, the multiplier will rise to a maximum as more and more of the associated activities are encompassed by the area included in the analysis. At some point, increasing the size of the area considered begins to reduce the multiplier because the places will be included in the economy from which activity is being displaced. Finally, when the area considered becomes so large as to be identical with the entire national economy, all displaced activities will be encompassed. The only multiplier effect in this case is the net addition of the project to national income—i.e., the estimated secondary benefits become identical with primary benefits.

Conceptual analysis of the effects on multipliers of coefficient errors can be used in an analysis of effects of industrial composition and area size, since both types of analysis have to do with the effects of magnitude of input-output coefficient on regional multiplier. In addition, a further conceptual analysis is needed which will identify income streams and component submultipliers and lead to an understanding permitting improved judgments about differences in multipliers between regions. This should also lead to refined estimates for the effects of entire sectors, rather than only individual coefficients, on multipliers.

The following remarks report on the progress that the study group has made on the conceptual analysis of aggregation, coefficient errors, and multiplier components. Much of the thinking to be reported here is due to Frank M. Goode, who participated in early phases of the project. A. A. Daghestani is continuing the research on multipliers.

Aggregation

As Fisher and others have emphasized, it is possible to combine two or more industries into one sector with little error if the industries have similar cost structures or if the relative outputs of the industries remain constant [ref. 1]. The following example indicates another case when it is possible to aggregate with little error. Consider a four-sector model in which the first and second industries are to be combined. The rows of Table 1 show the distribution of output for each sector and the columns show the purchases, i.e., X_{ij} is output of ith sector sold to the jth sector.

465

TABLE 1.

Flow of Goods and Services

Purchases \ Sales	1	2	3	4
1	X_{11}	X_{12}	X_{13}	X_{14}
2	X_{21}	X_{22}	X_{23}	X_{24}
3	X_{31}	X_{32}	X_{33}	X_{34}
4	X_{41}	X_{42}	X_{43}	X_{44}
	X_1	X_2	X_3	X_4

The X_j's are the total purchase of each sector. Aggregating industries one and two would result in Table 2. The first input coefficients for sector $1'$ from Table 2 may be expressed as follows because $a_{ij} = \dfrac{X_{ij}}{X_j}$.

$$a'_{11} = \frac{X_{11} + X_{12} + X_{21} + X_{22}}{X_1 + X_2} \tag{1}$$

or

$$a'_{11} = \frac{(a_{11} + a_{21}) + \dfrac{X_2}{X_1}(a_{12} + a_{22})}{\left(1 + \dfrac{X_2}{X_1}\right)}. \tag{2}$$

TABLE 2.

Aggregated Flows of Goods and Services

Purchases \ Sales	$1'$	$2'$	$3'$
1	$X_{11} + X_{12} + X_{21} + X_{22}$	$X_{13} + X_{23}$	$X_{14} + X_{24}$
2	$X_{31} + X_{32}$	X_{33}	X_{34}
3	$X_{41} + X_{42}$	X_{43}	X_{44}
	$X_1 + X_2$	X_3	X_4

Similarly,

$$a'_{21} = \frac{a_{31} + \dfrac{X_2}{X_1} a_{32}}{1 + \dfrac{X_2}{X_1}} \tag{3}$$

$$a'_{31} = \frac{a_{41} + \dfrac{X_2}{X_1} a_{42}}{1 + \dfrac{X_2}{X_1}}. \tag{4}$$

The derivatives of a'_{11}, a'_{21}, a'_{31} with respect to $\dfrac{X_2}{X_1}$ are as follows:

$$\frac{da'_{11}}{d\frac{X_2}{X_1}} = \frac{(a_{12} + a_{22}) - (a_{11} + a_{21})}{\left(1 + \frac{X_2}{X_1}\right)^2}, \tag{5}$$

$$da'_{21}/d(X_2/X_1) = (a_{32} - a_{31})/[1 + (X_2/X_1)]^2, \tag{6}$$

$$da'_{31}/d(X_2/X_1) = (a_{42} - a_{41})/[1 + (X_2/X_1)]^2. \tag{7}$$

As already pointed out, if the ratio X_2/X_1 remains the same as the ratio for the values at which the aggregate coefficient is calculated, the multiplier obtained in the aggregates will equal the true multiplier. Expressions (5), (6), and (7) indicate the effects of departures from constancy of X_2/X_1 on the aggregate input-output coefficients. As an example of how these might be used, express (7) in elasticity form:

$$\frac{da'_{31}}{d(X_2/X_1)} \cdot \frac{X_2/X_1}{a'_{31}} = (w_1 w_2)\left(\frac{X_1 + X_2}{X_{41} + X_{42}}\right)(a_{42} - a_{41}), \tag{8}$$

where $w_1 = X_1/(X_1 + X_2)$ and $w_2 = X_2/(X_1 + X_2)$. The first parenthesis on the righthand side indicates that there will be a small relative effect on the aggregate coefficient of departure from constancy of X_2/X_1 if the sectors being combined are disproportionate in size. The second parenthesis indicates there will be a small effect if the sales of the two sectors being aggregated to a third sector are a large proportion of their total sales; from $a_{ij} = X_{ij}/X_j$ this depends on the absolute sizes of the input-output coefficients. The third parenthesis indicates there will be a small effect if the difference in input-output coefficients is small.

The above derivatives can be utilized further in analyzing the effects of aggregation on multipliers, by studying the effects of changes in the ratio of output of the aggregated sectors.

Coefficient Errors

The discussion of multipliers so far has considered errors due to aggregation. More generally, there may be additional sources of errors in coefficients due to inaccuracy of sales and purchase data. Consider now this more general problem of how to investigate the effects of coefficient errors on multipliers.

Let X be the vector of industry outputs; let A be the matrix of the input-output coefficients a_{ij}; and let Y be the vector of final demands for output of each industry. Then

$$X = (I - A)^{-1}Y. \tag{9}$$

Let α_{KL} refer to the element in the Lth row and K^{th} column of the $(I - A)^{-1}$ matrix; i.e., it is the effect on the output of the Lth industry resulting from a one-dollar increase in final demand for the output of the

K^{th} industry. The total effect on regional output, i.e., the total regional multiplier, of a change in final demand for output of the Kth industry is the sum over K of α_{KL} . The present analysis will work with the submultipliers α_{KL} from which the total multiplier can be obtained. The problem then is to consider the effect of a change in a coefficient of the matrix A on an element of the inverse matrix $(I - A)^{-1}$. The expression for α in terms of the a_{ij}'s is

$$\alpha_{KL} = A_K^L / |I - A|. \tag{10}$$

Differentiation with respect to one coefficient, a_{RS}, gives

$$d\alpha_{KL}/da_{RS} = \alpha_{SR} - (A_{KS}^{LR}/A_K^L), \tag{11}$$

where A_{KS}^{LR} is the algebraic complement (cofactor) of the elements of the Lth and R^{th} rows and the Kth and S^{th} columns of the $(I - A)$ matrix, and A_K^L is the algebraic complement of the element in the Lth row and K^{th} column of $(I - A)$. Expression (11) indicates that the change in a submultiplier due to a change in one coefficient is the difference of a second submultiplier and a ratio of two cofactors that has a meaningful economic interpretation. The ratio of cofactors is the value of the second submultiplier in a hypothetical economy where all inputs of L are imported and where the output of the Kth industry is constrained not to change.

A second procedure may help to identify the sensitivity of multipliers to coefficient errors. The foundation for this procedure was advanced by Watanabe, and is pertinent because it utilizes the constraint that the sum of the coefficients is one [ref. 2]. This restraint requires that the change in a coefficient be compensated for by changes in at least one and possibly all of the other coefficients of that sector. The sensitivity of multipliers to coefficient changes or errors may well be dependent on whether or not the compensation is in the endogenous or exogenous sectors. Watanabe approached the problem as follows:

$\bar{A}$ = the coefficient matrix obtained in some base period,

A = the coefficient matrix at some later date, and A differs from $\bar{A}$ in that the coefficients of one of the columns have changed,

Y = estimated final demand vector,

$\bar{X} = (I - \bar{A})^{-1}Y$ = predicted output at some future period utilizing the base period coefficients,

$X = (I - A)^{-1}Y$ = predicted output at some future date utilizing the coefficients that have changed.

$$k = (\bar{A} - A) \tag{12}$$

$$u = \bar{X} - X = (I - \bar{A})^{-1}Y - (I - A)^{-1}Y \tag{13}$$

$$(I - A)u = (I - A)\bar{X} - Y \tag{14}$$

$$(I - A)u = (I - \bar{A} - k)\bar{X} - Y \qquad (15)$$

$$(I - A)u = (I - \bar{A})\bar{X} - k\bar{X} - Y \qquad (16)$$

$$(I - A)u = Y - k\bar{X} - Y \qquad (17)$$

$$(I - A)u = -k\bar{X} \qquad (18)$$

$$u = -(I - A)^{-1} k\bar{X}. \qquad (19)$$

Operating on both sides of (18) by (e), which is a row vector of 1's of the appropriate order,

$$e(I - A)u = -ek\bar{X}. \qquad (20)$$

If the product of the e vector and the k matrix is equal to zero (i.e., the sum of the changes in the coefficients sum to zero), then the sum of the changes in the predicted outputs sum to zero under the weighting system of the vector $V = e(I - A)$. According to Watanabe,

> This derivation can be interpreted as indicating that over-estimation and under-estimation of the solution level have to appear simultaneously under the condition of $ek = 0$, and also this statement would approximate for the case of $ek \neq 0$ unless changes are drastic, which may not happen frequently during the period considered. [Ref. 2, pp. 328, 329.]

If additional investigation of the procedure produces a meaningful expression of the sensitivity of predicted outputs to coefficient changes, the expression can be altered to indicate the sensitivity of the multipliers to coefficient changes. This is possible because the predicted outputs are the products of the multipliers and a known final demand vector.

Continued study of these two procedures should produce insights into, and expressions for, the relation between coefficient errors and multipliers. Integrating this result with the effect of aggregation on coefficients will, it is hoped, result in a systematic and quantitative method to determine the optimum aggregation procedure.

Multiplier Components

From (10), it is possible to express α_{LK} as follows:

$$\alpha_{LK} = (A_L^K/A_L^L) \cdot (A_L^L/|I - A|) \qquad (21)$$

$$= (A_L^K/A_L^L) \cdot \alpha_{LL}. \qquad (22)$$

Formally, K and L can refer to any two activities. For purposes of economic interpretation, let L refer to households. Then equation (22) shows how any submultiplier α_{LK} can be expressed as a multiple of an interindustry impact on factor payments in the region and a factor payment multiplier. The interindustry impact is the effect on factor payments to households due to an increase in final demand for the Kth industry if household spending within the region were not affected by the factor payments. It can be shown that the interindustry impact is equal to A^K_L / A^L_L. The factor payment multiplier, which is a Keynesian effect, is the effect on household income of an exogenous increase in household income, taking account of the fact that the income induces increases in expenditures within the region by households. The factor payment multiplier is α_{LL}.

This separation of effects enables one to understand how differences in regional multipliers depend separately on industrial composition and on considerations affecting household spending within a region (such as the size of a region). One use of this understanding of sources of differences in multipliers is to check the reasonableness of multiplier estimates from empirical studies. Further, comparing from past studies the interindustry effects (to see the quantitative importance of different industrial structures) and similarly comparing factor payments multipliers (to see effect of variation in household spending within a region), could aid if one wished to search for areas where future projects would have the largest effects.

CONCLUSION

This paper has concentrated on some needs for evaluating water resource development proposals for depressed areas. It has not exhausted the list of needs for greater understanding to which the research at North Carolina is directed.

Recreation is an increasingly important purpose of projects, particularly in depressed areas. While much progress has been made in recent years in estimating recreation benefits, methods are still lacking to estimate adequately the value of recreation quality and competition between sites. V. S. Hastings and S. Sydneysmith are conducting studies on these subjects.

Provision of water for low-flow augmentation affects water available to industry as an intake and as a medium of waste disposal. The recognition of regional development as a project aim, in addition to national income aims, increases the need to understand effects of water availability on industry locations. S. Ben-David is researching on this subject.

REFERENCES

[1] Fisher, Walter D. "Criteria for Aggregation in Input-Output Analysis," *Review of Economics and Statistics,* Vol. 40, No. 3 (1958).
[2] Watanabe, Tsunehiko. "Comments on Mr. Sevaldson's Paper," in *Structural Interdependence and Economic Development* (Tebor Barna, ed.). New York: St. Martin's Press, 1963.

A Co-operative Water Research Program and the Nation's Future

*Roland R. Renne**

$\mathbf{B}$y the summer of 1965 the federal-state co-operative research and training program in water resources had been in operation less than a year. On July 17, 1964, President Lyndon B. Johnson signed the Water Resources Research Act. Congress made available the first funds for financing the program in the First Supplemental Appropriation Act of October 7, 1964, which permitted allotting the authorized $75,000 to each of fourteen state water resources research centers. The Second Supplemental Appropriation Act of May 3, 1965, made available a little over $52,000 for each of the remaining thirty-seven water research centers or institutes (hereafter referred to as centers). Thus, all fifty-one of the centers were in operation with their programs before fiscal year 1965 closed.

Fiscal year 1966 is the first full year of operation under the co-operative arrangement with the federal Office of Water Resources Research for all of the centers. Some 316 projects were in operation under the funds for fiscal year 1965. The 1966 program showed that 27 were completed or converted to matching-grants support and that 92 other projects were added, making a total of 381 projects in operation under the allotment program.

Similarly, there was a marked increase in the number of matching-fund projects submitted by the centers; ninety-nine were submitted for fiscal year 1966 funding, more than triple the number submitted in fiscal

* Director, Office of Water Resources Research, U.S. Department of the Interior.

471

year 1965. The amount requested was considerably in excess of appropriated funds. These developments indicate there is no lack of interest or lack of research ideas among the centers in dealing with water research problems. This promises well for the program being productive and useful in helping solve the more perplexing water problems to be faced in assuring the nation of water sufficient in quantity and satisfactory in quality to meet the requirements of an expanding population and industry.

BACKGROUND OF THE ACT

A review of the background of the Water Resources Research Act of 1964 is necessary for an understanding of the implementation of its provisions. The ideas which may be considered the seed from which the Act has developed were generated by the comprehensive study of national water resources conducted by the Senate Select Committee on National Water Resources of the 86th Congress. That committee, commonly referred to as the "Kerr Committee," in its report of January 1961 to the Senate [ref. 1] stressed the need for co-ordinated scientific research programs on all aspects of water use and control and the need for co-operative federal-state approaches to planning the development of water resources.

Several other groups expanded the ideas of the Senate Select Committee regarding water research needs. For example, the 1962 report of the Water Resources Study, headed by Abel Wolman, to the Committee on Natural Resources of the National Academy of Sciences–National Research Council, pointed out the pressing need for training in water resources:

> The most critical shortage in the field of water resources by far is the very real shortage of broadly trained people capable of planning and executing effective research programs. At present, we have no institutional structure in the United States to take care of multi-disciplinary research in water. [Ref. 2, p. 33.]

The report of the Task Group on Coordinated Water Resources Research of the Federal Council for Science and Technology, issued in February 1963, recommended:

> There is need to strengthen support of graduate training and research by developing university research centers or groups in different regions of the country. Such centers should be characterized by purposeful organization for research in water resources by having a multidisciplined faculty and staff skilled in the fields of engineering; the physical, chemical, biological, and social sciences; and management. [Ref. 3, p. 189.]

472

The foregoing studies and reports, as well as the growing problems associated with increased pollution of our lakes, streams, and estuarian areas, and with our expanding industry and rising population, obviously has had considerable influence on congressional legislation such as the Water Resources Research Act. The Task Group of the Federal Council for Science and Technology recommended that, if adopted, the water research centers in each state should be set up in a way parallel to the Agricultural Experiment Stations established by the Hatch Act of 1887. Those experiment stations have had such marked success in increasing the efficiency of American agriculture, that it is logical that many similar provisions would have been advocated for the establishment of state water research centers.

PROVISIONS OF THE ACT

The 1964 Act is much broader than the Hatch Act, however. In addition to authorizing annual federal appropriations to assist each participating state in establishing and carrying out work of a competent and qualified water resources research center, it provides for annual matching grant funds to the centers. It also authorizes funds for annual grants; contracts; matching or other arrangements with educational institutions other than those establishing centers; private foundations or other institutions; private firms and individuals; and local, state and federal government agencies; for the purpose of undertaking research into any aspects of water problems related to the mission of the Department of the Interior which may be deemed desirable and are not otherwise being studied.

The opening paragraph of the Act states that it is the purpose of the Congress, by passage of the Act, to stimulate, sponsor, provide for, and supplement present programs for the conduct of research, investigations, experiments, and the training of scientists in the fields of "water and of resources which affect water." This is indeed a very broad authorization and explains why the term "water resources research" is used in referring to this program.

The main responsibility of the federal government in this joint partnership undertaking is to stimulate, advise, assist, help finance, guide, and co-ordinate needed water resources research by the various institutions and agencies mentioned above. The Office of Water Resources Research, at Washington, has already published a set of guidelines for the state centers to help them in working out sound procedures and needed research programs. It has also published a catalog of ongoing research projects which are federally supported. This catalog covers 1,545 water research projects and should help to avoid duplication of effort. A second catalog covers non-federally funded water research projects.

The Office in Washington will help state centers and the other institutions and agencies mentioned above to conduct an adequate water research program. It is hoped that a close and effective working relationship can be firmly established between the federal office and each of these centers and agencies undertaking water research work.

The centers provide an institutional structure conducive to a multi-disciplinary attack on water research problems which has been lacking, generally, up to now. Through the state centers, the research programs will encourage and make possible a more effective water-scientist training program—a further important purpose of the Act.

The Office in Washington looks to the state research centers as focal points for planning and carrying out the partnership program. It is expected that the centers will take the initiative in arranging with other institutions and agencies, both public and private, in their respective states for participation in the water research and water-scientist training programs. In attacking regional water problems, the centers work with other state centers in the region under study.

CARRYING OUT THE PARTNERSHIP PROGRAM

The 1964 Act provides for three specific types of funding: (1) Under Section 100, the annual allotment authorized for each state center is $75,000 for the fiscal year 1965, $87,500 for the fiscal years 1966 and 1967, and $100,000 for the fifty-one centers (the 50 states and Puerto Rico) in fiscal year 1968 and thereafter. (2) Under Section 101, matching funds are authorized in the amount of $1 million for fiscal year 1965, $2 million for fiscal year 1966, $3 million for fiscal year 1967, $4 million for fiscal year 1968, and $5 million thereafter. (3) Under Title II, Section 200, funds are authorized for making grants; contracts; matching or other arrangements with educational institutions other than those establishing centers; private foundations; private firms and individuals; and local, state, and federal government agencies.

Funds were appropriated under Sections 100 and 101 for allotments and matching funds, but none were appropriated under Title II. Appropriations for fiscal year 1966 permit allotments of $87,500 for each center and $1 million for matching grants.

The federal Office of Water Resources Research presently consists of a total of twenty persons—seven water scientists, administrative personnel including a grants and contracts officer and a statistician, and secretaries, typists, and clerks. It is not contemplated that the Office will at any time have a large staff but, rather, a relatively small number of competent water scientists and professional people who can work closely with the water research agencies and centers throughout the nation to achieve maximum results from funds made available for water research programs by the Congress.

STATE WATER RESOURCES RESEARCH PROGRAMS

Progress in establishing state water resources research programs is evident in the 381 projects, funded under the allotment program, that are now in operation.

Nearly nine-tenths of the projects submitted by state research centers fall into four of the nine major categories of water research developed and used by the Committee on Water Resources Research of the Federal Council for Science and Technology. These four categories are: Water Cycle—including precipitation, evaporation and transpiration, ground water and hydrogeology, and forecasting (40 per cent); Qualitative Aspects—including characterization of wastes, effects of pollution on water uses, interactions of wastes, disposal of waste effluents, effects of development on quality, quality characteristics, and aqueous solutions (28 per cent); Reuse and Separation—including saline water conversion, advanced waste treatment, improved treatment of waste, treatment of water, and use of water of impaired quality (12 per cent); and Water and Land Management—including water movement in soils, water and plants, watershed protection, water yield improvement, erosion and sedimentation, irrigation, and drainage (8 per cent).

The Office of Water Resources Research has found that the response to the Water Resources Research Act of 1964 is excellent; the high quality of the initial proposals and of the staffs that will carry out the research augurs well for the future of the programs. The research proposals received from the centers are well related to the water problems and needs for water research of the respective states, and several deal with key problems common to many states.

A committee of the American Geophysical Union (the Committee on Status and Needs in Hydrology), in reporting its findings, developed sixty-three research areas in hydrology, of which the first nine were considered to have priority. That more than half the projects submitted by state research centers fall in these nine categories indicates an excellent awareness of nationwide as well as local priority considerations.

Some idea of the range of research being undertaken at the centers is indicated by the disciplines in which the investigators (82 per cent of whom hold doctoral degrees) are working. In the following distribution, the first percentage applies to academic disciplines for fiscal year 1966; the second, in parentheses, to the 1965 program: civil engineers, 25 per cent (23 per cent); life scientists, 23 per cent (23 per cent); agricultural engineers, 11 per cent (12 per cent); geologists, including geological engineers, 11 per cent (10 per cent); soil scientists, 8 per cent (10 per cent); economists and social scientists, 7 per cent (9 per cent); chemists, 5 per cent (6 per cent); all others (lawyers, political scientists, etc.), 7 per cent (10 per cent).

The employment of graduate students as research assistants on projects is also encouraging. One or more graduate students (many working toward doctoral degrees) are being employed as research assistants on each of the more than 300 projects supplying such information. This indicates an excellent response to the training objectives of the Act. Through the concerted efforts of federal, state, and local governments, public and private agencies and firms, universities, experiment stations, research institutes and individuals, we should be able to solve many of our more perplexing water problems. As President Johnson stated, this can be done "if we maintain a continuing and effective research program."

CONCLUSION

The outstanding record of the land grant institutions, not only in the conduct of research but in the training of able scientists, promises well for the future of water resources research under the 1964 Act, which places heavy emphasis upon full use of the competence of these institutions. The federal program of assisting the institutions to develop water resources research, together with their own efforts toward co-ordinating their research with that of other universities in each participating state, should not only enlist the scientific and engineering competence of universities in problem-solving water resources research, but also provide a much-needed reservoir of scientists and engineers trained in the sciences most closely related to water resources.

The land grant institutions and state universities have demonstrated their effectiveness in advancing and disseminating knowledge widely throughout the nation and throughout their individual states. The Act will enable them to strengthen their participation in natural resources management. These are sound reasons for establishing broadly based water resources research centers at land grant institutions in each state.

Another special benefit of the program will be the increasing ability of

476

the fifty-one water resources research centers to provide informed professional assistance to state and local officials and others concerned with state, local, and regional water resources problems. As these activities move forward, state and local governments and non-governmental interests will take an increasingly active part in them. This participation needs expert professional assistance that is informed on local conditions and local problems.

The federal-state partnership principle is a sound one, but to be fully effective the program must have imaginative, creative scientists and leadership. There is a growing need for research which will be useful for programming, planning, and development work. State agencies and state leaders and federal agency representatives in the states can be helpful in pointing out areas of greatest research need. Those in the Office of Water Resources Research are confident that in the next few years a major contribution can be made toward solving some of our most difficult water problems by the federal-state partnership as carried out through the state water research centers, the matching fund grants, and Title II funds to provide needed support for competent research by universities; private organizations and individuals; federal, state, or local governments; and other concerned agencies.

REFERENCES

[1] Senate Select Committee on National Water Resources. *Report.* 86th Congress, 1st Session, Report No. 29. Washington: U.S. Government Printing Office, 1961, p. 24.

[2] Wolman, Abel. *Water Resources.* Report to the Committee on Natural Resources of the National Academy of Sciences–National Research Council. Publication 1000-B. Washington: National Academy of Sciences–National Research Council, 1962.

[3] Task Group on Coordinated Water Resources Research of the Federal Council for Science and Technology. *Report.* Washington: U.S. Government Printing Office, 1963.

Major Research Problems in Water Quality

*Earnest F. Gloyna**

T here are conflicting demands for water. Today the three leading water users—municipalities, industries, and agriculture—are being challenged by fish and wildlife, recreation, flood control, power, and navigation. While each contestant exerts its influence on both quality and quantity, the effects of water use become more pronounced. To provide for a continued supply of usable water there must be an accelerated flow of ideas from the research laboratory to the field of application.

This paper describes the nature of pollution, some dimensions of the quality question, the current status of water renovation, and research needs. Considerable background information is provided, for research requirements are all too often based on a limited interpretation of pollution.

THE NATURE OF POLLUTION

Water pollution may be obvious or rather subtle. Pollutants may be classified as disease-causing, conservative, and non-conservative. Within these three groups there seem to be eight general categories:

1. Infectious agents
2. Oxygen-demanding wastes
3. Plant nutrients
4. Organic chemicals
5. Inorganic chemical and mineral substances
6. Sediments
7. Radioactive materials
8. Heat

* Director, Center for Research in Water Resources, and Professor of Civil Engineering, University of Texas.

479

Disease-causing Pollution

The most important public health aspect of wastewater is the potential pathogenicity of the receiving waters. A list of pathogenic entities associated with domestic wastewaters includes the following:

1. Viruses
   a) Poliomyelitis
   b) Infectious hepatitis
   c) Adenovirus—upper respiratory and ocular diseases
   d) Epidemic gastroenteritis
2. Protozoa
   Endamoebic histolytica—amebic dysentery
3. Bacteria
   a) *Salmonella*—typhoid and paratyphoid
   b) *Shigella*—dysentery
   c) *Spirillum cholerae*—cholera
   d) Acid-fast bacteria—tuberculosis

The epidemiological evidence relating these diseases to man through water-contact sports, swimming, and ingestion of aquatic foods is somewhat meager; however, the potential is significant. Numerous reports discuss standards relative to bacterial content [ref. 1, 2, 3].

Conservative Pollution

Conservative pollutants are considered to be relatively stable and are not altered by the normal biological processes that occur in natural waters. Typical of this latter category are the inorganic chemicals such as chlorides which, once they enter the receiving water, may be diluted but not necessarily reduced in quantity. Some industrial wastes contain numerous conservative pollutants, including metallic salts and substances which are toxic, corrosive, colored, and taste-producing. Domestic wastes contain chlorides, phosphates, and other dissolved salts. Similarly, return flows from irrigation carry non-degradable dissolved solids.

Non-conservative Pollution

Non-conservative pollutants are changed in character by the biological, chemical, and physical forces that are exerted in a natural aquatic system. Domestic sewage, a highly unstable, organic waste, can be converted to inoffensive carbon dioxide, inorganic materials, and cell substances through the action of bacteria in treatment plants or rivers. Some industrial wastes contain decomposable organic substances and nutrients necessary to support bacterial growth. Agricultural runoffs frequently add to the organic load of a stream.

Essentially, a wastewater treatment plant systematizes, controls, and accelerates the processes that would have occurred in any case in a natural aquatic system. A treatment plant can only limit the self-purification burden that may be put on a receiving body of water.

DIMENSIONS OF THE WATER QUALITY PROBLEM

As the economic pressures become greater for more usable water the interrelationships between quantity and quality become more clearly defined, but the solution for a particular problem area becomes more complex. The quality of water is influenced by usage, natural pollution, drainage of urban and agricultural lands, waste-solids disposal practices, recreational activities, and certain political implementations. These factors are briefly discussed.

Relationship of Quality to Use

The usual quality study is made to determine if the water can be rendered satisfactory for a proposed use at an economical cost. However, the greater the urbanization of a region and the more advanced its economy, the more pronounced is the interdependence of water supply and wastewater disposal. As an example, consider some problems involving only the three dominant water users.

For domestic use the water must not contain harmful, biologically active entities. The water should be free from color and turbidity and should have no unpleasant odor or taste. The goals usually quoted in the United States for drinking purposes are based on the U.S. Public Health Service Standards [ref. 1]. However, there is considerable misunderstanding of these federal drinking water standards. While the 1963 standards recommend that water for drinking should contain less than 500 parts per million dissolved solids, they also imply that when such water is not available, more highly mineralized water may be used. Actually there are more than 100 public supplies in the United States that provide water with more than 2,000 ppm of dissolved solids. There is no limit placed on the sodium or bicarbonate content of ground water. The recommended limit of chloride (250 mg/l) is based on considerations of taste and corrosiveness. Many people will not be able to detect this level of chloride. The effect of many other mineral constituents in drinking water supplies have not been studied in as much detail. The California State Water Pollution Control Board Reports [ref. 4] are the most comprehensive publications on water quality criteria to date. More recently, water quality criteria and guides have been suggested by the

U.S. Public Health Service to meet the objectives of a particular water use [ref. 5].

Agricultural use of water includes the water for livestock, the irrigation of crops, and the operation of machinery. Most animals seem to be able to use water of considerably poorer quality than would be satisfactory for human beings. However, the total concentration of the dissolved matter, concentration of individual ions, and relative proportions of some of the constituents in water are important factors to be considered in evaluating its usefulness for irrigation. Certainly, this is an area of water quality research where much work has been done. Yet it is very difficult to predict on the basis of water analysis what may take place in the complex mineral assemblages of most soils.

Industrial water uses, quality requirements, and wastewater releases vary greatly. Research needs are generally directed toward treating the myriad process-waste streams so that the water can be recycled or released to a waterway. One specific quality problem which may require close watching is that of heat dissipation. For example, future power plants will most certainly be located near empoundments and embayments. In both cases hot waste streams will have a material effect on other water uses. The limnological changes bear watching. Approximately one gallon of water is evaporated for each 8,800 Btu dissipated in a cooling tower, or 0.61 gallon is evaporated for each kw-h. [ref. 6]. Based on studies at seventeen weather stations in Texas, between 49 and 58 per cent of the heat which is added to a reservoir results in evaporation [ref. 7]. The solids, of course, accumulate.

Natural Pollution Sources

To the above list must be added the natural sources of pollution which present some exceedingly difficult problems. Water, the universal solvent, dissolves minerals in concentrations that make the water unsuitable for many purposes. Salt springs and by-products of the mining industry, such as oilfield brines and acid mine drainage, are but a few examples.

Adverse Effects of Drainage

Pollution resulting from the drainage of agricultural lands and urban areas should be of concern. In a recent study it was demonstrated that irrigation return flows, rather than industrial waste and domestic sewage discharges, were the major factors influencing the over-all water quality of the Yakima River [ref. 8]. Drainage from this irrigation project raised the ground-water table and increased the salt content of the ground water to five times that of adjacent surface waters. Evapotranspiration increased the salt concentration by a factor of about 1.7, but leaching and ion exchange were primarily responsible for the increased concentration and changes in composition of salts in the return flows.

Of growing importance in maintaining over-all water quality is surface runoff from developed urban areas. Street washings include relatively high concentrations of pollution indicator organisms, biochemical oxygen demand, and plant nutrients. Reportedly, runoff from Seattle, Washington, contained 0.53 mg/l (NO_3-N) and 0.076 mg/l (soluble P) as compared to runoff from forested areas which contained 0.065 to 0.20 mg/l (NO_3-N) and 0.004 to 0.009 mg/l (soluble P). [Ref. 9.] In the same State, surface irrigation return flows from diversified farming contained 1.19 to 1.90 mg/l (NO_3-N) and 0.127 to 0.210 mg/l (soluble P). Contributions from drainage pipes were 0.9 to 3.9 lbs. (total P) per acre per year and 2.5 to 24 lb. (total N) per acre per year. As a comparison, the estimated nitrogen deposited via atmospheric dropout is 5.5 lb. per acre [ref. 10].

Solid-Liquid Waste Conversions

The magnitude and the impact of solid-waste disposal on both surface and ground waters is usually underestimated. As urbanization continues with the population explosion, organic solid wastes, whether garbage or animal refuse, will be generated in increasing amounts. Wherever refuse is deposited on land, there will be an opportunity for the waters of the land to intermingle with these wastes.

Today, agricultural wastes—both manures and field trash—are not wastes separate from the rest of society's discards. Consider the modern feedlot problem [ref. 11, 12]. At present, both disposal practices and design considerations are far from adequate. The relative degree of potential pollution from animal waste may be seen in Table 1.

TABLE 1.
Population Equivalents of Animal Wastes

| Species | Dry weight basis | Biochemical oxygen demand basis | | Carbon/ nitrogen basis |
		Human excrement baseline	Domestic sewage baseline	
Man	1	1	0.55	1
Hog	26.1	1.6	0.9	1.9
Hen	1.50	0.32	0.17	0.014
Turkey	4.97	—	—	—
Cow	114.5	6.4	3.5	16.4

Source: Elby [ref. 13], Henderson [ref. 14].

Municipal refuse totals about 250 billion pounds or one billion cubic yards annually. Collection and disposal costs are approximately $2.5 billion annually. In Los Angeles County the dry weight of suspended solids in the liquid wastewaters has been found to average about 0.23 lb. per capita per day, whereas other solid wastes average about 3.2 lb. Reportedly the cost per capita per year for collection and disposal, including operating costs and amortization, are $4.95 and $5.65, respectively, for wastewater and refuse.

Recreational Aspects

Herbert Hoover once said, "Next to prayer, fishing is the most personal relationship of man." According to the Outdoor Recreation Resources Review Committee, over 40 per cent of this country's population prefer water-based recreation to any other. Swimming has become one of the most popular outdoor activities, and boating and fishing rank among the top ten.

Changes brought about by water use may create a series of chain reactions which may adversely influence the usefulness of a body of water for recreation. The most obvious may include changes in pH, increases in turbidity, accumulation of sludge deposits, tainting of fish flesh, release of excessive nutrients and toxic compounds, increases in temperature, and decreases in dissolved oxygen.

The Single-Purpose Complex

The use of water for a single purpose must be given careful attention. For example, reservoirs built for flood control alone may detract from the efficient use of water for other purposes, including low-flow augmentation. Hydroelectric power for peaking purposes may conflict with downstream use of a stream for aquatic and wildlife propagation, water supply, and waste disposal. Diversion of stream flows for irrigation may drastically influence the quality of downstream flows. Uncontrolled releases from deep reservoirs which have stratified may provide oxygen-deficient water and thereby impair aquatic life. The use of waterways for municipal and industrial waste disposal and agricultural return flows may conflict with almost all other uses.

Political Implementation

Engineers and scientists can calculate only so long before some decision must be made. Ultimately, this decision will be moderated by political implementations. The decision process embraces the Hamiltonian principle: "The science of policy is the knowledge of human nature," i.e., a body politic will be responsive to public pressures.

CURRENT STATUS OF WATER RENOVATION

The status of wastewater renovation is not void of considerable accomplishments. It is possible to use most streams as a source of drinking water although pollutants are contained therein. Industry, with appropriate nudging, is cleaning up some of its effluent streams.

Probably over 40 per cent of the U.S. population is using water that has been used at least once for domestic or industrial purposes, and 60 per cent of the population now using public water supplies is using water which has been used upstream. It should be recognized, however, that many industries within a municipal complex may not have the legal right to reuse water, thereby depleting the downstream flow and effectively increasing the solids concentration. In several cases downstream users have taken legal action to prevent upstream municipalities from reusing their effluents for various purposes other than drinking water. On the other hand, upstream municipalities presently feel little responsibility to exercise a high degree of wastewater reclamation or quality improvement, particularly if the only beneficiaries are to be the downstream users.

Industry is spending considerable sums of money to treat effluents. A National Association of Manufacturers' survey found that industry spends about $100 million a year to operate wastewater treatment equipment, representing an investment of some $1 billion. The chemical industry is in the middle of crash investment in water-pollution control facilities. According to the Manufacturing Chemists' Association, 125 companies with 875 plants have invested $264 million in equipment and plan to spend another $70 million by the end of 1969. Operating costs for present facilities are about $40 million per year.

The first major legislative action for advanced waste treatment research came with the passage in July 1961 of the Amendment to the Federal Water Pollution Control Act (Public Law 87–88). Although no specific mention is made of treating agricultural return flows, storm-water runoff, and pollution resulting from increased temperature, the broad definition as set by Congress appears to be applicable to all cases.

It has been shown repeatedly that even domestic sewage, when properly treated, can be put to any of the normal beneficial uses. However, the reuse of municipal wastewater for direct public use is not one of the normal objectives for it is not usually economically feasible. However, indirect use after dilution is common practice.

485

As practiced today, the problem of water renovation becomes one of developing specific treatment units. Some progress has been made in the development of conventional and even new processes, but more rapid progress is needed. Due to the historical manner in which municipalities have approached the water and wastewater problem, most of the research and plant redevelopment effort has been to improve the efficiency of previously used processes. For example, consider the problem from a process point of view, Table 2. Because of technical breakthroughs, new processes may now be feasible.

While some laboratory advances may be expected in secondary biological waste treatment, the point of no return is rapidly approaching because, in general, operational supervision is not available at many municipal installations. This operational aspect has led regulatory agencies to become ultra-conservative in accepting new processes. Consequently, a

TABLE 2.

Upgrading via Additional Process Units

Water treatment plants		Wastewater treatment plants	
Conventional	Possible add. or substitution	Conventional	Possible add. or substitution
Sedimentation	Fine screening Super chlorination	*Primary Treatment* Sedimentation Sludge digestion	Fine screening Incineration Wet combustion
Chemical treatment	Use coagulant aids Removal of nutrients and taste and odor compounds	*Secondary Treatment* Aerobic-biological	Biological
Sedimentation		Sedimentation	Sedimentation
Filtration	Electrodialysis Ion exchange or demineralization Dechlorination		
			Polishing Treatment Coagulation Nutrient removal Adsorption Filtration Demineralization Underground recharge
Chlorination		Chlorination	Super chlorination Ozonation Ionizing radiation

486

third stage of wastewater treatment, in addition to sedimentation and aerobic stabilization, is considered necessary.

The cost of wastewater handling as presently considered is that incurred for collection, treatment, and disposal, as shown in Table 3. In general, the disposal costs reflect a desire to maximize the stream's assimilative capacity. However, should waste treatment become a means of producing water, i.e., not solely a means of removing contaminants, a different set of cost criteria must be used.

TABLE 3.

Transport and Treatment Costs

System	Average[1] (¢/1,000 gal.)	Range[1] (¢/1,000 gal.)
Source development and transmission	5	0–30
Water distribution	17	
Water treatment	6	0–9
Waste collection	6	
Sewage treatment	6	0–8

[1] Represents total cost including operation and maintenance, plus amortization of the original investment.

Source: Summary Report, The Advanced Waste Treatment Research Program [ref. 15].

Since some aspects of water-supply and waste-treatment costs are built around water distribution and waste collection, this fraction of the total cost of the water-use cycle is likely to remain fairly uniform for all modes of treatment. Obviously these costs do not relate the net cost of water, for such might include short-range depletion costs, waterway impairment, etc.

Estimated water renovation costs for various operations and processes have been computed [ref. 16]. Costs for a complete wastewater treatment plant capable of providing municipal-quality water may range between 54 and 57 cents per 1,000 gallons, depending upon the mode of inorganic solids removal. These costs include operation and amortization. An electrolysis plant (10 mgd) processing 1,700 to 3,000 mg/l of salinity is said to produce enough fresh water for all the domestic needs of 60,000 people at a cost of only 20 to 30 cents per 1,000 gallons. By contrast, a seawater distillation plant of the same size would produce fresh water at 70 to 75 cents per 1,000 gallons [ref. 17]. The newly developed Kunin ion exchange process reportedly can demineralize water for 11 to 22 cents per 1,000 gallons if the dissolved solids do not exceed 1,100 mg/l [ref. 18].

487

RESEARCH NEEDS

From the preceding discussion, it would appear that the focus of the research problems depends upon whether pollution is the discharge of wastes that impose an external cost on subsequent users, or a discharge that interferes with the optimum use of water resources, or a discharge that interferes with the well-being of selected groups. Probably all three conditions independently or collectively must be met in some areas. Thus to economically renovate water for all uses, water quality research must be conducted on a broad front. The following list suggests some of the most pressing water quality research needs.

- Improvement of treatment processes,
- Translation of theory to design,
- Optimization of water quality management,
- Development of stream use criteria,
- Ground-water quality management,
- Improvement of marine disposal systems.

Improvement of Treatment Processes

Many organic and inorganic contaminants that enter water resist present-day treatment processes. New treatment processes that may not have been practical at one time must be re-examined. Combinations of conventionally used unit operations must be re-evaluated and possibly a new arrangement established. Perhaps it is now desirable to add processes typical of water-treatment plants to wastewater-treatment plants. Higher efficiencies are required for removing well-recognized pollutants, and new schemes are needed to remove exotic but recognizable contaminants. Within the treatment and operations framework the following factors and processes need to receive detailed attention:

1. Biological factors
   a) BOD loading and removal relationships
   b) Oxygen requirements
   c) Oxygen transfer relationships
   d) Sludge production and accumulation
   e) Solids—liquid separation
   f) Sludge handling and disposal
   g) Eutrophication
   h) Elimination of aftergrowths
   i) Indicator organisms
   j) Ecological stability
   k) Taste and odor control

2. Physical and chemical processes
   a) Adsorption
   b) Electrodialysis
   c) Evaporation
   d) Extraction

488

e) Foaming
f) Emulsion separation
g) Freezing
h) Hydration
i) Oxidation
j) Ion exchange

k) Electrochemical degradation
l) Coagulation
m) Wet combustion
n) Liquid-solids separation
o) Ionizing radiation

3. Facilities and systems operation
   a) Industrial plant and product modification
   b) Optimization of industrial reuse, recycle, and disposal
   c) Optimization of municipal treatment plant design and operation
   d) Treatment by surface and ground-water interchanges
   e) Low-flow augmentation

Translation of Theory to Design

Probably one of the greatest problems in water treatment is the matter of translating fairly well-developed theoretical and laboratory data into economical designs. There is a logical process by which theoretical concepts can be moved through a laboratory study, pilot plant, drawing board, and field evaluation. Some way must be found to accelerate the process. The solution possibly lies in diverting more research monies to developmental research and establishing a premium on novel and efficient processes.

Optimization of Water Quality Management

This topic deals with water and wastewater management. Important research problems that must be undertaken in this area include:
1. Assimilative capacities of present and projected water systems;
2. Impact of reuse and recycle on water quality of present and projected water systems;
3. The degree of treatment, type of treatment, and location of unit processes for treating wastewater and municipal and industrial waters;
4. Development of treatment cost relationships between soluble organics and inorganics, insoluble materials, toxic pollutants, and other potentially objectionable pollutants;
5. Evaluation of minimum cost alternatives.

A number of engineering-economic studies are beginning to appear. These exploratory studies are probing for solutions which must come from the interaction of a variety of disciplines. Answers are being sought to such questions as, "How do you evaluate the social cost of pollution?"

and "Why is it that under certain sets of values minimum stream disposal rather than maximum stream disposal becomes the over-all cost alternative?" One of the more recent efforts in this area was to find the optimum division, on an economic basis, between the waste-treatment plant of one community and the water-treatment plant of another [ref. 19].

In the management of wastewater and water resources there is strong reason to suspect that the time has come when municipalities should seriously think about going out of the wastewater-treatment business. Because water quality transcends the corporate limits of a city or even a metropolitan area, this quality management can be done more effectively by a higher water-control unit. Such an authority most logically would be the river authority. The latter could provide more expert planning, operation, and maintenance to individual treatment plants. Funding for treatment would be more systematic if planning were done on the basis of a river basin. This is an area where basic and applied research should receive the highest priority.

Development of Stream Use Criteria

What constitutes stream classification? Presumably, this means the classification of streams so as to assure their best use for the greatest number of people. To maximize this simply stated concept in terms of economics or any other parameter is exceedingly difficult if not impossible under the present state of the art. Based on today's vision, we see streams that are clean and should be kept that way, especially if recreational values are important. Some streams, especially tidal streams, are seemingly beyond either the technical ability or the people's willingness to pay for the restoration of the stream for all types of recreation. For example, although it is easy to restrict open sewers today, is a tidal estuary that is subjected to highly industrialized activities, massive domestic developments, and use by ocean-going vessels likely ever to support game fish from its headwaters to its mouth the year round? Needless to say, mature and comprehensive research is needed on this matter of stream classification. The economy and welfare of an area, possibly the affluence of the state concerned, will surely be affected adversely if classification is attempted without the benefit of exhaustive research.

Ground-water Quality Management

The same arguments hold for the management of water quality in ground waters as for surface waters. Unfortunately, definitive research in ground-water pollution, prevention of pollution, and maximization of use is much more expensive than research dealing with surface waters. In general, the understanding of ground water is considerably less than surface waters. Areas of needed research are listed:

1. Selective transport of pollutants through underground aquifers;
2. Evaluation of exchange relationships under natural and induced recharge systems;
3. Role of ground water in reuse programs;
4. Effective removal of interfering microorganisms such as slime formers, algae, iron bacteria, sulfate-reducing bacteria, and fungi;
5. Equipment development, corrosion control, etc.

Improvement of Marine Disposal Systems

There is a growing realization by large water-using industries that plant sites near oceans or estuaries provide one answer to the wastewater problem. Large amounts of water are available for cooling and dilution purposes. This fact is becoming increasingly significant because changes in technology permit both the economical transport of raw materials and use of brackish waters. The limited availability and restricted use of fresh water will probably enhance the industrial migration to coastal areas. This increased domestic and industrial water-use load in the tidal areas may reduce the value of these waters for recreational use, sports and commercial fishing, and spawning or nursery grounds. Research for water quality protection is needed in the following areas:

1. Development of detailed mathematical models relating waste transport through embayments and coastal areas, i.e., development of predictive techniques for dispersion and mixing;
2. Accumulation and critical evaluation of a wide variety of background data, including ecological as well as physical information;
3. Development of economical, rugged, and sensitive monitoring equipment;
4. Statistical assessment of present and future recreational use.

SUMMARY

In summary, pollution need not be the penalty of progress. Water renovation is possible. However, the methods for allocating the cost of water supply, quality improvement, recreation, etc., are not well understood. Certainly the present fees for water use are not adequate, if water must be readily available for use by all categories of users.

Improvements in pollution control are necessary. Differences of opinion exist over the criteria or level of standards, the timing of regulatory action, and the allocation of costs.

There is a real distinction between pollution, which causes economic inconvenience and aesthetic distress, and contamination, which is the addition of substances that endanger the health of humans. However, the inability to trace all substances through the food chain periodically raises a question as to what constitutes contamination. The term "pollution" hinges on the unreasonable impairment of the water's value to other users. All attempts to agree on an interpretation will be influenced by economic, sociological, and political factors.

Today's standard of wastewater treatment cannot economically re-establish the original quality of water. Present treatment facilities can only limit the burden that may be put on a receiving body of water. For example, undue enrichment from highly polished wastewaters may bring about biological excesses that are inimical to recreational and other uses.

Both fundamental and applied research on a broad basis are needed to solve tomorrow's water quality problems. Processes must be improved; laboratory discoveries must be expedited; optimization techniques must be developed; stream-use criteria must be re-evaluated; ground-water quality problems must be overcome; and better marine disposal schemes must be found.

REFERENCES

[1] *Drinking Water Standards* (revised). U.S. Public Health Service. No. 956, June 1963.

[2] Garber, W. F. "Bacteriological Standards for Bathing Waters," *Sewage and Industrial Waste Journal,* Vol. 28 (June 1956).

[3] Ludwig, H. *Collation, Evaluation, and Presentation of Scientific and Technical Data Relative to the Marine Disposal of Liquid Wastes.* Report submitted to California State Water Quality Control Board. Sacramento, 1964.

[4] McKee, J. *Water Quality Criteria.* Sacramento: State Water Quality Control Board, 1952.

[5] Burk, G. W., Jr. "Water Quality Criteria." Paper presented before the National Task Committee on Industrial Wastes. San Francisco, November 18–20, 1964.

[6] *Steam-Electric Plant Factors.* National Coal Association, Vol. 22, Washington, 1963–64, pp. 16–17.

[7] Drew, H. W. *A Projection of Per Capita Water Use for Electric Power Generation in Texas.* Report prepared for Texas Water Commission. Austin, May 15, 1965.

[8] Sylvester, R. D., and Seabloom, R. W. *A Study on the Character and Significance of Irrigation Return Flows in the Yakima River Basin.* University of Washington Report, May 1963.

[9] Sylvester, R. D. "Nutrient Content of Drainage Water from Forested, Urban, and Agricultural Areas," *Algae and Metropolitan Wastes.* Cincinnati: U.S. Public Health Service, Robert A. Taft Sanitary Engineering Center, 1960, pp. 80–87.

[10] Hutchinson, G. E. *A Treatise on Limnology.* New York: John Wiley and Sons, 1957.

[11] Hart, S. A. "Processing Agricultural Wastes," *Proceedings, National Conference on Solid Waste Research.* University of Chicago, December 1963.

[12] Taiganides, E. P. "Agricultural Solid Wastes," *Proceedings, National Conference on Solid Waste Research.* University of Chicago, December 1963.

[13] Elby, H. J. "Manure Lagoons," *Agricultural Engineering,* Vol. 43 (1962).

[14] Henderson, M. "Agriculture Land Drainage and Stream Pollution," *Journal,* Sanitary Engineering Division, American Society of Civil Engineers, Vol. 88, SA6 (1962).

[15] *Summary Report, The Advanced Waste Treatment Research Program.* Cincinnati: U.S. Public Health Service, Robert A. Taft Sanitary Engineering Center, May 1962.

[16] Stephan, D. G. "Water Renovation, Current Status on the Technology." Paper presented at Southern Water Resources Conferences, Chapel Hill, North Carolina, April 15, 1965.

[17] Ionics, Inc. *Electrochemical Processes for Water, Food and Chemicals.* Cambridge, Mass., March 1965.

[18] "Brackish Waters Treated by Ion Exchange." Editorial in *Chemical and Engineering News,* Vol. 43 (April 19, 1965), p. 72.

[19] Frankel, R. J. "Water Quality Management: An Engineering-Economic Model for Domestic Waste Disposal." Unpublished Ph.D. dissertation, Division of Sanitary-Hydraulic Engineering, University of California, Berkeley, 1964.

Major Research Problems in Hydrology and Engineering

*William C. Ackermann**

Hydrological and engineering research has been stimulated in recent years by the increasing attention given to all aspects of water resource problems. Government and professional institutions alike have contributed an impressive amount of research effort, but much remains to be done. Before discussing some specific areas which press for further hydrological and engineering study, it may be useful to mention the large body of recently published work that is available to the student of water resource problems in general. The sources of information to which I refer have the advantage of representing the combined judgment of many informed people.

BACKGROUND FOR RESEARCH

Government Publications

The springboard for current research in the water resources field is the report of the U.S. Senate's Select Committee on National Water Resources, published as Committee Prints in 1960 and 1961 [ref. 1]. The report did far more than identify needed research. It projected water supply and demand and thus identified the problems the nation will have to face in this century; and it called for comprehensive planning as well as a co-ordinated scientific research program for water.

In 1961, President Kennedy asked the National Academy of Sciences

* Chief, Illinois State Water Survey.

to undertake a thorough and broadly based study and evaluation of the present state of research underlying the conservation, development, and use of natural resources (including water). Also the Academy committee was asked to inquire into the formation, replenishment, and substitution of resources. Further basic research needs were to be given particular attention. The resulting report, *Water Resources* [ref. 2], suggests priority research areas for improving present water use practices and for increasing scientific understanding. Prominent among the measures recommended are: increasing the production of skilled professionals, improving techniques of water management, and understanding the thermodynamics of the water cycle. Particular emphasis is given to ground water, pollutants, and demineralization of brackish and sea waters.

President Kennedy also directed his science advisor and the Federal Council for Science and Technology to review ongoing federal research activities and determine ways to strengthen the total government research effort. The resulting three published reports document the current research efforts of about twenty-five agencies and represent the combined judgment of many as to the water problems which bear on the missions of those agencies. The first of these reports, *Federal Water Resources Research Activities,* was prepared by a Task Group on Coordinated Water Resources Research and appeared in print in 1963 [ref. 3]. This significant report of the Federal Council is the first comprehensive statement of the objectives and activities of all federal agencies engaged in water resources research and provides policy guidance for such research within the executive branch. In addition to examining the interrelationships among the agency programs and the degree of their co-ordination, it presents an inventory of ongoing programs and points to some weaknesses in the research effort. The weaknesses particularly cited are in the areas of training and of research in ground water, socioeconomics, and water quality.

The second report in this series, *Federal Water Resources Research Program for Fiscal Year 1965* [ref. 4], documents the federal program for the fiscal years 1964 and 1965 according to some fifty categories of research and by agencies. Like the first report, this report also is much concerned with co-ordination. The Council's third report is essentially an updating of the second, *Federal Water Resources Research Program for Fiscal Year 1966,* and was published in February 1965 [ref. 5]. Some of the problems it identifies as needing priority research are discussed later in this paper.

Meanwhile, the Federal Committee on Water Resources Research is developing a long-range research program which shortly, it is hoped, will be publicly available.

A rich source of information on the needs for and character of water research is to be found in the records of Congress. These include the hearings and debate during 1962, 1963, and 1964 relative to the Water Resources Research Act of 1964 [ref. 6], and the extensive hearings before the Subcommittee on Natural Resources and Power of the House Committee on Government Operations, which examined water quality and pollution research problems and programs [ref. 7].

Activities of Professional Organizations

Through the meetings and writings of its Section of Hydrology, the American Geophysical Union contributes to the advancement of hydrological research. The Union's Committee on Status and Needs in Hydrology prepared a first draft of the U.S. program for the International Hydrological Decade and later developed a list of "63 Priority Areas of Research in Hydrology" [ref. 8]. The Committee met in July 1965 to consider the over-all needs for data and instrumentation. Its conclusions were published at the end of the year [ref. 9].

The International Hydrological Decade (1965–74) is directing the attention of scientists and the world at large to the importance of water science. Its program is excellently summarized by Nace in the AGU *Transactions* [ref. 10]. In this country, the program is guided by an ad hoc U.S. Committee for the International Hydrological Decade in the Division of Earth Sciences of the National Academy of Sciences. Internationally, eighty countries have declared their intentions to participate through a Co-ordinating Council established in the United Nations Educational, Scientific, and Cultural Organization. The Council held its first meeting in Paris, May 24–June 3, 1965. The Decade program includes consideration of basic data, inventories and water balances, research and education, and supporting activities too extensive to report here. At the international level, the areas judged to have priority importance are indicated by the subjects considered at meetings held or scheduled to be held early in the Decade:

Hydrological Networks, Quebec, Canada, June 1965;

Hydrology of Representative and Experimental Basins, Budapest, Hungary, September–October 1965;

Hydrology of Fractured Rocks, Belgrade, Yugoslavia, October 1965;

Hydrology of the Unsaturated Zone, Waageningen, Netherlands, June 1966.

Other symposia have been scheduled or proposed dealing with: physical limnology, in Garda, Italy, October 6–11, 1966; artificial recharge of ground water, in Israel during March 1967; and the use of analog models and digital computers in hydrology, probably in the United States.

Among the many professional organizations that are concentrating on research and development in the water resources field, mention should be made of the American Society of Civil Engineers. This organization, through its various divisions, is now in the process of assessing research needs in water resources. The report of one ASCE group, "Research Needs in Surface-Water Hydrology" [ref. 11] deals with stochastic hydrologic procedures, runoff from small areas, channel losses in ephemeral streams, water use by natural vegetation, economical flow records of desert streams, conservation of flood runoff, electronic digital computers, improved quantitative measurement of precipitation, and radioactive and chemical tracers. In July 1965, the ASCE sponsored a Seminar on the Hydraulic Engineering Research Aspects of Water Quality Management in River and Reservoir Systems, at Vanderbilt University; and in August, held a Gordon-type Conference on Urban Hydrology at Andover, New Hampshire. The subjects of the two meetings suggest that the Society views water quality and urban hydrology as areas that are in critical need of study and accelerated research.

Since the reports and activities I have described are the product of able minds counseling together, the resulting recommendations represent a wide consensus and can be regarded as having considerable validity. From among these recommendations I have selected a few problems that, in my opinion, require immediate attention. They are confined to the areas of hydrology and engineering, but it should be recognized that other areas of water resources research, particularly those of socioeconomics and water quality dealt with elsewhere in this section of the volume, are equally important. Nor should it be overlooked that there is urgent need for improving education and training in all aspects of water resources use and management.

RESEARCH PROBLEMS NEEDING SPECIAL ATTENTION

River Forecasting for Water Resource Management

The need to research, develop, and implement a sophisticated and integrated system of river and reservoir forecasting and management is of pressing importance. The next generation will see more structures built for more purposes than in the entire history of the country. Besides the requirements of flood control, hydropower, navigation, and irrigation, our water resources will have to provide water supply for an increasingly industrial society, waste dilution, recreation, and a suitable environment for fish and wildlife. Every year the number of agencies—federal, state, and local—that wish to manage the flow and storage of our waters grows larger. The consequences of these programs, many of which are at cross purposes, will be disastrous unless a high order of knowledge is available to all interested agencies. Knowledge of the natural variables, such as precipitation and runoff, is, of course, involved; but to an increasing extent we also need to know more about the regulation and control of the waters by the works of man. For forecasting, more complex and realistic hydrologic models than have been employed in the past are possible today through the use of high-speed electronic computers, but considerable educational effort will be required in order to realize the full potential of such new and developing technology.

Urban Hydrology

The field of urban hydrology is almost devoid of modern research investment. Here, empirical methods developed before the turn of the century are still in general use. Research on small or experimental watersheds, such as that done by the U.S. Department of Agriculture, has been chiefly devoted to agricultural, forested, or wild lands, and the results of these studies are not applicable to the urban environment characterized by paved areas and rapid collection systems. In view of trends in urban growth, it is clear that substantial attention should be given to this area of research. It has been predicted that between today and 1990 the nation will spend between $30 and $45 billion on the construction of urban storm drainage systems alone. Large economies of design are possible if a major program of research were undertaken in this area.

Engineering and Geology of Dams

Recent failures of dams and dam foundations in the United States and abroad have dramatically demonstrated the need for expanded research in the fields of soil mechanics, engineering geology, and construction materials.

Dams and other structures built over the past thirty years have utilized the best sites, the most favorable foundations, and the most suitable and economically available materials. Construction agencies are now faced with the problem of designing and building safe and adequate structures of unprecedented size and complexity on foundations and with materials of less than optimum suitability. Research in these areas will have an important bearing on the integrity of the nation's water resources development.

Evaporation and Transpiration

Of the water resource received as precipitation, some 70 per cent, on the average, is lost by evapotranspiration. The large amounts of water involved are an inducement to finding ways of improving efficiency in managing precipitation, including reductions in water use by plants. Research on evaporation and transpiration is expected to take a number of directions, among which are plant breeding, chemical applications to soil and plants, the timing of water applications, and land use management. This area is now ripe for an intensive research effort.

Research on Prime Water Resources

Finally, there is the need to shift more research effort to the valuable resources that are usually taken for granted. Supporting the underdog is a strong tradition in this country, and one which seems to carry over into the field of natural resources. For example, where soils are concerned, great effort is expended on marginal or problem situations, but little consideration is given to Class I soils until they, too, become marginal or problem cases. In the field of water resources, the Great Lakes can be identified as a uniquely valuable resource that has been taken for granted to the point of abuse. More has been expended in legal efforts than in constructive hydrologic or engineering study. Recent signs indicate that we are paying for our indifference in lowered water levels and water devoid of oxygen. What is happening to the Great Lakes is a conspicuous example of our need as a nation to place greater emphasis on conserving and wisely developing the prime resources of water upon which so much of our strength depends.

REFERENCES

[1] U.S. Senate, Select Committee on National Water Resources. *Water Resources Activities in the United States*. Committee Prints 1–32. Washington: U.S. Government Printing Office, 1960–61.

[2] Wolman, Abel. *Water Resources*. A Report to the Committee on Natural Resources (series 1000-B). National Academy of Sciences–National Research Council. Washington, 1962.

[3] Senate Committee on Interior and Insular Affairs. *Federal Water Resources Research Activities*. Committee Print, 88th Congress, 1st Session. Washington: U.S. Government Printing Office, March 25, 1963.

[4] Federal Council for Science and Technology. *Federal Water Resources Research Program for Fiscal Year 1965.* Progress report of the Committee on Water Resources Research. Washington: U.S. Government Printing Office, February 1964.

[5] Federal Council for Science and Technology. *Federal Water Resources Research Program for Fiscal Year 1966.* Washington: U.S. Government Printing Office, February 1965.

[6] *Congressional Record,* various issues, 1962–64.

[7] U.S. Congress. "Water Pollution Control and Abatement." Hearings before a subcommittee of the Committee on Government Operations. House Doc. No. 1636, 88th Congress, 1st Session (Committee Report No. 21). Washington: U.S. Government Printing Office, 1963, 1964.

[8] Linsley, Ray K. "Meeting of American Geophysical Union Committee on Status and Needs in Hydrology," AGU *Transactions,* Vol. 45, No. 4 (1964).

[9] Ackermann, William C. "Committee on Status and Needs in Hydrology: A Look at Data and Instrumentation," AGU *Transactions,* Vol. 46, No. 4 (1965).

[10] Nace, Raymond L. "The International Hydrological Decade," AGU *Transactions,* Vol. 45, No. 3 (1964).

[11] "Research Needs in Surface-Water Hydrology," *Journal* of the ASCE Hydraulics Division, American Society of Civil Engineers, January 1965.

Major Research Problems in the Social Sciences

Stephen C. Smith*

The research dealt with in this paper is concerned mainly with issues that have had scant attention in the water resources field. Little need be said about the necessity for continuing research in the broad field of benefit-cost analysis, related regional analysis, and economic-engineering analysis. Since these approaches have often proved their usefulness in evaluating projects and water systems, the probability is high that research of these types will continue and that support for it will not be too difficult to obtain.

With water, as with other natural resources, the central problems revolve around man—his knowledge, institutions, and objectives [ref. 1]. Thus, all of the social sciences have their place in helping to solve problems of water management. Indeed, as Allen V. Kneese has pointed out in the Introduction to this volume, the contribution of some of the social sciences to the field of water resources has been unique during the last thirty years when compared with their contribution to other applied resource fields. Opinions differ in assessing the impact of this contribution. At the least, however, fresh and vigorous thinking has been stimulated about multidimensional problems that will yield to no single disciplinary approach.

When the social scientist surveys water resource problems, he is faced with a two-way challenge. First, by using his tools of analysis in this

* Director, Natural Resources Center, and Professor of Economics, Colorado State University.

field, he can contribute toward the solution of problems so basic that if they remain unsolved, they will degrade the level of living within our economy. Second, he can regard water resource problems as a laboratory in which to test hypotheses, develop new concepts and tools, and evaluate the precepts of his discipline in the context of man's capacity for adaptation and readaptation.

The term "social scientist" is used in an inclusive sense, for the economist, political scientist, sociologist, psychologist, historian, lawyer, and geographer each can make an important contribution to research in the water resources field. But care must be utilized in that the professional disciplines do not obscure an understanding of the observed behavioral pattern by centering on technique rather than on substance.

There is a close intertie between each of the social sciences as well as between the social sciences and engineering or the physical and biological sciences. Exploration of these interties can yield several types of payoff— the amelioration of conditions known to be undesirable; a redefining of situations to improve current practice; and an accretion to the body of social science knowledge. Research into these "points of intertie" should be given more emphasis.

A major task for social science research is to identify the significant systems and subsystems of organized social action with reference to water resources development and management, and to understand the dynamics of these systems and their interaction. Such a task is never ending, for the systems not only are internally dynamic but have dynamic relationships among each other. As Boulding has observed, "Social processes are always in some sense stochastic, they have chance elements built into them, and hence their course can not be predicted in detail. . . ." [ref. 2]. Even with these characteristics—indeed, one can argue *because* of these characteristics—a specification of the appropriate social system is essential for the criteria which social science might suggest to be useful. Criteria developed from the social sciences (benefit-cost analysis, for example) have been accepted, but they have sometimes been applied to an inappropriate social system or to one which diverges too greatly from the parent model. At other times, they have been applied in ways that do not recognize the intertemporal dimension of the uncertainty built into organizational dynamics. Since the dynamics are continually shifting the system boundary, this raises questions about the appropriateness of specified criteria.

Benefit-cost analysis was derived from the efficiency-competitive model. It has been applied usefully and with increasing rigor to public enterprise. Yet the decision maker who uses this and other criteria cannot jump from the criteria to hard decision without an uncomfortable feeling that he has just passed over a void which may engulf him. The old hand at making such jumps develops composure, yet he realizes he has taken that necessarily heroic leap across the unknown. True, we must learn to live with an unknown; but by reshaping, through research, the definitions of our working system, existing criteria will be utilized more effectively and intrasystem and intersystem tradeoffs may be more accurately assessed. Therefore, I suggest some fundamental multidiscipline studies in identifying the appropriate decision systems for the water problems in which social science performance criteria can function. For example, Gilbert F. White's research (part of which is outlined in his paper in this volume) has been attempting to reshape the system boundaries and the operational criteria for flood control.

For the West and for many other sections of the nation, the social role of water in both public and private behavior has not been properly perceived. Has the social scientist compared the concept of water development which says (a) "Governments invest to remove water as a constraint to private development," with the conventional implication deriving from the objective (b) "We seek an economically optimal water resource allocation within region x and time y"? History has been written on the basis of (a) and much of our effort to adopt (b) has only led to redefining the rules by which the game in (a) has been played, rather than moving to (b). Social science could perform a practical as well as scientific service by confronting this issue. The developmental and management criteria under the two systems are quite different and the social scientist should help clarify the differences. In performing this task, there is a role for each of the social science groups.

The significance of this line of research may be highlighted in the following way: Project evaluation with a system of political ordering has been the general rule. The weaknesses of this approach have been explored and have been made explicit. By contrast, research has stopped short of thoroughly integrating the dominant behavioral system. One reason for this may be due to having focused directly upon water resources rather than upon establishing the role of water resources within the socioeconomic system. Basic clarification in this area would permit us to take major strides in a whole sequence of subproblems. Yet it is often such basic types of work that fail to attract funding. We have not taken a tough enough look at studies dealing with the processes of social change as they relate to water with its variety of "regional taste." This people-and-process situation is illustrated by the events in Colorado in the summer of 1965. The floods called attention to a recommendation made over ten years earlier for the construction of dams on the South Platte system. But no action resulted. The clamor for effective flood plain zoning and for holding the flood plain free from development has been deafening by its absence. Is it not time the sociologist and social psychologist brought their talents to bear on these problems?

There are other problems needing their attention. In many areas, the level of water use is moving up the scale from that of previous decades. Scarcity of the type of water desired, with attendant increased demand and "prices," are forcing adjustments in water use. Along with this shift, the contribution of the sociologist in adapting the spread of "practices research" to water use would be useful. There has been a small beginning in this area but the results of further studies can aid in the adoption of the best water use practices by the individual user. Along with a focus on the adoption of the latest technology, a series of social behavioral studies would be beneficial. These would range from studies of the acceptance of organizational change to studies of attitudes toward water quality and recreation. The benefits from this area of research would accrue not only to the public decision-making entity, but to the individual user in attaining a higher level of water use. This is almost virgin territory for the social scientist.

Questions of social organization and the handling of conflict are another category of problems deserving attention. The economist, political scientist, and lawyer have been working on some of the problems, but rarely has the sociologist applied his tools to these issues within the context of water resources. It has been almost twenty years since Philip Selznick looked at the Tennessee Valley Authority and developed such useful concepts as co-optation [ref. 3]. Urging the sociologist into this field in no way implies that the economist, political scientist, geographer, and lawyer should vacate; only that a new perspective may add new insight.

Organizational studies have been an important part of research in water resources for many years and political scientists have contributed usefully to the literature. Yet, certain aspects of this area of study should receive greater attention than in the past. The political scientist can further understanding through thorough analysis of the power relationships among political entities vis-à-vis the use of water resources. The politics of water differs from party politics without differing in applicability of political thought. This difference has been only partially analyzed. Furthermore, water resources offer the political scientist a laboratory for testing many concepts with respect to the structure of government. This testing would be of practical value for the public hearing procedure, for enabling the voting public to evaluate a complex public investment in water, for simplifying intergovernmental relations, for administrative structure at all levels, and for dealing with the question of representation

506

of special interests as opposed to making more general tradeoffs—to give only a suggestive list.

Studies of this type cannot be divorced from economic, legal, and sociological analyses. The economist and the lawyer have long been making efforts to communicate. Their efforts should be continued. Without elaborating, it is my belief that the legal profession has been slow to come to research. This attitude is understandable, but I would urge the lawyer, the court, and the law-making bodies to take a much more careful look at what legal and scientific research can contribute to the solution of long-run and short-run water problems. There are many areas of difficult communication to be overcome, which run in several directions. The politician of today needs to learn the role of social science and how to use it; the social scientist must improve his ability to understand the subsystems of values and informational relationships significant to the politician. I have used the word "communication," but clearly the issues run much deeper than this. It is on these deeper substantive issues of dynamic intertie that the social scientist must concentrate.

In the West, water law has reached voluminous proportions; in the East, it is accumulating at a rapid rate. As a result, the social sciences— in combination with engineering and the physical and biological sciences —have a responsibility to analyze, interpret, and bring order to this tangled web. As I have already emphasized, in pursuing their goals individual problems and studies must be related to the larger concept of a system. One such area of research which needs clearer understanding is the integration of surface- and ground-water management. The whole concept of management is, in fact, often rejected.

Problems of surface and ground water with a narrower focus have received and will continue to receive prime attention. In addition, a few social scientists are continuing an old thread of interest in the interaction of climate and man. Atmospheric water and weather modifications pose a significant range of water problems frequently neglected. Man's power of adjustment and adaptation are so great, and these adaptations have been so capitalized within our social structure, that purposeful manipulation is fraught with resistance. Also, questions of social evaluation take on a new dimension in terms of the burden of choice placed upon man. Analysis of the complexity of this burden is a massive challenge for the social scientist. In facing such a challenge he must be alert to the necessity of (a) creating a purposive decision-making structure that will guide man's behavior in a world where his environmental influence is paramount, and (b) early identifying the multiplicity of side effects that could lead to unwanted ends.

Two final comments: (1) social science research should be carried

507

through to the operational stage where possible; and (2) research talent should be applied to making non-monetary criteria as explicit as possible. This does not imply any diminution of the importance of monetary criteria, but simply suggests that if we are dissatisfied with it as our sole criterion, other criteria must be developed from a firm research base.

REFERENCES

[1] Ciriacy-Wantrup, S. V. *Resources Conservation, Economics and Policies.* Berkeley: University of California, Division of Agricultural Sciences, 1963, pp. 28–29.
[2] Kahn, Robert L., and Boulding, Elise (eds.). *Power and Conflict.* New York: Basic Books, Inc., 1964, p. 136.
[3] Selznick, Philip. *TVA and the Grass Roots.* Berkeley: University of California Press, 1953.

INDEX

Index

Ackermann, William C., 495, 497, 501
Adams, F. Gerard, 130n, 175
Advisory Committee on a National Highway Program, 322
Aerojet-General, desalination pilot plant, 434–35
Agriculture: use of water, research needed, 482; western, and water utilization, 273–75 *passim*
Akron, Ohio, employment effects of hypothetical rubber project located in Appalachia, 460
Allee, David J., 224
Alternative cost, role in project design and selection, 33–37
Amberg, H. R., 157, 172
American Association for the Advancement of Science, 303
American Association of State Highway Officials, 322
American Chemical Society, 427
American Economics Association, 308
American Geophysical Union: Committee on Status and Needs in Hydrology, 475, 497; Section on Hydrology, 497
American Society of Civil Engineers, 308, 310, 498
American Society for Engineering Education, 307
Amidon, Elliot, 372, 373

Analog model (simulator), *see* Models, analog
Analytical models, *see* Models, mathematical
Anderson, E. A., 343, 345, 354
Anderson, Henry W., 355, 357, 358, 359, 362, 364, 365, 366, 368, 369, 371, 372
Animal wastes, relative degree of potential pollution from, 483t
Anis, A. A., 401, 411
Appalachia: hypothetical rubber project located in, 460; program, objectives and benefit-cost analysis, 312
Appalachian Act, 457
Arrow, Kenneth J., 15, 29, 31, 444
Arrow Lakes, 74, 78, 81n, 82, 84
Atomic Energy Commission, 435
Austin, R. J., 154, 172

Badger, W. L. and Associates, 426
Bain, Joe S., 51, 67
Baldwin-Lima-Hamilton Corporation, distillation plant, scale control study, 429
Bator, F., 176, 177, 179, 181, 188
Bechtel Corporation, 435, 437
Becker, G., 14, 18, 31
Beckman, R. T., 167, 173
Bell, D. A., 424, 426
Bellman, R., 22, 31

511